MENNONITES IN AMERICAN SOCIETY, 1930-1970

MENNONITE EXPERIENCE IN AMERICA SERIES

The Mennonite Experience in America series attempts to tell with disciplined integrity the history of the first three centuries of Mennonite and Amish in America. The four volumes are:

1. *Land, Piety, Peoplehood: The Establishment of Mennonite Communities in America, 1683-1790*
    by Richard K. MacMaster, 1985.

2. *Peace, Faith, Nation: Mennonites and Amish in Nineteenth-Century America*
    by Theron F. Schlabach, 1989.

3. *Vision, Doctrine, War: Mennonite Identity and Organization in America, 1890-1930*
    by James C. Juhnke, 1989.

4. *Mennonites in American Society, 1930-1970*
    by Paul Toews, 1996.

MENNONITES IN AMERICAN SOCIETY, 1930-1970

MODERNITY AND THE PERSISTENCE OF RELIGIOUS COMMUNITY

Paul Toews

HERALD PRESS
Scottdale, Pennsylvania
Waterloo, Ontario

Library of Congress Cataloging-in-Publication Data
Toews, Paul.
    Mennonites in American society, 1930-1970 : modernity
and the persistence of religious community / Paul Toews.
        p. cm. — (The Mennonite experience in America ; v. 4)
    Includes bibliographical references and index.
    ISBN 0-8361-3117-7 (alk. paper)
    1. Mennonites—United States. 2. Sociology, Christian
(Mennonite)
    I. Title. II. Series.
    BX8116.T64 1996
    289.7'73'0904—dc20   96-21253
                                                    CIP

The paper used in this publication is recycled and meets the minimum requirements of American National Standard for Information Sciences—Permanence of Paper for Printed Library Materials, ANSI Z39.48-1984.

COVER PHOTO: Mennonite Central Committee archival photo.

MENNONITES IN AMERICAN SOCIETY, 1930-1970
Copyright © 1996 by Herald Press, Scottdale, Pa. 15683
    Published simultaneously in Canada by Herald Press,
    Waterloo, Ont. N2L 6H7. All rights reserved
Library of Congress Catalog Number: 96-21253
International Standard Book Number: 0-8361-3117-7
Printed in the United States of America
Book and cover design by Jim Butti

05 04 03 02 01 00 99 98 97 96 10 9 8 7 6 5 4 3 2 1

To Barbara

CONTENTS

Series Introduction

In 1683, when the Mennonite experience in America began, there was no United States. Thereafter, Mennonites and Amish, like their fellow Americans, came to the so-called New World at different times and for different reasons, with varied backgrounds, customs, polities, languages, and dialects. Along with other immigrant groups they eventually began to ask who they were as a people. Like others, they searched for identity and mission. And provincially, in fragments, they began to tell their stories. Now they see more and more that their separate Mennonite and Amish stories weave into one story which in turn is interwoven with national and world history.

Mennonites have always understood history as a statement of faith, a tracing of God's ways with God's people. The Mennonite Experience in America volumes seek to be history with disciplined integrity. They portray both failure and faithfulness, shadow and light.

In four volumes the series savors the meaning of the Mennonites' three hundred years in the New World. That meaning tells also of America. In America Mennonites and Amish have found both paradox and promise. The MEA books invite us all to come, read, learn tales never before told, and reflect on how Mennonites fared during three centuries of growing nationhood. As the story proceeds into the second half of the twentieth century, Mennonite windows have opened to a world beyond the nation, an international world.

In this volume a gifted historian of ideas, Paul Toews, offers rich interpretive insights on the journey of a people through a traumatic period of lows and highs, theological and cultural, in-

cluding quarrels, depression and world war, prosperity and explosive institutional growth, backlash of Vietnam and social
upheaval, and efforts to clarify self-understanding. Along with the
first three volumes in the series, this book offers an alternative
reading of the American experience. It tells of a people who for
three centuries both resisted and yielded to the conformist pressures of American society. Their story invites comparisons with
studies of other peoples of the American mosaic.

With this the fourth and final volume in the Mennonite Experience in America series, writers and editors welcome a widening conversation on the findings. What essentials have been
omitted? What further questions beg for careful study? What do
the perspectives of these four volumes mean for a people entering
a new century, a new millennium?

Let a hundred studies bloom. Let a thousand conversations
begin.

Robert Kreider
North Newton, Kansas

Editor's Foreword

This and the three earlier books in the Mennonite Experience in America series are about Mennonites but also more than Mennonites. In their parlance "Mennonite" includes "Amish." And far beyond the Amish, the MEA books are about America and the ways American policies, patterns, and culture have been the setting for a particular family of churches. Often the members of this family have seen themselves as a people apart. As they knew at least dimly, their roots went back to the Anabaptists, who in the sixteenth century were the strongest of dissenters.

In America, Mennonites have often not been a people apart, nor dissenters. They have woven themselves intricately into their communities' economic lives and patterns. In large extent they have taken on their neighbors' political attitudes, sometimes becoming politically quite active. Most of their children and youth have attended public schools and more and more the public universities. Mennonites have adopted American patterns of denominational identity and institutions. Influenced heavily by the nation's dominant Protestantism, they have gotten caught up in America's religious quarrels.

At times of war, however, the nation has suddenly reminded Mennonites of their apartness after all. For while by no means pacifist to a person, in their churches' teachings and in percentages refusing military service Mennonites have retained at least one form of dissent: a stubborn, deeply rooted pacifism. So, especially in times of war and draft, they have recovered a sense of their own peoplehood and cast about for new ways to express their group identity.

Such is the story Paul Toews tells in this final book of the initial four MEA volumes. At his story's outset at 1930, memories of World War I were fresh. It was a war in which American intolerance and harassment of conscientious objectors had reached an all-time peak. Soon another war, then two others, would keep raising the question of whether pacifism, and conscientious objectors as persons, had any real place in the nation's psyche and the institutions that embodied that psyche.

At the story's outset also, Mennonites were eagerly trying to achieve their goals the American way, that is, by building and developing institutions. So they were developing ever more structured denominations, with publishing houses, colleges, and an ever-expanding list of mission and benevolent agencies. Before Toews' story is over, a considerable number of inter-Mennonite professional groups and other service organizations have arisen. Meanwhile in the souls of persons, congregations, and those young institutions there raged what now are fashionably called "culture wars." There were struggles that often were outwardly ideological but inwardly quite largely clashes of different cultural experiences. Since in the fifty years before 1930 Mennonites (except their Old Order groups) had widely opened themselves to Protestantism and its culture wars, and since Mennonites had deep respect for a direct, literal biblicism, it is no surprise that one major idiom for their cultural wars was a strong echo of Protestant Fundamentalism. If the fundamentalist-liberal encounters were partly cultural, they also expressed deep religious convictions. As in many other denominations, among Mennonites "fundamentalism" and "liberalism" had peculiar flavors growing out of the groups' own faith traditions. One major theme of Toews' book is that, under pressures from modernity and secularism, Mennonites drew from the American context as well as from their own special histories and convictions. Thus they shaped and developed their own faiths and responses.

With American influences always evident, Toews might easily have told his story as one constant, straight-line process of acculturation—that is, of Mennonites becoming ever more American. He has not done that, for the story is not so simple. For one matter, there are three major wars in his story, each again a reminder that Mennonites are always to some degree a different people, and dissenters. For another, the story includes vigorous new developments in Mennonite thought, especially around a historical-theological understanding of faithful peoplehood captured in the slogan "the Anabaptist Vision." And the "Anabaptist Vision" story includes new recognition, at least in America's churches, that Mennonites might not only be influenced but might influence America. Still another matter is institutional development, in ways that gave new visibility and structure to peoplehood even while in other ways the same institutions reflected acculturation. And finally, although America and America's own global reach was always the context, Mennonites were not identifying entirely with the nation. More and more their ideas of service, cultural identity, and even self-definition were global. For many Mennonites (although by no means for all), skepticism about Americanism and nationalism became part of the new Mennonite identity.

Such are the themes of Toews' book. Because Mennonite institutions, programs, and diversity of ideas proliferated greatly from mid-to-latter twentieth century, and because of large developments in the American context, his was an especially complex story to write. But he is a skillful historian, especially in interpreting changes in ideas and culture. With his skills he has drawn out very well the major themes of Mennonites' interaction with America from 1930 to 1975. The aim of the MEA volumes has been to tell both of Mennonites and of America. Like its predecessors, the newest MEA volume does exactly that.

For such a task, many thanks are due the project's donors and other supporters. To mention names without unfair omissions is impossible, and to mention only a few large donors might violate the example Jesus made of the widow who gave only a mite. The same is true of the many librarians, archivists, and others whose help for this kind of book is absolutely crucial. Perhaps we can mention the colleges who gave direct support and cooperation for this project. These were especially Fresno Pacific College for Toews as author and Goshen College for me as editor. The Institute of Mennonite Studies at Associated Mennonite Biblical Seminary acted as financial manager and overall host of the project. To all these, named or unnamed, our hearty thanks.

Theron F. Schlabach
Goshen College, and the Young Center
for the Study of Anabaptist and Pietist Groups,
Elizabethtown College

Author's Preface

If eighteenth-century titles were still in vogue, this would be called a "Prolegomenon to a History of American Mennonites in the Twentieth Century." Like the other three volumes of the Mennonite Experience in America series, it offers a more inclusive history than have most accounts of Mennonites heretofore. The history is inclusive, at least in the sense that groups all across the Mennonite spectrum are fair game for the story. It is a prolegomenon in the sense that it is the first such attempt to lay out an interpretation for the mid-twentieth-century American Mennonite story. It is also a prolegomenon in that many things are left out. That is partially because I do not know enough about some subjects, partly because the sheer amount of archival materials that Mennonites have generated for this period could take several lifetimes to digest, partly because important documentary materials are still inaccessible, and partly because we do not yet have the perspective that time will bring to the recent past.

What I have attempted is a description of some of the main currents of the Mennonite passage through several critical, and in many ways transforming, decades of this turbulent century. Those currents are diverse, just as the American Mennonite universe is diverse. During these decades most Mennonites became fuller participants in American society; yet they kept a sense of being a separate and distinguishable community. The differing ways in which the various Mennonite groups have sought to sustain themselves has been the story's dominant motif. Other historians will offer different motifs for understanding the period.

My debts are many. Surely there will be some special reward in the hereafter for Mennonite librarians and archivists who preserve, make accessible, and, in my experience, rendered exceptionally kind service and competent direction. The list of people and institutions who have helped is long: James and Dorothy Lehman, the late Grace Showalter, and Harold Huber at Eastern Mennonite University (Harrisonburg, Virginia); Carolyn Wenger at Lancaster Mennonite Historical Society (Lancaster, Pennsylvania); Joseph Miller, and Joel Alderfer at The Mennonite Library and Archives of Eastern Pennsylvania (Harleysville, Pennsylvania); John Oyer, John Roth, and Joe Springer at the Mennonite Historical Library (Goshen College, Goshen, Indiana); Leonard Gross, Bryan Kehr, Rachel Shenk, and Dennis Stoesz at the Archives of the Mennonite Church (Goshen, Indiana); David Haury, John Thiesen, and Rosemary Moyer at the Mennonite Library and Archives (Bethel College, North Newton, Kansas); Peggy Goertzen at the Center for Mennonite Brethren Studies (Tabor College, Hillsboro, Kansas); Amos Hoover at the Muddy Creek Library (Denver, Pennsylvania) and in a particular way Kevin Enns-Rempel at the Center for Mennonite Brethren Studies (Mennonite Brethren Biblical Seminary and Fresno Pacific College, Fresno, California).

My conversational partners about all things Mennonite, including the themes of this volume, have been many. Colleagues at Fresno Pacific College—Delbert Wiens, Robert Enns, and Steven Brandt—over many years have been part of a mutual exploration of all kinds of related issues. John B. Toews and John E. Toews, father and brother respectively, though formally trained in theology and biblical studies, are also historians; hardly a family gathering passes without sustained reflection about the history and current state of the Mennonite world. In the Mennonite Experience in America network, James C. Juhnke, Robert Kreider, and particularly Rodney J. Sawatsky shared abundantly from their wealth of insights.

A number of scholars read the entire manuscript and offered innumerable valuable suggestions: James C. Juhnke, John Lapp, C. J. Dyck, Robert Kreider, Donald Kraybill, Leo Driedger, Peter Klassen, and Wesley Prieb. Rachel Waltner Goossen read the chapters on World War II. Theron Schlabach, as editor, read it more than once. The book is stronger because of his tenacious pursuit of accuracy, nuanced interpretation, and intelligible prose.

The entire Mennonite Experience in America series has been underwritten by a series of generous donors. Among the most generous have been Dr. Velma Dyck and her late husband, Dr. William Dyck of Fresno, longtime friends and supporters of many kinds of scholarly activity.

A project such as this one becomes akin to a long-term guest in one's household. My wife, Barbara, and children—Renee and Matthew—were supportive, gracious, and unfailingly kind in responding to this guest who stayed longer than he should have.

With all of this good help, this should be a perfect book. Of course it is not and for that I am responsible.

Paul Toews

Mennonites
in American
Society,
1930-1970

CHAPTER

1

∾

MODERNITY AND THE PERSISTENCE OF RELIGIOUS COMMUNITY

In January 1930 the office of a Philadelphia law firm was an unusual meeting place for any group of Mennonites. Most Mennonites still lived on farms or in villages. Few had professional training and even fewer were lawyers.

Yet on January 25 a meeting of the Mennonite Central Committee (MCC) Executive Committee in the law offices of Maxwell H. Kratz brought together a group of people comfortable in that setting and quite prepared to discuss issues that roamed across the world—issues which involved negotiations with numerous governments, large business firms, and international investment companies.

Those present—Kratz, Peter C. Hiebert, Orie Miller, and Levi Mumaw, plus Harold S. Bender—brought impressive professional biographies, educational degrees, and global experience. Kratz, the oldest, had been born in 1875. He had graduated from Princeton University in 1899 with academic honors, then attended the University of Pennsylvania Law School. Bender would soon be awarded a Ph.D. degree from the University of Heidelberg and become the foremost articulator of twentieth-century Mennonite identity. Hiebert, who had studied at the Baptist Seminary in Rochester, New York, under Walter Rauschenbusch, a major theologian of the American Social Gospel movement, was a founder of Tabor College (a Mennonite Brethren school in Kansas) and chair of MCC for its first thirty-three years, 1920-1953.

By 1930 Miller, Hiebert, and Bender had all traveled exten-

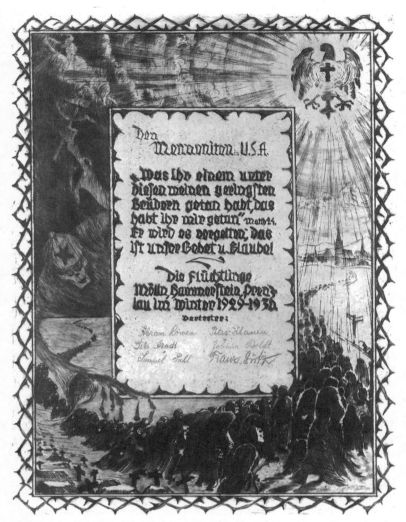

**Thank-you note from Russian Mennonites in refugee camps in Germany
in 1929-1930 to Mennonites in the USA. Translation: The Mennonites
in the United States. "What you have done to the least of these my brethren, you have done it to me."** Matthew 24. **It will be repaid, that is our
hope and prayer! The Refugee Camps Möllin, Hammerstein, and Prezlau
in the Winter of 1929-30.** Credit: MCC Collection, Archives of the Mennonite Church,
Goshen, Indiana.

sively in Europe. Miller had gone to Beirut, Lebanon, in 1919 to work at post-World War I relief. In 1920 he had been among the first Mennonites sponsored by MCC to travel to the Soviet Union to investigate the plight of coreligionists following the Soviet revolution and to arrange for American Mennonite assistance. In 1922 Miller and Hiebert made a follow-up visit to examine how Mennonite relief was going. Bender not only had studied in Europe on several different occasions during the 1920s; he also had been deeply engaged in negotiation with various European and American governments to arrange for the resettlement of Russian Mennonite refugees to Canada and South America.

In 1930 Hiebert, Mumaw, and Kratz had already served ten years each on the MCC Executive Committee. And for the next twenty-five years Miller and Bender would be MCC's dominating figures. If the leaders of this MCC meeting were atypical, in its own way the meeting was also a harbinger of things to come. Here were Mennonites from three different denominations working together again to assist their religious compatriots caught in the turmoil of the Russian empire. Kratz's lifelong affiliation was with the General Conference Mennonites (GC). Hiebert was a Mennonite Brethren (MB). Mumaw, Miller, and Bender were members of the Mennonite Church (MC).[1]

The five leaders' meeting in January 1930 concerned thousands of Soviet Union Mennonites, mostly from the Ukraine, who had traveled to Moscow in hopes of securing an exit to Western countries. Stranded in desperate conditions, they faced deportation to Siberia unless Western governments altered immigration quotas and extended financial credit for their passage. In the weeks prior to the meeting, Bender had been in Washington, D.C., to explore emigration for these stranded people. Possibilities included emigration to the United States, Canada, Brazil, and Paraguay, as well as colonization in waste lands in East Prussia.[2]

MENNONITE DIVERSITY

While diverse in some ways, the five leaders of MCC did not fully represent the motley lot of their twentieth-century kinsfolk called Mennonites. North American Mennonites are an extended family of groups, and even at the end of the twentieth century they include some who still seem to reject Western civilization, resist modernization, and live in their own separated ways. Others take part in the central institutions of American society and are inte-

Original MCC headquarters. Credit: MCC Collection, Archives of the Mennonite Church, Goshen, Indiana.

grated into the technological, urban, and global culture. Some of these sit in the largest stock brokerage firms, hold prominent positions in government, acquire directorships on boards of the largest corporations, teach at distinguished universities, dine at fashionable restaurants, and vacation on Greek islands. They feel quite at home in the world.

Lancaster County, Pennsylvania, home of MCC, is historically one of the U.S. counties with the largest Mennonite population. It provides further contrasting images of its Mennonites. For the past several decades, people from around the world have traveled there to see Mennonite and Amish culture. Large tour buses wind through backcountry roads in search of quaint ways. Many visitors are children or grandchildren of Eastern European immigrants coming to smell, taste, and touch the ancestral ways. A trip from New York to Lancaster is much cheaper and easier than a trip back to Bulgaria, Poland, or Yugoslavia.

So the people come in busloads. They come for nostalgia and for a sense of how far their own families have come. Here they can relive the past without its harshness and tragedy. They think of the Amish and plain-clad Mennonites as bearers of the world they once knew. And indeed some Mennonites do seem to be stage pieces out of history. Some Mennonites are old-fashioned. Some live in a world defined by the limits of horse-drawn carriage travel. Some seem strangely unaffected by the twentieth century. Some Amish and Mennonites have proven that the pace of change is controllable; the essence of the past need not necessarily yield to modern ways.

In the rolling hills of Lancaster County is the rural village of Akron, home of MCC. In the MCC offices the traveler finds a different Mennonitism. The unpretentious buildings include several converted residences. Yet these modest structures are the center of a relief, development, and service agency that meets human need on every continent. MCC aids refugees around the world and when necessary assists their relocation to new homelands. One MCC exchange program supports Mennonites or like-minded teachers in educational institutions in the People's Republic of China. A "People to People" exchange program brings "trainees" from various parts of the world to North America. With other denominations and often working through the Canadian Foodgrains Bank, Mennonites use MCC to ship tons of grain to needy countries. In many countries MCC seeks to bring appropriate seeds and technologies for agricultural development. Elsewhere it works to improve health and sanitary conditions.[3]

The MCC offices are a center of world information. Staff members, many of them volunteers working only for expenses, talk knowledgeably about a myriad of global issues. They meet with many kinds of the world's leaders to discuss economic, religious, and political matters. A small library has the world's major newspapers. Staff members come and go from the earth's far corners. Coffee conversations bound across the world's geography. Telexes and faxes relay urgent messages to and from Nicaragua, Vietnam, Lesotho, Russia, and elsewhere. Telephones carry a plethora of languages. Delegations move in and out, conveying MCC knowledge and concerns to U.S. congressional committees, State Department planners, embassies, and sometimes the U.S. president's Oval Office. Or they converse with United Nations representatives and offices in New York, Geneva, and elsewhere. The staffers live and work next to Mennonite and Amish farm families who still move by horse and buggy. But these coreligionists are deeply engaged with the global political issues of the day.

Few tourists who search out the quaintness of Mennonites and Amish seem to know that many Mennonites are thoroughly modern. While some travel with horses to a family farm to worship in time-honored ways, others gather in fashionable churches to debate the latest trends in Western theology. Some congregations, singing a cappella, repeat traditional melodies from a sixteenth-century hymnal known as the *Ausbund.* Other congregations occasionally sponsor contemporary rock or Bach cantatas with full orchestral accompaniment. Even in Lancaster County, some Mennonite congregations are populated by bankers, lawyers, psychiatrists, professors, and businessmen whose firms do annual business in the hundreds of millions of dollars. And while the more modern members inhabit a different cultural and economic universe, they too are bearers of the Mennonite tradition. In the Mennonite world, English tweed and MCC-volunteer fatigues are as typical as broad-brimmed Amish hats.

Twentieth-century Mennonites live both on the margins of American society and in many of its central institutions. Social scientists emphasizing cultural pluralism can use Mennonites as good copy, but so can those who emphasize cultural assimilation. Mennonites are a distinguishable community—yet they are not. Many pass through theaters, airports, hotels, and banks unnoticed. Others break the visual uniformity of American dress and convey their continuing sense of estrangement from much of their national culture.

Such diversity was a fact already as Mennonites entered the middle third of the twentieth century. Although few in number, Mennonites moved into the 1930s with differences in histories, ethnicities, nuances of theology, and patterns of immigration and assimilation into American society. And even where they shared histories and ethnicity, past schisms and quarrels divided them still further. A U.S. religious census in 1936 recorded 114,337 Mennonites divided among seventeen denominational groupings. The total was about twenty-seven thousand more than a decade earlier, with the various denominations growing at roughly the same rate. Fifteen of the groups each had fewer than ten thousand members—nine had fewer than two thousand. The smallest, the Stauffer Mennonite Church, had only 161 members.[4]

SWISS AND DUTCH BACKGROUNDS

Although the seventeen denominational groups represented distinct religious communities, the more fundamental divisions were ancestry and degrees of cultural adaptation. An important divide separated Mennonites and Amish whose roots were in Switzerland and southern Germany from other Mennonites whose an-

cestry was in northern Germany and The Netherlands. Mennonites sometimes bridged the gap between Swiss-south German
and Dutch-north German, and in the twentieth century they
would bridge it even more. But through much of their history the
gap was wide and contacts across it were limited. The gap separated two differing stories, two differing patterns of relating to the
various nations in which Mennonites had lived.

In the sixteenth and seventeenth centuries, an expanding
western Europe sent populations migrating both east and west.
Generally Swiss and south-German Mennonites moved north and
west. In 1683 some arrived at Germantown in Pennsylvania, William Penn's haven for religious dissenters, and began the first permanent Mennonite settlement in the new world. Until the middle
of the nineteenth century, almost all Mennonites and Amish who
went to North America were Swiss and south-German.

Historically the Dutch and north-German Mennonites sought
political refuge farther east in Europe. As early as the 1530s they
began moving along the North Sea until they found toleration in
Polish and subsequently Prussian territories. In the 1780s the
Russian czarina offered a special set of privileges. This prompted
many Mennonites to move farther east into the Ukraine.[5] Unfortunately for these Mennonite colonists, their cherished privileges, or
Privilegium, lasted scarcely a century. In the 1870s the Russian
government withdrew the guarantees of cultural seclusion and exemption from military conscription. Largely in response, in the
late nineteenth century, some eighteen thousand Dutch-Russian
Mennonites emigrated to North America, settling mainly on the
U.S. and Canadian plains.

The histories of both the Swiss-south German and the Dutch-
north German Mennonites are in part stories of searching for separation from worldly society. Mennonites of north-European origin arrived in North America after a long search for places to live
peacefully in their own enclaves. By contrast, Swiss-south German
Mennonites lived much more among the general European and
North American populations. Especially in the U.S., they fashioned
their patterns of separation through nonconformity rather than
in spatial isolation. Throughout history those differing models of
separation, now largely gone, underlay much discussion, misun-
derstanding, and even disagreement between the two groups.[6]

MENNONITE-AMISH DIVISIONS

Among the groups of Swiss origin, a deep fracture had taken place already in Europe in the late seventeenth century, dividing Mennonites from Amish. Then in the United States in the nineteenth and early twentieth centuries, there were many more schisms. Numerous disagreements turned on whether or how much to accept or reject some typical religious patterns. Did revivalism, or Sunday schools, or denominational institutions and missions represent the profanation or the revitalization of the tradition?

Some of the groups, such as the Stauffer Mennonites and various emerging Old Order fellowships, saw themselves almost entirely as preservers of tradition. Others—the Reformed Mennonites; the Mennonite Brethren in Christ; the Conservative Amish Mennonites; the Central Conference of Mennonites; the Defenseless (now Evangelical) Mennonites; the General Conference Mennonites; and the Church of God in Christ, Mennonite (or Holdemans)—all worked for one blend or another of tradition and innovation. Although these groups usually worshiped in different places, they settled in adjacent territories where they shared rural and small-town life. The cultural patterns and ethical values they shared surpassed the theological differences segregating the groups on Sundays.

The Dutch-north German stream coming by way of Russia was also divided. The Russian *Privilegium* made schism more difficult because, by providing for Mennonite cultural islands, it tended to produce elites who consolidated power. They governed both secular institutions and the main Mennonite church—eventually nicknamed the *Kirchliche.* Despite that control, however, other groups broke off. These included in 1812 the Kleine Gemeinde (today's Evangelical Mennonite Conference); in 1869 the Krimmer (Crimean) Mennonite Brethren; and most importantly, in 1860 what is now the third-largest Mennonite group in North America, the Mennonite Brethren. With continental Pietism and Evangelicalism raising many of the same issues as American revivalism, those divisions were analogous to schisms among Swiss-south German Mennonites and Amish in the nineteenth-century United States. Still, as with the "Swiss Mennonites" (our shortened label for those of Swiss-south German origin), the common cultural inheritance of the so-called Russian Mennonites often bridged their religious differences. Denominational differences scarcely touched the social patterns of Russian Mennonite villages on the plains and in the far-western states of the United States.

LARGER MENNONITE GROUPS IN AMERICA IN 1930

The four largest Mennonite and Amish bodies reflected both the separate ethnic origins and the ethnic consolidation that American life encouraged. The largest, today's Mennonite Church (MC), which numbered 46,301 in the 1936 U.S. census, was still made up almost exclusively of people descended from Swiss or south-German immigrants who had arrived between 1683 and the mid-nineteenth century.

The next largest, the General Conference Mennonite Church (GC), which numbered 26,535 in the U.S. in 1936, bridged the two streams. The GC church had begun in 1860, in movements for change among U.S. Mennonites largely of the Swiss-south German stream. But in the 1870s its numbers swelled by taking in congregations of *Kirchliche* from the Russian empire. Third largest were the Mennonite Brethren (MB), numbering 7,595 in the United States in 1936. Virtually all the MBs were of Dutch-Prussian-Russian background.

As for the Amish, by 1936 many of them had merged into the Mennonite Church (MC); others were in GC congregations, in the Central Mennonite Conference, in the Defenseless Mennonite Church, or elsewhere. The largest group still bearing the Amish name were the highly traditional Old Order Amish (9,887 in the United States in 1936). All Amish were of Swiss and south-German descent.

Thus of the four largest groups, only the General Conference Mennonites bridged the basic ethnic gap inherited from the Mennonite past. The Church of God in Christ, Mennonite, or Holdemans (2,024 in the U.S. in 1936) was the other group which bridged that gap.[7]

In the 1930s the four largest groups—MC, GC, Old Order Amish, and MB—were indeed members of one Anabaptist-Mennonite family. Yet they also reflected the pluralism of the North American denominational system. Each group had its own traditions. The MCs lived predominantly in the eastern half of the U.S. Their general conference, created in 1898 as a biennial meeting of regional or district conferences, provided overall organization. Although by the 1930s the general conference had considerable power, its function was supposed to be advisory and in fact district conferences still retained great authority. The dispersal of authority permitted considerable cultural and theological variation—much to the dismay of both the progressive and the conservative wings of the church. Generally the eastern districts, located in Pennsylvania, Maryland, and Virginia, tended to be more traditional. Conferences from the Allegheny Mountains westward were somewhat more open to change.

MC Mennonites thought of themselves as the center between the traditionalist Old Order groups on the one hand and the more innovative Mennonites on the other. They were suspicious both of those who seemed to hold rigidly to the past and of those who seemed too quick to adapt in the changing cultural environment.

From their 1860 beginnings the GC Mennonites seemed in some ways to typify the North American Mennonite future. The fracturing of North American Mennonitism, the isolation of some nineteenth-century immigrant groups, and frontier scattering left numerous congregations without conference affiliation. Different strategies of adaptation and change to American society set congregations adrift in different directions. The General Conference quite deliberately drew together various immigrant generations and congregations more ready to adapt.

The GCs had adopted a highly congregational polity, which allowed considerable difference in culture and religious practice. The founders aimed to deepen Mennonite faith, but through freedom and autonomy rather than authority and control. They understood congregationalism, even a radical variety, to fit a believers' church and its high doctrine of individual responsibility. From 1860 to the 1930s and beyond, the General Conference was also the most ecumenically minded of the larger Mennonite groups.

The MBs, also formed in 1860 but in the Ukraine, had originated from mixed influences. Some of their early leaders drew from neighboring theological traditions—especially European Evangelicalism and Pietism—while others had reached back more to sixteenth-century Anabaptism. Like the GC's, the MB founders had been restive with the way their Mennonite world seemed bound by tradition and encased by culture. The tensions they had experienced during the early years in Russia with the parent Mennonite church, the *Kirchliche*, had made it easy for them to fraternize elsewhere rather than with kindred Mennonites.

Among the Amish, most did not become "Old Order." From mid-nineteenth century onward, the Amish diverged more and more in their attitudes toward their inheritance. In a gradual pro-

cess beginning in the 1860s, those who insisted on a strict construction evolved into the Old Order Amish. Their hallmark was
conservation. Most of the others, best called Amish Mennonites,
found more and more fellowship in the Mennonite Church. These
participated in the MC general conference from its beginning in
1898. During the 1920s their district conferences in the United
States formally allied with MC district bodies. But although they
were now Mennonites rather than Amish, many—although not all
—were a conservative element in their new church.

RADICAL ORIGINS

Mennonite and Amish of all varieties followed the Anabaptist
movement of the sixteenth century, a movement that arose out of
the larger Protestant Reformation. Anabaptists stood with the An-
glican, Lutheran, Calvinist, and other Reformers in rejecting many
practices in the Roman Catholic Church of that day. But they also
called for additional, more radical reforms. Scattered in numerous
places (but especially in Switzerland, Holland, and Germany) and
subject to the sectarianism and pluralism of dissident movements, these "radicals," for which the sixteenth century was not
ready, foreshadowed some modern developments. Rejecting state
Christianity, they called for religious commitment and hence
church membership to be voluntary. By establishing new religious
communities apart from the territorial churches, they implicitly
moved Western culture toward religious pluralism and toleration.
In such ways Anabaptists unwittingly planted distinctly modern
notions.[8]

Unlike mainline Reformers, Anabaptists made a radical
break from the medieval idea of a "Christian society." In its place
they thought of the church as a distinctive people, based on adult
religious commitment rather than automatic infant membership.
In so doing they incurred the wrath of virtually all religious and
political authorities, Catholic and Protestant. Hence, severe persecution and martyrdom befell them. Later the seventeenth-century
search for religious toleration and the eighteenth-century Enlightenment would integrate some of these ideas into Western culture. But by then the Mennonites who would form the twentieth-
century North American Mennonite and Amish population had
dispersed to the remote corners of Europe or to the English colonies in North America.

With that dispersion, the Mennonite story (except in Holland) became largely one of living at the fringes of various social and political systems. In the words of historian James Stayer, Mennonites became "a minority hermetically separated from the fallen world and the coercion necessary for its preservation."[9] If that position made it more difficult to penetrate society and culture with religious values, it did make experimentation possible for a purer kind of Christian community. Also, in the face of religious and political persecution, Mennonite theology soon saw the exercise of power in society as contrary to religious virtue. That meant a strong inclination to separate from worldly society and a clear ethical distinction between church and world. The result was sharp boundaries, with more and more Mennonites living in cultural enclaves, in political isolation, and even in segregated spaces.

When Mennonitism took shape, Western history itself was largely fragmented. The integration of economic, political, and cultural life into the modern nation-state was just starting and thus only beginning to pull smaller and diverse populations segments into the larger national culture. In that pre-national world, geographical and cultural separateness was the protective barrier in which Mennonites could nourish their ideals and continuity with the past.

In the U.S. at mid-nineteenth century, Mennonites were still largely on society's margins. Rural isolation, village patterns, and some cultural withdrawal following the Revolutionary War all reinforced the prevailing ethic of separation.[10] There were exceptions to be sure, yet for most Mennonites, like most Americans, small community life was normative. Face-to-face communities were like a loosely connected series of islands. There was exchange of news and goods and a strong sense of neighborhood, yet still a sense of living independently.[11]

MODERN INTRUSION

The new modernizing order of the late nineteenth century, with its industrial and urban revolutions, required greater contact between different people groups. With the building of national economic and social networks, pressures for cultural assimilation and integration increased. Urban patterns of interaction and interdependence distorted older, more provincial loyalties and identities. Whether by choice or by intrusion, modernity created an expansive society and fractured the small Mennonite world. A fracturing that began with the Reformed Mennonite break in

1812 accelerated throughout the nineteenth century until there were successive, almost continuous schisms.

Hence by the 1930s those seventeen identifiable subgroups had emerged. Such fracturing was a response to the new conditions of modernity. Mennonites were not the only minority responding that way. Jewish scholar Jacob Neusner has argued convincingly that modernity brought the death of Judaism and the birth of Judaisms. He identified eight strands that emerged during the nineteenth and twentieth centuries. James D. Bratt, a historian of Dutch Calvinism in North America, found four different "mentalities" defining the Dutch Calvinist tradition during the last decades of the nineteenth century and the first of the twentieth. For both Jews and Dutch Calvinists, the problems posed by modernity resulted in new alignments and self-definitions.[12]

Among Mennonites and Amish in the nineteenth and early twentieth centuries, the clearest tension was between traditionalism (represented best by the Old Orders) and progressivism (represented best by the GCs). Faced with modernity, those two groups expressed different ways to meet the pressures for cultural conformity and homogenization. The progressives thought they could revitalize the Mennonite imagination by borrowing elements of modern society. Traditionalists thought renewal required disciplined resistance to acculturation and its profane ways.

These differing responses shaped much of the twentieth-century Mennonite story. Traditionalist Mennonites and Amish remained on the margins of North American society. Skillfully and purposefully, they preserved or adopted forms of worship, church life, dress, authority, and technology that marked their boundaries and insured some separateness. Some progressives also were schismatic, to be sure; but generally in U.S. religious history the various forms of separatism or withdrawal have been in conservative regimentation against the seductions of the world. Mennonite and Amish traditionalists were no exception.

The more progressive groups, on the other hand, assumed that Mennonite faith need not be encapsulated in cultural forms. Moreover Mennonite faith and peoplehood could exist more near the center of society, not only on the margins. For most of the twentieth century this progressive vision numerically triumphed. More Mennonites live as participants in the dominant culture and for them supplemental forms of unity became necessary. Those that emerged were institutional, ideological, and ecumenical. Church institutions, new theological formulations, and inter-

Mennonite alliances forged a new sense of community to replace the one disappearing with the demise of village unity.[13]

TRADITIONALISTS AND PROGRESSIVES IN 1927

In 1927 two sets of events signaled how the traditionalists and progressives each sought in their own way to preserve a sense of community. Progressives began publishing *The Mennonite Quarterly Review (MQR)*. The *MQR* quickly became the forum for an ideological reconstruction of the meaning of Anabaptist-Mennonite life. Meanwhile among the traditionalists, in Pennsylvania two schisms occurred. In an old, established Mennonite community in the eastern part of the state, still another denomination emerged: the Wenger Mennonites. In an Amish congregation, Casselman in Somerset County farther west in the state, another appeared: the Beachy Amish. Although the leaders and specific issues in the two schisms were different, both stories suggested the trajectory of continuing separation.

By the end of the nineteenth century there were already three different Amish communities. The Old Order Amish—the *Alt Amisch* ("old" Amish)—strongly emphasized the Alt Ordnung (old order, old regulations, old discipline). They were increasingly characterized by strong maintenance of tradition and by shunning of those who failed to keep the strict convictions. A second group, largely of Alsatian origin, was more open to change. Many of them eventually joined with the progressive GC church, some via creating their own Central Conference of Mennonites, which eventually merged into the GC group. A middling group, the one often called Amish Mennonites, favored moderate changes and organized into three regional conferences. Most of them eventually merged with the MC.[14]

The 1927 schism of the Casselman congregation in Somerset County divided an Old Order Amish congregation. Earlier, in 1895, there had been another division in the same county and neighboring Garrett County in Maryland, also over how to respond to changes. At that time the questions were whether Amish young people might attend courses conducted by Daniel H. Bender, a popular Mennonite preacher, and whether to begin a Sunday school. The conservatives applied the ban to the innovators. In so doing the leading bishop, Moses D. Yoder, upheld a tradition of strictness among Somerset County Amish.[15]

But there were dissenting voices in Yoder's congregation, at least from 1912 onward. In 1927, soon after Yoder died, those voices gained strength, especially around the issues of accepting Sunday schools, electricity, and automobiles. Those seeking change did so cautiously. The congregation's new leader was bishop Moses Beachy; late in 1926 Beachy's brother Rufus, a self-educated veterinarian, advised the bishop that "we are living in a progressive age, in which times and ways of doing things are changing most rapidly." Rufus Beachy thought that to navigate through such "rapidly changing times" called for care.[16]

Cautious change became a Beachy Amish hallmark. A middle way between accepting change and maintaining separation from the dominant culture was sought. In 1927 the group accepted the traditional Amish haircut and a full beard. They wanted to maintain German as the language of faith. Attire and language were important ways to express peoplehood and yieldedness to God. They could accept more new technology than did Old Order Amish, if they could alter it enough to reflect Amish humility.[17] Automobiles were all right, but they should be black. Convenience need not undermine separation.[18]

The second fracture of 1927 happened among the Old Order Mennonites of Lancaster County. By then the United States and Canada had various groups of Old Order Mennonites, who since mid-nineteenth century had been separating from the larger Mennonite church over questions of change and modernization. The 1927 schism occurred in the Lancaster Conference's Weaverland District, among an Old Order group that had formed in 1893. It centered in the use of automobiles.

In 1925 the 1893 founder, bishop Jonas Martin, died. Martin had held the line against automobiles, but his two main successors, bishops Dan Wenger and Moses Horning, disagreed on the point. Wenger feared the automobile, seeing it as dangerous and as associated with the "proud" and the "fashionable." To him and his supporters, convenience was less important than maintaining the Old Order principles of plainness, humility, and yieldedness.

Horning, by contrast, saw automobiles as practical rather than as ethically threatening. A fellow minister, John Kurtz, who was also a businessman and inventor, defended motor vehicles even more. He echoed other Old Order defenses of technology during the past century. Kurtz granted that it was often worldly people—people "puffed up" and with "high heads"—who accepted innovations at the outset. But, he implied, the symbolic meaning of new devices diffused over time. Once the symbolism dissipated, less-than-fashionable versions of the devices were acceptable.[19]

The two positions were not easy to harmonize. After Martin died, Horning stopped excommunicating members who bought cars. With communal discipline thus relaxed, a splinter group led by Wenger withdrew. In the late twentieth century in that district, there still are two Old Order groups—the "team" Mennonites (using horses); and the "black-bumper" Mennonites (so-called because their cars must be so severely black that they paint over even the chrome parts).

In the schisms of Somerset and Lancaster County in 1927, the separating groups thought of themselves as being faithful to the old traditions. They both used boundary maintenance for survival against threatening changes.

The key progressive event of 1927, the beginning of *MQR*, also grew out of events of mid-to-late nineteenth century. At that time the progressives were very receptive to institutional forms typical of North American Protestantism. The three largest groups—Mennonite Church, General Conference Mennonites, and Mennonite Brethren—each had undergone an institutional renaissance whose effect was to transform the group more and more into a modern American-style denomination. Thus by the late nineteenth century, those groups had begun Sunday schools, church periodicals, mission societies and boards, revival meetings and other special services, church colleges, publishing houses, and other new practices. Other parts of this institutional revival were conference structures and bureaucracies.

Creating denominational institutions clearly infused the affected Mennonite groups with new, activist vitality. It also served to demarcate the denominations more clearly. Each major Mennonite denomination developed an impressive array of its own institutions. Denominational institutions, activities, and leaders became articulators of denominational identity and were new forms of distinctiveness and loyalty.[20]

However, when Harold S. Bender and a group of younger intellectuals at Goshen College began publishing the *MQR*, their strategy for preserving Mennonite faith and life was not so much institutional as ideological. They understood that ideas could create a corporate sense of belonging. Moreover, they were part of a fraternity of Mennonite or closely related historians, who included especially C. Henry Smith, John Horsch, Ernst Correll, Robert Friedmann, Cornelius Krahn, Guy F. Hershberger, Edmund G. Kaufman, Bender's wife (and Horsch's daughter) Elizabeth Horsch Bender, and of course Bender himself. Those persons all worked in institutional contexts, mainly Mennonite colleges. They reconceptualized the Mennonite past and in the process articulated an ideological vision that simultaneously protected the distinctiveness of the Mennonite past and encouraged greater engagement with the larger society.

By the 1920s the Mennonite belief system had become more conflictual than unitive. Like other denominations of the time, although in their own ways, they were caught up in the quarrels between Protestant Fundamentalists and liberals, who offered sharply different responses to modernity. But both Fundamentalism and theological liberalism or Modernism were ideologies foreign to Mennonites. Neither was suitable to be the carrier of Mennonite identity.

Ideological unity might replace the eroding primordial unity, but only if it was congruent with the past as well as with future needs. In January 1927 the first *MQR* issue made clear that the journal's editors intended to fashion an ideology that would avoid the seductions both of Fundamentalism and of liberalism.[21] By choosing history to define the new ideology, Bender made possible a marked shift in Mennonite thought and social reality. Bender and other Mennonite historians instinctively knew that articulating a usable past was a means of defining the present and shaping the future.[22]

Mennonites had long used history to shape their self-identity. Now scholars needed, as Bender wrote his father-in-law John Horsch, to fashion a more "clearly defined and integrated Mennonite worldview." Doing so would open the way to more engagement with the larger society even as it preserved the distinctiveness of the Mennonite past. To function without a more systematic Mennonite understanding was to face "the constant danger of drifting . . . and simply becoming like the rest of the world."[23]

Bender's new use of history would come to be known as "The Anabaptist Vision"—the title of a landmark address he would give in 1943. As an ideological construct, the Anabaptist Vision came to provide ideological justification and reinforcement for the continuation of the Mennonite tradition. Even more, it did so precisely when the social environment increasingly threatened the survival of spatially-defined Mennonite communities.

The Anabaptist Vision was a call for a different kind of people and different kinds of institutions. Using words implying transiency and alienation—pilgrims, sojourners, strangers, exiles—to describe the people of God, the vision was a warning to a people increasingly comfortable in the dominant culture. Bender would conclude his 1943 address with a call to withdraw. "The Christian may in no circumstance participate in any conduct in the existing social order which is contrary to the spirit and teaching of Christ and the apostolic practice. He must consequently withdraw from the worldly system and create a social order in the fellowship of the church brotherhood."[24]

But like many ideas, this one had a dual quality. Even as it moved Mennonites inward to create a "Christian social order," it legitimated an outward missional activism. The decades that followed the introduction of the Anabaptist Vision brought a witness and service activism that vastly enlarged the scope of Mennonite benevolence. Ironically, a sense of the past alleviated much Mennonite fear of cultural adjustment and change—fear that had been strong among Mennonites as late as the first third of the century. History became the paradoxical handmaiden of the Mennonite modernizers.

If the first impact of modernity was to fracture Mennonitism into different Mennonitisms, a later effect was to bring Mennonites back together. After the building of denominational institutions and the ideological reconstruction, another means by which the progressive Mennonites revitalized their self-identity was through a Mennonite ecumenical renaissance in the Mennonite family. Inter-Mennonite activity and fellowship would become a hedge against subtle pressures for conformity that smaller distinctive denominations feel in American society.

The 1936 Census Bureau compilers were certain that the future would witness the greater cultural and theological assimilation of Mennonites. The introduction to their report included comments probably common to many external observers of the small Mennonite world. According to the compilers, the Mennonite conviction that civil law and its requirements might conflict with Christian teachings was a product of past persecution and present "clannish qualities."[25] What they seemed to suggest, although not explicitly, was that as Mennonites experienced the freedom of this pluralistic society and assimilated out of their clannish communities, such distinctive beliefs would dissipate.

The census report's perspective offered both a good and a poor forecast of the coming decades. Paradoxically, Mennonite distinctives would become both stronger and more tenuous. And the compilers were accurate with their second prediction—that the schismatic and divisive history that produced these innumerable smaller denominations would give way "to closer union and cooperation along certain common lines of gospel work. . . ."[26] Although the Mennonite ecumenical renaissance would not dissolve many denominational groups, it did bridge both theological and cultural differences.

CONCLUSION

The two sets of events in 1927—the redefinition of traditional boundaries and the creation of new ideological and institutional networks—along with both sets' outworkings, took progressive Mennonites and Old Order Mennonites and Amish in different directions. In the twentieth century, the social distance between the two kinds of Mennonites would widen. Events from the 1930s to the 1970s tested the ability of both strategies to maintain Mennonite identity in an increasingly nationalistic and integrated society.

CHAPTER

2

BALANCING TRADITION AND CHANGE
DURING THE GREAT DEPRESSION

Mennonites entered the 1930s amazingly optimistic and buoyant. During the 1920s they had suffered all too many disagreements and schisms over questions of adaptation and change. Adding to the harshness of their own quarrels, they had joined in the Fundamentalist-Modernist quarrels of U.S. Protestantism. Now, in the 1930s, came the worst economic depression in all U.S. history. Mennonites might have been thoroughly discouraged. But offsetting their discouragement was a new generation of leaders, plus a growing sense of mission and benevolent activism which connected them more and more to peoples and places far beyond their own limited numbers and narrow borders.

The small number of U.S. Mennonites was deceiving. They had strong connections with their coreligionists in Europe, and so enjoyed a wider sense of peoplehood. As the 1930s began, they were helping fellow-Mennonites emigrate from a very harsh Soviet Union, first to refugee camps in Germany, then more permanently to regions in North or South America which Mennonites in the United States, Canada, and Europe were helping to search out. Such work involved them in complex politics and arrangements on several continents. The demands of an international peoplehood, even a small one, made for breadth.[1]

At home Mennonites were still very rural—their four largest bodies were 76.9 to 94.2 percent rural in 1936, according to the U.S. religious census. Only two small fellowships, the Evangelical Mennonite Brethren and the *Kleine Gemeinde*, were slightly more urban, and even their "urbanism" was that of towns such as Steinbach, Manitoba, not of cities such as Chicago or Ottawa. Many Mennonites and Amish did indeed still live by old, premodern village traditions. Yet they were also becoming more modern. By 1930 many of them enjoyed electricity, household appliances, running water, and automobiles.[2]

Amid such change some old and basic themes continued. As they had been doing at least since their first settlement in America, Mennonites were both resisting and accommodating various pressures to Americanize. This required them constantly to judge whether or not this change, this new American attitude, involved compromise. So during the 1930s and beyond, strong clashes continued between traditionalists and innovators. Many of the old ways yielded; but along the way, Mennonites also refined some past treasures.

IMAGES

In the easternmost counties of Pennsylvania, north of Philadelphia, there are two district bodies: the Eastern District Confer-

William S. and Nancy Gottschall family, c. 1935, members of the (GC) Eastern District Conference. Credit: Mennonite Library and Archives of Eastern Pennsylvania, Harleysville, Pennsylvania.

Joseph and Katie Hackman family, c. 1945, members of the (MC) Franconia Conference. Credit: Mennonite Library and Archives of Eastern Pennsylvania, Harleysville, Pennsylvania.

ence (GC) and the Franconia Conference (MC). In the 1930s each had its own texture. Along with the nearby Lancaster Conference, Franconia was one of the two oldest Mennonite conferences in America, dating apparently from the eighteenth century. The Eastern District had begun in 1847, when a group who wanted certain changes had broken with Franconia.[3] In the 1930s many families and neighborhoods had members in both conferences. By then the Eastern District Conference, always more open to change, allowed women to be delegates at their annual convention. The Franconia's sessions were still all-male.

From the beginning the Eastern District, in modern fashion, had demanded that decisions be put in writing. In the 1930s the annual report and proceedings of the District filled a booklet of thirty-five pages, while the cryptic Franconia proceedings fit on a single page. In the Franconia Conference, although all ministers and deacons as well as bishops were delegates, decisions depended heavily on consensus among the bishops. Again by contrast, the far more modernized Eastern District sessions featured lively par-

**Harvest meeting, Deep Run meetinghouse, Franconia Conference (MC),
1938.** Credit: Mennonite Library and Archives of Eastern Pennsylvania, Harleysville, Pennsylvania.

liamentary maneuvers, debate, and long reports from committees.[4] And whereas ordained men of Franconia were all from traditionally Mennonite families, the Eastern conference's leaders included converts from various backgrounds.[5]

In 1928 an estate auction at Franconia Square, in the heart of the two conferences' territory, illustrated typical contradictions. A journalist noted that women wore clothes and bonnets which, although "subdued" in color, were as expensive as any from a good tailor or hatmaker. Over plain dresses they draped "expensive black shawls." Meanwhile men in the MC Mennonites' distinctive lapel-less coats bought the deceased Mary Bechtel's "gilt-edged securities." The people were plain, the journalist observed, but they paid "fancy" prices—then left in expensive cars.[6]

In many MC congregations, especially in the old communities of the East, worship services echoed the past two centuries. Song leaders led from the pews. There were multiple ministers sitting on a bench behind the pulpit. To pray, worshipers knelt between the pews. However in the Sunday schools, which had begun only in the nineteenth century with a more modern flavor, practices were different. The song leader stood to conduct the singing. Increasingly there was music from small groups (duets, quartets, etc.) although the stronger tradition was still a cappella congregational singing.[7]

Such changes often brought subtle forms of individualism that might threaten equality and the bonds of community. In 1927 the Franconia Conference ruled that those who sang in small groups outside the church were not to participate in communion. In its own boundaries, the church was trying to resist and control individualism. It was even more perturbed when members carried on their new practices outside the church, in the larger culture, away from corporate discipline.[8]

A long way from Franconia was the Mennonite Brethren congregation of Hillsboro, Kansas. Hillsboro was an important MB center with a rural village character. Mennonites there were not as distinctive in dress, but they could still mark boundaries between themselves and their neighbors. In 1930 the congregation decided that lead minister Peter E. Nickel, plus another ordained minister and a deacon, would visit all members who had married outside the MB fellowship. Up to World War I the MBs had strictly forbidden such marriages, but by 1930 the automatic ban was eroding. The Hillsboro MBs worried also about Sunday sports, the cutting of women's hair, and exchange of rings during weddings. In 1931 the church decided ring ceremonies were still not acceptable.[9]

GC Mennonites also incorporated elements of the old and the new—as was clear a few miles from Hillsboro at Hutchinson, Kansas, during the triennial sessions of their general conference in 1929. In some ways it was the GCs' first modern conference. It met in a convention hall rather than at a church. Delegates stayed in hotels instead of homes. They dined in restaurants. Yet it was still the old conference, divided for instance by language.

Especially the delegates from the East, of Swiss-south German ancestry and generations away from immigration, could not get along in German. The more recently immigrated "Russian" congregations on the western plains, could not do well in English.[10] Other issues were religious modernism and lodge membership. It was neither the first nor last conference troubled by those matters. At stake in both issues were cultural transitions as much as theology.[11]

In all Mennonite groups, many of the ministers had no formal training. Reuben Weaver, pastor during the 1930s of the Pleasant

Valley MC congregation near Harper in south-central Kansas, was typical of rural pastors. A farmer and a father of fourteen, he reserved Saturday evening to study his Bible and prepare his sermon. If he was not sure what a word meant, he turned to a member who was the local schoolteacher.[12] Most Mennonite congregations chose ministers from their own ranks instead of hiring them from seminaries or other congregations. Many MC congregations still used the lot to select leaders. Men of insight rather than of education, the leaders passed on the proverbs and homilies of rural truth they inherited from past generations.

The homilies contained wisdom, but they could be shopworn and uninspired. One exceptional MC diarist, classics professor Edward Yoder of Hesston College, found refreshment from a sermon by a quite different kind of Mennonite preacher, missionary and Yale graduate Martin Clifford (M.C.) Lehman. The reflective Yoder thought Lehman had delivered one of "the most uplifting and inspiring sermons . . . that we have heard for some time." But, he noted ruefully, such preaching was "not the rule here." It was true that some preachers did "put real work, study, and preparation" into their sermons and "sometimes" offered "real spiritual food." But others scarcely offered "any crumbs of fresh thought or ideas that do not smell of fifty years ago."[13]

DEPRESSION

For the United States the great stock market crash of 1929 plus the Great Depression largely shaped the 1930s. However for many rural Mennonite congregations those two developments had less immediate impact. At the end of 1929, at Kidron in eastern Ohio (Wayne County), a scribe of a Swiss-dialect GC congregation, Salem, began the congregation's annual report with the words "this was an ordinary year." The congregation had just increased the minister's salary from $1320 to $1560. Mission efforts, revivals, special services, and other activities prominent in the 1920s—a "decade of flourish," according to the congregation's historian James O. Lehman—continued smoothly into the 1930s. At a business meeting early in 1931, the pastor noted that although 1930 had been a depression year for the country, it had been "a good average year" for his flock. Financial contributions had stayed about even. Clearly these Mennonites lived apart from the impact of the stock market crash.[14]

Flourishing would hardly be the way to describe the nearby

Harold Burkholder, pastor in the pulpit of the East Swamp Mennonite Church, Eastern District Conference (GC), c. 1943.
Credit: Mennonite Library and Archives of Eastern Pennsylvania, Harleysville, Pennsylvania.

Sonnenberg congregation, mother of the Kidron Swiss. Sonnenberg belonged to no Mennonite conference but was moving more and more toward a quite conservative one, the MCs' Virginia Conference (which Sonnenberg finally joined in 1952). In 1886 a progressive group had split from Sonnenberg and formed Salem. Now, in the 1930s, Sonnenberg suffered another major fracture, again over questions of change and tradition.

As the decade began, the congregation still chose its leaders by lot. When the congregation wanted to add a minister, members voted and nominated candidates, and one vote was enough to put a man in the lot. The method of casting the lots was by a slip of paper in one book, with as many books (usually hymnbooks) as candidates. In 1925 and 1931 the congregation had used that method, and it turned out that the new leaders thus chosen were more conservative than many other members.

Indeed, Sonnenberg's leaders were so conservative they frowned on what had become common in many MC congregations: laypersons teaching Sunday school; literary societies for the youth; church libraries; choruses of singers giving special programs on Sunday evenings at a nearby old people's home; and the like. In 1931 the large (500-member) congregation had been so restless that only seventy-five members nominated any candidates, but the seventy-five named twenty-five different men for the lot.

Five years later the congregation split. About half the members—generally the more progressive ones—withdrew, built a meetinghouse a mile away, and formed a new congregation, Kidron, which promptly joined the MC Ohio and Eastern Conference. But the Kidron church, like the Sonnenberg, continued to spurn fellowship with the still more progressive, GC-affiliated Salem. Salem seemed to have accommodated too much with the world. Among members of the three Swiss congregations, family and business interchange continued. Yet the ethnically bonded Swiss community could not overcome its internal differences about how much religious change it could accept.[15]

Much literature pictures Kansas as hit hard by the Great Depression. Yet even in Kansas the Pleasant Valley congregation was able, like Salem in Ohio, to remodel its meetinghouse. During the 1920s and early '30s, the congregation levied a tax on each member for the upkeep of the building, scaling the tax according to the families' different economic levels. In 1934, with the depression worsening, the congregation's trustees rented eighty acres which members farmed collectively for money to maintain and improve the church facilities. Apparently the plan worked. By 1937 the congregation had remodeled and considerably enlarged its meetinghouse.[16]

For the MC Pike Mennonite congregation near Elida in western Ohio, the depression years were difficult. In 1930 their meetinghouse burned. They immediately began a fund to rebuild, and soon bought a vacant church building not far away, for its lumber. But then the banks in Elida and Lima, like many others, closed. The work stopped and the lumber languished in old sheds designed for sheltering horses during services. In 1932 Benjamin B. King became the congregation's bishop, and new leadership brought new determination. Yet not until the summer of 1935 did the congregation begin using its new building.[17]

More deeply than from economics, the Pike congregation suffered from the traumas of change. To be sure, in the 1920s and '30s they carried on their routines of vacation Bible schools, revival meetings, young people's meetings, and other activities—but conflict simmered. As was happening throughout much of the MC church, leaders in the Pike congregation, and not least the forthright Bishop King, wanted stricter adherence to codified rules than they saw in various neighboring congregations. Successive bishops found their authority challenged. Amid that tension, in 1936 the congregation temporarily withdrew from the Ohio and Eastern (MC) Conference. That action in turn helped stimulate some members to split away and start a new MC congregation,

Bethany Mennonite Church. Thus for Pike the depression's economic troubles added to older-style church tensions to create a most troublesome decade.[18]

At Henderson in eastern Nebraska, a "Russian" Mennonite community had been established by immigrants in the 1870s. In 1934 an editor in nearby York, writing as if Henderson were free of the depression, declared that it was the "wealthiest settlement in the county" with lots of "fine automobiles and indications of luxury."[19] But appearances may have been deceiving. To be sure, the economies of Henderson and other Mennonite agricultural communities were not tied directly to stock markets. However, the nation's agricultural prices, which especially affected farmers on the drought-troubled Great Plains, tell their own story. Already in the 1920s they experienced a downturn from the high prices of World War I. And the decline worsened in the 1930s.

	Wheat prices	Corn prices
1920	$2.08/bu.	$1.56/bu.
1929	$0.97/bu.	$0.77/bu.
1932	$0.27/bu.	$0.13/bu.

By 1933 few farmers could purchase autos and farm machinery. Many had bought land during the prosperous years of World War I and immediately following, with short-term credit; now they and others fell behind in land and machinery payments. In thirteen southeastern Nebraska counties, including York County, creditors foreclosed on 136 farms in 1932 alone. During that one year, 8.2 percent of the land changed hands.[20] Before the depression abated, quite a few Mennonite farmers lost their farms. However their farms usually went to fellow church members. So while individual Mennonites suffered, as a community the Henderson Mennonites did sustain themselves during the depression years.[21] For Mennonites in Henderson and probably for others as well, the depression had the net effect of widening social differences. Some of the poor got poorer and some of the rich got richer.

Kansas agriculture responded much like Nebraska's. In the 1920s farm prices had never reached pre-World War I levels. Even in 1929, the boom year, they only reached 86 percent (adjusted for inflation) of the earlier high. In the first years of the depression farm tenancy climbed nearly 10 percent—and would have climbed much higher had not the 1933 Kansas legislature passed an eighteen-month moratorium on mortgage foreclosures. For Mennonite farmers in both Nebraska and Kansas, as on most of the Great Plains, depression woes came mixed with dustbowl drought. From 1932 to 1939 rains were scarce. Too often, the only clouds were dustclouds. By 1934 the U.S. Soil Conservation Service estimated that 300,000,000 tons of soil had blown away.[22]

Near Hesston, Kansas, the experience of an MC congregation named "Pennsylvania" (after the origin of its people, distinguishing them from "Russian-Mennonite" neighbors) was similar to that of the Mennonites at Henderson. Member Elmer White lost his farm when he could not repay a $4000 loan he had made to buy more land and the bank refused to renew his note. But whereas quite a few others in the area were suffering such loss, White's experience was rare among the Mennonites. Most of them managed to hang on. The Pennsylvania congregation had no formal mutual aid program, but its members helped each other as individual cases arose.[23]

Edward Yoder, the Hesston College professor and diarist, moved to Goshen College in 1933. Unable to sell his house, he rented it out. In the following year, four or five oil-worker families lived in it one after another, paying him a total of $56. Out of that amount, Yoder paid a mortgage company $25 to service a $1000 loan; he paid nothing on the loan itself.[24] Such were the strains of the depression. Yoder felt his idealism threatened. Already in June of 1932, he lamented in his diary that he might have to give up teaching and become a farmhand—"a dismal prospect." What, the professor asked, of time for reading and study? What of money for books and travel? He feared he must "throw away all such ambitions and dedicate myself body, soul, and spirit to the job of getting food, clothing and shelter."[25]

Other Mennonite communities in Kansas reflected the decade's uneven economics. Compared to some more rural areas, Newton remained reasonably well-off and increased its population. In 1928 the First Mennonite Church (GC) had begun planning for a new building; and in 1931, despite the depression, it started to build. Some members were suffering, but not enough of them to cripple the congregation's finances. So $45,600 and eleven months later First Mennonite dedicated its new 700-seat sanctuary. The new building—a kind of "Mennonite Gothic"—even communicated a certain grandeur, with decorations uncommon to most Mennonite meetinghouses. From special gifts it had stained-glass windows costing $200 apiece and a bell tower with a $500 bell.[26]

In contrast to such gifts, a few miles away at Hillsboro, the large MB congregation in 1930 bought a cow for a family and a funeral casket for another, shingled the roof of a poor family, and each month paid for the care of an aged woman at the local old people's home.[27] In the Pennsylvania MC congregation between Newton and Hesston, a man bought a Model T Ford from a fellow member. By the time the check reached the bank, six individuals had endorsed it. Six people had been able to pay off $5 debts.[28]

Ironically, congregations of the West sometimes benefited from the Midwest's troubles. Fleeing the dust bowl were not only the "Okies" and "Arkies" of John Steinbeck's great novel *Grapes of Wrath* but also some Mennonites, especially MBs. At Reedley, in California's San Joaquin Valley, the MB congregation's membership more than doubled in the 1930s, to 931. Indeed the church became, for decades, the largest Mennonite congregation in America. Of 481 new members in seven years, 435 were transfers, mainly out of the dust bowl. Meanwhile membership at an MB congregation at Ingalls, Kansas, dropped from 83 to 45; at Fairview, Oklahoma, from 115 to 89; and at Balko, Oklahoma, from 125 to 92. If they did not go to Reedley, quite a few went to other California MB congregations at Dinuba, Rosedale, Bakersfield, and Shafter.[29]

THE DEPRESSION AND MENNONITE INSTITUTIONS

Hard as it was on some congregations, the Great Depression was perhaps even harder on Mennonite institutions—especially colleges. Already plagued by the fundamentalist-modernist conflicts (although none was really modernist or even theologically liberal in a technical sense), Mennonite colleges bent dangerously from the fierce winds of depression economics. Hardest hit, perhaps, were the three in Kansas: Bethel (GC), Hesston (MC), and Tabor (MB). Troubles in all three caused presidents to resign.

At Hesston in the late 1920s enrollment had peaked at 248 students. By 1930-1931 it was at 148 and in 1931-1932 down to 70. Part of the drop was surely due to tragic personal circumstances that forced the president, Daniel (D. H.) Bender, to resign in the summer of 1930. Two years passed before the Hesston trustees were able to appoint Milo Kauffman as the new president. Fortunately, Kauffman would have a long and successful tenure. But in the interim, faculty salaries had fallen by 29 percent. Annual deficits had roughly doubled and pushed the college's debt to the then-large sum of almost $20,000.[30]

In 1931 the state of Kansas withdrew accreditation and the MCs' Board of Education seriously considered closing Hesston College down. As much as anybody, women of the surrounding congregations saved it from that fate. Throughout the depression, they made bed and window coverings for the dormitory rooms. They also laid in supplies of food. Even with enrollments down, meeting young appetites with homegrown and canned foods took some doing.[31]

For nearby Bethel College, the depression made three perennial problems—accreditation, enrollment, and finances—even more severe. Accreditation was already a large issue, for in 1926 the Kansas State Board of Education had refused to certify junior- and senior-level courses. And even before the state's refusal, the college's own GC Mennonite constituency was complaining. Its complaints turned more on cultural issues than on questions of quality: intercollegiate athletics, insufficiency of German courses, and differing disciplinary standards.[32]

Such troubles of course made it hard to accumulate endowment funds, which in turn were necessary for full accreditation. During 1927-1931, a simmering economic crisis hampered various creative efforts to gather funds. So Bethel College had gone deeper into debt: from $32,000 in 1926 to $141,000 in 1932. That debt, huge for that time, worsened the strains between church and college to a point of almost complete rupture. In spring 1932, Western District Conference, Bethel's main official backer, voted on whether to recall $100,000 it had invested in the college's governing corporation. The motion lost, but only by the narrow margin of 131 to 149. Earlier Bethel's president, John W. Kliewer, had weathered the turmoils of World War I, then of Fundamentalism. But in 1932 he resigned, and his post went to Edmund G. Kaufman, a missionary-scholar. Young, energetic, and resourceful, Kaufman began a twenty-year presidency during which Bethel surmounted the depression and much more.[33]

Tabor College, twenty miles northeast from Bethel and Hesston, was less fortunate. During 1934-1935 it closed. The immediate cause was depression economics, but as usual the deeper roots were theological and cultural controversies between the school and its supporting church. Begun in 1908 by MBs who organized as an educational corporation, the college had been seeking official denominational sponsorship for years. In the 1920s it had much trouble raising money, and MB conferences heard a steady litany of motions calling for direct conference subsidies.[34]

Then in 1930-1931 a downward spiral began. The conference established a separate Bible institute housed in the college but administered through the Board of Missions. Henry W. Lohrenz, president since Tabor's founding, resigned in 1931. Adding to the woes, in the same year the state of Kansas withdrew senior-college accreditation, reducing Tabor to a junior college. Many of Tabor's most gifted faculty members then left. The climax of these difficulties was the 1934-1935 closing.[35] Although Tabor reopened in 1935, it was years before the school regained the academic standing it had enjoyed during the 1920s.

The fact of three Mennonite colleges in a thirty-mile triangle, all struggling to survive under the depression, augured for new forms of cooperation. And indeed, between 1930 and 1933 Tabor's and Bethel's leaders discussed ways to affiliate or even merge. Lohrenz, a faculty member at Bethel after he resigned at Tabor, fostered the discussions. But the proposals never moved beyond a few key faculty and board members at each institution.[36] Mennonite denominational boundaries were too high in the 1930s to be bridged even by the traumas of prospective college closings.

MENNONITE THOUGHT

Intellectually, Mennonites responded to the depression's deprivations in predictable ways. It was easy to express pieties that defined those deprivations in moralistic terms. At the same time, a long tradition of aiding the unfortunate galvanized Mennonites to act, both for mutual aid in the Mennonite communities and to help others.

The MC denominational magazine *Gospel Herald*, more than other Mennonite periodicals, explained the depression moralistically. It did so by reprinting an article from a provocative Protestant Fundamentalist paper *The Defender*. Preaching against the profane 1920s, the *Defender* piece said "it was a glorious spree—while it lasted," then treated the depression as a morning-after hangover.[37]

The *Gospel Herald* also printed from the pen of John H. Martin—who suggested that the drought was God's answer to an over-zealous work ethic. Christians had been so busy producing abundant crops, Martin wrote, that God had sent dry years to give "time for spiritual matters."[38]

The same paper ran a moralistic analysis by its influential editor Daniel Kauffman himself. "Covetousness lies at the bottom of this world's poverty," Kauffman opined in 1935. The editor saw the sin partly as institutional, "the grasping policies of organized capital and organized labor." But the sins were also personal, stemming from "the love of ease." As for solutions, he thought that government's assistance money ended up in "drinking resorts, the gambling den, the tobacco barns . . . and the moving picture shows." So, Kauffman seemed to say, the depression called for no particularly new economic or cultural practices. Christians simply "should not become discouraged." If they would just be "diligent in every good work, [and] stop spending money 'for that which is not bread'. . . this old world will blossom as a rose. . . ."[39]

Such language permeated the *Gospel Herald*. Meanwhile its GC counterpart, *The Mennonite*, was generally more restrained in its moralizing. Yet it too attributed the "sad condition" of the world to the "materialistic spirit of the age."[40] Seldom did Mennonites call for genuinely political solutions to pressing social and economic needs. Indeed they rarely spoke out politically except on questions of how nonresistant peoples related to the state and to war. Or they spoke very generally.

In private, however, a Mennonite could be more pointed. In an analysis that had moral overtones but went beyond them, Edward Yoder reflected in his diary that the prosperity of the 1920s had been a "fool's paradise." Deep technological and other changes seemed to make "unemployment a perpetual problem. One almost despairs of ever again seeing anything like a stable and balanced order of life in the world. . . ." As for New Deal president Franklin D. Roosevelt, Yoder considered his popularity an example of "*gullibilitis Americana.*"[41]

In Canada the depression stimulated Mennonites to organize quite a few producer and consumer cooperatives. But Mennonites in the U.S. developed few such structural innovations, at least not until they organized Mennonite Mutual Aid in the mid-1940s. Instead, the answer of U.S. Mennonites to personal and social distress was largely that members should be frugal in their own affairs and charitable to the unfortunate.[42] In 1945 church leaders set up a multi-faceted, inter-Mennonite organization, Mennonite Mutual Aid, Inc. (MMA). The depression played only a minor role in the founding of MMA, which grew more out of the "recovery of the Anabaptist vision" and from looking ahead to postwar conversion needs.

MENNONITE MISSION

Despite the troubles of the 1930s, Mennonites continued with missions and benevolence at a surprising pace. Historically Mennonites had found that their distinctive cultural traditions, language barriers, demanding theology, and implicit or explicit separatism made growth through evangelism difficult. Perhaps as a consequence, for decades Mennonite missions had seemingly been more successful in foreign lands than in home communities or neighboring towns. During the 1930s in the U.S., most Mennonite conferences grew—but the limited data suggest that the growth came largely from Mennonites' own families. Such growth was quite constant through the century's early decades.

Mennonite missionary activism had begun in the nineteenth and early twentieth centuries with "quickenings" and "denomination-building" in various Mennonite branches. By 1930 mission structures were in place. Not only the denominations but their district conferences had mission boards and mission newsletters which offered powerful images of both need and opportunity. Among the MCs, by the 1930s a key slogan was "every congregation an outpost." New MC "mission outposts" doubled from 71 in 1930 to 140 in 1940. For MC home-mission activity the 1930s was the most active decade up to that time.[43] In 1928 the Conservative Amish Mennonite Conference, loosely affiliated with the MC but generally even more traditional in dress and attitude, began home mission work in Flint, Michigan. Then in the next decade it opened outposts in Sebewaing, Michigan; Vassar, Michigan; and Williamsville, New York.[44]

Like outposts of other Mennonite groups, some of the Conservative missions were rural and some urban. In cities, Mennonites' missions were usually among people of relatively low incomes, often immigrants. However, some seemed designed more to follow rural Mennonites who were drifting cityward. In some cases one hardly knows whether an outpost was truly a mission or just a Mennonite haven. In the 1930s the MBs had city missions in Winnipeg, Manitoba, and Minneapolis, Minnesota. The Minneapolis one tried genuinely to reach an alien population, but the Winnipeg one was largely a center for young Mennonite women who had come to the city to feed their families' depression-starved budgets.[45] Among the GCs in the first half of the century, their home mission board often debated whether it had found the proper balance between following Mennonites and inviting new people.[46]

New outposts easily brought influences that clashed with established Mennonite practices. In 1915 GC Mennonites had established a mission in Los Angeles which by the early 1930s was a thriving congregation. In 1931 it sought to leave the board's tutelage and become an independent congregation. But living as it did in the shadow of the Fundamentalistic Bible Institute of Los Angeles (BIOLA), the congregation had taken on a theology the GCs considered doubtful. So the board held back from handing over the property. A GC mission in Chicago had a rather similar story. It had begun in 1914, partly through the efforts of twenty-two Mennonites studying at the increasingly Fundamentalistic Moody Bible Institute. By 1929 there was a congregation of mixed ethnic background and a Sunday-school attendance of more than 300. In 1934 the congregation split because of new methods of ministerial control instituted by William Clyde Rhea, a BIOLA graduate.[47]

Some Mennonites took up "child evangelism," although not usually in extreme form. In the 1930s and '40s, MCs widely used vacation Bible schools and boys' and girls' clubs to reach out to newcomers. By contrast the Mennonite Brethren did not take up child evangelism much until after World War II. Evangelism that urged children to see themselves as sinful and decide for Christ at a tender age took its cue largely from conservative Protestantism and its doctrines of innate depravity and original sin. Mennonites, by contrast, had traditionally seen children as innocent, and had emphasized responsible, voluntary commitment to faith.[48]

These varied mission activities brought various new people into Mennonite congregations and conferences. Ex-moonshiners, ex-gamblers, and ex-prostitutes now joined, as well as many whose sins were less dramatic. Persons came of various racial, ethnic, and cultural stocks. In the Franconia MC conference a reference to mission described it as a "league of Nations." In 1932 the same conference discussed, apparently for the first time, whether to receive blacks as members (a practice the nearby Lancaster Conference had begun in 1917, a first for MCs). The decision was "that a colored applicant applying for baptism at the Rocky Ridge Mission [should] be baptized and received into the Mennonite church."[49]

It was not necessarily easy to incorporate new and culturally different people into the Mennonite fellowships. Few such people moved into leadership. However the outposts offered some release for Mennonites' own youth. Being at the churches' boundaries (or beyond), they gave youthful workers and other adventurers places to experiment in ways not yet acceptable at home.[50]

NEW ROLES FOR YOUTH AND WOMEN

Other new activities brought change and its pains. More and more, congregations offered weekly activities for the young, including Sunday-evening young people's meetings, literary societies, Christian worker bands, and more. In 1924 the youth of the Pleasant Valley MC congregation at Harper, Kansas, had organized a "Ciceronian Literary Society"—as was happening in many MC congregations. The societies offered social activities and built skills and self-confidence through recitations, musical performances, debate, office-holding, and procedures based on *Robert's Rules of Order.*

About 1927 the MCs' general conference increased its attention to the literary societies, which then gradually took on a more religious tone. Thus in a reorganization in 1932, the Pleasant Valley group decided to limit itself to topics of Christian faith. In that same year a more service-oriented Christian Workers' Band began channeling youths into missionary and related activities.[51]

From 1920 to 1923 a Young People's Conference flourished among the MCs. Led by young persons who had college training and were strongly progressive, the movement it represented quickly ran head-on against an older generation of leaders who had codified the church's doctrines and disciplines and had turned conference structures into more modern, more effective means to enforce both belief and practice. Out of concerns for the directions that this young people's movement might take, in 1921 the MC general conference formed a new, parallel "Young People's Problems Committee." In 1923 it instructed the newer committee to work with the unofficial Young People's Conference, but thereafter the youth conference never reconvened. The official committee continued; the floating, autonomous Young People Conference disappeared.[52]

Meanwhile many GC congregations, more ecumenical than the MC, sponsored chapters of the Protestant interdenominational Christian Endeavor organization. About the time of World War I, the GCs' general conference began to take a more direct interest, and in 1920 it appointed a Young People's Committee. Three years thereafter, the official GC periodical *The Mennonite* began a youth page that was more or less a voice for the committee. Later, in the mid-1930s, a movement began for a still-stronger church-sponsored youth organization. Somehow it took six years (two general-conference intervals) for the organization to form. Finally in 1941 it got underway—officially connected to the denomination and named the Young People's Union. Meanwhile among the MBs, between 1933 and 1936 a Youth Committee of the general conference took form. Soon it was sponsoring Christian Fellowship chapters in the congregations and promoting youth camps and other activities. A youth paper, the *Christian Leader*, which it began in 1937, eventually became the denomination's main English-language periodical.[53]

Mennonite youth organizations developed under a Christian rubric, but they also followed changes in American culture. As the nation industrialized and modernized, it more and more segregated its youth from adults for education and other purposes. Increasingly, youths were a distinct category in the population. Before, during, and after the 1930s, the pattern was spilling into Mennonite culture.

For women, unlike for youth, the 1930s were neither expansive nor a time of new autonomy in Mennonite religious culture. In the larger American culture, the 1920s and 1930s brought both

First General Conference Young People's Retreat, Camp LaVerne, California, 1935. Credit: Mennonite Library and Archives, Bethel College, North Newton, Kansas.

Women of the Lancaster area Associated Sewing Circles meeting, at the Paradise Cutting Room, Paradise, Pennsylvania, c. 1925. Credit: Lancaster Mennonite Historical Society, Lancaster, Pennsylvania.

liberation and repression. In 1920 women gained the vote in national elections. During the following decade they joined the workforce in unprecedented numbers; also, they were allowed somewhat greater freedom in dress and behavior.

U.S. religious conservatives generally resisted such changes. In 1930 two key institutions of Protestant Fundamentalism, the World's Christian Fundamentals Association and Gordon Divinity School, each took steps to keep women only in auxiliary positions or to limit them by quotas. Also, conservatives held women more and more responsible for society's morality. They and many other Americans had long accorded women the honor of being society's chief moral guardians. When many saw moral standards as declining in the 1920s, they easily made women the scapegoats for moral decay.[54]

As for Mennonites, their families, congregations, conferences, and institutions were highly patriarchal—many almost absolutely so. So Mennonites were more likely to sympathize with religious conservatives' anxieties than with anyone who wanted to widen women's roles and rights.

Officially, Mennonites' position on women's place in both home and church was a matter not of social or economic theory but of biblical prescriptions. During the 1930s the MC and culturally related conservative groups were much more preoccupied with those prescriptions than were some of the culturally more progressive groups. In 1929 MC bishop Jacob (J. K.) Bixler of Indiana, writing in the *Gospel Herald*, spelled out that place in words that pleased *Herald* editor Kauffman. While many congregations were not so strict in practice, surely many Mennonites were equally pleased. Bixler stated categorically that women should lead or speak publicly only in women's and children's groups—and then only with men's prior consent. Women could teach young boys, but Bixler was sure it was "unscriptural, and unfitting otherwise, for a woman to instruct and lead young men." In larger church gatherings, women were to be silent. Bixler and Kauffman thought women should not even ask questions if men were present.[55]

In the MC and various other conservative Mennonite groups, a crucial symbol for acknowledging women's submission was the devotional head covering. During the 1920s MC publications ran many articles to advocate and explain it, almost always based on the apostle Paul's advice in 1 Corinthians 11:3-10.

For instance in 1930 Oscar Burkholder, a prominent bishop in Ontario and member of the General Problems Committee, wrote that the covering's "greatest meaning is its recognition of woman's relationship. In these days," the problem-minded Burkholder lamented, woman was "usurping man's position and power." In so doing she was "scorning her God-given position of motherhood." A sign of such a woman was that she was "unwilling to wear anything that shows . . . she is second to men in God's order. . . ."[56]

The view, inferred from the Corinthians passage, was that in God's order of creation there were not only differences between the sexes but primary and secondary places. Some women were quick to concur. Lina Zook Ressler, a former missionary who soon would endear herself to children throughout the MC church by answering letters to the children's paper *Words of Cheer*, wrote, "We submit not because we must but because it is natural and right."[57]

This MC concern for maintaining the gender hierarchy took organizational forms. In 1912 some progressive MC women had formed the Mennonite Women's Missionary Society—the only MC organization above the congregational level which women fully controlled. Almost from the beginning, its autonomy troubled denominational leaders. Were women to pray, speak, and preside at such meetings? For many local chapters, the obvious answer was no. Reports of meetings mention men who came and performed these functions. With the men's blessings, women then turned to crafting materials. Apart from the gender issue, leaders clearly were troubled at any kind of freelance organization: the same generation brought John F. Funk's publishing company under a new Mennonite Publishing Board and Elkhart Institute (remained "Goshen College") under a new Mennonite Board of Education. But whether the concern was gender or freelancing, in the 1920s MC church leaders brought the Women's Missionary Society under the control of their male-dominated Board of Missions and Charities. Organized to support mission, by 1921 the Women's Missionary Society provided full support for four missionaries on the field. Between 1921 and 1929, despite conflict over control (and a change in name to "General Sewing Circle Committee") the women doubled that number.[58]

In the more remote parts of the Amish and Mennonite world, such consolidation did little to change local practice. In Lewis County, New York, a formerly Amish settlement relatively isolated from other Amish communities was changing in ways that obscured distinctions between Mennonites and Amish. In 1933 its Mennonite women organized their sewing circle more formally than before. The depression was on them, and they could not ignore the area's needy families and institutions. When a hospital opened in Lewis County in 1936, women from the Croghan and Dadville congregations assisted by mending and folding gauze. The reorganized sewing circle also kept records and took minutes of its meetings, in the fashion of modern organizations. Charity might be from the heart, but modernity dictated that there be accounts of the good being done.[59]

Among the GCs and the MBs, local women's missionary associations also had a long history. Like their counterparts in other Mennonite denominations, they provided material and money for both foreign and domestic outreach and nurtured interest in mission. Into the 1920s the societies' main activity was sewing garments and bedding. But during the 1920s, the GC and MB women's groups began to fund specific projects. In 1931 GC local societies across North America cooperated to raise monies for an automobile for China, a school building in India, a hospital building in Winnipeg, and aid for Russian Mennonite refugee students.[60] In that same year, at the depression's depth, the GCs adopted a "Two Cents a Week Plan" whereby each member was to give that amount for a missionary pension fund. Their annual budget for projects during the 1930s remained at about $10,000 per year. MB women's groups were responsible for much of the relief material and money that was raised during the 1920s and 1930s to support the refugees from the Soviet Union as they resettled in Europe and in North and South America.[61]

GC mission leaders actively sought the women's cooperation rather than trying to dominate them. Beginning in the 1930s, their mission board invited two members of the women's missionary association to its meetings. The practice quickly became standard. Also, projects that the women initiated became integrated into the work of the board and other conference agencies.[62] Samuel Floyd Pannabecker, GC historian and missiologist, observed that in these varied activities "the sisters may well have done more to popularize 'mission' than their brothers on the Mission Board."[63]

TWO VIEWS OF THE MENNONITE FUTURE

In 1929 and 1930 two thoughtful Mennonites made quite different predictions. Together they summarized Mennonite optimism and pessimism as the middle third of the century approached. Both were accurate. But the two wrote from different realities and mentalities.

Paul Whitmer, dean of the GCs' Witmarsum Seminary in Ohio, had earlier been an MC Mennonite teaching at Goshen College. In August 1929 he delivered a major address at the triennial sessions of the GCs' general conference as it met at Hutchinson, Kansas. Calling his remarks "The Future of the Mennonite Church: In the United States and Canada," he articulated a position held by many progressives in whatever Mennonite denomination. He began with the past, for in the Mennonite imagination, past and future always intertwine. The past of which Whitmer spoke was one of persecution and migration—experiences which had fractured Mennonites into "fifty-seven varieties."[64] While humorous, his use of the Heinz company's slogan underlined a Mennonite tragedy. In reality Mennonite divisions were as much the consequence of religious and cultural schisms as they were of persecution and the search for asylum.

However, for Whitmer the future promised greater unity. The American environment would diminish past differences of language and culture. However painful the current transition from German to English, in the long run Mennonite Anglicization was good. He said the process was "inevitable and we might just as well accept it good humoredly." In any case, "one of the greatest forward steps ever taken by Mennonites in America" would be greater fraternal relationships between the six or eight larger Mennonite denominations. To expect such cooperation was realistic, said Whitmer; from his "rather extensive acquaintance among five or six Mennonite branches" he thought "such an achievement in the next twenty-five or thirty years is by no means visionary."[65]

Whitmer was optimistic also about the institutions—publishing houses, mission agencies, schools, and more—Mennonites had built over the previous seventy-five years. They offered church-related vocations, an enticement to Mennonite youth which previous generations could not dream of. All in all, Whitmer offered a most hopeful reading of the Mennonite future. Anglicization, inter-Mennonite cooperation, and institutional developments—these were the bedrock for optimism.

From the denomination that featured "Problems" committees came a considerably less sanguine and more troubled set of predictions. The pen was that of Noah Mack, a bishop in the conservative Lancaster MC conference. Labeling his piece "The Situation in American Mennonitism," Mack published it in *The Sword and Trumpet*, an MC-related but freelance conservative paper whose editor, George R. Brunk I, was determined to fight laxity in both doctrine and practice. Mack wrote in a mood of apocalypse. "There is now a doom and an overthrow threatening the Mennonite Church in America. . . ." During past centuries the church had stood "against the onslaught of the enemy." It had "passed through the severest of trials and persecutions"—even to the point of martyrdom. More recently it had "held out" against war and bloodshed, life insurance, lodge membership, and "many other worldly ideas." But now the armies of Satan were threatening. Already that army had "gone through the more popular churches"— although in some "independent bodies" there were "still remnants who are standing for the gospel simplicity."[66]

Mack saw the rise of mass advertising and mass media posing new dangers for the church. Their glitz was finding its way into Mennonite homes and imaginations. Too many Mennonites were deaf to their church leaders' warnings. Instead they "have read all their magazines," including the "fashion plates." Their radios were bringing in "the Jazz music and Amos and Andy and other interesting matter." As a result, Mack wrote, "they have no taste for good instructive literature; it tires them and makes them sick."[67]

Thus Mack found threatening the very developments that

Whitmer found so promising. The impact of American culture on Mennonites was not a healthy Anglicization or new opportunities but something pagan and insidious. He feared the increasing autonomy and independence of church institutions. Greater cooperation among Mennonites would lead the faithful ones to relax their nonconformity and boundaries.

Mack's conservative analysis was the Mennonite counterpart of a deep pessimism in many American denominations. In the 1920s, among Protestants, Fundamentalists expressed similar fears. Mack was a Mennonite fundamentalist. In the 1930s and beyond, a version of fundamentalism shaped the outlooks of quite a few Mennonites.

CHAPTER

3

MENNONITE FUNDAMENTALISM

The different Mennonite futures Mack and Whitmer projected came partly from the contrast between conservative and progressive outlooks. In 1927 Guy F. Hershberger, a young historian at Goshen College, observed to a friend that the Mennonite church hardly knew what it meant by conservatism and progressivism. But he thought his church had "a splendid opportunity . . . to work out a sound religious and social philosophy in which these two elements are properly related." The way to do it, he thought, was to address the "Peace Problem."[1] In fact Hershberger would have a notable career as a teacher, thinker, and writer on Mennonite social ethics, blending theological conservatism with a rather progressive social outlook and integrating them around the doctrine of peace.

Another problem the young professor saw in 1927 was that instead of addressing up-to-date issues, Mennonites wanted to "creep inside a tortoise shell." He was referring to parts of the "old" or MC Mennonite church, but he could have said the same of other Mennonites. Many Mennonites were indeed looking for protection against an intrusive culture. And they were not alone. Often their attitudes coincided with a rather fearful outlook in Protestant churches known as Fundamentalism. For numerous Mennonites, Fundamentalism held considerable attraction.

CULTURAL AND THEOLOGICAL FUNDAMENTALISM

Interpreters have long understood that Protestant Fundamentalism was both cultural and theological and have explained it in various ways.[2] In recent years historian George Marsden has offered an especially complex (and well-received) interpretation that presents it as integrating many strands of the American religious past—nineteenth-century revivalism, pietism, evangelicalism, a congealing Presbyterian theology nourished by Princeton Seminary, millenarianism, Common Sense or Baconian philosophy and science, denominational conservatism, and more.[3]

In Marsden's telling Fundamentalism, as a historic movement[4] in American Protestantism, emerged as various people who commonly thought of themselves as evangelical responded to a profound religious and intellectual crisis of the late nineteenth and early twentieth centuries. More and more the enemy was Modernism, both theological and cultural.

Theologically, Modernists were willing to question key beliefs Fundamentalists saw increasingly as bedrock—most notably Scripture as God's unique, inerrant revelation, uncontaminated by being transmitted through human culture; a literal understanding of the Genesis account of creation, the virgin birth, the resurrection, and other miracles; Christ's substitutionary atonement as the central act and meaning of salvation; and biblical understandings of eschatology, or how history would unfold and end.[5]

Culturally, Fundamentalists thought Modernists were diminishing God's role in the social and cultural changes of their day. Some other Christians, not just Fundamentalists, might have been uneasy with Modernism; but Fundamentalists challenged it militantly, vehemently, in a spirit of battle. Nonetheless, more profoundly than the surface conflicts, Marsden saw Fundamentalism as a movement of both theological and cultural opposition to the drift of North American culture. It was partly a search for an appropriate relationship between culture and Christianity.[6]

MENNONITE CULTURAL AND THEOLOGICAL FUNDAMENTALISM

For Mennonites, Fundamentalism was also a way to reassess cultural and theological issues. People who understood themselves as separate from their culture should have been put off by it. Furthermore Mennonites had traditionally read the Bible more as a guide to life than as a body of rigorous propositions. Yet since they took the Bible literally and seriously, they easily saw Fundamentalists' views of Scripture as their own.[7]

As for issues such as creation, virgin birth, resurrection, and the saving efficacy of Christ's shed blood, Mennonites had taken orthodox positions for granted more than developing them into systematic doctrines.[8] But if (as Fundamentalists strongly implied) there were only two choices on such points—the Fundamentalist and the Modernist—Mennonites certainly felt drawn to the Fundamentalist side. Moreover, Mennonites (like some in many other denominations) might shape fundamentalism their own way by adding their own favorite doctrines, such as nonresistance and nonconformity, to the list of indispensable beliefs.

Whatever theological issues were present, for Mennonites fundamentalism was more an effort to redefine the relationships between culture and Christianity than a strictly theological crusade. It was one Mennonite response to modernity and its cultural changes. Mennonite fundamentalism was generally an attempt to resist Americanization, reinforce cultural separatism, and purge out alien ideologies and practices whether theological or cultural. Paradoxically, however, scholarly interpreters of early-twentieth-century Mennonite fundamentalism have suggested it really was also a part of the Americanization process—for it accelerated the integration of Mennonites into the larger society and hastened cultural accommodation.[9]

The truth surely lies somewhere in between. Mennonite fundamentalism helped both to tighten and to loosen boundaries. Through it, Mennonites accepted a larger dose of varying American theologies, but they also tightened theological boundaries by making both dogma and discipline more precise.

By emphasizing their own historic distinctives and concerns, Mennonites gave their fundamentalism a Mennonite cast. Except for John Horsch, the MC writer and historian, hardly any Mennonites participated in the larger Fundamentalist movement. Among Mennonites there was almost no real theological modernism. In Mennonite soil it remained exotic, far from the everpresent weed that some conservatives feared. Indeed it is a puzzle to know exactly who it was that militant Mennonite fundamentalists feared. Theron Schlabach has aptly described John Horsch, the leading Mennonite crusader, as often "aiming elephant guns to kill flies."[10] Horsch's son-in-law Harold Bender, who was surely keen and competent, observed in 1926 that "as far as the Old Men-

John (J. E.) Hartzler, 1921. Credit: Mennonite Historical Library, Goshen College, Goshen, Indiana.

nonite Church is concerned, there is no Modernism."[11]

Among the various Mennonites, fundamentalism took hold only after some Mennonite "awakenings" or "quickenings." In the late nineteenth and early twentieth centuries, Mennonites borrowed heavily from revivalistic and sometimes other American Protestants. The largest groups (MC, GC, MB) and some smaller ones created the institutions characteristic of American denominations—stronger conferences; Sunday schools; colleges; publishing houses; revival and other special meetings; mission boards and missions; youth and women's organizations; etc. Such institutions often increased Mennonites' contacts with the larger Protestant world. Some contacts were with conservative and Fundamentalist Protestants, some with the more mainline.

Mennonites who wandered in the larger Protestant world came back bearing many things. Some found new ways of expressing old truths. Many refused to adopt Fundamentalist formulas and language, and they soon bore the criticism of being "liberal." But there was more than one liberalism to borrow. Writing of American religion generally, scholar Kenneth Cauthen has distinguished between "evangelical liberals" and "modernistic liberals." Both were liberal in the sense of accepting change and adapting religion to modern culture; but the evangelical kind, while liberal in spirit, was orthodox in theology. Evangelical liberals continued to believe in such doctrines as Jesus' full divinity and felt a deep sense of continuity with the past.[12]

John (J. E.) Hartzler, who into the early 1930s was chief

spokesman for MCs charged with liberalism, was the evangelical kind of liberal. A graduate of Goshen College, he earned advanced degrees from Union Theological Seminary, the University of Chicago, and Hartford Seminary. He was an evangelist and then successively dean of the Goshen Bible School (1910-1913) and president of Goshen College (1913-1918). In 1918 he left for Bethel College, was its president for a short term, then from 1921 to 1931 was president of Bluffton College's Witmarsum Seminary. His leaving Goshen in 1918 for these GC schools was an event in a fundamentalist-versus-liberal tension within the MC world.[13]

In 1925, reflecting on the conflicts in his church, Hartzler lamented that extreme conservatism "exalts human authority above the Scriptures and above reason." By contrast he thought that while the liberal spirit was "overthrowing much of the religious tradition, and most of the religious educational method," such an "overturning of things" was not all bad. At least it was "not entirely unwelcome to the rising generation."[14] Nonetheless, at least into the 1930s Hartzler was not a theological modernizer. But he was a cultural modernizer, and his Mennonite critics did not always make that distinction. It was easy to confuse and misidentify the two.

Conservatives also came back with new modes of thinking. Conservative devotional books, *The Sunday School Times*, items from a conservatively religious press known as David C. Cook, and the dispensationalist Scofield Bible found their way into many Mennonite homes and churches. A Mennonite tradition of direct "biblicistic" thinking increasingly gave way to a self-conscious, intellectual theologizing. A new emphasis on Protestant doctrines of justification and sanctification now appeared alongside older motifs like discipleship and obedience.[15] Some conservatives returned with the militancy that echoed Protestant Fundamentalism's fighting spirit. Even Daniel Kauffman, strongly allied with the conservative cause, recognized that in his church the "impulsiveness of some conservatives" made both unity and a sensible conservatism quite difficult.[16]

Two conservative borrowings that generated a great deal of discussion were premillennialism, a doctrine that Jesus will return to earth before he then literally reigns as a king for a thousand years; and dispensationalism, a belief that God has worked differently in human affairs in different epochs of history.

To Mennonites these beliefs were historically foreign. In North America and in the Russian empire some key future leaders

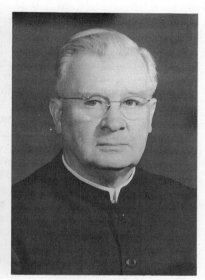

Chester K. Lehman, c. 1965   **John L. Stauffer, c. 1950**

picked up such ideas while attending various schools. Young American MCs such as Amos (A. D.) Wenger, Aaron Loucks, and Samuel (S. F.) Coffman learned them while studying at Moody.[17] The MCs never officially adopted premillennialism. But in 1928 Harold Bender thought Daniel Kauffman's 1928 *Doctrines of the Bible*, which effectively codified MC theology, "skated rather close to the brink on premillennialism"—even if it "did not quite skate in."[18] Bender, an amillennialist (or nonmillennialist) rather than a premillennialist, advised Kauffman that he had no objection if a fellow Mennonite advocated premillennialism in a proper spirit. The trouble was, he said, "usually premillennialists become intolerant and radical."[19] Kauffman, however, thought that "pre's and anti's" were equally guilty.[20]

The millennial controversy embroiled MC colleges. Goshen College drew strong criticism for amillennialism.[21] Eastern Mennonite School, guided by presidents Amos (A. D.) Wenger and John (J. L.) Stauffer and others, was strongly premillennialist but had a strong amillennialist dissenter in the person of Chester (C. K.) Lehman, dean since 1922.[22] The central issue was the premillennialists' suggestion that nonmillennialism smacked of liberalism. To the "pre's," nonmillennialists' failure to interpret some scriptural passages literally put them on a slippery slope toward liberalism and modernism. The charge grew directly out of Fundamentalism's sharp dichotomies.

Among Mennonite groups, only the Defenseless Mennonites and the Mennonite Brethren in Christ made premillennialism their official doctrine. The Krimmer Mennonite Brethren allied closely but not officially. Among GC Mennonites by the mid-1940s premillennialism found favor among a minority who aligned with Grace Bible Institute in Nebraska.[23]

As for the Mennonite Brethren, their leading historian John A. Toews has identified dispensationalism as the chief theological influence from outside the group between 1925 and 1950. Already in the Russian empire in the late nineteenth century, MB leaders attended meetings in Germany known as the Blankenburg Alliance conferences, which dispensed the ideas of John Darby of Plymouth, England, founder of the highly dispensationalist "Plymouth Brethren." One who then sowed Darby's ideas was William Bestvater, a turn-of-the-century immigrant from the Russian empire to North America and one of the first MBs to enroll in the correspondence courses of Charles I. Scofield of Scofield Bible fame. In the 1920s MB premillennialism in North America got a boost from the Soviet Union's Mennonite emigrants in Canada.[24]

Cultural fundamentalism was as pervasive as theological fundamentalism. In the three large groups cultural rigidity was more deeply ingrained among the MCs and MBs than among the less-insulated GCs. In 1930 nearly all Mennonites lived in communities that spatially isolated them to some degree. MCs into the 1950s reinforced that separation by visual or dress segregation, and MBs reinforced their distance by continuing use of the German language into the 1940s. The GCs dropped distinctive attire in the nineteenth century and during the 1920s largely completed the switch to English. For MCs and MBs, fundamentalist-related theological controversies often made the cultural conflicts more intense.[25]

The Old Orders also practiced distinctive dress. But their adherence to visual distinctions is better understood as traditionalism and should not be confused with the growing dress conflicts among the MCs during the twentieth century. By resisting many American Protestant patterns, the Old Orders also remained aloof from the fundamentalist controversies that engulfed the progressive denominations during the 1920s and on into the 1950s. Those Mennonites who stepped on the escalator of change in the late nineteenth century more easily confused cultural and theological fundamentalism than those who stayed more aloof from social change. Cultural fundamentalism and cultural conservatism were two different kinds of responses. Cultural fundamentalism among the groups embracing change was an attempt to regulate or even halt the social changes that an earlier generation had applauded.

MC and GC fundamentalism tended to be nourished by Presbyterian sources, while MBs turned more to the Baptists for the articulation of their fundamentalism. The Baptist version, at least the Augustus H. Strong and Charles Y. Mullins one that became prominent in MB circles, was a more irenic form. Less militant or conflictual, it more easily became subtly diffused. The Presbyterian form, allied most prominently with J. Gresham Machen, was more militant, confrontational, and divisive but also more easily discernible as a foreign substance.[26]

Controversies around fundamentalism came to focus especially in the denominations' colleges, seminaries, and publishing houses—a pattern that Mennonites shared with Protestant bodies. From 1913 to 1951 at least seven Mennonite college presidents resigned partly due to such conflicts. Meanwhile Mennonites formed several new institutions of higher learning: Eastern Mennonite School (MC) in the East in 1917; Grace Bible Institute (largely GC) in the plains states in 1943; and Pacific Bible Institute (MB) in the West in 1944.

The three new schools reflected regional needs, but another motive was fear that the existing Mennonite colleges were not sufficiently orthodox. Mennonites were following a pattern whereby Protestant Fundamentalists created their own institutional structures either interdenominationally or within denominations.[27]

MC FUNDAMENTALISM

MC Mennonites entered the 1930s more deeply bruised by the fundamentalist controversy than any other Mennonite group. In 1923-1924 the board of Goshen College closed the school for a year largely because many of its constituents feared for its orthodoxy. In the 1920s, among MC district conferences, Indiana-Michigan (at whose center the college sat) lost four congregations, six ministers, and an eighth of its members due to quarrels over what some thought was "liberalism."[28]

In 1924 the MCs' official publishing house released *The Mennonite Church and Modernism*, by John Horsch. An unabashed polemic, the book departed sharply from a Mennonite tradition of theological civility. Horsch explicitly identified John E. Hartzler, Noah E. Byers, Samuel K. Mosiman, Lester Hostetler, Samuel K. Burkhart, and Vernon Smucker as modernists.[29] He also fingered the *Christian Exponent*, a 1924-1928 publication that gave voice to these and other MC and GC progressives. All of Horsch's "modernists" except Mosiman were graduates of Goshen College. Byers and Hartzler had been Goshen presidents. A number on Horsch's list had grown up in the MC church, then shifted to the GC, often to Bluffton College. Shifts of loyalty from MC to GC seem to have troubled Horsch as much as the "modernists" theology did.[30]

In January of 1929 other MCs, led by George R. Brunk I and colleagues in Virginia, began a journal they named *The Sword and Trumpet*. The astute diarist Edward Yoder soon observed that the journal's "method and spirit" were "pugilistic and almost quixotic."[31] In fact Brunk's polemicism was not frivolous, for it surely grew out of deep and sincere conviction. Yet the title and style he chose were strange indeed among a people known as pacifist and "the quiet in the land." Paradoxically, the journal's tone, approach, and even title seemed to violate some of the very Mennonite traditions the journal earnestly upheld.

The MCs suffered deeper fractures than other major Mennonite groups because their historic resistance to change was more refined, and therefore modernity seemed more threatening. Schlabach has noted that the late-nineteenth-century "quickening" caused breaches in the Mennonite fences which let "the horses . . . [begin to] run in different directions."[32] If he was right, surely Mennonite fundamentalists were trying to close the holes. They tried to do so by codifying doctrine, centralizing church authority, and giving new rigidity to cultural nonconformity.[33]

In the process, doctrines long held as equals became unequal. This distortion, typical also of how Protestant Fundamentalists treated classic doctrines such as the atonement, especially affected Mennonites' principle of separation from the world. In the MC church, attire took on new importance. Conferences, district and general, passed detailed descriptions of the permissible and the unacceptable. Melvin Gingerich, MC historian, tallied 237 resolutions on dress by various MC conferences. Exactly half (118) passed between 1918 and 1951.[34]

Chief among the demands were the lapel-less "plain" or "regulation" coat for men (at least for church leaders and church employees) and the cape dress and bonnet for women.[35] It seems that as other forms of separatism receded, costume became ever more important.[36] Moreover it was easy to confuse costume fundamentalism and theological correctness. In 1932, commenting on "hats-for-women," Daniel Kauffman, chief guardian of MC orthodoxy, assured Eastern Mennonite School's J. L. Stauffer that such deviation was "the outward slogan of an inward liberalism."[37]

In 1924 Vernon Smucker, the first editor of the *Christian Exponent*, lamented privately to Harold Bender about a tendency to classify anyone as a "modernist" who resisted the dress standards and other conference rulings.[38] From a position somewhere between Kauffman's and Smucker's, Sanford C. Yoder—who in the 1920s and '30s had been president of Goshen College and chief executive of the MCs' main board of missions—later observed of those times that men who had "refused to wear the plain coat were declared infected with the spirit of liberalism."[39]

From an outlook similar to Yoder's, Guy F. Hershberger later wrote that "cultural change . . . [had been] more basic than theological questions in the minds of most Mennonite Church leaders." The "fundamentalist spirit," he thought, had been a way to guard against change.[40]

Eventually John (J. C.) Wenger, MC historian and bishop, would symbolize for many the connection of dress with orthodoxy. He became a symbol because by the 1970s, when most MC church leaders had changed to ordinary business suits, he continued to wear the lapel-less coat or at least a clerical vest, always in solid black. But in 1935, when a student at Princeton Seminary, he confided to Harold Bender that the prospect of having eventually to wear the regulation coat troubled him. He understood that any MC man who wanted to do "Christian work" in his church would have to wear it. But to Wenger, doing so was only a "peace offering to those driving the issue so hard." Which should he do—"please the conservatives like the Virginia bishop" or do what he thought "best" in his "everyday living"? Wrote Wenger, "I greatly deplore all this emphasis on dress." The more he studied history, he said, the more he thought "we are not true to the faith of our fathers when we draw such hard and fast lines at Conference" and then "force the regulations of a few bishops upon the brotherhood."[41]

In the short run, linking liberalism with wearing anything other than the plain coat did increase dress uniformity. But it did so at the cost of undermining a nonconformity doctrine long cen-

tral to Mennonite theology. Preservation, held too close and too te-
naciously, can trivialize and undermine.[42]

For conservatives, however, the issue was not simply preserving dress restrictions. They saw a threat to the very future of the
church. Unless the church clearly defined the "apparel for disci-
ples of Jesus," wrote Eastern Mennonite School professor Jacob
(J. B.) Smith, "she will soon be swallowed up by the gaudy votaries
of fashion." Church history demonstrated that such a process led
to "apostasy."[43]

Along with the confusion of cultural and theological liberalism, the controversies around Mennonite fundamentalism to
some degree reflected a struggle also between the MCs' East and
West. There were conservatives in the West, but generally the congregations and districts east of the Alleghenies were more so. For
decades a major concern of those who led the MCs' general conference was preserving a fragile unity. In retrospect Elizabeth Horsch
Bender, like her husband, Harold, a keen observer, thought that
during the troubled 1920s Daniel Kauffman was more concerned
with church unity than doctrinal orthodoxy.[44]

Meanwhile MC conservatives, wanting strength against the
liberals, tried persistently to get three eastern conferences who
had never joined their church's general conference—the large and
old Franconia and Lancaster bodies, plus the smaller Washing-
ton-Franklin—to join. In 1931 Virginia's J. L. Stauffer assured
John H. Mosemann, Sr., a leading Lancaster Conference bishop,
that the conservatives had "already whipped" the liberals. Lancaster's joining would "keep them on the run."[45]

The rivalries were partly a matter of Eastern Mennonite
School versus Goshen College, partly conformity versus individuality, and partly centralized versus local authority. After its closing
in 1923-1924, a reorganized Goshen College took a moderately
conservative course under president Sanford Yoder. Nevertheless
in 1933 Daniel Kauffman chided Harold Bender, then dean, that
Goshen still was, "in some point, too far away from the accepted
standards of nonconformity and kindred standards that the Mennonite Church holds to." A " 'fight to the finish' between Goshen
and Warwick [George R. Brunk I]," Kauffman thought, "might form
the nucleus for a church-wide rend that would be disastrous."[46]

The conservatives were correct in perceiving that Goshen was
moving toward a different definition of Mennonitism. With Bender, Elizabeth Horsch Bender, Guy F. Hershberger, and others as intellectual guides, Goshen was trying to guard Mennonite identity

through the articulation of a history-based ideology soon labeled "the Anabaptist Vision."

As for individuality versus conformity, George R. Brunk I once wrote: "We have a closed policy as to all that the Bible teaches—all that the church rules—all that a bishop rules."[47] And regarding central versus local authority, ever since the late-nineteenth-century quickening, MC church leaders had been strengthening the denominational machinery, with the effect of centralizing power. In 1932 Edward Yoder reflected that "one cannot make a slightest move without bumping into a committee"; committees and boards had "multiplied like a plague in Egypt."[48]

The rules and tensions were not only about dress. For instance in 1931 the Virginia Conference asked members to rid themselves of all radios. In 1932 it reaffirmed a ban against attending various kinds of fairs, commercial exhibitions, and patriotic gatherings, and against being in civic clubs such as Kiwanis and Rotary. J. L. Stauffer, in the lead sermon of the 1933 conference, warned against the "unequal yoke," whether in marriage, economic organizations, religious fellowships, or political contacts.[49] Such admonitions were by no means limited to Virginia. And many of them, such as the warnings against attendance, affiliations, and the "unequal yoke," were traditional and longstanding in MC district conferences.

In the MC general conference during the 1930s and 1940s, the chief body dealing with matters of change was the General Problems Committee. The conference created the committee in 1929 and charged it with, among other duties, "investigation and solution of any . . . irregularity . . . affecting the peace, unity, and spiritual welfare of the church."[50] From then until 1944 the committee gave its main energies to drawing lines of separation. Its work was consolidation and conservation, not adaptation or change. Leading the committee was a prestigious and staunchly conservative set of figures: Daniel Kauffman, Oscar Burkholder of Ontario, Daniel (D. A.) Yoder of Indiana, Harry A. Diener of Kansas, and John (J. L.) Stauffer of Virginia.[51]

The committee's 1935 report, although rather shrill, was typical. At its heart were seven protests against "selfishness," "carnality," "growing indifference toward our historic and biblical principles," "immodest and fashionable attire," "worldly and fashionable headwear worn by some of our sisters," "world conformity" via members' belonging to various associations, and a growing practice of individuals keeping membership in distant congregations rather than yielding to the standards of local ones. Other points, often more specific, were against joining unions, purchasing life insurance, and frequenting worldly amusements. The 1935 report concluded, in bold print, that "ACTION IS NOW NEEDED." But instead of specifying action it merely exhorted the church to do better.[52]

In 1943 the committee did come to the conference with proposed concrete action. It recommended that nonconformity and nonresistance be made tests of membership. Nonresistance had been such a test in Mennonite congregations historically. In the middle of World War II, 1943, was an appropriate time to reaffirm it. Nonconformity by contrast had not been so codified and not so much a litmus test of faithfulness. But now the committee recommended that "the doctrine of nonconformity to the world" be required for church membership. Specifically, a member might violate the doctrine by "holding of life insurance, membership in labor unions, immodest and worldly attire (including hats for sisters), the wearing of jewelry (including wedding rings), [and/or] attendance at movies and theaters."[53]

Lacking time to debate the proposal at its 1943 meetings, the MC general conference held special sessions in 1944. For conservatives—those seeking to consolidate the authority of the church and to arrest its changing profile—the sessions promised to be a defining moment. J. L. Stauffer thought they were a "crossroads" and called for action to stop "compromise with and surrender to the world and worldliness."[54] Paul Erb, new editor of the *Gospel Herald*, feared quarrels about dress threatened to set off another church division.[55]

The conference vibrated with discussion. Some conservatives challenged the legitimacy of the Illinois district conference's membership in the MCs' general body because of its laxity on dress questions.[56] Guy F. Hershberger later described the sessions as the "last desperate attempt" to rein in the MC variations.[57] Actually the conference was hardly the last attempt of MC cultural fundamentalists. Their cause and their sincerity would continue. But no longer would they dominate.

GC FUNDAMENTALISM

MC quarrels were bound to influence the General Conference Mennonites. Relationships between MC and GC, although often distant, were rather close in the colleges because of a drift of dissatisfied MC academics to either Bluffton or Bethel College. Nonetheless in the late '20s and early '30s the conflicts at Bluffton, Bluffton's Witmarsum Seminary, and Bethel were different from MC ones as well as similar. Without the question of visual nonconformity—that is, of attire—GC quarrels were more like those in North America's Protestant denominations.

At Bluffton, concerns about modernism surfaced in 1922, when a committee of the GCs' Middle District Conference circulated a doctrinal questionnaire to various GC schools. President Samuel K. Mosiman's response seemed inadequate to Peter R. Schroeder, pastor of a large and powerful GC congregation at Berne, Indiana. So Schroeder and others produced a series of letters and reports that the Berne congregation printed in 1929 as *Evidences of Modernism at Bluffton College*. Authors of the printed documents included William S. Gottshall, a pastor in the Bluffton area from 1900 to 1924; Peter H. Richert, longtime pastor at Goessel, Kansas; Rudy Gehman, who had left the GCs for the Brethren in Christ; and the MCs' leading anti-modernist, John Horsch. Most of the correspondence was about how the Bluffton and Witmarsum faculties treated inspiration of Scripture, incarnation, resurrection, and atonement.[58]

That same year, 1929, at the triennial sessions of the GCs' general conference, the critics somewhat hesitantly made formal charges against Bluffton. Privately to Richert, Gottshall predicted that the conference would formulate some common articles of faith but in the end each faction would go its own way. Sure that the GC church would soon be "in the middle of the stream of Liberalism," he asked: "Should conservatives hang back, to avoid a break in the ranks? Is our denominational loyalty stronger than our loyalty to the Truth?"[59]

Much as Gottshall predicted, in the end the conference passed a rather innocuous declaration of "loyalty to the faith of our fathers." And it appointed an investigative committee. Beyond the work of skillful church politicians, depression economics and other issues seem also to have deflected the discussion.[60] In 1933 the committee made an inconclusive report which the conference accepted.[61]

By that time, however, the conservatives had enjoyed a real victory. In 1931 Witmarsum Seminary ceased to exist, surely due in part to the controversies swirling around Bluffton. Some of the seminary's troubles were financial. Others had to do with a flamboyant president, John E. Hartzler, who was not always adept at building consensus and connecting well with constituents. There was also a question of whether the more prudent course was not to use funds to strengthen Mennonite colleges rather than seminaries.[62]

But the deeper cause was theological whirlwinds. Samuel F. Pannabecker, later president of Witmarsum's eventual successor, the Mennonite Biblical Seminary, defined the whirlwinds as coming from a "sterile liberalism and a dogmatic orthodoxy." A faculty committed to neither had found it difficult "to mediate between the two current positions."[63] The same winds would prevent the GCs from establishing an effective seminary until after World War II.

The Witmarsum Seminary story illustrated a larger truth. Not only were Mennonites caught between conservatism and liberalism; even more, they had not articulated a theological system appropriate to their history and position in society. Protestant Fundamentalism and liberalism were both alien to them.

Bethel College also passed through a crisis over fundamentalist-related questions. That crisis, shortly after World War I, clearly grew partly from cultural difficulties German-speaking Mennonites had experienced during the war and its aftermath.[64] By the 1930s, however, the issues were less cultural and more theological.

In 1930 John W. Kliewer thought of resigning as Bethel's president. Bethel's troubles were various. Not least, Bethel faced an accumulated deficit of more than $100,000, and its accreditation was shaky. But Kliewer also was having difficulty balancing, as he put it, the "liberal and [the] conservative elements of our constituency."[65] Peter H. Richert, the nearby Goessel pastor, was writing to various people with a list of concerns. He scored guest speakers who deviated from fundamental standards; faculty who were not vigorous and explicit enough about the authority of Scripture; and permissive, inappropriate activity in student athletics, dramas, and campus socials.[66]

Moreover Richert had an ally in the influential Henry (H. P.) Krehbiel. In the 1920s Krehbiel had tried to resurrect a proposal first put forward in 1905 by his father,[67] church leader Christian Krehbiel, calling for a Bible school.[68] Now H. P. Krehbiel argued once more for the Bible school on grounds that denominational colleges were "utterly failing" to turn out "consecrated spiritual" workers. He accused Bethel of caring more about the regional accrediting association than about the welfare of the church.[69]

In a widely circulated "Overture" for the proposed Bible

school, Krehbiel argued that liberal arts colleges contributed only "to the things of this perishing world"; they offered students nothing about "the eternal Kingdom of God and the realm of the soul."[70] The strategy of Krehbiel and others was to try to take $100,000 which the Western District Conference held as endowment for Bethel College and shift it to the new Bible school.[71] The conference, however, rejected the idea and kept the endowment with Bethel.[72]

Nonetheless some GCs were unwilling to give up on creating a Bible school. By 1943 they were able to open Grace Bible Institute (GBI) at Omaha, Nebraska. Although technically an interdenominational school, Grace was really a school for GCs of fundamentalist bent. Its origins were in proposals to expand Oklahoma Bible Academy (OBA), a GC secondary school at Meno, Oklahoma. Discussions between OBA and a variety of GC ministers (especially Peter A. Kliewer of Albany, Oregon; Albert Schultz of Butterfield, Minnesota; and Cornelius H. Suckau of Berne, Indiana) suggested that there was a broad GC constituency who might support a conservative school. In the summer of 1943, ten like-minded Mennonite conservatives met at Omaha. Some of the ten, all male, were graduates of Bluffton and Bethel but many also had Bible school training. Their discussion quickly turned to forming a new school.[73]

Three features of the Mennonite landscape during the 1930s and 1940s troubled the group. First, in their perception the Bible departments in Mennonite colleges "were becoming increasingly liberal in their theology and secular in their educational programs." Paul Kuhlmann author of a GBI history, likened the trends at Bethel and Bluffton to the histories of Harvard and Yale, which also had once been denominational schools for religious training. In the language of Protestant Fundamentalism, those present charged the faculties of the "secularized" Mennonite colleges with questioning the inspiration of the Scriptures, the virgin birth of Christ, and other central orthodox affirmations while teaching "humanistic foundations for their faith."[74] They thought that of all Mennonites, the GCs were most in danger. But Suckau at least hoped "to unite the fundamental groups in the various Mennonite churches."[75]

A second issue was Mennonite students attending various non-Mennonite Bible schools, especially BIOLA, Moody, and Northwestern. The problem the conservatives saw was not that such students absorbed bad theology; the educations they received were good. Rather it was that they tended to take up careers in non-Mennonite missions, schools, and other agencies. So they did not become leaders of Mennonites.[76]

The third issue involved the Mennonite responses to World War II. It is no accident that the Bible school movement grew strong during a war. Behind the founding of GBI in 1943 were Mennonites who were tolerant toward military service. Instead of advising Civilian Public Service, GBI—especially Suckau, GBI president beginning in 1944—advocated noncombatant service within the military.[77]

Suckau never quite achieved his goal of uniting Mennonite fundamentalists behind GBI. However, in the early 1950s he could claim that ten Mennonite groups were part of its constituency. Dominant were certain segments of the GC. Further important support came from the Krimmer Mennonite Brethren, the Evangelical Mennonite Brethren, and some MBs.[78]

MB FUNDAMENTALISM

Among the Mennonite Brethren, the Fundamentalist-Modernist conflict first surfaced at Tabor College. The conflict simmered in the 1920s and '30s and erupted in 1942 as Peter E. Schellenberg became president. Roots of the conflict were in the eclectic nature of MB theology and in events of the 1920s.

Ever since their beginnings in the Russian empire in 1860, MBs had blended Anabaptist, Pietist, and evangelical theologies.[79] Those in North America always considered themselves theologically conservative; they identified with revivalism, one of Fundamentalism's roots. So by the early twentieth century they easily absorbed Fundamentalism's language—quite unreflectively, without examining how it fit their own theological heritage.[80]

Throughout the 1920s and '30s MBs generally assumed their church had not been tainted by modernism—not even Tabor College.[81] Then in the 1940s the tenor changed. In 1942 Schellenberg became the school's first nonordained president. Within a year the first suspicions surfaced. And in five years a paper—"How to Detect the First Signs of Modernism," read at an MB ministers conference, then published in the denomination's English-language paper *The Christian Leader*—signaled fear that Tabor was no longer safe.[82] However, that article was just a surface event; more important were longtime pressures that tended to squeeze the MB progressives and work for the conservatives.

Examples of the squeeze were experiences of four Tabor facul-

Peter E. Schellenberg, c. 1945. Credit: Center for Mennonite Brethren Studies, Hillsboro, Kansas.

ty. All four—Adolph Frantz, Marvin S. Schlichting, Peter S. Goertz, and Abraham J. Harms—were Tabor graduates who attended Yale Divinity School, returned during the 1920s to teach at Tabor, then left by 1930 after finding the environment too restrictive. The departure of the four Yale-trained teachers dealt Tabor an intellectual blow from which it did not soon recover.[83] Moreover, in 1931 Tabor lost its senior college accreditation and was reduced to a junior college—an event which in turn helped induce other intellectually strong faculty to depart, including Schellenberg.

After leaving Tabor in 1931, Schellenberg taught for ten years at nearby Bethel College, returned in 1941 as dean, then became president in 1942. To his discomfort, just as he began as president there was a flow of aspiring MB teachers and ministers to Central Baptist Seminary in Kansas City—twelve of them by 1950.[84] Such persons wanted more clearcut statements of MB theology and were quick to see signs of modernism. Schellenberg came under fire, so that in 1943 he was called to testify at the MBs' general conference about his own religious experience; declare publicly the limits of psychology, his academic field;[85] and defend his and his college's orthodoxy before a conference committee.[86] In this case the fear was not of theological modernism but of a modernism via the social sciences. Finally, in 1951, Schellenberg resigned—although even his critics came to realize he was no modernist.[87]

Theological modernism was not creeping into the MB church, but other currents were, including fundamentalism. MB fundamentalism came not because there was theological modernism to root out; it came as part of the larger cultural transition. A loosening of traditional authorities, a shift from lay to professional ministry, and greater participation in society brought uncertainty and anxiety. In their anxiety, MBs embraced the certainties of theological fundamentalism. During cultural transition it was easy to misperceive the threats and purge those who in fact represented a new order that would soon engulf the church.

Tabor's troubles partly explain why in 1944 MBs of their Pacific Coast Conference opened Pacific Bible Institute. Other motives were also clearly present. The conference's district— California, Oregon, and Washington—was a long way from Kansas; too many Mennonite students in Bible institutes of non-Mennonite sponsorship did not return to MB communities; and World War II required more concentrated teaching on nonresistance. A committee of older, trusted leaders—Nicholas Hiebert, John H. Richert, Peter N. Hiebert, William Bestvater, John P. Rogalsky, and others—tried from before World War I and through the 1930s to establish a school. Finally just before World War II the project gained strength under new leaders. The new leaders—notably Henry D. Wiebe, Jonas D. Hofer, George B. Huebert, and Jacob J. Toews—had training at BIOLA or in Baptist seminaries. They felt comfortable with a more expressive piety, and among other goals, they sought a more clearly defined theology.[88]

CONCLUSION

In the 1940s and after, Mennonite fundamentalism persisted. For MCs it remained a brake on cultural change. For MBs it served those who strongly emphasized conversion and new birth. For many Mennonites fundamentalism seemed a shelter for traditional elements in their identities. After all, virtually all Mennonites valued fundamentalist concerns for orthodoxy, revivalism, strong preaching, and a warm pastoral spirit. And young Mennonites attending Fundamentalist schools such as BIOLA and Moody Bible Institute nurtured inclinations long present in Mennonite congregations. But even as fundamentalism sheltered, it distorted. Truths that had been part of Mennonites' theology but heretofore treated only equally among other truths suddenly began to overwhelm.

For all Mennonites, fundamentalism tended to deflect them from having to face up to interpretive and hermeneutical questions that nineteenth- and twentieth-century scholarship made inevitable. For at least a generation, from the 1920s into the 1950s, Mennonite scholars equipped to deal with historical-critical methods of biblical study held back from many critical questions. They did so partly because the churches so often spurned the very intellectuals who had the requisite skills. The exodus of scholars from Bethel, Goshen, and Tabor is part of that story.

For important parts of the Mennonite world, fundamentalism offered a transitional theology between what MC scholar C. Norman Kraus has called "pretheological biblicism" and "theological biblicism."[89] Embracing fundamentalism was a safe way for Mennonites to begin to theologize; then, after a time, they moved on to other forms of theological biblicism and made fundamentalism marginal.

As the Mennonite social boundaries became more permeable during the early decades of the twentieth century the churches built sharper, more distinct doctrinal boundaries. The substitution of ideological boundaries for shifting or vanishing social boundaries has been part of the continuing history of Christianity almost from its inception. Historian George Marsden has suggested that Fundamentalism served a similar purpose for many Americans.[90] Mennonites were no exception.

For Mennonites allied with either theological or cultural fundamentalism, 1944 seemed a good year. In that year, groups of Mennonites established Grace Bible Institute and Pacific Bible Institute. Also, the MCs' general conference reaffirmed its commitment to nonconformity. Yet 1944 was hardly a year for fundamentalist Mennonites to cheer. In all three of the large Mennonite denominations new changes were afoot.

The year 1944 was in the middle of World War II. The war brought a different set of challenges that had far more substance than the imagined threat of modernism. Its challenges galvanized Mennonites to consider a new, emerging redefinition of themselves. Two expressions, both published that year, were Harold S. Bender's now-classic essay, *The Anabaptist Vision*, and a book by Guy F. Hershberger, *War, Peace, and Nonresistance.*[91] In such writings Mennonites were fashioning a usable past more suitable to their identity as a separate people and more appropriate than fundamentalism for their functioning in the twentieth century. Many Mennonites turned to Anabaptism, not fundamentalism, for their dominant ideology. In future decades it would both integrate Mennonites into and separate them from their society.

CHAPTER

4

SEARCH FOR A USABLE PAST

On December 28 and 29, 1943, the American Society of Church History held its fifty-fifth annual convention, a gathering that included some of North America's most distinguished church historians.

On the first evening the august group met at the University Men's Faculty Club for the Society's annual dinner and presidential address. The president: Harold S. Bender. His topic: "The Anabaptist Vision." That evening Bender delivered a discourse that would reshape the Mennonite historical imagination. For Mennonite scholarship and self-understanding, it was a *kairos* moment, a moment of breakthrough. No other single event or piece of historical writing has filtered so deeply into Mennonite thinking. The phrase "the Anabaptist Vision" became the identifying incantation of North American Mennonites like no other set of words.

It could be such a kairos moment because for Bender's generation it summed up how Mennonites should live and position themselves within modernizing North America. That H. S. Bender offered the statement was most appropriate. He was the undisputed intellectual leader of his generation. No other person was so well positioned to prescribe a new Mennonite identity. The "Anabaptist Vision" address was surely Bender's. Yet like so much in Mennonite life, it can hardly be thought of as one individual's triumph. Rather, it crowned a Mennonite system of ideas that was emerging through a nineteenth- and twentieth-century Anabaptist renaissance.

Records of the Church History Society note that the ensuing

discussion was "very lively"—but that unfortunately it was cut short because "President Bender had to leave soon afterwards by plane to attend a meeting in Chicago."[1] Even in his moment of fame, Bender found other business more pressing. As late as December 16 he had informed the program chairman that he was uncertain whether he would be able to attend the sessions at all. He might just send a manuscript for someone else to read, if by so doing he would not be "anathematized."[2]

The business in Chicago was the annual meeting of the Mennonite Central Committee (MCC). Historians in their tweed jackets might have time for two days in the oak-paneled rooms of the University Club, but Bender in his straight-cut coat needed to do the business of his church. December 1943 was in the middle of World War II. The Civilian Public Service program for conscientious objectors and MCC relief to war sufferers was more important than basking in honor from fellow scholars.

That judgment was entirely consonant with an earlier lament by Bender that his historical work was suffering because of commitments to current issues. On May 1, 1932, he told a friend that he had hardly been in Goshen's historical library since the previous summer. A research project on Conrad Grebel, a sixteenth-century Swiss Anabaptist leader, had suffered. Bender's heart had been with needy Mennonite refugees who had fled from the Soviet Union to Harbin, China, and with colonies of other refugees in Paraguay. He thought "living Mennonites ought to be saved first before dead ones are revived by historical research anyway."[3] Always Bender's first concern was the needs of his church, his people.

Bender's selection as the Society's president and his choice of topic for the presidential address were both rather curious. Up to that time his published scholarly writings on sixteenth-century Anabaptism were scant—a short biography of Menno Simons and six articles. All the articles were published in his own journal, *The Mennonite Quarterly Review*, and all were taken from his doctoral dissertation, a biography of Grebel.[4] His other writings, in American Mennonite history and general topics in Mennonite studies, were at least as important. They included one book, a bibliographical listing of American Mennonite imprints. His presidential address might easily have been on American Mennonite history.

Also curious was the fact that in 1943 Bender was not the chief Mennonite reinterpreter of the sixteenth century. For readers of *The Mennonite Quarterly Review* and by implication for the Mennonite church, John Horsch held that honor. Since the *MQR*'s beginning, Horsch had provided twenty-three articles defining early Anabaptism. Yet with the Anabaptist Vision address, soon published in both the Society's journal and the Mennonite press, Bender became the singular definer of that sixteenth-century movement.

On the other hand by 1943 Bender had already built the Mennonite Historical Library at Goshen into the finest collection of Mennonitica in North America. *The Mennonite Quarterly Review*, which he edited, was a respected journal. He was also the main founder and editor of the Studies in Anabaptist and Mennonite History book series and a leader in turning important European publication efforts—the Täuferakten-Kommission's work and the *Mennonitisches Lexikon*—into trans-Atlantic projects. No one in America surpassed him as an entrepreneur of sixteenth-century Anabaptist studies.

Beyond a personal triumph, Bender's election to the Society's presidency reflected church historians' new respect for Mennonite historical scholarship. In recent years scholars had gained a new understanding of Mennonites' forebears, the sixteenth-century Anabaptists and their role in history. In the nineteenth and early twentieth centuries, various historians had altered the general view of those Reformation radicals.[5]

Opening his address, Bender said that the Anabaptists had offered "a program for a new type of Christian society which the modern world, especially in America and England, had been slowly realizing." His distinguished listeners did not demure. The Anabaptists were no longer the unfortunate relics of the past. More and more, scholars saw them as progenitors of an ideology that had done much to shape American Protestantism and democratic society.[6]

If Bender's selection as president was curious, the fact that Mennonites' kairos moment came through history was not. Since the sixteenth century, an understanding of God's people remaining faithful through harsh periods of history had been central to Anabaptist and Mennonite understandings. Through history more than through any system of theology, they understood the relationship of God to his people and how to be faithful and obedient to Christ and Scripture. Moreover, Bender's vision provided twentieth-century Mennonite people with a way of linking the church to the heroism of the sixteenth century. Anabaptism rather than fundamentalism came to define the center of twentieth-century American Mennonites. A rediscovery of the past permitted a different future.

That rediscovery, which became a Mennonite historical renaissance, began in the mid-nineteenth century with two European scholars, Carl A. Cornelius and Ludwig Keller, and books they published between 1855 and 1885. Keller's work especially would strongly influence a series of European and American Mennonite historians, notably Christian Hege, Christian Neff, John Horsch, and C. H. Wedel. Central in Keller's work was a thesis that the Anabaptists had been part of a much larger movement in Christian history—a movement whose principles, doctrines, and loose institutional connections had perpetuated a continuing evangelical tradition. Keller named the groups in that tradition the *"altevangelische Gemeinden"* (old evangelical fellowships). In his recounting, these groups included historic figures ranging from the great medieval mystic Meister Eckhardt; through Johann von Staupitz, Martin Luther's Augustinian prior; to Protestant mystics such as Johann Arndt, so-called "father of German Pietism."[7]

It is no wonder that Keller attracted Mennonites. With an emphasis on spirituality and piety, his thesis could fit well with influences from American revivalists. Moreover, the groups and persons of whom he wrote had all cultivated their religiosity and piety apart from the state churches. And central in his analysis had been the Waldenses and the Anabaptists. Indeed Keller's interest was more than historical; he wanted to bring kindred spirits together around the tradition. And of that new fellowship, nineteenth-century Mennonites were to be at the core.[8]

Church historians at large rejected Keller's thesis, but for Mennonites it was compelling. Hermann G. Mannhardt, a Prussian Mennonite pastor and publisher, and Peter M. Friesen, a Mennonite historian in the Ukraine, incorporated Keller's interpretation into Mennonite histories.[9]

More directly for Mennonites in America, Keller deeply influenced John Horsch. Having immigrated from Germany in 1886 and joined the staff of MC publisher and leader John F. Funk, Horsch was an accomplished Mennonite historian well before he took up the crusade against modernism. His pages in Funk's *Herold der Wahrheit* were full of writings from Catholic and Protestant mystics. Horsch offered accounts of history that used the Keller thesis, emphasized the Anabaptists, and linked them ecumenically to spiritualist reformers such as Hans Denk.[10] At the turn of the century Mennonites were not separating true Anabap-

Elizabeth Horsch Bender and Harold S. Bender, c. 1958. Credit: Harold S. Bender Collection, Archives of the Mennonite Church, Goshen, Indiana.

tists from spiritualists, as Bender and other Anabaptist Vision scholars would later do.

The Goshen Historical Renaissance
During the 1920s, Horsch and Bender collaborated (a pattern enhanced by the marriage, in 1923, of Bender and the Horsches' able daughter Elizabeth, eventually a scholar in her own right). Soon they were offering a substantially different interpretation of the Mennonite past, changed from that turn-of-the-century one.

Historical scholarship had eroded Keller's linkage of Anabaptists and Mennonites to the various other groups. And perhaps as importantly, the character and needs of the Mennonite church had changed. Scholarship now took place in an environment charged with the fundamentalists' battle to purify the church. Such was the atmosphere when Bender joined the Goshen College faculty in 1924 and—with the help of colleagues, notably his wife Elizabeth, Guy F. Hershberger, fellow Anabaptist historian Ernst Correll, and speech professor John Umble—launched the Mennonite Historical Library, *The Mennonite Quarterly Review*, and the Studies in Anabaptist and Mennonite History book series.

From the moment of his arrival at Goshen, Bender called for the founding of a new Mennonite journal. With Bluffton and its Witmarsum Seminary offering an alternative to Goshen, the context called for a progressive yet orthodox forum for reflective persons in the MC church. Appearance of *The Christian Exponent* in January 1924 only intensified the need.[11]

Where the *Exponent* frequently criticized the MC church as led by Daniel Kauffman and other conservatives, the *MQR*, appearing in 1926-1927 with Bender as editor, called for scholarship in a framework of loyalty. The January 1927 issue (first with the *MQR* title) declared that the mission of the new journal was to be "a servant to the truth and to the historic ideals and faith of the Mennonite Church," a church with "a high calling in the Kingdom of Christ in the present world."[12] Just inside its front cover the same issue carried an invitation "To the Youth of the Mennonite Church" as they faced a world full of difficult and persistent problems. The piece expressed confidence that Mennonite youth were equal to the world's challenges if they maintained faith in their church's organization and historic ideals.

Thus Bender appealed to both organizational and ideological loyalty. He was offering a history which would provide ideals for a generation tempted to leave the church or at least to flirt with new ideas. Awareness of the past, Bender wrote, would "stir hearts to loyalty and devotion" and make the loyalty "more intelligent and well-grounded." To the many influences eroding such loyalty, the *MQR* would be a counterweight.[13]

That Bender's formulation made loyalty a key function of history was a sign of deep conservatism in the historical renaissance of the mid-1920s. In context, loyalty language was the property of the conservatives, who used it mainly to restrict change and to buttress an older cultural order. Bender's appropriation of this language was deft. He implied a historical consciousness but appealed at the same time to a historic traditionalism that had been trying to maintain cultural rigidity in the face of encroaching modernity. Thus he was making the new history acceptable to Mennonite fundamentalists and conservatives as well as to a generation seeking a new meaning and vocation for the church. The rediscovery of history would be an important part of a process that would transform twentieth-century Mennonites. But at least the Goshen-related scholars of that history needed to be careful to invoke themes which the church's conservative majority could accept.

In the mid-1920s loyalty was only one of various stimuli awakening historical interest. The year 1925 was the 400th anniversary of Anabaptist beginnings in Switzerland, a time for commemorations and addresses. The recent war also helped by rekindling an interest in the origins of Mennonite pacifism.[14] And if Mennonites were to be respectable in the family of American denominations, they needed their history retold. For too long most church historians had offered a perverted version of Mennonite history, one in which Anabaptists had been only fanatical extremists "guilty of rebellion and uprising," engaging in "wicked and lustful practices," and promoting disloyalty. A different history might clear the church's reputation and correct centuries of polemics.[15]

In 1926 John Horsch unlinked the Anabaptists from earlier reform movements such as the Waldenses. He did so in a way that tended to give Anabaptists a different character. In "The Origins and Faith of the Swiss Brethren," an essay published in the *MQR*'s brief predecessor *The College Record: Review Supplement*, Horsch laid out a line of historical interpretation that would dominate the first two decades of the Goshen-led historical renaissance. Horsch rooted Anabaptism in a group of "Swiss Brethren" who had coalesced during intense debates surrounding the reformation led by Ulrich Zwingli at Zurich in the early 1520s.[16] A follow-up article by Baptist historian Albert H. Newman further repudiated the Keller thesis.[17] Now instead of linkage to Waldenses, various spiritualists, and others, Horsch and Bender were finding Anabaptist origins that were Protestant and a return to biblicism.

In subsequent articles Horsch sharpened both his ideology and his historiographical interpretation. In 1926 he advanced the theme that the Swiss Brethren and the Anabaptists of The Netherlands had genetically different origins. He conceded that between the two groups there had been a "vital unity in faith and practice." Nevertheless he argued that the two had been "distinct bodies."[18] In Horsch's analysis three different historical strands made up Anabaptism: the Swiss Brethren, the Hutterian Brethren, and the Brethren of The Netherlands. Among them, he said, there were such great "differences and contrasts in doctrine and practice" that it was "impossible to speak of a vital characteristic that was common to all."[19]

In 1930 and 1931, in a long-running article in four issues of *MQR*, Horsch set forth what he named "The Faith of the Swiss Brethren." However, instead of faith as historically understood by

Mennonites, he actually set forth a theology organized in categories familiar to twentieth-century Fundamentalism: the doctrines of Scripture, Trinity, sin, salvation, and sanctification, plus some other topics. His analysis made the Swiss Brethren entirely safe and orthodox. He scarcely mentioned martyrology, discipleship, ethics, and the communitarian nature of faith—points that later became the identifying topics of the *MQR* interpretation.

In sum, Horsch carefully delineated and separated the Swiss Brethren from sixteenth-century Anabaptists whose theology Mennonite fundamentalists might not find orthodox. Clearly the sectarian Horsch, wanting to distinguish his people from the more liberal Dutch and General Conference Mennonites, found them a different intellectual parentage. His treatment of the Swiss Brethren was akin to the way Daniel Kauffman had systematized the doctrines of Mennonite fundamentalism.

Guy F. Hershberger, an interim editor of the *Review* in 1930, pleaded with Horsch to make his articles history, not advocacy, and to be "moderate" rather than "emphatic."[20] Much later a fellow scholar of Anabaptism, Robert Friedmann, judged that Horsch's version of Anabaptist theology was scarcely more than "a proof that the Anabaptists were essentially Fundamentalists."[21]

Harold Bender, however, used three editorials to endorse his father-in-law's articles and to describe the Swiss Brethren as "consistent biblicists, evangelical, soundly moderate and practical, free from fanaticism or doctrinal aberrations."[22] In light of Horsch's portrait, he found it ever more difficult to understand how others misinterpreted the story so egregiously. To him it was self-evident that the Swiss Brethren showed "the purest and most original form of Anabaptism."[23]

So now the faith once delivered needed to be preserved from alternative scholarship. If history was to serve the search for a viable identity for MC people, then it had to insure some key distinctions—between the Swiss Brethren and the more radical sixteenth-century Anabaptists; and between the twentieth-century MC church and the more liberal Mennonites in the General Conference church or in Holland.

A rich example of the urge to distinguish and separate was the *MQR* response to a work by Wilhelmus Johannes Kühler, *Geschiedenis der nederlandsche Doopsgezinden in de zestiinde eeuw* (1932)—the first of a two-volume general history of the Dutch Mennonites.[24] Kühler was a Mennonite, a professor at the Mennonite Seminary in Amsterdam, and librarian at the Menno-

nite Library. He had long studied the Catholic antecedents to the
Dutch Reformation and had examined the relationship between
Mennonites and some Anabaptists who had carried out a violent
revolution at Münster in Germany.[25]
       When his *Geschiednis* appeared, *MQR* was quick to let John
Horsch publish a long, two-part article in reply. "Is Dr. Kuehler's
Conception of Early Dutch Anabaptism Historically Sound?"
Horsch asked by way of a title.[26] The answer: an emphatic no.
Among other points, where Kühler saw connections among various groups of Anabaptists, Horsch again wanted to keep them dis-
crete and separate.[27] He argued that the aberrations at Münster
"had more in common with the state church than with evangelical
anabaptists."[28] He also rejected a Kühler argument that before
Dutch Anabaptists had turned conservative, there had been an
initial period of *vrijzinn*, or theological liberalism.
       Ironically, in Kühler's work Horsch saw a problem that was a
mirror image of his own treatment of the Swiss Brethren. Kühler's
interpretation, he wrote, was not history. Instead it was an "attempt to seek an historical Anabaptist parentage for the advanced
theological liberalism" of most twentieth-century "Netherlandic
Mennonites."[29] Aptly enough, in an editorial introducing Horsch's
critique, Bender invoked the problem of historians' writing history
to suit the zeitgeist, that is, the mood of one's own times. But he
applied that criticism only to Kühler. Of Horsch's work he said the
evidence was "the sort that cannot be gainsaid."[30]
       Bender's editorials and the whole attempt at refuting Kühler
conveyed both insight and naïveté. To recognize the role of ideology, cultural attachments, and religious conviction in fashioning
historical interpretation was insightful—a promise of maturity
and openness in the historical dialogue. And indeed the young
MQR communicated a mood of expectancy. Not only did it open to
Mennonites in America new documentary historical materials of
Europe; it promised historical understandings free from the zeitgeist.
       The naïveté was in the failure to apply the zeitgeist criticism
to one's own efforts. Horsch apparently never understood the limits his own ideological commitments imposed on his work. Apparently Bender understood but believed that for history to serve his
people, its ideology had to be masked. Generosity in historical debate was too great a luxury for a church struggling to be free from
the doctrinal absolutism of Fundamentalism.

GC Mennonite Historical Renaissance

The Mennonite Church was not the only denomination trying to meet its ideological needs through the search for a usable past. Among General Conference Mennonites a parallel and different reading of the Mennonite past was developing.

Into the 1920s the Keller thesis was also a starting point for several GC historians,[31] most notably Cornelius (C. H.) Wedel, founding president of Bethel College. Traveling in Europe in 1898, Wedel unsuccessfully tried to visit Keller, and he freely credited Keller for much of his historical inspiration.[32] In an 1899 book, *Bilder aus der Kirchengeschichte für mennonitische Gemeindeschulen* (Portraits from Church History for Mennonite Church Schools), and then in a much more ambitious, four-volume *Abriss der Geschichte der Mennoniten* (Summary of the History of the Mennonites) published 1900-1904, Wedel used the Keller thesis to trace a continuity between the Anabaptists and the earlier apostolic age in Christian history. Keller provided Wedel with a way of seeing the Mennonite story as part of the larger record of God's work to fashion his kingdom. The carrier of that kingdom was the *Gemeindekirche* (congregation-based church) or *Gemeindechristentum* (congregation-based Christian culture), which Wedel distinguished from Roman Catholic *Priesterkirche* (priestly church) and the Protestant *Staatskirche* (state church).[33] Around such concepts Wedel constructed a progressive Mennonite history in which "world history relates to salvation history in the way the oute© court relates to the sacredness of the temple."[34]

Succeeding Wedel as the GCs' interpreters of history were C. Henry Smith, eventually of Bluffton College, and Edmund George (E. G.) Kaufman, eventually president of Bethel. They rejected the Keller thesis yet offered conceptual categories very different from those of the emerging MC interpretation. The result, from the 1920s to the 1940s, was a spirited dialogue on the nature of Mennonite history.

The strain between the two interpretative frameworks appeared already in 1925. In that year Goshen held celebrations for the 400th anniversary of the beginnings of the Anabaptist movement. John Horsch was an obvious speaker for the occasion. By that time the other notable American Mennonite historian was C. Henry Smith. Born in 1875 in the Amish Mennonite community of Metamora, Illinois, he had taught at Goshen College (and at Goshen's predecessor, the Elkhart Institute). He then attended the University of Chicago to become, in 1907, the first U.S. Mennonite to earn a Ph.D.[35]

Smith returned to Goshen, saw his dissertation published by the MC press in 1909 as *The Mennonites of America*, and served as dean and professor of history until 1913. With the troubles at Goshen brewing, in 1913 he and Goshen's president Noah E. Byers resigned and transferred to Bluffton College and to the GCs. At Bluffton he was a professor of history until he retired in 1946. By 1925 he was the author of a second book on American Mennonite history and would publish two more before 1930.

Smith's work was of such quality that at a time in the latter 1920s when some MC leaders wanted a new book written on Mennonites in America, Bender demurred—saying it would be hard to match Smith's work.[36] Yet despite Smith's credentials, in 1925 Horsch refused to share the 400th-anniversary platform with a Bluffton professor. He protested that "Bluffton is the citadel of religious modernism among the Mennonites of America" and said he would "not feel free to have a part in a meeting in which a Bluffton professor would have a part."[37] Bender replied that Smith was not "an active part of the crowd . . . whose influence is for modernism." But Bender did not prevail. Instead of a GC historian, the planners invited the Baptist Albert H. Newman.

Cooperation among Mennonites to publish certain items floundered on the same disputes. Bender hoped for instance that a project to print the writings of the Anabaptist Pilgram Marpeck could be inter-Mennonite and intercontinental as the Täuferakten-Kommission and the *Mennonitisches Lexikon* projects had been.[38] For Horsch it was inconceivable to solicit Bluffton support. And in light of Horsch's frontal attacks, C. Henry Smith found cooperation equally difficult to imagine.[39]

Surely the Bluffton-Goshen tensions were a factor in an attack from Bender himself, this time against a book by J. E. Hartzler, *Education Among the Mennonites of America*, published in 1925. Hartzler was another of the educators who had left Goshen for Bluffton. His history of Mennonite education showed that he was not a particularly careful or meticulous scholar, and it certainly was partisan. Given such an opening, Bender wrote a ten-page review that spared no words in exposing what he perceived to be misstatements of fact and interpretation.[40]

The attack on Hartzler was so strong that it won Bender the praise of eastern conservatives. John Mosemann, Sr., the prominent Lancaster Conference (MC) bishop, informed him that his review had been well received in both the Lancaster and Virginia conferences. "It seems the good Lord has raised you up for a spe-

Edmund (E. G.) Kaufman, c. 1940. Credit: Mennonite Library and Archives, Bethel College, North Newton, Kansas.

cial purpose among us, a sort of John the Baptist, 'to prepare the way of the Lord and make his paths straight'," the bishop declared.[41] If history was preparing the way of the Lord, it was indeed serving a high purpose. In fact however, history had gotten all too entangled with the ideological conflicts of the 1920s.

The Mennonite Past: Conservative or Progressive?

The ideological dialogue around "What kind of history?" continued as GC authors published two further works: Edmund G. Kaufman's *The Development of the Missionary and Philanthropic Interest Among the Mennonites of North America* (1931); and C. Henry Smith's *The Story of the Mennonites* (1941).[42] But unlike the Kühler-Horsch exchange, the dialogue was no longer about fundamentalist orthodoxy. Instead it turned to the intellectual challenge of twentieth-century Mennonites to position themselves in American society without being either marginalized or assimilated. Mennonites' deepest quest was not for doctrinal certainty but for a social posture somewhere between complete withdrawal and complete engagement. In World War II the search for a middle ground would increase even more; however, the intellectual framework that emerged from the controversies of the 1920s set the conversation in motion.

Kaufman came to Mennonite history after returning in 1925 from eight years as a GC missionary in China, then earning a B.D. from Garrett Biblical Institute and a Ph.D. from the University of Chicago—two institutions highly suspect to antimodernists. In his Ph.D. dissertation, which became his 1931 book, he was the first American Mennonite scholar to apply key ideas of Swiss sociologist Ernst Troeltsch on distinctions between churches and sects and on stages of the sect cycle.

Using those ideas, Kaufman presented Mennonites in America as having been, until the nineteenth century, in retreat into rural communities. In that stage, a sectarian mentality of the *"kleiner aber reiner"* (smaller but purer) reinforced attitudes of resignation and withdrawal. Consequently Mennonite communities had become "stagnant."[43] But at midcentury, with a revival of missionary interest, they had moved into a revitalized stage. Clearly Kaufman's allegiances were with progressive Mennonites emerging from self-imposed isolation. Interested in missions and education, he was restive with parochial Mennonitism, past or present. He found little or no value in the doctrine of nonconformity; it was an "exclusive idea" that resisted missions and littered the past with schisms. Kaufman's book was an affirmation of the more open, cosmopolitan, and ecumenically-minded GC tradition.[44]

The book was a natural for publication in the Studies in Anabaptist and Mennonite History series, its scholarship being on par with books by Bender and Horsch already in the series. But to Horsch, the mere use of sect-cycle theory was evidence of modernism.[45] Moreover, Horsch asked Bender, "is not this book probably the hardest knock ever given the principle of separation from the world unto God?"[46] Its interpretation should not bear "the imprint of one of our church institutions."[47]

Bender responded more generously. He thought that sect-cycle theory offered interpretative possibilities and that certain parts of the Mennonite experience indeed supported the theory. "As honest men we must say that truth is truth, whether we like it or not," he told Horsch, "and what Kaufman has to say must be judged from that basis, pleasant or unpleasant as it may be."[48]

What was unacceptable to Bender was the position that the necessary conflict between separation and mission interests was the starting point for understanding Mennonite history.[49] In the end, instead of SAMH and the MCs' publishing house, two GC agencies cooperated to publish Kaufman's book. And *MQR* did not review it.

Publication of Smith's *The Story of the Mennonites* in 1941 occasioned another, more public discussion of how to interpret Mennonite history—not just Anabaptism but the whole Mennonite story. Horsch died in 1941, and by then Bender was clearly the leader of the Goshen school of interpretation. Smith was the acknowledged dean of Mennonite historians and *The Story of the Mennonites* was his magnum opus. The book covered the entire sweep of Anabaptist-Mennonite history, and its greatest contribution was Smith's construction of a synthesis around a definite interpretation.

That interpretation argued in effect that Anabaptists and Mennonites had contributed significantly to Western freedom and progress. Mennonitism, like other social movements, had both conserving and liberating elements. In Smith's narrative the liberating elements became the main story. The great Anabaptist-Mennonite contributions were the twin ones of church-state separation and religious toleration. Both stemmed from the understanding that "religion is a matter of individual conscience"—which Smith said was the commitment at "the very heart of . . . Anabaptism."[50]

Of the two, church-state separation was more a political contribution. Toleration was more religious, for it legitimated many separatists, including not only the European Anabaptists but also English nonconformists and Baptists in America. The historic Anglo-European struggle for religious liberty had emerged from the logic of Anabaptism.

After the Anabaptists, according to Smith, Mennonites had made other contributions to Western culture. Logically and historically, their refusal of coercion in religious matters had become nonresistance in individual and political life. Moreover, in various countries Mennonite industry, frugality, agricultural skill, and simple virtue had stimulated economic development. And in Holland, Mennonites' contribution to high culture, commerce, and industry had few rivals from other small religious groups.[51]

As the Holland example suggested, not all Mennonites had contributed equally. Smith divided twentieth-century Mennonites into conservatives, moderates, and liberals. He was referring to cultural, not theological, divisions. Essentially he offered a scale of acculturation on which the more liberal Mennonites had rendered the greatest contributions to Western culture.[52]

Smith's progressive reading of the Mennonite tradition was different from the emerging MC interpretation. In a joint review, Bender and Ernst Correll, a German-born, European-trained colleague, complimented many aspects of Smith's work. Yet the reviewers wanted more. What they asked for was "more interpretation of the essence of Mennonitism and the changes in its content which have taken place through the centuries under the impact of the changing environment." Further, they yearned for a "more thorough and systematic description of the basic principles of Anabaptist faith and life."[53]

Except for a brief plea to be more understanding of the Amish, Bender and Correll did not defend the conservatives, but they thought the moderates had been better carriers of the Mennonite future. By "moderates" they clearly meant mainly moderately progressive MCs. They suggested that Smith had put too much faith in the "liberal," General Conference path. They reasoned that the moderates' "stronger group solidarity," "greater steadfastness under test," "deeper sense of historical tradition," and "stronger resistance to 'worldly' influences" held greater promise than did the posture of the liberals.[54]

By framing their review in such terms, Bender and Correll were searching for a way to guard basic Mennonite principles against the erosions of cultural change. Important among those changes, they noted, were the rural-to-urban transition, the impact of higher education, and changing conceptions of the "brotherhood" ideal.[55]

In a response, Smith sharpened the discussion. He thought that Mennonites' future lay with their colleges and other church schools. These were "still equally beacon lights of pacifism in their respective constituencies, and no doubt the most effective guardians of the essentials of the traditional Mennonite faith." Schools and pacifism were more appropriate guardians than "a back to the farm movement, or a particular cut of dress, or even a spirit of worldliness." To be sure, retaining a distinctive tradition was easier in a solid farm community that was a "seclusive religious unit," but he rejected that choice. Smith was seeking to distance himself from the emerging "Mennonite Community" movement, which he saw as separatist.[56]

The discussion continued with one of the finer Mennonite historiographical exchanges. The April 1944 issue of *MQR*, the same one that carried the first Mennonite publication of Bender's Anabaptist Vision statement, included an exchange between Anabaptist scholar Robert Friedmann, who was then at Goshen College, and Smith. Friedmann's primary concern was to establish the *Geistesgeschichte* (inner history, capturing the essence or spirit) of Mennonites. Discerning that essential "*Geist*," or spirit, was important because, wrote Friedmann, "Mennonite history is not simply another history in which a sympathetic but academic objectivity is all that is required. Its very subject, as I understand it," he continued, "is a religious concern of timeless actuality."[57]

Smith responded by calling for objectivity. *Geistesgeschichte* he dismissed as a first cousin of "philosophy of history" in which "you often leave real history behind and enter the realm of speculation." It led all too easily to "a distortion of fact, from a special point of view, and with a definite aim in mind."[58]

At least for the time being, the discussion about Smith's book marked an end to the MC-versus-GC debate over history-based ideology. Smith was near retirement, and no GC historian would quite take his place as a proponent of the progressive and liberal usable past. Moreover, Bender's Anabaptist Vision would soon all but overwhelm competing views. In the 1950s MC, GC, and Mennonite historians of every kind would work collaboratively to produce *The Mennonite Encyclopedia*. By and large, the 1920s had run their course.

Sociological Recovery

The exchanges in *MQR* contained the essential issues out of which Mennonite scholars were forging a more singular and, for a time, all-but-normative interpretation of the Anabaptist-Mennonite story. However, historians were not the only ones defining Mennonite identity. By 1944 both Smith's and Bender's interpretations were interacting with a sociological reading of Mennonites' past and their present. What might be termed the sociological recovery was a second phase of American Mennonites' ideological reorientation.

At the time, sociologists and other U.S. scholars were looking for ways to revitalize traditional communities amidst the nation's growing urbanization.[59] The Mennonite phase of this movement for community rediscovery and revitalization began in the late 1930s, when scholars rediscovered the tradition of Mennonite mutual aid, and when the Mennonite church came face-to-face with a growing labor union movement. Leading the rediscovery of mutual aid was J. Winfield Fretz, a GC Mennonite and graduate student at the University of Chicago, who published articles on the subject in the *MQR* issues of January and July 1939.[60]

Introducing Fretz's work, Bender suggested that mutual aid, although "largely overlooked," was "one of the outstanding characteristics of Mennonitism throughout its history."[61] Its roots were in Anabaptism's concern to imitate Christ, reject legal and formal associations, resist state dependence, and insist on the right of in-

J. Winfield Fretz, c. 1945. Credit: Mennonite Library and Archives, Bethel College, North Newton, Kansas.

dividual conscience. From such concerns had come fraternal associations ordered on the principles of love and brotherhood instead of an order constituted by legal, coercive, and even violent regulations.[62]

Mennonite history is indeed rich in mutual aid. Examples include Hutterian communalism; Dutch assistance to Swiss Mennonites bound for colonial America; the *Waisenamt* (widows' fund, which evolved into much more) in the Russian empire and in countries to which Russian Mennonites emigrated; various old-age homes, orphanages, hospitals, and fire, storm and burial insurance societies in North America; and more. How much was really an outgrowth of Anabaptist principles and how much a product of social and historical circumstance may be debated. After all, many immigrant groups, post-Civil War African-Americans, and others—groups who had both needs and distinct identities—developed programs of mutual aid.[63]

Whatever the origins, Fretz saw both theology and sociology. He believed that mutual-aid societies embodied "a literal interpretation of the Sermon on the Mount" and also provided social life in Mennonite society.[64] In mutual-aid networks, people could define their "social status in the community" and "enjoy . . . Christian fellowship."[65] The societies were instruments of "social solidarity and social cohesion" and tended to bring under control the "great economic and social inequalities within Mennonite communities."[66]

In mutual aid, Fretz saw a gift Mennonites might give to others. He wrote that Mennonite mutual aid might "have significant implications for the development of a growing universal Christian community."[67] In fact Fretz was critical that too often Mennonites had made "mutual aid and its other virtues an end in themselves." They should make it "the means whereby the Christian circle is ever extended."[68]

More pessimistically, Fretz feared that urbanization posed a threat—not only to mutual aid but to the future of a distinctive Mennonite cultural system. His research indicated that of Mennonites migrating to Chicago, only 10 percent remained affiliated with Mennonite congregations. The conclusion was clear. Fretz noted that

> the discovery of these facts . . . impressed upon me the disruptive influences that a city environment has on Mennonite ideals and teachings and therefore, on the church itself. The urban soil is not the kind of soil in which the Mennonite church can grow. It is literally true that the city soil is too hard, stony and shallow for Mennonite ideals to take root.[69]

Other social science scholarship among Mennonites reinforced these concerns. A 1942 study of "Secularization Among the Mennonites," by Karl Baehr, a GC Mennonite, examined Mennonites in Elkhart County, Indiana. It identified both centripetal and centrifugal forces in the Mennonite universe. Foremost among the centripetal ones—those that held Mennonitism together—were mutual aid and community organization. The opposite, centrifugal forces included education, mixed marriages, fundamentalist Bible institutes, and, above all, urbanization. Baehr believed that Mennonites drifting to urban areas would undoubtedly secularize faster than those remaining in the protective sheath of the more isolated village.[70] In 1942 Melvin Gingerich, an MC historian teaching at Bethel College and soon a strong supporter of the Mennonite Community movement, joined the lament. "Our former rural security is disappearing, we are becoming secularized, our community life is breaking down, and our culture is losing its distinctive qualities."[71]

Part of the pessimism about urbanization was a fear that if the prevailing social ethics of Mennonites dissolved, so would their theological ethics. Fretz thought that most Mennonites still held to the authority of the Scriptures, the centrality of Christ, separation from the world, and refusal to give too much subservience to the political order. Yet with youths leaving the Mennonite communities, the principle of "social responsibility . . . [and] the idea that the welfare of one member becomes the concern of all" were eroding. What was needed was a vigorous program of land acquisition and community formation to keep the youth on the land. Mutual-aid organizations, set up alongside of and parallel to the church, would nurture both social and theological ethics.[72]

Fretz and Baehr and other Mennonite intellectuals came to these issues from the milieu of the Chicago Theological Seminary and the University of Chicago. Arthur E. Holt, professor of social ethics at Chicago Theological Seminary from 1924 to 1942, was one of the foremost Protestant educators concerned with rural issues and the training of ministers for country parishes.[73] Reinforcing his fears was a school of urban sociology that flourished in the same years at the same university, led by Robert E. Park. Park and others hoped that even city neighborhoods might learn how to preserve the order, social bonds, restraints, and primary associations of the village.[74]

In that milieu Mennonites studying in Chicago called a meeting on December 31, 1941, to discuss "Mennonite Sociological Problems." A new organization, eventually renamed the Conference on Mennonite Cultural Problems, met annually from 1941 to 1967 and became the key inter-Mennonite forum for intellectuals to discuss community problems, secularization, and more general sociological and educational trends.[75]

A leader among such intellectuals was Guy F. Hershberger. Ever concerned with nonresistance and peace, in the late 1930s Hershberger (with others) had been mulling the question of how Mennonites should respond to labor unions. New Deal legislation had recently invigorated unions, but unions used methods which were all too coercive and sometimes even violent. Yet the modern industrial order and its urbanization were pulling at least a few Mennonite workers into situations where they might have to join unions to keep their jobs. Unlike a 1938 MC statement which leaned toward the rights of employers,[76] Hershberger understood the union movement in more lofty terms as "a fight for power with which to achieve social justice."[77]

But there was still a problem. Even if for social justice, the unions' quest for and use of power violated the prevailing Mennonite interpretation of nonresistance. By that interpretation, nonresistance included submission, even to injustice if necessary to avoid conflict or coercive use of power. Labor union's strikes, boycotts, and other nonviolent coercion were still coercion. And so, Hershberger declared in a landmark address to the MCs' general conference in 1939, Mennonites could have no part "in the struggle for economic power, either on the side of the class-conscious workers or on that of their industrial overlords."[78] Yet nonparticipation was hardly an option. Hershberger was realistic enough to see that the church had to devise practical alternatives. A questionable alternative already existed. Since 1935, MC church officials had had an agreement with the United Mine Workers in the Pittsburgh-Johnstown area which allowed Mennonite miners to work. They did not have to become union members or participate in union activity, but they did have to pay dues to the union.[79]

In the next decade Hershberger and other Mennonite church leaders would negotiate numerous such arrangement with local unions—some, however, with provisos that Mennonites' dues would go to pension funds or other benevolences.[80] The arrangements, at least those without the proviso, were a compromise at best. In 1939 Hershberger pointed out that nonresistants' money went into union treasuries and thence to purposes "altogether out of harmony with the nonresistant way of life."[81] The church should seek other alternatives.

Hershberger suggested that the problem for Mennonite employers was simpler. They could keep their businesses small enough to retain the intimate and wholesome relationships between workers and the managers and owners. Such intimacy combined with Christian attitudes would make unions unnecessary.[82] But the real solution, for both Mennonite workers and Mennonite employers, was to cultivate the rural life.

Before many years, Hershberger would speak more of the "small community" and less of the rural community.[83] But in 1939 Hershberger evoked Thomas Jefferson, Hector St. John de Crèvecoeur, and others who had rhapsodized the virtues of the farm and rural communities. As historic practitioners of rural life, Mennonites should revitalize their traditional communities and evade the conflicts of the large-scale industrial order. That called for cooperative planning. Needed were a system of mutual aid, a community social security program, Mennonite-operated community medical facilities, assistance to young people to begin farming, and other forms of community wealth-sharing. The Mennonite Central Committee had lent American Mennonite money to purchase three hundred thousand acres in Paraguay so Mennonite refugees from the Soviet Union could settle there. Was it not as reasonable for a Mennonite organization to purchase land at home for the aid of "their refugee brethren who are about to flee to the city, or who would like to flee from the city, or who ought to do so"?[84]

Like many other matters the dream of community-refurbishing and rural revitalization, while articulated in the immediate prewar years and during World War II, was put on hold until the conclusion of the war. The wartime experience nourished the ideal but the practical necessities of the alternative service system also left little energy and even fewer dollars for rebuilding rural communities.

The sociological recovery proved to be less divisive than the historical renaissance. To be sure, C. Henry Smith and E. G. Kaufman were troubled by its anti-urbanism. The Mennonite Community movement was rooted primarily in the MC academic community, but most other Mennonite scholars were tolerant or even participated. Still, despite that acceptance, the community movement as a movement lasted only about fifteen years. Postwar Mennonites retained considerable social consciousness, but they did not organize that consciousness around the Mennonite Community ideal.

Bender's "Anabaptist Vision"

The historical recovery had much greater staying power. At least into the 1970s, the Anabaptist Vision, historically defined, remained at the center of Mennonite reflection. It became the "regulative principle" of Mennonite thought, and insofar as ideas can affect practice, it regulated practice as well.

It was Harold Bender's version of Anabaptism that carried the day. That version defined the essence of Christianity as discipleship (ethical faithfulness); a gathering together of the faithful in voluntary churchly communities that practiced mutuality and accountability; and an ethic of love and nonresistance that governed all relationships, civil and religious.

The purpose of Mennonite history, according to Bender's 1943 address, was to make those principles visible in the life of a Christian community, a Christian people. Christian faith was not mystical; it was ethical and to be realized in identifiable human communities. Community was after all an important antidote to the social direction of twentieth-century Mennonites.

Compared to either doctrine or individualism, this vision offered more continuity with the past. Doctrinal definitions of faith, however useful against the seductions of free thinking and cultural change, had been a fundamentalist graft onto the Mennonite tradition. Individualism too was a graft, introduced by modernity. It seemed appropriate for persons such as Smith who were seeking freedom from the authoritarianism in the Mennonite past. In the end, however, their approach was too ecumenical and too loose to give clear direction to a drifting people. Bender's was a more churchly vision. As such it could promote the continuity of a tradition more effectively than either of the alternatives.

Bender's conception reflected a conviction that modernity's real threat was ethical more than doctrinal variance. Moreover, ethical faithfulness (discipleship) made possible a discernible religious community. For Mennonites, belief has always been important, but practice has been equally or more important. The modernity threatening Mennonites was more sociological than ideological.

So, in his historic address to the Society of Church History, Bender concluded with a plea for the church to be a distinctive Christian social order. He did not call for radical withdrawal. He did not propose to reverse the slow but steady social drift of Mennonites into American society. The form of Christian community that Bender had in mind was paradoxically a strategy for both separation and integration, for withdrawal and engagement, for consolidation and dispersion. He did not wish to reify the traditional boundaries of the past. Instead he offered Mennonites in America a new ideological self-consciousness. He did not reject tradition. Instead he believed that distinct communities could embody a witness. They could show the world that corporate ethical discernment, and reconciliation, were indeed possible.

Anabaptism, as it came to function in American Mennonite life, carried a dual meaning. It offered distinct community but also witness. It promoted particularity but also ecumenicity. It integrated Mennonites into the world but preserved a rhetoric of difference. It brought respect but gave new eloquence to the language of dissent.

Bender delivered his address at the height of World War II. In that context, Guy F. Hershberger and others were doing for peace theology what Bender and his colleagues did for historical theology. Both efforts provided new categories for traditional understandings. Bender, Hershberger, and their co-laborers not only redefined the past; they also positioned Mennonites to face the future with new confidence about themselves and their role in American society.

The combination of the new scholarship and the opportunities that World War II presented for transmitting the reshaped tradition to the next generation were the updrafts on which a new Mennonite zeitgeist could spread its wings and fly.

CHAPTER

5

∼

RETHINKING PEACE, 1925-1944

Ever since the sixteenth century, Mennonites have worked at shaping a theology for understanding how the people of God should relate to the people and the political orders of the world. In doing so, they have distinguished sharply between the obligations of citizenship and those of God's kingdom. If God's people are faithful, they live by a different ethics than do the people of the national culture.

This idea of separate ethics was forged out of a hermeneutical tradition but also nourished by a cultural dualism. So long as Mennonites lived on the fringes of various host societies they could easily think that the requirements of faith were in conflict with participation in the social system. The state lived in its realm and acted appropriate to its calling; the church, at least the true church, occupied its own realm.

As the twentieth century opened, Mennonites and Amish, living comfortably in the United States, did not feel it necessary to articulate their peace theology very much or to transmit it very formally to their children. Instead they treated it more as a part of the cultural and theological inheritance, deeply embedded but often unconscious.

Then came World War I, with the shocks of having sons taken to camp and prison and of Mennonites even at home often feeling harassed for their various combinations of Germanness and pacifism.[1] Thereafter Mennonites did discuss and debate their peace theology. During the 1920s and '30s the debates were far from serene. Both of the largest Mennonite denominations found it urgent to rebuild their conference peace committees. In 1925 the MCs' general conference reorganized its Peace Problems Committee, which had become inactive after the war. The next year the GC church also reactivated its Peace Committee. These committees and other individuals began a process of rethinking—a phase that lasted until World War II and the writings of Guy F. Hershberger.[2] At least three realities now impinged on the American Mennonite peace discussion.

The first reality was World War I and the deep shock it had inflicted. Much more than in any previous war, the U.S. government had violated the civil liberties of anyone who would not give support. After all, the war was a global crusade—the war to end all wars and make the world safe for democracy. Dissenting minorities dared not stand in the way. So Mennonites along with certain others felt the wrath of a state which required conformity.

In Mennonite homes and churches during the 1920s and '30s, memories of indignities and abuses ran deep. Mennonite historians believed that the war had permanently altered the relationship between nonresistant peoples and the state. By 1938 C. Henry Smith saw a new, more difficult future in which governments would make few concessions to distinctive minorities.[3]

In 1935 Guy Hershberger likened the situation facing American Mennonites to what European Mennonites had confronted in the nineteenth century as nations militarized their societies and withdrew exemptions based on conscience. Also, he feared that under pressures of strong new militarisms, Mennonites might compromise.[4]

In 1939 Harold S. Bender feared Mennonites' prospects in a coming war might be analogous to the martyr tradition of the sixteenth century.[5] For all, the conclusion was inescapable: Mennonites could no longer count on the tolerance that had characterized their past relationships with American political institutions.

The second reality was the modern industrial order. Few peoples could live apart from it or escape its intrusiveness. In modern societies diverse peoples become politically and culturally intertwined. By the 1930s Mennonites were being pulled into the national society, and not entirely against their wills. Nor was the process a matter only of religious laxity. For nearly a century they had been moving toward greater involvement partly because certain ways of participating seemed to offer new vitality for their own religious traditions.[6]

This closer contact would challenge not only the cultural patterns of semi-isolation but also the theologies nurtured in that isolation. Traditional nonresistance defined the ethical obligations of a people culturally separated from the larger society and possessing only a limited sense of identification with that society. While the war dampened the sense of fraternity with America, it could not undo much of the previous half-century's movement into American society.[7]

The third reality affecting the shape of Mennonite peace discussions was a new popularity for the national peace movement. Mennonites were not used to having pacifism be fashionable, but after World War I it was. Literary works from John Dos Passos' *Three Soldiers* to Erich Maria Remarque's *All Quiet on the Western Front*, and many others, portrayed a brutal and senseless slaughter that had sacrificed one generation for little gain.[8] In the 1920s and early '30s revisionist historians often presented World War I as the work of avaricious businessmen, munitions manufacturers, and other merchants of death.[9] Many Americans agreed, and millions rallied more or less to the pacifist cause.[10]

These three realities—the war, the modern industrial order, and the new popularity of pacifism—all impinged on the Mennonite discussion of peace theology between World Wars I and II. As Mennonites discussed, they raised three sets of troubling issues.

Set one had to do with how much Mennonite pacifism applied to the larger world. Was reconciliation possible outside the church's boundaries? Should Mennonites advocate policies based on the idea of ending war? Should they give a peace witness to public officials at all? Was that too much mixing of religion and politics? Or should they assume, as many conservative Mennonites did, that wars were inevitable and any attempt to restrain the state was politically naive?

Set two was questions of how much Mennonites should fraternize with fellow pacifists. For some Mennonites, imbued as they were with Jesus' words that the broad road leads to destruction, the very popularity of pacifism was troubling. Meanwhile Mennonite fundamentalists were disturbed that many in the new wave of pacifists were theological liberals. So, how ecumenical or sectarian should Mennonites be in pursuit of their own pacifism?

Set three had to do with an appropriate theology of nonresistance. What should Mennonites say in a society that could militarize itself and its citizens as rapidly as the United States had done in World War I? If and when another war came, how could Mennonites find breathing room? In peacetime, what must they do to protect the rights of the peaceable conscience in time of war?

THE INTERWAR PEACE DISCUSSION AMONG THE MCs

In 1925 the MC Mennonites' general conference was on the verge of dissolving its Peace Problems Committee. The committee had begun as an emergency "Military Problems Committee" during World War I. Now its members—Aaron Loucks, and bishops Daniel (D. D.) Miller, and Eli (E. L.) Frey—considered their task completed. But when one of Miller's sons, Orie O. Miller, heard the news, the younger Miller found such an idea inconceivable.[11]

Orie O. Miller was a graduate of the old Goshen who had become a businessman (by joining his father-in-law as a shoe manufacturer). He also had done relief work in the Soviet Union and Lebanon under a fledgling Mennonite Central Committee (MCC), the organization of which he would be chief executive for most of his life. By 1925 this businessman-activist was already a Mennonite peace leader with a remarkable ability both to articulate ideas and to translate them into practice. In that year, in Washington, D.C., he attended a National Study Conference on the Churches and World Peace that stimulated him further. With other churches showing new interest in peace, he argued, Mennonites might have new contributions to make.[12] So the younger Miller counseled persuasively for continuation, got his wish, and was made the Peace

Orie O. and Elta Wolf Miller family, c. 1933. Credit: Orie O. Miller Collection, Archives of the Mennonite Church, Goshen, Indiana.

Problems Committee's secretary. Between 1926 and 1929 he produced a series of articles for MC papers that defined the committee's work and much of the subsequent MC dialogue.[13]

Miller's concerns were various. For one, the war had shown that young Mennonite men facing wartime decisions had hardly been well prepared. Draftees who returned from the camps were virtually unanimous that the church had neither prepared them nor properly positioned itself. Miller was distressed by what he termed the "utter lack of literature covering the Church's four centuries of nonresistant faith and practice."[14]

Moreover Miller thought the church had given no "consistent witness against war and militarism in peace time," and so had none to point to as it requested CO status.[15] It had not acted on its belief in the "practicability of love and good will as conquerors of wrong and evil." The war had shown that the church should shift from the negative posture of mere nonparticipation. It should speak positively, emphasizing the social value of the peace principle. Doing so would help generate greater toleration for the nonresistant position.[16]

Second, Miller wanted his church to show greater interest in ecumenical conversation and peace witnessing. For four centuries, he charged, the Mennonite church had not produced a single book designed to explain Mennonite peace theology to others. Now the moment was right, especially for conversations with other churches. Miller's ecumenical interests extended to the many new and older peace societies and organizations. He urged the church to keep in touch with the larger body of peace literature and to be represented at peace conferences.[17]

Third, Miller wanted the committee to represent the church's position to the government. He and others frequently framed that concern as keeping in touch with pending legislation of interest to Mennonites. Actually, they saw an opening for Mennonites to become more active in the political process.[18]

Miller's initiatives drew quick responses, both public and private.[19] In the *Gospel Herald* bishop John Mosemann, Sr., of the Lancaster MC conference denounced the modern peace movement as a front for modernists. To him it was "nothing less than a Satanic delusion" intended to lead the church "headlong into the clutches of modernistic and liberalistic leaders." Mennonites had no business fraternizing with organizations that included prominent modernists such as Shailer Matthews, Harry Emerson Fosdick, and other "semi-infidels."[20] Before long George R. Brunk I was using his new *The Sword and Trumpet* to make similar points. "False peace propagandists" of all kinds—"Infidels, Socialists, Bolsheviks . . . talk against war in time of peace but bellow for war when peace is broken," he warned. Some were "even foolish enough to urge nonresistance upon the civil powers." Brunk argued that "nonresistance was given to the church"; it had never been "intended for the unconverted nations."[21] Hardly anyone could have drawn a sharper line than did Brunk, between sectarian nonresistance and active pacifism.

To such critics, the idea of making political statements to Washington was anathema. In 1927 the *Gospel Herald* printed a letter that Peace Problems Committee leaders E. L. Frey and Orie Miller had sent to the U.S. Secretary of State and to the chairman of the Senate Foreign Relations Committee. They argued that a nation under Christian influence should act with good will toward its neighbors. Mosemann immediately warned that Frey and Miller's course would lead the church "astray," taking it "into the mire of politics, to the mire of modernism, to the mire of trust in man."[22]

Mosemann's objections were largely rooted in a premillennialist reading of Scripture. By that reading, in the present age the demonic powers were loose and all efforts to promote peace were misguided.[23] Since Christ had taught that wars and rumors of wars would continue until his return, Christians should not try to prevent them.[24] The only acceptable course for the Peace Problems Committee was to represent Mennonite self-interest to Washington and to "show the utter fallacy of the Modern Peace Movement."[25]

In a private letter to Mosemann, Orie Miller defended his own orthodoxy and argued that the church needed to work at building God's kingdom in whatever age.[26] Nonetheless he yielded more than a little to the Mennonite fundamentalist voices and pressure. In the 1920s and early '30s, in the view of antimodernists such as Mosemann, even meeting with persons from other historic peace churches in an organization called the Conference of Pacifist Churches (CPC) was likely to contaminate. Not only were some Quaker and Church of the Brethren pacifists contaminated, but the conference included "old Goshen" people (persons connected with Goshen College before the 1923-1924 closing and reorganization) no less prominent than former president N. E. Byers.[27]

Miller was on the CPC's Continuation (executive) Committee, and Mosemann warned that his position "cannot but impair your own usefulness among us in the East."[28] This warning was both truth and threat, and Miller quickly resigned from the CPC committee. But under his direction the MCs' Peace Problems Committee continued its connections with the CPC and many other organizations. Objections continued to come, and by 1927 Miller concluded that committee members' attendance at peace conferences should be done quietly. The committee should make clear that it was sending only observers, not full delegates.[29]

In 1935 a number of MC leaders and thinkers met at Goshen College for an important "Mennonite Conference on War and Peace."[30] There, not surprisingly, the ecumenical versus the sectarian stance vis-à-vis the larger American peace movement was a major issue. In a major address, John Horsch argued that the Anabaptists had never hoped to abolish war and that any hope to convert the world to peace was futile. He insisted that Mennonites should stay aloof from America's larger peace movement, including the pacifism found in many churches. One should see the American churches' current flirtations with peace against their long history of providing sanction for war—and against their "curious supposition" that individual Christians were "not responsible for the unchristian deeds" they committed in war. That history and that view were just too deeply ingrained. The churches might be repudiating twentieth-century forms of warfare, but they were not yet repudiating their own history and its twisted logic. So despite others' pacifism, the Mennonites of America were "well-nigh the only defenders of the vital Christian principle of nonresistance."[31]

The Goshen conference was a closed MC affair, but in fact Horsch spoke for some in other Mennonite denominations as well. In 1938 Jacob (J. B.) Epp, an MB who had been an editor, missionary, pastor, and college teacher, voiced the same concern in the MB's new English-language periodical, *The Christian Leader*. Epp noted that during the 1930s many mainline denominations passed resolutions indicating they would not participate in war. But they all had limited their self-imposed restrictions by approving defensive wars. For Epp that left "the back door open to war."[32]

Epp was prescient. History would shortly prove that he, Horsch, and others were correct when they cautioned that many religious pacifists of the 1920s and '30s would not be so pacifist in case of real war.

At the Goshen conference, two speakers who wanted to be more open to the larger peace movement were Melvin Gingerich, at that time a high school teacher in Iowa, and Harold Bender.

Gingerich reasoned that the distinction between religiously based and secular peace organizations was not always clear. An organization such as the American Peace Society included a commitment to the Christian gospel in its charter. And many leaders even of the Socialist party were "deeply religious." It was right for Mennonites to be suspicious, for many such organizations had indeed compromised their pacifism in times of actual war. And Mennonites were right in their conviction that lasting peace was predicated on religious conversion.[33]

Gingerich thought, however, that Mennonites could profit from such organizations. The organizations offered factual information, scholarship, and other resources Mennonites as a small group could not bring. The historical record showed that curbing social evils was the business of many civic organizations as well as of the church. Such organizations had been able to reduce "the burnings of witches, slavery, drunkenness, and duelling." At the very least, Gingerich believed, Mennonites should not condemn or disregard the peace organizations. Every Mennonite minister's library should contain some of the organizations' literature.[34]

Harold Bender, despite his father-in-law's alarm, agreed with Gingerich. In 1935 Bender's reputation was still being made, but soon he would be a dominant voice in such discussions. He called forthrightly for the church to link more with people beyond its own boundaries. Choosing a theme that was almost irresistible, he made the issue a question of mission. "Does the Word of God require that believers teach the world the Gospel principles on peace and war?" he asked. What indeed was the Christian's "testimony . . . for the world?"

Answering his own questions, Bender rejected the fundamentalists' limitation of the church's witness only to conversion. Invoking verses dear to Mennonites, he noted that Scripture tells us to "teach all nations to observe *all things*" which Christ had commanded (Matt. 28:19), and also, "not shun to declare the whole counsel of God" (Acts 21:27). Those who insisted that the church's only task was to preach salvation, he said, had been influenced by "extreme premillennial groups."[35]

Yet Bender agreed that the church called its members to a righteousness which no one should confuse with political lobbying, social reforms, or attempts to Christianize the social order. Thus he made peace work a matter of witness and teaching, yet hedged on the question of any really collaborative or political work. He drew a fine line: Mennonites would be ecumenical in their witness but sectarian in their alliances.[36]

By the latter 1930s and World War II, for fundamentalistic MCs there had been a hardening of the course that Mosemann and Horsch advocated—a hardening, that is, in the radical separation of politics from nonresistance, and of Mennonites from other pacifists. Conservatives continually objected to an interMennonite group, the Mennonite Central Peace Committee; to connections among the historic peace churches; to what the conservatives considered political activity on the part of the Peace Problems Committee; and finally to the Mennonite Central Committee as it negotiated the particulars of the new system of an alternative to military service, the Civilian Public Service (CPS) arrangement. The conservatives continually warned against yoking MCs to anyone else, even other Mennonites.

In the end, the conservatives largely lost. The ideas that triumphed were those forecast in the 1920s by Orie O. Miller and defended in 1935 by Bender. But the finest expression of those ideas would come only in World War II, with the CPS system and a 1944 book by Guy F. Hershberger, *War, Peace, and Nonresistance.*

THE GC DISCUSSION

Among GC Mennonites, in 1926 their general conference replaced its wartime Committee on Exemption with a new peace committee consisting of Henry (H. P.) Krehbiel and Andrew (A. J.) Neuenschwander, a pastor-teacher. Unlike the MC church, the conference told its committee explicitly to cooperate with other pacifist churches and organizations whose principles were in harmony with those of their own church.[37]

In a major address at the same 1926 conference, Jacob (J. H.) Langenwalter, until recently the president of Bethel College, strongly called on both the conference and GC congregations to affiliate with the Conference of Pacifist Churches, to read peace-movement literature, and to take the peace witness to American political institutions. Langenwalter believed world peace was "a practicable goal of human effort," and that its time was at hand.[38]

Nonetheless, there were GCs who wished to keep clear the distinction between political and religious pacifism. H. P. Krehbiel, prominent on the Western District's Peace Committee and in the entire GC church, represented that position well. Even though earlier he had served in the Kansas State Legislature,[39] in the 1930s he took a firmly nonpolitical position.

For several years Krehbiel had been planning for what eventually became the 1935 Historic Peace Church Conference, held at Newton, Kansas. In 1933, writing to Rufus Bowman of the Church of the Brethren, he counseled that the peace churches should concentrate on the witness they could contribute most naturally. By that he meant they should "abstain from political programs and anti-military propaganda and devote their whole thought and endeavor to the cultivation and propagation of the spirit of peace."[40]

In 1929 Krehbiel had published "An Overture to the Historic Peace Groups of the World." It was his own work, although no doubt stimulated by the Conference of Pacifist Churches. In it Krehbiel recounted the history of the peace churches, who at great cost had kept alive the "absolutist" teachings of Jesus. In doing so they had paid the price of isolation—from the larger society and from each other. But now, freed from persecution, the "friends of peace" could touch each other. The time for sectarian isolation was past.[41]

Cooperation should proceed according to four principles: (1) "Laying the Christ-foundation of the spirit of peace, upon which may rest and out of which can grow the will to peace for human society"; (2) the historic biblical faith as summarized in the Apostles' Creed; (3) a historic as well as present commitment to nonresistance; and (4) a "non-political" character.[42]

Between 1929 and 1935 Krehbiel revised the Overture several times, making it more christological than historical. In its meetings (1922-1931) the Conference of Pacifist Churches had worked under the label "pacifism," but at the final meeting (at Mount Morris, Illinois, 1931) Krehbiel delivered an address asking, "What Is a Pacifist?" To answer, he distinguished between political pacifism and Christian peace. In contrast to the political approach, Christian people were to win "the souls of men for Christ," then teach the "love-life." Such Christ-followers Krehbiel labeled not pacifists but "Amitists."[43] Thus he too segregated nonresistance from popular pacifism.[44]

In the fall of 1935 a new successor to the Conference of Pacifist Churches, now called the Historic Peace Church Conference, met in Newton, Kansas. Although Krehbiel was its leader, the meeting mixed religious and political concerns. The largest public inter-Mennonite peace gathering since World War I, the conference was a series of discussions rather than formal addresses. Its stated objectives were to study together the biblical basis for Christian peace; to "seek recovery of lost ground on Peace Conviction and attitude"; and to explore what might be the appropriate role of the historic peace churches amidst the rising militarism of the 1930s.[45]

The conferees moved quickly from the biblical basis of peace to dangers facing the peace churches. In a findings statement, three of four sections explained the concept of patriotism, announced the establishment of a Joint Committee of the Historic Peace Churches, and called for a "Plan of United Action in Case the United States Is Involved in War." The latter two sections in effect joined peace churches into what eventually became the National Service Board for Religious Objectors.[46]

The section on patriotism suggested just how clearly the conferees recognized that their peace understandings were both political and religious. They were seeking a concept of citizenship that would link the pacifist ideal with love for nation and doing patriotic duty. The statement suggested that there was no conflict between pacifism and patriotism. Applying "the principles of peace, love, justice, liberty, and international goodwill" simply contributed to the "highest welfare of the country," and the nation should regulate its affairs accordingly. Pacifists were the "true patriots" because they had the courage to stand for these correct principles.[47]

This pacifism was neither separatist nor sectarian. By invoking the terms of patriotism, the conference was not mainly offering a political agenda for policymakers. Rather, it was answering a frequent charge that the people of peace were marginal citizens. In fact in another resolution the conference reiterated the ancient peace-church conviction that, in practice, pacifism and the nation's demands might indeed be in conflict. The delegates resolved unequivocally that if a future war were to come, "we cannot cooperate in military service."[48]

The statements foreshadowed positions that some Mennonite denominations, including the three largest, would take in subsequent years. The 1937 MC general conference at Turner, Oregon; the 1941 GC general conference, Souderton at Pennsylvania; and the MB general conference of 1943 all passed resolutions indebted to the 1935 statement. All three denominations stated explicitly that members should not perform even alternative service if it was under the direct command of the military, nor should they buy war bonds or help voluntarily to finance war in other ways. One way or another, the three denominations also affirmed their peoples' patriotism or allegiance or loyalty and their gratitude to

Emmett (E. L.) Harshbarger, c. 1933. Credit: Mennonite Library and Archives, Bethel College, North Newton, Kansas.

the country.[49]

The resolutions of the 1935 Historic Peace Churches conference at Newton were more ecumenical than those of many Mennonite gatherings. Yet the pattern of attendance showed the sectarian wariness regarding collaborative activity. Of seventy-nine persons who attended, forty-seven were Mennonites. Fifteen attended from the Church of the Brethren and fourteen were Quakers. The MC delegation consisted only of Orie O. Miller, Harold S. Bender, and three people from Hesston—Paul Erb, Milo Kauffman, and Maurice Yoder. Miller and Bender were regulars at such interchurch meetings; no doubt the Hesston people came largely because of proximity. Even other members of the MCs' Peace Problems Committee did not attend. Only two MB persons attended, Peter (P. C.) Hiebert and Peter S. Goertz, both members of the denomination's Peace Committee. A third committee member was not present, and even Hiebert and Goertz were hardly representative of Mennonite Brethren. Hiebert taught at a Presbyterian school, Sterling College; and Goertz was dean at Bethel College. No one came from any other Mennonite denomination. Forty of the forty-seven Mennonites present were GC.[50]

Among peace leaders in Kansas, one especially strong voice that ran counter to Krehbiel's was that of Emmett (E. L.) Harshbarger. A GC Mennonite reared in the MC church at West Liberty, Ohio, Harshbarger was a history professor at Bethel College from 1933 until he died in 1942 at age forty. Earlier he had studied Mennonite history under C. Henry Smith at Bluffton College and absorbed a revisionist approach to history during graduate work at Ohio State University. His work at Bethel combined both perspectives.[51] And he brought credentials from his church, for in 1935 he succeeded Krehbiel as chairman of the GC denomination's Peace Committee, a post he kept until his death. In that position he acted as the quintessential GC progressive, quickening the committee's pace. He gathered around him some persons who, after World War II and their administration of Civilian Public Service, would be the next generation of GC peace leaders.

In 1936 in *The Mennonite*, Harshbarger published a "Mennonite Program for Peace"—partly in response to the Historic Peace Church Conference six months earlier. In his view, that conference had revealed the Mennonites as "the most backward of all the historic peace churches." Perhaps reflecting a bias against more folkish ways of maintaining faith and nurturing convictions, Harshbarger charged that Mennonites held their peace conviction by reflex, without critical thought about its meaning. And they gave it neither programs, agencies, nor institutions.[52] Moreover, Harshbarger strongly rejected the belief that if the church gave more attention to converting people, peace would result. "We have been evangelizing for 400 years and wars have become larger, more numerous, and more deadly," he reasoned.[53] The most arduous evangelistic efforts could not avert a global war.

Harshbarger did not reject evangelism, but he called additionally for education and the building of international alliances. Rightfully understood, these tasks belonged to the church.[54] To embody his ideas, Harshbarger set up at Bethel College a "Kansas Institute of International Relations"—one of eight such institutes conducted under the auspices of the American Friends Service Committee to promote peace education and activism.[55] Beyond increased education, the Institute also addressed a different and deep need of Mennonites in the interwar period. A new peace activism could cushion future requests for military exemption. In a letter of appeal Harshbarger asked: If Mennonites did not do their "utmost to help prevent another war," were they not "hypocritical in professing to have conscientious scruples against war"? The new activism, he wrote, would show they were good and sincere citizens.[56]

The Institute lasted only from 1936 to 1940. After four years it was in debt. Under pressure from community and constituents, Bethel College withdrew its support. Apparently Harshbarger's ecumenical and activist vision had failed. However, one institute's failure did not mean an end of Mennonites' political activism for peace.

NEW FORMS OF MENNONITE PEACE ACTIVISM

By the end of the 1930s different kinds of activism were catching Mennonite imaginations. Two important kinds were work camps in North America and a beginning of MCC relief work to people other than Mennonites in or from the Soviet Union.

The concept of short-term Mennonite voluntary service or work assignments already had a long history. Since the nineteenth century volunteers had worked for varying lengths of time in city missions and missions to Native Americans. But the more organized and deliberate programs of voluntary service had their origins in World War I and in a work-camp program begun by a Swiss activist, Pierre Ceresole. After World War I an American Friends Service Committee (AFSC) reconstruction unit in France attracted forty-six young Mennonite men who wanted to express their pacifism actively.[57]

During the interwar years, the Friends (or Quakers) and the Fellowship of Reconciliation drew other Mennonites into volunteer programs for work in detention homes, migrant work camps, settlement houses, schools for black children, and other settings. Among those participating were some GC persons who would later be important in administering Civilian Public Service and Mennonite voluntary service: Henry A. Fast, Robert Kreider, William Stauffer, Donovan Smucker, Esko Loewen, Edna Ramseyer Kaufman, and Elmer Ediger, to mention a few.

In 1938 Carl J. and Martha Landes, GC Mennonites with Bluffton and Quaker education, led the first Mennonite-sponsored work camp. Carl Landes had previously worked under the AFSC and been a pastor of the First Mennonite Church of Philadelphia. The work camp was a project of a Bluffton-based Mennonite Peace Society of which Landes was executive secretary.[58] The camp was attached to the Twenty-Sixth Street Mennonite Mission in Chicago, a work of "Central Conference" Mennonites,[59] a largely-Illinois denomination which would later merge with the GC. In the Volunteer Community Citizenship Camp, fourteen volunteers worked mornings on renovation of buildings and spent afternoons on field trips or doing surveys to investigate social injustice and study ideas for nonviolent reform. With slogans like "YOUTH HAMMERS WAR" and "overcome evil with good," they expressed their pacifism and gave dignity to their manual labor.[60]

An MB leader, Otto B. Reimer of Reedley, California, was not as successful as Landes in starting a work camp, but he thought such a project would be both an appropriate expression of Mennonite biblicism and a way to position Mennonites for a forthcoming war. So in 1936 he implored the MB peace committee to begin a work camp of some kind. He said he sensed among the young people a kind of "agitation or movement" for such activity. "They wish to take decisive steps which will be of a help to them in war, which everyone feels is, 'just around the corner.' "[61]

OVERSEAS RELIEF WORK

During the interwar years, the most important outgrowth of the activists' vision was relief work overseas. The history of Mennonite benevolent activity among both European and American Mennonites is long. The aid frequently was to assist fellow Mennonites suffering from persecution, special taxes, loss of civil liberties, or other hardships related to their dissenting and pacifist stance. The most recent large-scale assistance was the relief effort in the Soviet Union following the 1917 revolution and subsequent local anarchy, which led to a famine in the Ukraine in the early 1920s and eventually to emigrations which, by the early '30s, relocated some 20,000 Mennonites in Europe, Canada, and South America. For such relief, the main agency came to be the Mennonite Central Committee (MCC). Well into the late 1930s its efforts were mainly for fellow Mennonites, but quite a few Mennonites were eager to extend the same benevolence to others.

An important expression of that impulse was the response of Mennonite young people who went to work in the so-called Near East in cooperation with the semiofficial American Relief Administration. During the 1920s and 1930s twenty-seven Mennonite men and two Mennonite women worked with Near East Relief in Turkey and Lebanon. Mennonites contributed some $340,000 to the Near East Relief effort. From work in the Near East as well as from the aid to Mennonites of the Soviet Union came the birth of the Mennonite Central Committee (MCC) and the leadership of Orie O. Miller.[62] Also, beginning in 1937, Mennonites collaborated with the American Friends Service Committee to get relief to Spain during the Spanish Civil War.[63]

With the outbreak of World War II in 1939, a new phase of relief work began which lasted until the United States entered the war in December of 1941. During that phase MCC developed an extensive program of relief to war sufferers. Planning began at a September 30, 1939, meeting of the MCC's executive committee. By November 1 the agency's constituent denominations had given approval. Soon they appointed Martin (M. C.) Lehman, longtime MC missionary to India, to be the first administrator (or "commissioner") of Mennonite relief to Europe.[64]

Orie Miller's instructions to Lehman defined what would become MCC policy around the world. MCC relief, Miller wrote, "is entirely nonpartisan" and is "to be extended without preference as to race, nationality, or otherwise, with particular attention to relief needs among war suffering women and children." Any "relief needs among the Mennonite folks of Europe . . . should also receive prior consideration."[65]

In early 1940 the relief program began in France and in England. In France, MCC mainly supplied meals to refugees and clothing and shelter to children, doing so through existing distribution centers and government schools and nurseries. In England it distributed food and warm clothing for the winters.[66] Meanwhile it investigated whether and where it might work in other allied

Martin (M. C.) Lehman visiting an MCC-assisted relief kitchen in Warsaw, Poland, c. 1939-1941. Credit: MCC Collection, Archives of the Mennonite Church, Goshen, Indiana.

countries. By June of 1940 MCC was committing $10,000 per month in addition to personnel costs. Thus began a relief program which by the war's end would reach parts of Europe, the Middle East, Asia, and Latin America.

On the German-controlled side, MCC worked in Poland, mostly through the Polish and the German Red Cross. Authorities allowed Lehman to visit Warsaw and other sites bimonthly to oversee distribution that included milk, lard, serums, and some specialized relief packages for certain families. MCC won the ability to designate particular families through an agreement which Harold Bender negotiated at least partly in response to Mennonite visits at camps in England and Canada, where the Allies held German prisoners of war. For such designated distribution, MCC worked through a firm owned by Mennonites in Berlin—A.P. Fast Company—and through Polish-American friendship societies. The Fast firm had a history of working with German relief agencies.[67]

The nonpolitical nature of the relief also permitted Lehman to visit a German Mennonite congregation at Kazun, near Warsaw, as late as October of 1940. This small, ethnically German community had been plundered by Polish soldiers, who had executed seventeen of its members. There MCC was able to give special gifts of milk, lard, and monies to assist and comfort the Mennonite survivors. However by August 1941, with the United States and Germany practically at war, relief efforts in Poland became difficult. In December, when Germany and the United States formally declared war, M. C. Lehman (like various U.S. diplomats and humanitarian workers) found himself interned in enemy territory.[68]

PEACE THEOLOGY IN WARTIME

In 1940, with the United States on the edge of the war, Mennonites' domestic peace energies were drawn more and more toward politics. But it was not the optimistic politics of abolishing war; rather, it was negotiating for what became the Civilian Public Service system, so that draftees who were conscientious objectors might help the nation through alternate, nonmilitary forms of service. Conservatives' efforts to stop any statements to government and any collaboration with other pacifists faltered, but so did the activists' effort to abolish war as an institution.

Denominational peace discussions temporarily become less contentious. There were various reasons. One was that negotiating for and operating the CPS system made the historic peace church-

Guy F. and Clara Hooley Hershberger and children Elizabeth and Paul, 1947. Credit: Guy F. Hershberger Collection, Archives of the Mennonite Church, Goshen, Indiana.

es a separated fellowship. They were the privileged. The government let them run their own camps, a pattern that tended to isolate them from other pacifists. Leaders put their energy into shaping the CPS system.

An air of exhilaration caught Mennonites as they began to tackle CPS administrative and organizational challenges. Never had the Mennonite churches in the United States managed anything of this scope. Never had so many young men been drawn into active military or alternative service. The systems also drew young women into related roles. The defining of Mennonite peace now proceeded from thousands of young persons enmeshed in the relationships within or surrounding these new military or CPS units.

The peace dialogue also changed because Guy F. Hershberger offered a way out of the seeming impasse between the nonpolitical-sectarian path and political-ecumenical pacifism. His first large book, *War, Peace, and Nonresistance*, which the MCs' publishing house released in 1944, did not please conservatives, but it did define a position that would hold for the next generation. A conceptual triumph, the book articulated both the church's new scholarship and its wartime necessities. Written under the auspices of the MCs' Peace Problems Committee, it drew more readers, both in the Mennonite world and from the larger American religious public, than had any previous exposition of Mennonite peace theology.

Part of the book's appeal was its broad sweep. It combined biblical exegesis, general church history, the story of Mennonite nonresistance, an analysis of various forms of contemporary pacifism and their relevance to political culture, and reflection on where and how the Mennonite doctrine of nonresistance was applicable to modern life. The controlling idea was that nonresistance was central throughout the Bible and equally central to the church which would be faithful to its calling.[69]

To present nonresistance as central to the biblical story, Hershberger argued for a progressive view of revelation. The teachings of the New Testament could supersede those of the Old. Hershberger divided the Old Testament into three distinct parts—the fundamental moral law; the civil law; and the ceremonial law. The civil and the ceremonial laws represented "concessions on the part of God to the lowered moral state and the spiritual maturity of the people of that time."[70] War in the Old Testament was part of that concession; the fundamental moral law, even under the old covenant, was "thou shalt not kill." While by his "permissive will" the Old Testament God allowed even the Israelites to engage in war, even then God wanted all humankind to live in peace.[71]

Since the Ten Commandments were the fundamental moral law, one had to assume historically that there were two "levels of humanity, which today would be called the Christian and sub-Christian levels." God's real hope was that all humans would live on the higher level. In the new covenant God had empowered his people with the hope that they could indeed live—and draw all others to live—by the fundamental law. "The new and perfect covenant has invalidated the old imperfect one, and restored all conduct to the level of the fundamental moral law. . . . The law of Jesus went out freely to all men; it knew no restrictions of race or nationality or of station in life."[72]

Not all Mennonites agreed. With their more wooden doctrine of inspiration, Mennonite fundamentalists reacted uneasily. In 1938 George R. Brunk I died and *The Sword and Trumpet* lapsed. But in 1943 the paper was revived and now its new editor, J. Irvin Lehman, objected. Hershberger, he wrote, had not quoted all of the Scriptures which were relevant to his subject. He had philosophized with "false logic and improper analogies . . . until what God says is explained away."[73] On at least one point Lehman was correct. Hershberger had indeed raised questions about how to read the Bible. If Hershberger's way of reading the Bible was correct, then how much authority did certain elements of the Old Testament carry in the life of the church? Even more troubling to conservatives was a hint that God expected not only the church but the world's nations to live by peace instead of vengeance. If state violence did not carry God's sanction in the old covenant, then it surely did not in the twentieth century.[74]

Despite his hint about the nations, Hershberger wrote that "the outlook of the New Testament is entirely unpolitical"; it had "nothing to say about how the affairs of state should be conducted."[75] The early Anabaptists had understood this and had been "altogether nonpolitical in faith and practice."[76] Biblical nonresistance did not seek to direct the state. Even conscription was a legitimate right of the state so long as government accommodated its religious dissenters.

Thus biblical nonresistance as Hershberger defined it was sharply different from nonviolent resistance. That distinction, central to Mennonite peace discussions for the next decades, separated most Mennonites from various pacifists who sought social justice through peaceful but direct action. The distinction rested on the difference between "doing justice" and "demanding justice." Modern pacifists—William Lloyd Garrison, Leo Tolstoy, Mahatma Gandhi—demanded justice. By Hershberger's formula, Mennonites should do justice in their own individual and corporate lives. They should do justice submissively, however, and eschew every kind of resistance. Rather than making social change their commitment, Christians' ultimate commitment should be "obedience to the divine will." "New Testament nonresistance is concerned first with obedience to God and the creation of loving brotherhood," wrote Hershberger. To that, "desired advantage and social change are secondary."[77]

Few Mennonites objected to Hershberger's position on grounds that it was too withdrawn. However, Donovan Smucker, a younger GC minister, writer, graduate of Bluffton College, and sometime worker with the FOR and the AFSC, did object—on several grounds. He wrote Hershberger that the distinction between doing and seeking justice was one "for which you did not give Scripture." And pragmatically, doing justice would look like seeking justice. For instance, a Mennonite who lived in a racially segregated community and really did justice, even in the mode of "radical quietism" that Hershberger suggested, would really be practicing a "radical doing-ism." Besides, Smucker thought, Mennonites in history had gone beyond only "doing justice." In both Europe and America they had sometimes "sought justice for their brethren elsewhere."[78]

If Hershberger presented his approach as nonpolitical, it nevertheless embodied a prophetic witness that gave it pragmatic relevance. As nobody had before him, Hershberger positioned historic Mennonite understandings to make them relevant for the larger ecumenical world and even for the nation at large. He was traditionally Mennonite in his argument that Christian ethics was for Christians only, yet he enlarged the boundaries in which nonresistance had effect.

Hershberger did this partly by incorporating into the Mennonite narrative the writings of some people (T. S. Eliot, Adin Ballou, Gandhi, Pitirim A. Sorokin, Arthur Morgan) who had argued for the political relevance of nonresistant communities. Hershberger readily embraced their reading of the "curative" influence of nonresistance. "It is to bring healing to human society" and

to prevent its further decay through a consistent witness to the truth. This world needs the ministry of nonresistant Christians whose light, set on a hill, stands as a glowing witness to the way of truth and righteousness. A people who provide this witness are not parasites living at the expense of organized society. They are its greatest benefactors.[79]

Hershberger offered a radically two-kingdom theology but one in which Christians clearly contributed to the social order. Smucker, while objecting to some elements, embraced *War, Peace, and Nonresistance* as a "new biblical social gospel." He saw that its impact would be to move the church from its somewhat inactive and self-protecting posture to more active forms of reconciliation.[80]

In his rearticulation of biblical nonresistance, Hershberger surely drew from Mennonite history and theology. But, with training as an American historian, he also pointed to a long American tradition of prizing the dissidents who set out to build the model community separate from and over against the dominant society.[81] Much of Hershberger's career was devoted to building an alternative community.[82] In time he would find a different metaphor. Christians, he would write, were to be "colonies of heaven."[83]

Thus defined, Hershberger's nonresistance was both Mennonite and American. It suited a people who wished to retain their disengagement from political activity, but it also appealed to pacifists who feared they might be political parasites. Some Mennonites could find new freedom to be ecumenical because they had defined their own political contribution. Under attack in the war years, Mennonites were both redefining their peace theology and finding a place in the American political system.

CHAPTER
6

"WILL A NEW DAY DAWN FROM THIS?"
A PACIFIST PEOPLE IN WORLD WAR II

Early in 1941, when the new system for conscientious objectors, Civilian Public Service (CPS), was just getting started, a GC Mennonite minister, Peace Committee member, and church leader offered praise for a political order that granted alternative service for conscientious objectors. Writing to Henry A. Fast, who had recently been appointed as the first administrator of Mennonite-run CPS camps, Andrew (A. J.) Neuenschwander rejoiced that Mennonites could now serve, yet do it apart from the military system. It was remarkable that a wartime government was so generous. Now Mennonites could demonstrate to themselves and the nation that their pacifism was constructive, not destructive. Mused Neuenschwander, "Will a new day dawn from this?"[1]

Seldom if ever have Mennonites worked as closely with the state as during World War II. Traditionally, war had set the two at odds. Now by a strange paradox the war drew the two together. An unusual partnership emerged between the historic peace churches and the political order. More than most religious pacifists, Mennonites brought to this partnership a theology that separated church from state. Yet Mennonites embraced the CPS system with fewer reservations than did other historic peace churches. Whatever the strains on their theology, Mennonites said little about compromises inherent in the new partnership.

For the political order too, World War II offered a novel venture into the rights of religious dissent and national tolerance. For the first time, the rights of conscientious objectors had a legitimate place in a war society. Lewis B. Hershey, director of Selective Service for most of the war and a friend of conscientious objectors, labeled the venture "an experiment in democracy . . . such as no nation has ever made before." This experiment would test "whether our democracy is big enough to preserve minority rights in a time of national emergency."[2] Secure in an almost universal belief that World War II was just and right, Americans showed a new tolerance for ethnic diversity, religious pluralism, and even dissent.

The war was also remarkable as a transforming context for twentieth-century American Mennonites. General Hershey encouraged the pacifist churches to accept the Civilian Public Service system for two reasons: the public respect they might gain by performing service of national importance, and a likelihood that the program would enhance the religious and educational ideals of their own peoples.

Hershey was right on both counts. Mennonites emerged from wartime with a new confidence about their place in the national society and with a revitalized sense of their own religious mission. Paradoxically the war nourished an ideal of service and produced administrative agencies to channel that ideal. The demands that wartime benevolence put on Mennonites matured into a theology of active reconciliation that in turn redefined Mennonites' public life.

Years later Studs Terkel would produce a bestseller on World War II and call it *The Good War.* Of course no war is good. Yet peoples can profit in many ways from war's tragedy. In the "Good War," Mennonite peace people were among those who profited.

For millions of English, French, Germans, Russians, Chinese, Japanese, and peoples of Eastern Europe, the war meant incredible devastation and a remapping of their world. But for Americans it brought a great age of self-confidence. Americans could now dream of a "Pax Americana." They were in the "American Century." A week after the United States dropped its second atomic bomb on Japan, Britain's Prime Minister Winston Churchill told his House of Commons that "America stands at this moment at the summit of the world." Soon U.S. president Harry S Truman told his countrymen that they possessed "the greatest strength and the greatest power that man has ever reached."[3] In 1945 neither statement was an exaggeration.

The roots of Mennonite self-confidence early in the war were not in the prospect of military victory but in the extraordinary national system worked out to accommodate the pacifist conscience.

During the 1930s, as the second great war loomed, Mennonite thinking focused on preventing a repeat of the draft experiences of World War I. Memories of Mennonites' unpreparedness for World War I and their harassment in military camps and even in some home communities pierced their psyche and left it deeply insecure about Mennonites' place in America. So the 1930s' signals of a new global conflict prompted Mennonites to work actively to protect conscientious objectors in any new draft law.[4]

In 1935 Guy F. Hershberger articulated the working Mennonite position. The occasion was the Mennonite Conference on War and Peace sponsored by the MCs' Peace Problems Committee and held at Goshen College. If the draft were to come, Hershberger identified four possible responses. One was to accept regular military service, but of course with its deep convictions and long pacifist history, the church could not approve that alternative. Another possibility was noncombatant service within the military, and during World War I some Mennonite men had indeed chosen this option. Noncombatancy, however, was an integral part of the military system: even if "not one of actual killing," noncombatants' work was "auxiliary" to it. Thus, Hershberger advised, there was virtually "no difference between this and the acceptance of military service."[5]

A third and historic position was to refuse any kind of service. Mennonites considered this option honorable, and new circumstances might again require it.[6] But during the interwar years, Mennonites were exploring a different path.

The way being contemplated was alternative service—service, but in forms that would neither contribute directly to the war effort nor be under military direction and control. Hershberger preferred this position,[7] and it would soon have the support of virtually all Mennonite leaders. Mennonites found it acceptable because it fulfilled scriptural commands to relieve suffering and was in line with such efforts in their history. Amid the destruction of war, its moral example would be a witness to the nation.

Hershberger spoke against a background of historic peace church collaboration that had intensified during World War I and continued into the interwar years.[8] At the 1935 conference in Newton, Kansas, the peace churches moved to form a standing committee composed of Robert W. Balderston for the Friends, C. Ray Keim for the Church of the Brethren, and Orie O. Miller for the Mennonites. The committee continued interchurch contacts and tried to educate draft-age youth and to prepare politically for what

Historic Peace Church delegation to President Franklin D. Roosevelt, January 10, 1940. Left to right: Clarence Pickett, Friends; Walter Woodward, Friends; Rufus Jones, Friends; Peter C. Hiebert, Mennonite; Harold S. Bender, Mennonite; Rufus Bowman, Church of the Brethren; Paul Bowman, Church of the Brethren. Missing is Mennonite Emmett L. Harshbarger. Credit: Mennonite Library and Archives, Bethel College, North Newton, Kansas.

seemed like an impending war. Twice, on February 12, 1937, and January 10, 1940, representatives of the committee visited President Roosevelt to represent their respective churches' convictions on militarism and conscription.[9]

In 1939, with interchurch and governmental consultations quickening, Mennonites created a Mennonite Central Peace Committee. Although inter-Mennonite and a forerunner of the MCC Peace Section, until 1942 the new committee was independent of MCC. Yet the memberships overlapped, with P. C. Hiebert, E. L. Harshbarger, and H. S. Bender making up the new body's executive committee.

In 1939 the committee quickly began to prepare for conscription. On September 30, 1939, the executive committee drew up "A Plan of Action for Mennonites in Case of War." According to the Plan, Mennonite young men should register for conscription but indicate that they wanted nonmilitary service. The church could cooperate so long as the forms of service were acceptable, approved by the church, and under its supervision.[10]

The Mennonite plan was the core of the January 1940 Mennonite-Quaker-Brethren communication to Roosevelt. It recounted the groups' efforts since World War I for humanitarian relief and rehabilitation, a determination to keep working "for suffering humanity," and a hope that the U.S. Government would authorize "such nonmilitary humanitarian service to be substituted for military service."[11]

Although all three groups—Mennonite, Church of the Brethren, and Friends—signed and offered it, the letter obscured conflicts among their approaches. The main division was between supporters of alternative service and absolutists who wanted no complicity with the conscription system at all, including registration. Should the churches seek guarantees for the absolutists? Mennonites adamantly refused. Harold Bender called the absolutists' position "negative" and "diametrically counter to the philosophy which we [Mennonites] have been operating on so far."

For Raymond Wilson, an American Friends Service Committee staffer, the fact of nonpolitical Mennonites refusing to support those who would not participate in conscription was ironic. Besides, he countered, "to some of our young people," would the proposed statement not smack all too much "of the historic peace churches trying . . . to save their skins from the rigors of conscription?"[12]

With the letter went a memorandum that pleaded more openly for the absolutists. Yet its main thrust was to spell out more precisely the peace-church aspirations for an alternative system. Two elements were central. (1) At the stage of draft classification, there should be a civilian agency to judge the merit of conscientious objector claims and make the initial classifications. (2) The historic peace churches must be allowed to establish their own organizations to administer their conscripted men. A third point was that the government and not the churches should deal with absolute resisters who could not cooperate at all with the conscription system.[13]

As for the service cooperative men would perform, it was to be in line with the humanitarian work the peace churches had been doing in peacetime. Appropriate examples included relief of war sufferers, refugees, or evacuated civilian populations; reconstruction of war-stricken areas; resettlement of refugees; forestry or land-reclamation service; reconstruction work in local communities; nonmilitary medical and health service; and farmwork.[14]

Like the Friends and others, Mennonites came into 1940 with an active record of humanitarian work. As they entered negotiations with the government to shape the draft system, they hoped government would recognize that record. But they soon saw that negotiations would not be easy. To the U.S. government, there were other realities more substantial than the hopes and private charities of a few peace people.

NEGOTIATING THE CIVILIAN PUBLIC SERVICE SYSTEM

In June of 1940 swift victories for Nazi Germany climaxed in the fall of The Netherlands, Belgium, Luxembourg, and France. Now Hitler ruled Europe from the North Sea to the Mediterranean. Britain stood alone. The U.S. public's sentiment for neutrality, deep throughout the 1930s, now waned. The Roosevelt administration turned more and more to military preparedness. Reporting on a June 6, 1940, meeting with Francis Biddle, the U.S. Solicitor General, Orie O. Miller wrote that "the trend in Washington is definitely toward preparation for the entry of the United States into the European War."[15]

On June 20 Congress took up the Burke-Wadsworth bill, a measure which would eventually become the Selective Service and Training Act of 1940. Its original language on conscientious objection was close to that of the World War I law. That version would have exempted only members of those "sects whose creed or principles forbids its members to participate in war in any form." It also would have required them to perform noncombatant work the U.S. president decided was suitable.[16] However, by September 16, 1940, when Congress had finished the bill and the president signed it, it was more acceptable.

The change was due largely to persistent efforts of the conscientious-objector community. The Friends, more sophisticated than either the Brethren or the Mennonites in the ways of Washington, led the lobbying. Yet crucial to the lobbying's success was the fact that diverse elements managed to join in support. By late summer 1940 Mennonites were actively linked with peace-minded Catholics and Episcopalians, War Resisters, the Fellowship of Reconciliation, and many other religious groups; pacifist organizations; and others wanting to protect the rights of individual conscience.[17]

Paul Comly French, right, standing with Joe Weaver, c. 1943. Credit: Mennonite Library and Archives, Bethel College, North Newton, Kansas.

The new Selective Service and Training Act improved on World War I legislation in various ways. Those conscientious objectors who "by reason of religious training and belief" were "opposed to war in any form" were allowed either to serve as noncombatants in the military or to engage in "work of national importance under civilian direction." Yet since it provided only for persons of "religious training and belief," the phrase seemed to exclude secular pacifists, or at least to leave the law open to various interpretations. Unlike British law, legislators made no real provision for the absolutists. Instead, all conscientious objectors had either to participate in some way or face punishment for refusal. Unlike the wording of the World War I law, the term "training" did not put the historic peace churches and their members in a special category, yet it hardly prevented their enjoying a favored position.[18]

Administration of the new law rested almost entirely with a new Selective Service System. While technically a civilian agency, the System's business was clearly to mobilize people for the armed forces. One victory for anyone who might resist was that appeals went ultimately to the Department of Justice rather than to the military. But that victory was small. Theodore Wachs, in a study of World War II conscientious objection, has assessed the entire structure and observed correctly that "pressures of time, political concerns, misconceptions about pacifism, and general ignorance about conscientious objection" all combined to defeat some of the pacifists' fondest hopes.[19]

The meaning of "work of national importance" and the administrative structure necessary to run the alternative service system remained for the U.S. president to clarify. During the fall of 1940, the peace churches mobilized to influence the as-yetundesigned regulations. On October 11, 1940, MCC representatives met with Michael R. Ziegler of the Brethren Service Committee and Paul Comly French, representing both the Friends War Problems Committee and the American Friends Service Committee. The Mennonites were Orie O. Miller and Henry Fast (a GC Mennonite who had recently earned a Ph.D. degree from Hartford Seminary and was now the new director of MCC camps). The four delegates established what would become the central agency to deal with all matters related to religious dissent from military service.[20] First called the National Council for Religious Conscientious Objectors, two months later the agency became the "National Service Board for Religious Objectors" (NSBRO). Eventually its name would be "National Interreligious Service Board for Conscientious Objectors" (NISBCO).

In ensuing discussions, no players did more to shape the outcome than did Lewis B. Hershey and Paul Comly French. Hershey was descended from Swiss Anabaptists who had emigrated to Lancaster, Pennsylvania, in 1708 to practice the pacifist ideal. His branch of Hersheys were no longer pacifist, and he was a Brigadier General in the U.S. Army. Nonetheless, he was unusually tolerant of conscientious objectors.[21]

Hershey somehow had extraordinary freedom to manage Selective Service, and the peace churches and their people benefited. Even before the Burke-Wadsworth law was signed, he and his associates had the system virtually in operation. The president and his close advisers played only minor roles in devising particulars. One reason for Hershey's freedom was his considerable ability to charm both the public and the system's critics. George Flynn, Hershey's most recent biographer, notes that "with his gold-rimmed glasses dangling off one ear, he rivaled President Roosevelt in playing with the press." By such tactics he made the system seem fairer and more democratic than it really was. Astute enough to stay out of trouble with both the military and Congress, he ran a draft system that was decentralized and remarkably autonomous.[22]

As early as the Burke-Wadsworth hearings, Paul Comly French was spokesman for the Friends War Problems Committee. Thereafter, from 1940 to 1946, he was executive director of NSBRO. French was a former journalist with deep commitments to the pacifist cause. In a 1940 book *Why We Won't Murder*, he had indicted the government's handling of conscientious objectors during World War I. A workable alternative service system, he believed, would preserve both pacifist consciences and American democracy.

But beyond such ideals, establishing a system to coordinate "work of national importance" involved many technicalities. What would be its structure? What roles would the government and the conscientious-objector community each play? How closely could the peace churches work with the government before feeling—or in fact being—co-opted and compromised? Who would fund the program? During September and October 1940 it quickly became clear that the government had not thought many of these issues through. Lack of clarity let the peace churches make many crucial suggestions.[23]

The peace churches responded quickly and cooperatively. On October 4 the Mennonite Central Peace Committee met in Chicago with ten Mennonite denominations represented. The conferees contemplated a program of "service projects . . . for our Mennonite draftees directed by the church," and asked Mennonite Central Committee (MCC) to assume responsibility. Further, they approved cooperation with the other historic peace churches in establishing a system acceptable to the government. In the same month the American Friends Service Committee and the Brethren Service Committee took similar positions.[24]

On October 22 the new National Council for Religious Conscientious Objectors proposed a National Selective Service Board and a dual system of units, some governmentally and some privately administered. Government, the Council suggested, should pay for transportation, materials, and maintenance, plus military-level wages to draftees in both kinds of units. The private operating agencies would be allowed to set standards for what conscientious objectors they would accept. Domestic units would operate under the jurisdiction of the Public Health Service, the Department of the Interior, the Department of Agriculture, and the Office of Education. A series of overseas units would work in refugee settlement, feeding of displaced persons, and reconstruction.[25]

On October 29 Selective Service accepted the proposal in essence. But there was a large hurdle. President Roosevelt's approval would come only at a considerable price. In early December the usually affable Roosevelt responded, by French's account, with "instant and aggressive opposition." If young men were dying in battle, he would not permit COs to go to former Civilian Conservation Corps (CCC) camps.[26] He opposed both the proposed structure and any notion that government should fund an alternative-service plan. In Congress also the idea of government funding seemed to evoke wide rebuff.

Thereupon French, Clarence Dykstra (first and short-term director of Selective Service) and some of the president's advisers decided they could not depend on Congress for funding. If the peace churches hoped for a system with at least partial autonomy they themselves would have to pay—not only for their own members but for all who took up alternative service. The planners proposed that NSBRO, as the central administrative agency of the peace churches, might "supply subsistence, necessary building, hospital care, and generally all things necessary for the care and maintenance of the men."[27]

Dykstra put his new proposal—an enormous reversal—to the peace churches as an all-or-nothing proposition. If the government funded the program, it would have complete control; if the churches wanted to retain some control, they would have to supply the funds. The peace churches responded quickly. On December 21 Mennonite Central Committee voted to accept Dykstra's memorandum. By the time the CPS system would end in 1947, the decision would cost MCC more than $3 million. But at the moment of truth, there was no eye-blinking. In a note to Clarence Pickett of the American Friends Service Committee, Orie O. Miller pledged that Mennonites "would gladly pay their share of the bill. They would do it even though every Mennonite farmer had to mortgage his farm."[28]

Miller was not a man of empty words. He gauged the sentiments of his people correctly. Nearly a year after this decision, John Mosemann, Jr., son of the Lancaster Conference bishop and initial director of the first Mennonite camp at Grottoes, Virginia, mused that to have "actually paid our own fare has amazed even the severest of critics." For the peace churches to serve the government while footing their own bill "has in large measure been the sufficient rebuke to enemies of the conscientious objector position."[29] Mosemann surely was right. MCC extended its commitment even to draftees not from MCC churches if they could not pay their own costs.[30] Self-funding made alternative service acceptable and in part insulated COs from their severest critics.

MENNONITE EMBRACE OF THE CPS SYSTEM

On February 6, 1941, President Roosevelt signed Executive Order 8675 and thereby established the Civilian Public Service

Henry Fast. Credit: Mennonite Library and Archives, Bethel College, North Newton, Kansas.

program. For six years that order linked the government and the pacifist community in a rare and strange partnership. The overwhelming majority of conscientious objectors would serve in camps under the general administration of NSBRO but with churches operating specific units. Church and state worked together by gentlemen's agreements rather than under explicit contracts.

Such imprecision invited interminable bickering. Were the church agencies autonomous or agents of Selective Service? Were religious communities that historically shunned governmental responsibilities now agreeing to perform governmental functions or not? At the beginning and throughout, the partnership was ill-defined.

In late 1940 and early 1941, such questions caused little concern. Mennonites were euphoric. With World War I memories still fresh, the relative autonomy of CPS seemed good indeed. The drafted men could serve under the guidance of the church. In January 1941 a widely-circulated statement by the Mennonite Central Committee suggested that CPS offered a chance to witness to the nation. Feeling "grateful to our government for these privileges," MCC was "happy to be able to render a constructive service . . . as 'unto God' and not only as 'unto men.' "[31]

Surely, MCC said, both the churches and the individual young men would respond to this opportunity "in a sacrificial spirit." Such a spirit, plus a "patriotic devotion on the part of all to the welfare of our country," would assure success. In the same month a lead editorial in the GC paper *The Mennonite* was as effusive. It spoke of "our beloved United States" being moved "under the guid-

Albert Gaeddert. Credit: Mennonite Library and Archives, Bethel College, North Newton, Kansas.

ance of our kind heavenly Father." Under such guidance, the United States had given Mennonites "the privilege of doing service of real benefit to our land, entirely under civilian control."[32]

MCs expressed similar sentiments. In 1941 their Peace Problems Committee contrasted the action of "our government" with the worldwide "tendency toward totalitarian and dictatorial methods." Even in "national emergency" and under "the threat of war," the government had made "generous provisions for the consciences of nonresistant Christians." Its generosity "should be a matter of deep appreciation and gratitude by the entire church."[33]

Henry A. Fast also expressed admiration by invoking a paradox: wartime service might be good for peace peoples. "If the people in our churches can catch a vision of the wonderful opportunity God, through this arrangement of the government, has placed at their disposal," he wrote, "they will thank God for the opportunity and undertake it with the determination to make the most of it." It was as the apostle Paul had said: "All things work together for good to them that love the Lord."[34]

Fast thought that Mennonites were at a high moment. "The question before American Mennonitism now," he wrote, was how Mennonites "will answer the challenge of their present choice." Their answer, he thought, "will not only test the reality and depth of their loyalty to Christ and their faith in His way of love"; it would also "determine very largely the whole future of Mennonitism in this country."[35]

The fact was, Mennonites had long wanted to prove their good citizenship. They had long wished to demonstrate the "constructiveness" of their resistance to militarism and to define for themselves a different place in American society. Now was the chance.

Mennonites' understanding of the CPS system tended to be different from those both of the government and of quite a few other conscientious objectors. The Mennonites did not see CPS as rooted in the requirements of statecraft or even in the legal rights of citizens in a democratic society. Rather, CPS was an act of witness. To be sure, work performed in a spirit of charity and goodwill and compassion for human welfare made a contribution to the nation's well-being. But more importantly, the work was an expression of biblical faith. Mennonites would accept a system that kept their young men out of war, but to be at peace with the system, they needed to go "the second mile."

To Albert Gaeddert, the second director of Mennonite camps, that was the way of biblical nonresistance. "In place of gaining its point by law," he wrote in 1946, biblical nonresistance "operates on the level of love . . . ; in place of using the tactics of pressure to gain its point," it acted "on the basis of principles involved; it does not insist on personal rights, but rather gives thought to . . . [one's] obligations and duties. . . . When compelled to go one mile, the nonresistant Christian does not resist the compulsion, but rather stands prepared to volunteer the services of the second mile."[36]

Another motive lay in yet another paradox—a sense that CPS was good because the camps could be places for Mennonites to develop community, faith, and character. Church leaders saw CPS as more than a period of service to fulfill one's draft obligations or even to go the second mile. From the start, Mennonite planners expected CPS to reinvigorate the church. A generation incarcerated by government and sequestered under the church's considerable control of the units could be educated in the recently refurbished idealism of the Mennonite world. Those ideals, rooted in the history and culture of Mennonite peoples and recently refined by Anabaptist-recovery scholarship, could be passed to the youth of the church. In effect, CPS could be a Mennonite university experience. History would prove such aspirations far from wrong.

Mennonites were not the only ones to embrace the CPS system. Many pacifist leaders were willing to support at least some parts of a church-based system. They assumed that the arrangement would permit COs to express their conscience more completely than would a system with the government in day-to-day control. However, a group such as the War Resisters League accepted the arrangements for the sake of unity but with reservations. The League's executive Secretary, Frank Olmstead, was troubled. To force members of his League to report to a camp run by Quakers, he told a friend, was as "distressing" as making a Quaker "report to a camp run by Jews or Theosophists."[37]

Yet on the more optimistic side, Olmstead wrote also that CPS was "a sermon on peace preached in terms of life itself . . . a reservoir of liberty."[38] And Paul Comly French stayed with the NSBRO for six years at least partly because he too thought the CPS experiment would advance America's traditions of freedom. Out of the diverse peoples who would come to each camp, he thought CPS could both preserve individual rights and forge model communities who would demonstrate how humans should live.[39]

The camps, wrote French, would "create a pattern of life that will demonstrate the way that nations can live together in peace and harmony." Such utopianism, which some in the NSBRO constituency shared, was hardly appropriate. It was surely too much to think that the CPS venture in communal living would become a model for global conflict resolution. But the fact that conscientious objectors were an exception did not daunt the visionaries. French was sure that "Civilian Public Service has the chance to develop the new Third Order—not by formal educational courses nor by idealistic pronouncements but by the ability to live and work together."[40]

Once the presidential order had been signed, Mennonites were eager to begin. Orie Miller regretted that "through February [1941] we have simply marked time."[41] The first CPS camp opened on May 15, 1941. At the opening ceremony, twenty-six conscientious objectors and fifty-four photographers participated, in what some dubbed a "gold fish bowl." The first Mennonites, eight young men, reported seven days later to a Mennonite camp near Grottoes, Virginia.

EARLY CPS WORK

Before the CPS program ended in March of 1947, nearly twelve thousand conscientious objectors served in it. More than forty-six hundred were Mennonites. In addition roughly twenty-five thousand (thirty-nine hundred of them Mennonites) served in the military as noncombatant conscientious objectors.[42]

The CPS system also involved about two thousand women. Some worked in the campus, employed mainly as dietitians, cooks, and matrons. Others followed their husbands, fiancés, and boy-friends to unit locations; many found employment in communities near the units. Some women worked in the same places as their men, particularly in the more social-service-oriented locations such as mental hospitals. About one thousand children of CPS couples also lived in or near the units.[43]

Camp Grottoes, just outside Shenandoah National Park, quickly showed MCC the size of its task and some possible frustrations. Selective Service was supposed to provide usable camps. Yet before it opened the camp, MCC spent $2500 on physical facilities and local congregations provided labor to repair and clean up the camp. Elsewhere—often using a "Camp Kit" folder from MCC that suggested what items were needed—women's groups in congregations across the country prepared sheets, towels, soap, sewing packets, and other items for individual campers.

At Grottoes the workday was from 7:30 a.m. to 5:00 p.m., five days per week. Planning schedules and activities for other times was the task of whichever church agency was in charge of the unit. That included activities designed to make the men's stay more comfortable and enriching. At Grottoes MCC developed a laundry, a library, a reading room, a barber shop, prayer rooms, recreation rooms, a craft room, a photography darkroom, outdoor recreational courts (basketball, volleyball, tennis, softball, horseshoe), and a canteen with a few items for sale.[44]

Grottoes (like most of the early camps) was under the jurisdiction of the Soil Conservation Service of the U.S. Department of Agriculture. Through NSBRO, Mennonites had expressed interest in soil conservation, and the rural roots of most Mennonite men seemed to match that work. After a year and a quarter of CPS, some 1147 of the 1725 Mennonite men in CPS were in soil-conservation camps—66 percent, although by the end of the war the 66 would drop to 19. The Soil Conservation Service continued depression-era projects, such as constructing water reservoirs and drainage systems, building dams, erecting fences, terracing farmlands, and planting trees. Sometimes its CPSers also helped harvest crops as emergency workers. Amid wartime shortages of labor, communities turned to the camps for assistance.[45]

Other early units were under the jurisdiction of agencies such as the U.S. Forest Service, the Bureau of Reclamation, and the Federal Security Administration. As the war went on, units operating under the U.S. Department of Agriculture became prominent. In the spring of 1943, some 250 Mennonite CPS men fanned out to

Smoke Jumpers, Missoula (Montana) CPS Unit. Credit: Mennonite Library and Archives, Bethel College, North Newton, Kansas.

selected dairy farms, mainly in Wisconsin, Ohio, Michigan, and
Pennsylvania. There they replaced hired hands who were now often at war. Those 250 CPSers lived isolated and apart from camp
experience.[46]

Under the Forest Service MCC operated six units, and
throughout the war 12 to 14 percent of Mennonite CPS men
worked in them—mainly at tree planting, fire control, and forest
pruning. A camp that won exceptional publicity was one near Missoula, Montana, from which men flew out and parachuted to fight
fires in five western states. The Smoke Jumpers, as the men were
fondly known, were organized in the spring of 1943 with Friends,
Brethren, and Mennonites in about equal numbers but under
MCC administration. The Jumpers were for Mennonites almost
what fighter pilots were for nonpacifists; few government assignments were nearly so glamorous.[47]

In mid-1942 and following, opportunities became available in
both mental hospitals and in public-health projects. The numbers
of CPS people employed in mental hospitals grew rapidly. By October 1943, one out of six in CPS was working in such an institution.
By the end of 1945, more than 1500 men from Mennonite units
had worked in mental institutions. The public-health units involved lower numbers in a variety of programs and places. Projects
included hookworm eradication in Florida, privy installation in
Mississippi, a medical clinic in Puerto Rico, and medical-guinea-
pig units in various university and government hospitals.[48]

CHURCH vs. GOVERNMENT TENSIONS
IN CPS ADMINISTRATION

The structure of CPS administration was untidy. One CPSer
later called it an "ad hoc enterprise, hurriedly contrived and im-
plemented."[49] Official authority rested with the U.S. president. He
delegated it to Selective Service, which turned over large parts of it
to NSBRO—which in turn split the actual management of the
camps among the three service agencies of the historic peace
churches. At the outset of the war, the three agencies administered the CPS system for all COs regardless of church affiliation.
MCC ran almost sixty camps. The Friends and the Church of the
Brethren each ran about thirty. In 1943 and 1944 the government
created several camps of its own and also permitted other agencies to establish units.[50]

The demands of the state inevitably clashed with the consciences and wishes of individual conscientious objectors. When they did, the state assumed—and never forgot—that its claims were superior.[51] In contrast, the CO community generally assumed that rights of conscience were paramount. In some ultimate sense, conscience did have the higher claim. But wars are not easy times for asserting ultimate, abstract values.

Peace people clearly wanted to contribute to society by doing work of national importance. But Selective Service much preferred to keep COs invisible. That preference practically insured that the objectors' work would not be very significant. Preventing a potential national embarrassment was more important than getting maximum benefits from a comparative handful of COs.

After all, veterans' organizations outnumbered peace people and had direct access to Washington policymakers. There was always a host of congressmen anxious to show their patriotism by backing anything military. Selective Service leaders attended the annual conventions of both the American Legion and the Veterans of Foreign Wars partly to deflect resolutions attacking the entire CPS program. At the American Legion national convention in 1943, delegates offered more than forty resolutions attacking conscientious objectors and CPS. Often such resolutions called for revoking COs' citizenship and making sure COs did not get paid.[52]

Particularly after Pearl Harbor, such pressure from veterans' groups pushed Selective Service and the church agencies into continual discussion over how tight, uniform, and military-like the administration of camps should be. Looking at local camps, veterans' groups professed to see various abuses, such as "sloppy housekeeping"; directors who had "no authority and have to ask the opinion of the men on every point"; and "men going home every two or three weeks when Army men may not get home for months."[53]

In 1943 a statewide American Legion conference in Michigan charged that "CO camps in the state resembled vacation resorts more than work camps." Finally, no camp lay beyond the scrutiny of the local press. A fairly remote unit was the Hill City Camp in South Dakota. Its relations with nearby towns were good. Yet from time to time a local editor reviewed its people's conduct and suggested that the "internees" had too much freedom, especially to leave the camp.[54]

Debates among administrators, both church and government, went on and on. Which campers could bring automobiles and under what regulations? How many weekend leaves? Should camps encourage athletic competition with teams from local communities? Should nonresistant people be flying the nation's flag in their camps? Should campers emulate or avoid military neatness?

Some of the Mennonites' own camp directors shared the American Legion's and the government's concerns about excessive democracy in the camps. One camp director, Albert E. Bohrer, wrote Henry Fast in 1942 that he often felt "that too much is left up to the boys to decide" and that "the discipline is a little loose."[55] Other Mennonite directors felt comfortable with the looseness.[56] But the questions were not only about standardization and flexibility; they were also about coercion and voluntarism. If they were doing the work of the state, how much enforcement could Mennonites exert without violating their consciences? If camps were to be model communities pointing the way to the future, what about coercion, what about democracy?

Hershey himself told French that camp structure should develop leaders for the postwar world's needs. French wholeheartedly agreed. Here was an opportunity to "develop the kind of leadership which . . . is necessary to organize any kind of an intelligent world."[57] Henry Fast could easily agree. The way to achieve the standards of the military camps was through education, not authoritarianism.[58]

However, the religious agencies administering the camps differed on the forms of camp life that would produce leadership, and on how far to accept the restraints inherent in their subservience to Selective Service. Mennonites approached the political system very much according to the apostle Paul's injunction to be subservient to duly constituted authorities. They tended to be grateful for the system. The Friends, more committed to radical individualism from their "inner light" tradition, were less willing to accept governmental restrictions or to discipline draftees who protested the system of conscription that incarcerated them. The system was especially frustrating to those young people who believed that CPS did not let them make an adequate contribution to society and who therefore found their inner convictions compromised. Between Mennonite acquiescence and Quaker protest stood the Church of Brethren, often trying to accommodate both principles.[59]

Paul Comly French, a Quaker, mediated the differing positions to Selective Service. Ironically, he felt more comfortable with the Mennonite approach. For one thing, he was sure General

Hershey, Congress, and most of the Roosevelt administration thought of the CPS program as a privilege rather than a guaranteed right. Even more, French believed that making the system work by keeping disparate elements hinged together was part of the new world witness CPS could make. In their work with Selective Service, the churches needed to show the "basic humility and sensitiveness that we should have as followers of Christ." Quakers threatened from time to time to leave the program. But to French, such departure would mean failure—not failure for Selective Service or the government, but an admission that "in a really difficult tension situation we did not have enough understanding and goodwill to carry us through." Making the system work in spite of outside criticism and internal conflict was a way to "demonstrate that there is something in the power of goodwill and understanding."[60]

No Mennonite could have said it better. Rooted in his hope that the CPS experience could be formative for the postwar world, French's views were in some ways like those of Guy F. Hershberger. Both pacifists formulated their peace theology to tie present acquiescence to a prophetic future.

PERSUADING MENNONITE YOUNG MEN

Working with government did not create the only problems the Mennonites faced as CPS began. Church leaders began with those high hopes that alternative service would transform the church, but such an effect depended on churchwide assent. Henry Fast correctly noted that while conscription required decisions by draft-age youths, "our churches more than our boys" were "being put to the test." Like others, Fast knew that some of the churches were "only half awake to the issue." He particularly worried that those Mennonites most influenced by American Fundamentalism were easily "indifferent to the issues of military training." Yet Fast was not pessimistic. While military pressures swayed some youth, others were "tremendously concerned and are eager for any help in thinking through this whole difficult problem of the Christian's relation to the state."[61] The problem was one of education. The churches had to continue and intensify their energetic peace education of the 1930s.

Other Mennonite leaders were less confident. In spring 1941, E. G. Kaufman feared "we will be losing some young men unless they are helped to get into the right channels at the very beginning."[62] Early reports on the young men's choices gave cause for concern. A Peace Problems Committee report to the 1941 MC general conference lamented "that a few of our young men have accepted full military service and a few more noncombatant service."[63] In summer 1942, Robert S. Kreider, then a young CPSer at Colorado Springs, presented a study on "The Environmental Influences Affecting the Decisions of Mennonite Boys of Draft Age." Of 179 case studies of Mennonite conscripts he had gathered, 102 were in the military and only 77 in CPS. As did others, Kreider blamed what in the 1990s would be called a growing Mennonite pluralism—more and more ethical, residential, and vocational diversity.[64]

A more complete census in November of 1942 showed that a disconcerting pattern was continuing. MC data showed that eight hundred members were in CPS and 320 in the military. Harold Bender was shocked. "A 30 percent failure is a bad record," he exclaimed. "Only 70 percent loyal! Is this a passing grade. . . ?" Bender (and others) did not blame only the youth. He said the dismal figures were a direct challenge to pastors, bishops, parents, and congregations.[65]

Early reports to Fast and other GC officials revealed similar deviation from their church's official positions. After meeting with Eastern District Conference ministers in the fall of 1940, one of Fast's correspondents indicated that for the most part he was "impressed with their attitudes." Yet he was distressed that he had had to devote one session to an effort "to convert" three ministers. "If the ministers do not know or do not believe in the principles of nonresistance," he asked, "how can the rank and file of the congregations believe in it?"[66] Similar concerns came from the West. In March 1941, John H. Langenwalter, pastor of a GC congregation at Reedley, California, advised Fast that "many of our people are imbued with the idea that Peace is not to be expected."[67]

Langenwalter believed that such pessimism about peace came because too many Mennonites held to " 'fundamental doctrines' which seem far from fundamental to me." Fast agreed.[68] So did the historian C. Henry Smith in 1942. Seeing all too many defections among his GC church, he wondered if his people were losing their peace testimony. The problem as Smith saw it was that "evangelists, missionaries and ministers" in various kinds of evangelistic efforts were inclined to stress only "a few of the fundamentals of salvation." The result: more and more members in many congregations "are utter strangers to the distinctive doctrines of Mennonitism."[69]

Noncombatant military service was an especially thorny problem; church leaders themselves disagreed. Fast advised one young man that in accepting noncombatancy he was linking up with a system whose "sole purpose is to train . . . men in the most effective system of destroying human life." Certainly, advised Fast, no Christian could be identified, "even as a hanger-on, with a method and an organization which is completely contrary to the way of Jesus."[70] With such words Fast spoke for most Mennonite leaders and certainly for the MCC position. In 1944 an editorial in the MCs' *Gospel Herald* defined a noncombatant as "simply one of eight or ten men who are required to keep every front-line soldier going."[71]

An open advocate of noncombatant service in the military was Cornelius H. Suckau, the pastor of the large Berne, Indiana, GC congregation and one who helped found Grace Bible Institute. In November 1942, preaching on "Service to God and Country," he said that what Christians should render to "Caesar" included even "our sons and daughters and husbands and wives." In Suckau's litany, "Render to Caesar the things that are Caesar's" and "Render . . . unto God the things that are God's" were equal.[72]

God had privileged America much like Israel. Suckau thought that noncombatancy was a way to serve America and still be consistent with Mennonite tradition. One result: only twenty of 150 men drafted from his large congregation listened to their denomination and chose CPS. The other 130 joined the military.[73] Nor was Suckau the only minister who favored noncombatant service.[74]

A perception that the CPS program was relatively easy may have helped Mennonite boys choose noncombatancy. Confusions arose through a lack of information or misinformation. In Oklahoma some Mennonites referred to the civilian camps as "picnic grounds" because of the location of the first camp in the "beautiful Shenandoah valley." If "picnic grounds" was meant as a joke, the consequences were serious.[75] Persuading young men to accept CPS remained an important concern throughout the war.

For some of the conservative groups, the question was not CPS or military service but cooperation of any kind with the conscription system. The Reidenbach Mennonites were a small Old Order congregation of about thirty-five members who split from the Wenger Mennonites (an Old Order group based in Pennsylvania's Lancaster County) over cooperation with the Selective Service System. Although one survey reported that 100 percent of the Old Order Mennonites went into CPS, David B. Hoover, a Reidenbach deacon, was extremely critical, suggesting that any Mennonite cooperation with Selective Service was analogous to the Gibeonites of the Old Testament "who by craft obtained a league with Israel, so as to escape the edge of the sword." Mennonites working with draft officials had done so "to escape imprisonment," whereas the true followers of Jesus "will rather suffer for righteousness' sake than to tolerate such insidious arts."[76] Six Reidenbach young men refused to register and were sentenced to two years in Federal penitentiaries. However, governmental authorities were reluctant to incarcerate, so the six were placed in a CPS camp under MCC jurisdiction.[77]

MANAGEMENT PROBLEMS

Mennonites had never undertaken a managerial task as large as CPS. Their own churches were structured into separate denominations with little bureaucratic machinery to harmonize the varying groups and interests into a cooperative union. Now the groups had to cooperate by appointing and apportioning representatives to new inter-Mennonite and interchurch agencies. Yet they still had to respect denominational structures and styles of administration. The demands of wartime would enlarge inter-Mennonite structures but also streamline the denominational ones.[78]

Finding adequate leadership to manage the camps was another critical need. An example was Paul Goering, a young GC Mennonite student at Hartford Seminary. Urging Goering to become a camp leader, Henry Fast reasoned that the moment required sacrifice and that "taking care of our boys" was just as important as any future church or missionary work.[79]

Complicating such appeals was the need to be sure camp leaders were theologically sound. MCC chairman P. C. Hiebert cautioned executive secretary Orie O. Miller about several candidates. Some able ones had studied at seminaries which were not avowedly conservative. "I would feel bad," he wrote, "if our boys would return from camps contaminated with modernism." Since "there will doubtless be some liberal thinkers among the boys, . . . we must be all the more careful about the directors."[80]

Suspicions between members of different denominations in the MCC family made problems for keeping the CPS system together. Persons who were active in the MCC network and in CPS administration almost all shared the vision of inter-Mennonite cooperation. They were frustrated at others' parochialism.

Through selective memory Mennonites would later look back on CPS as the great ecumenical event that brought Mennonites together. Yet, except for the GC, in whose ideology Mennonite cooperation and ecumenism were central, virtually all the Mennonite denominations challenged CPS's cooperative basis.

Caution from some smaller groups such as the Reformed Mennonites, the Amish, or even the MBs was not nearly as troubling as were some voices that came from the large MC church. At MC general conference sessions in August 1941, barely four months after the first camp opened at Grottoes, conservative leaders expressed dismay at mixing MC youths with pacifists of questionable beliefs. The Peace Problems Committee report assured the assembled delegates that the MC church retained "independence of action," and that the CPS arrangement "in no way committed" it to other Mennonite bodies. Nonetheless, at the urging of the Virginia district conference, the general conference established a "Civilian Service Investigative Committee." The committee was to look into the possibility of a program controlled by "those bodies" who believed in *biblical* nonresistance and in the standards of the church.[81]

Some MC conservatives feared the prominence of GCs in the system's management. They would have preferred more persons from their church as camp directors and in the MCC offices at Akron, Pennsylvania. In fact the GCs, perhaps more prepared for modern organizational roles, did provide camp leaders quite out of proportion to the numbers of their men who actually chose alternative service. However, the criticism was less about numbers than about fears that the GCs did not maintain distinctions between biblical nonresistance and the liberal sorts of pacifism.[82] In 1943 John E. Lapp, a rising bishop in the MCs' Franconia Conference, suggested to the Peace Problems Committee that MCC form two administrative divisions. One would run the camps whose men were mostly MC, the other would run the remainder. Lapp noted accurately that MC boys were serving under the jurisdiction of Mennonites who did not share the same disciplines of nonconformity.[83]

The MCs' Civilian Service Investigative Committee reported to the MC general conference of 1943. Parts of its report clearly expressed the concerns about lax religious conditions in the camps and too many speakers with unacceptable views. Another part treated linkage with pacifists through NSBRO as regrettable, even if working with the NSBRO was necessary and not quite a violation of the "unequal yoke." But the report raised another concern. CPS highlighted a large problem in some parts of the church, centralization of leadership. Without naming names, the report implied that Harold S. Bender, Orie O. Miller, and such people controlled too much. In the shaping of policy there had not been "sufficient representation and counsel." There was a "danger" that the "present organizational setup of Peace, Relief, CPS and related organizations" would become the "permanent mold for postwar operations." That pattern would "lead the Church away from her traditional ways of working and from some of her cherished doctrines and practices."[84]

The critique was astute and prophetic. The war did bring such changes. Indeed, even by 1943 the momentum toward them was too strong to stop. The report called for as much denominational segregation as possible without a real break from the CPS system.

CONCLUSION

If CPS was to transform the church as Mennonite leaders hoped, surmount the challenges inherent in Mennonites' own world, and avoid the pitfalls of alliance with government, Mennonites needed persuasive diplomacy and administrative skill. They had not wrangled so long and persistently with the government just so their young men could work in soil conservation and related projects tucked away in the country's backwashes. Direct service to human need and suffering would evoke much more Mennonite interest and be more in keeping with the tradition of Mennonite benevolence to war sufferers. It was also a more plausible way to bring the new day which Neuenschwander and others envisioned. And in fact that new day did require more than isolation in camps. It involved a shift in Mennonite ideology.

CHAPTER

7

~

NEW THOUGHT AND OUTLOOK
WITH WORLD WAR II

"So many things to do!— . . . Like-minded fellows representing various denominations!—All here for similar reasons!—Ahead of us— new experiences!—A broader view of life and our fellowmen . . . unlimited possibilities for living a positive Christian life devoted to peace!— . . . No looking back!—Enthusiastic hope for a greater, nobler future."[1]

In 1941 a new recruit at a Civilian Public Service (CPS) camp in Colorado had caught something like Mennonite leaders' vision that CPS might indeed transform the church. The next year, in Virginia, CPS draftee and future scholar Irvin Horst said much the same, although a bit more guardedly. For too long, he told comrades at Camp Grottoes, Mennonites had let "the so-called do-nothing attitude" isolate them from the world. But now, "no sincere, red-blooded CPS man will stand by indifferent when millions of other . . . [men] are sacrificing, even unto death, for a cause." Mennonites also had "a method of dealing with evil." CPS was not yet the fulfillment of that method, but it held the promise.[2]

Idealism there was. But Harry Van Dyck, initially a recruit at camp Fort Collins in Colorado, later remembered "no rising tide of pacifism or of peace."[3] No doubt many new arrivals felt less idealism than uncertainty and fear. For quite a few, it was the first time of living away from home. Especially if one came from a conservative group, the trip to camp might have been one's first train ride.[4]

Most draftees settled into the rhythm of camp life even if work was dreary and irrelevant. Life was quite regimented, yet the cases

Marietta (Ohio) CPS Camp. Credit: Mennonite Library and Archives, Bethel College, North Newton, Kansas.

of mistreatment and suffering were few. Friendship and camp routine filled the void of old and familiar people and places. Arguments there were, but fights and violence were rare. Mennonites were already a minority; now refusal to fight in a popular war reinforced that consciousness. Van Dyck later recalled that a "spirit of male camaraderie dominated" the psyche of Mennonite COs. And, he observed, a high philosophy of service did much to compensate for the disruption and denial that CPS required.[5]

Mennonite scholar Theodore Grimsrud has identified four different CO types in World War II—resisters, transformers, servants, and separatists.[6] Mennonites were virtually all servants. Albert Gaeddert's "second mile" philosophy was a good illustration. An unnamed writer in *The Olive Branch*, newsletter of a camp at Dennison, Iowa, noted that the campers found that doing work of national importance was less crucial than nurturing the religious self. Living by the Christian ethic in the camps was its own testimony, but being was even more important than doing. For CPS men, the first priority was "to be something fine." Whether or not they were destined to "great deeds . . . most important is what the CO's are in the daily life."[7]

Such words favored personal witness over political activism

and did not challenge the government's right to conscript young men and define their work. Mennonite men caused Selective Service relatively few problems. The servant attitude made them the "good boys" of CPS.

MENNONITES' DISSATISFACTIONS WITH CPS

To be sure, there were forms of Mennonite deviancy. Many men were in CPS less from strong personal conviction than because tradition weighed heavily, and they wanted acceptance from their home communities. In a discussion with his men on "what's wrong with our unit," one camp's educational director got the answer that became common. "Many of us do not know just why we are in CPS. We are here not so much on the basis of personal conviction about a Way of Life" as from "the desire and insistence of church and family."[8]

Perhaps it was unfair for observers to expect each young man to be verbal and articulate about his reasons. After all, many Mennonites, especially those from the more folkish, conservative settings, tested their ethics more by living than by speaking. They made and expressed their convictions as groups and by corporate witness more than as individuals and by individual witness.

Nonetheless, Bill and Helene Ramseyer, directors of a camp at Camino, California, wrote Henry Fast somewhat disappointedly that we "expected most COs to be mature in thinking and to have a fair picture of the total implications of this war and of what it means to be an objector." But unfortunately too often the conscientiousness expressed on war did "not carry over into other phases of their lives."[9]

In 1941 James Steiner of the Wells Tannery Camp suggested what some of those "other phases" were. Privately he wrote that some campers took liberty to "go to dances, shows . . . smoke on the ground[s] . . . and to live their own life." In 1944 another camp director reported that one-fifth of his men were smokers.[10] Often the camp directors who needed to deal with such matters were almost as young and inexperienced as the campers themselves and new at major administrative or personnel responsibilities.

Henry Fast, their superior, advised that "above all" they should "not invoke penalties which you cannot enforce."[11] Doing so would only weaken an authority system already precarious. His advice generally fit a cooperative style that he hoped to foster in camp management and discipline. The camps, Fast wrote on an-

other occasion, were to be "an experiment in the Christian democratic way of life."[12]

Some disciplinary problems related to ill-advised or inconsequential work the government had CPS men do. Contrary to their
idealism of "going the second mile" and doing the "moral equivalent of war," campers often found themselves faced with ineffi-
cient planning, work superintendents indifferent to the amount
of work accomplished, inadequate tools and vehicles, and other
management lapses. Camp leaders and staff might work ever so
conscientiously and well only to see the behavior or policies of government personnel undermine camp morale.[13]

Men sometimes reacted angrily to the way the government restricted the use of CPSers and to lack of pay. Indeed, in the end
these policies dissolved some elements of the CPS coalition. The
vociferous critics tended to be in Quaker and government-
sponsored camps—camps where emphasis on the individual and
on democracy underlay the men's pacifism. In that atmosphere,
mundane work and governmental control were all the less acceptable.

Arthur A. Ekirch, a CPSer with some graduate education who
eventually would be a noted American historian, had been reared
Lutheran but did service in Brethren and Mennonite camps. In
1944, writing in *Pacifica Views: A Weekly Newspaper of Conscientious Objectors*, a voice especially of CPS dissidents, he compared CPS to American slavery. Like slavery, he noted, CPS had its
apologists—the historic peace churches. Their "philosophy of voluntary service and of 'going the second mile' " permitted the entire system to function.[14]

It was true that Mennonites at least protested far less than
did Ekirch's type of pacifist. Yet Mennonites were not entirely content. Many years after the war, ex-CPSer and GC minister Esko
Loewen remembered the feeling of being "on the shelf and here the
last cataclysm was occurring and you were off digging postholes."
For him and his fellows, he said, that brought "some real
anguish."[15]

For camper Albert Foote the work itself was not the issue. The
"paramount concern," he wrote in 1941, was becoming "service-
rendering minded." CPS was "a training school" in which the
camper was "ever requested to lay aside his own interests."[16] In an
MCC publication, Donovan Smucker in 1945 offered the strongest
Mennonite defense of CPS and criticized various forms of resistance. Yes, the various complaints were justifiable, he wrote, yet

those who advocated resistance committed "a ghastly denial of Christian ethics." Christian ethics emphasized service not rights, giving not demanding. Compulsory service could always "be redeemed by audacious voluntary goodwill and love." For those unwilling to go the second mile, there was "no place whatsoever in Civilian Public Service."[17]

Other Mennonites were not as sure. Dissent among Mennonite campers persisted. It became most visible at a series of Conscription Institutes at which CPS unit leaders and representatives gathered early in 1945. Organized by MCC ostensibly to forge a policy regarding an anticipated peacetime draft, the Institutes became forums for assessing the CPS system. Some participants argued for accepting conscription and opposing it only if it forced conscientious objectors directly into service under or for the military. Others suggested that conscription was inherently designed for military purposes. In their view, CPS-like programs for COs were merely a way to silence a troublesome minority and prosecute the war more effectively.[18]

Unresolved in 1945, the debate persisted into the 1960s and beyond. In another generation and the context of the Vietnam War, those who argued against all complicity with conscription gained a new legitimacy. But in 1945, Mennonite leaders gave that position little hearing.

WOMEN AND FAMILIES

Whereas World War II conscription drafted only men, the war experience encompassed all Americans, including women and children. Mennonite women became part of the CPS system in three ways. Some were directly employed in the work of the unit; others moved, often alone and great distances, to be close to husbands, fiancés, or boyfriends; and many who stayed at home became involved in the sewing and food preparation necessary for the church to sustain the entire operation.

At least initially those who worked directly in the units were most often dietitians, nurses, and matrons. Dietitians supervised the kitchen operations, nurses established infirmaries, and normally the unit director's or the business manager's wife took the role of matron or host. But beyond the specific and important jobs they performed, the women became friends and counselors and even surrogate mothers to young men away from home for the first time.[19]

Many of the women who came as nurses and dietitians were graduates of nursing school and home economics programs. They came because they wished to identify with the CO position and because the church needed them. Some, particularly nurses, came realizing the potentially negative impact of the decision on their subsequent careers. The Red Cross was seeking every available nurse for the military effort, and there were at least implicit threats against those not volunteering for military duty.[20]

MCC was more successful in securing properly trained nurses than were the other peace churches. One reason was the formation of the Mennonite Nurses' Association (MNA) in 1942. It is perhaps the best Mennonite women's expression of wartime solidarity with the COs. Its constitution included a declaration of intent to "formulate a program for Mennonite nurses as conscientious objectors during a wartime crisis."[21]

Because of the outback locations of some of the CPS camps, the nurse sometimes provided the only firstline medical services available. One nurse later observed that she had been "the doctor as well as the nurse."[22] And that service sometimes even applied to the isolated surrounding communities. Rachel Waltner Goossen, historian of women in CPS, has recounted the story of a nurse living in a reclamation camp near Hill City, South Dakota. People living nearby might not be "the friendliest to our boys, but they knew where to come when they were sick."[23]

Matrons supervised a variety of tasks—hosting guests; laundry and ironing; the onerous job of trying to maintain orderliness in the barracks; and frequently, service as camp librarian. Beyond these specific duties, they also played the more elusive but important need of recreating some of the homelike and civilizing qualities of civilian life. In recruiting matrons, MCC looked for women who, as Henry Fast said, had the "ability to carry the spirit of the home and an atmosphere of refinement and culture into the camp."[24]

Dietitians faced the problem of providing food for people with varying tastes and backgrounds, and of doing so with limited budgets. The church agencies were financing the food costs, and they always encouraged frugality. Some units met the perennial problem of food shortages by maintaining their own gardens and in some cases even their own livestock. A good cook could make all the difference. Jesse Harder, camp director at Belton, Montana, reported a good spirit in his camp thanks in part to a new cook. The unnamed individual was "making a marked difference"—even

" 'plumamoos and zwiebach.' Excellent!"[25]

Not only the Belton cook but virtually every unit kitchen re-
lied on the generosity of home congregations. Women's groups in
congregation after congregation canned foodstuffs, made linens,
sewed new clothing, and repaired old garments for CPS campers.
Camp newspapers were full of appreciation for the women's contributions. At Grottoes in November 1942, the northern district of
the Virginia Conference furnished the campers "several months of
accumulation of warm . . . and needy garments" that had been
"patched and mended." In the fall of 1943, the Southwest Pennsylvania Conference donated ten thousand quarts of canned fruits
and vegetables for eastern camps. In September 1943, the Dennison, Iowa, camp reported receiving nine complete camp packs of
sheets, towels, soap, sewing equipment, and laundry bags from
Berne, Indiana; twenty pot holders and twenty-two tea towels from
two women's sewing circles at Wellman, Iowa; and thirteen
pounds of egg noodles from three families at Topeka, Indiana.
Camp Dennison was also a collecting center for other camps in
the upper Midwest. In fall 1943, the center received 32,793 quarts
of vegetables and fruits from congregations in Illinois, Minnesota,
Iowa, and Nebraska. A rail shipment from Pennsylvania's Lancaster County was expected to round out the winter supply at 60,000
quarts.[26] The list of congregational donations could be expanded
for virtually every CPS unit and region of the country. Between
April 30 and November 30, 1943, 234,126 quarts of congrega-
tionally prepared food was sent to the MCC-sponsored camps.[27]

Women on the move to join husbands and fiancés or relocat-
ing to be closer to families was part of the story of World War II.
Historian William Chafe estimates that more than seven million
women moved during the first three-and-a-half years of the war.[28]
The approximately fifteen hundred Mennonite women who were
part of this larger pattern often found themselves in unfamiliar
and even difficult circumstances. Aganetha Fast, a former missionary sent by MCC to visit the women of several CPS sites, reported that "many left nice homes behind and now live in primi-
tive homes and surroundings with their tiny tots. Some have as
many as four children. In most cases I found them living in only
one tiny room, on the third story, in a dark basement, a barn, or in
tourist cabins."[29]

The financial strains on women and children were inevitable,
given the absence of any government salaries for those in CPS. At
the outset MCC paid a small allowance of $1.50 per month ("tooth-

New Jersey State Hospital (Marlboro) nursery for CPS babies, 1944.
Credit: Mennonite Library and Archives, Bethel College, North Newton, Kansas.

paste money") to men in CPS. In a cost-cutting move, even that meager payment was eliminated in November 1941. In 1944 a combination of churchly or MCC support of $5.00 per month was reinstated.[30]

But of course $5.00 per month did not cover the needs of dependents. An incomplete census of September 1943 revealed 690 wives, 198 children, and 140 other dependents of Mennonite CPSers. To partly meet this need, in March 1944 MCC suggested that each denomination take care of its own at the rate of $25 per month for dependent adults unable to provide for themselves and $10 for children.[31] Given the inadequacy of these amounts and the consequent need to work, it was only natural that women would seek work as close as possible to their men.

Apparently MCC never formed an official policy discouraging or encouraging wives to follow spouses to camp. Certainly it was a boost for some campers' morale to have wives nearby. But their presence could also raise problems. For example, by fall 1944, the Colorado Springs unit had forty-five wives attached to the main camp and fifteen to an agricultural side-camp. The potential problem, as camp director David Suderman saw it, was that as their numbers increased, so would requests for greater freedom.[32]

Established policy permitted husbands to be with their wives on Saturday and Sunday evenings (not nights) each week and two weekend nights per month. Yet at the Three Rivers Camp in California some men were spending almost every night with their wives in the neighboring town. In 1944 the camp's leaders tried to restrict these privileges, only to have the townspeople come to the defense of a more liberal policy. The wives had become "part of community life," and as good citizens they were entitled to enjoy the company of their husbands.[33]

Enjoyable as that might have been for the young men in service, MCC officials worried that it diverted the men from camp activities. The common way to solve that problem was to encourage the women to visit their men at the camps rather than have the men go into town. That plan had the further advantage of drawing the women into the programs of the camp and broadening the educational impact of CPS.[34] But men were usually anxious to get off the camp grounds and into the neighboring town or city.

Wives following their husbands found work in a great variety of settings, often as household domestics, cooks, secretaries, teachers, or factory workers.[35] In mental health units, wives often worked as attendants in the same hospitals as their husbands. Fifty-eight wives worked at the New Jersey State Hospital at Marlboro. So many of the wives became pregnant and quit that the superintendent of nurses added a nursery to care for "CPS babies."[36]

MCC's "problem" of women following men to CPS locations paled in comparison with the potential problems of single CPS men dating local women. M. C. Lehman, who after returning from Europe became a divisional CPS director for MCC, worried that boys at the Mt. Pleasant camp in Iowa were dating women of "uncertain character." One camper was even dating a local married woman, a fact that might "develop a public relations problem."[37] Nor was Mt. Pleasant the only place MCC supervisors worried about their men's dating habits.

HOPING TO SERVE OVERSEAS

When the alternative service plan was taking form, pacifist groups wanted to include overseas relief. Many men who worked in domestic units hoped eventually to aid war victims and rebuild areas devastated by war. Early on, MCC began planning how CPS might prepare people for such work. If such service was not possible in actual wartime, then readiness to move quickly when peace came was all the more important.[38]

A Council of Mennonite Colleges, drawn together by the necessities of the war, anticipated an "unparalleled opportunity for relief administration and reconstruction work." Such a program could especially use persons with college training.[39] During the 1941-1942 academic year, some colleges began special training programs. In August 1942, Mennonite college presidents met and soon established a cooperative program.[40] Also, in the camps themselves there were programs for learning foreign languages, first aid, methods of disaster relief, and foreign geography.

At its annual meeting in late December 1942, MCC decided on a vigorous program of training for relief, confident that constituent groups would fully support postwar relief and bear the costs of training leaders.[41] A relief-training program would both reclaim some of CPS's early hopes and help Mennonites fashion an idealism relevant to global social systems. In March 1943, Selective Service approved a plan for letting up to 4 percent of CPS men participate in such training units at five peace-church colleges. A flurry of activity followed.

MCC's most ambitious relief-training school was one at Goshen College during the summer of 1943. A quota system limited the men to a total of sixty-five—carefully selected both from CPS ranks and from college students facing the draft. Included also were sixteen women, mostly persons already in professions. These young men and women were to be the talented, the elite corps, the vanguard of leaders for Mennonite relief and reconstruction work during and after the war.[42]

From June 12 to August 27, the school brought together the best of the combined Mennonite college faculties. Directed by Ernest E. Miller, Goshen College president (and a brother of Orie), the faculty was a who's who of Mennonite academics and of the articulators of the church's new idealism. Here was the moment for a new Mennonite brain trust to pass its ideologies and conviction to the brightest and best of the next generation. The curriculum consisted of courses in Christian Personality and Leadership; Mennonite Heritage; Community Hygiene and Nutrition; Relief Administration; the Contemporary World Needs of Central Europe, China, and South America; and Physical Fitness. The schedule was sixteen hours a day, six days a week—as rigorous as the academic expectations. Clearly the intent was to instill the same discipline in the pacifist "officers training school" as the military instilled in its own.[43]

Daniel Kauffman, not the editor but a young CPSer recruited at Grottoes to attend the school, later told fellow campers that the history and philosophy of Mennonite relief made it clear that giving such aid was "a direct outgrowth" of the doctrine of nonresistance. Previous efforts to limit nonresistance to not "bearing arms" showed Mennonites understanding the principle only in its "narrow form." For Kauffman, and by implication others, the school also "eliminated from our minds the idea that we are several different denominations, as some people think of it; rather we find that we are a brotherhood."[44] Nonresistance and Mennonite relationships, redefined in this fashion, would have transforming consequences.

The assumption behind the training at Goshen was that Mennonite young people would soon be working overseas. And at the same time it approved the training program, Selective Service agreed that seventy CPSers, drawn from all of the groups under NSBRO supervision, might go to China. In May 1943, even before the relief-training school convened, a seven-person advance unit including Mennonite Robert Kreider left and got as far as South Africa.

But the idea of U.S. dissenters against war fanning out into the world was far from popular among veterans' organizations and in the U.S. Congress. In June, just as the training school at Goshen was getting underway, Congress blocked the plans. To a military appropriations bill it attached a rider known as the "Starnes Amendment," which forbade Selective Service to use any monies either for relief-training or to send CPSers overseas. Overseas alternative service, a central hope for CPS, was dead.[45]

Mennonites acquiesced to the Starnes Amendment, just as they had yielded to other government regulation of their draftees. One-third of those in the Goshen Relief Training School went to Ypsilanti State Hospital in Michigan and Alexian Brothers Hospital in Illinois. Most of the rest went temporarily to the Grottoes camp, hoping to be reassigned to Puerto Rico. Meanwhile MCC, the American Friends Service Committee, and the Brethren Service Committee continued informal relief-training schools in various CPS units, mostly at mental hospital locations, by offering the equivalent of six college credit-hours per semester. By 1945 about 800 persons (about one-third women) had continued relief training in such schools.[46]

INTO MENTAL HOSPITALS

Denied the opportunity to do CPS work abroad, Mennonite draftees, women, and church leaders turned to the mental health field to find other meaningful work. Mental health work became the alternative to soil conservation, forestry, and agriculture.

Already in 1941 administrators of a state mental hospital at Elgin, Illinois, had inquired whether they might replace conscripted employees with CPSers.[47] The following March a unit of Roman Catholic COs began work in Chicago mental hospitals and with disabled persons. In months the historic peace churches began mental health units in Virginia and Maryland. Before CPS ended they had placed CPSers in fifty-two different hospitals and affiliated training schools. Of those, MCC supplied about fifteen hundred men to twenty-three hospitals.[48] Across the CPS coalition, CPSers and their sponsors felt that mental hospital work was one of their most significant contributions.[49]

Such work was not entirely new for Quakers and Mennonites. In 1910, in a Mennonite village in the Ukraine, the first known Mennonite mental hospital was established. The first one in North America opened in 1932 in Ontario.[50] When World War II broke out, other such hospitals were being planned.[51] Furthermore, some Mennonites had worked as noncombatants in medical corps both for the Russian government since the 1870s or for American forces in World War I.

Also during World War I, conscientious objectors had alleviated labor shortages in a number of civilian mental hospitals. And before the United States entered World War II, some Mennonite leaders advocated civilian emergency medical work. Peter H. Richert, a prominent GC leader in Kansas, feared that without such opportunities for medical work, some educated Mennonite draftees might turn to military hospitals.[52]

In mental hospitals across the nation in the 1940s, violence by staff against patients was all too common. By turning to mental health, CPSers had opportunity to address at least one kind of violence in the social system. Paul Comly French thought the testing of nonviolence in the hospitals would even "give us some of the answers to the problem of what to do with Hitler."[53] While that expectation was too grand, the CPS mental health units would at least do quite a bit to change how mental hospitals dealt with their patients.

In addition to their violence, many mental hospitals in the 1940s were deplorably overcrowded, underfunded, and often little

Arts and Crafts at Hawthornden Hospital (Cleveland). Credit: MCC Collection, Archives of the Mennonite Church, Goshen, Indiana.

more than holding wards for the retarded and the troubled—a "tragic human spectacle," as a CPSer described Hawthornden Hospital near Cleveland, Ohio.[54] An early unit, begun in October of 1942, was in the Philadelphia State Hospital; it had six thousand patients in facilities built for twenty-five hundred[55] and a staff whom wartime labor shortages had reduced from one thousand to two hundred. Nor was Philadelphia a great exception. Early CPSers in mental health often worked seventy hours per week and sometimes up to 100. Work might be for twelve to fourteen hours daily, seven days a week, as it was at Western State Hospital in Virginia. There one man worked seven months before getting a day off.[56] Of all CPS work, mental health care provided some of the severest tests of physical and psychic energies.

As for the CPSers' larger contribution, William Keeney, who worked in an MCC hospital unit and went on to become a peace scholar, has observed that they contributed on three levels. The first was more compassionate treatment for the patients. Moving away from attempts to control through fear and threat, CPSers used "more generous and humane" treatment.[57] And when they did, they demonstrated a truth that psychiatrists had long known

—relationships built on a measure of tenderness could help patients improve.[58]

The second was institutional reform. In many communities the CPSers allied with reform-minded individuals and agencies. As they did, they were in a position to give details about hospital conditions, to testify credibly against abusive attendants and errant administrators, and to ally with the journalists bringing the conditions to public attention.[59]

Systemic change was the third level of reform. While better treatment of the individual patient was important, CPSers faced with deplorable conditions wanted also to deal with fundamental, systemic causes. A CPS Mental Health Program evolved from a Friends unit in the Philadelphia State Hospital. This program eventually distributed its periodical, *The Attendant*, to more than 600 hospitals and medical training schools. The same program · also surveyed state laws governing mental hospitals and prepared a model legal code. Its people chartered the National Mental Health Foundation, which in turn became a permanent force for reform. From across the country they gathered firsthand data on maltreatment, and in 1946-1947 presented the data in a series of articles in the national press.[60] The program received further national attention when Eleanor Roosevelt, the nation's reform-minded First Lady, visited the Marlboro, New Jersey State Hospital, which had an MCC-sponsored unit.[61]

Mennonites participated actively in both the program and the subsequent Foundation, but their main contribution to systemic change came after CPS, in a network of mental hospitals. As Keeney has observed, the Mental Health Program fit the activist social and political ethic of Friends. Mennonites, true to their social ethic, established an alternative mental hospital system.[62] Indeed, even as the MCC managers set up mental hospital units for CPS, they like the Brethren and the Friends set up training schools along with the units—for instance, one at Marlboro early in 1945 with the theme "Psychiatry and Christian Service." As they invited CPSers to train at Marlboro, the managers promised that the school would benefit persons who would return to their communities and serve as ministers, teachers, and lay persons. They also said the study would help CPSers "who have been considering psychiatry as a profession."[63] Clearly the MCC managers were thinking in larger and longer-range terms than just fulfilling wartime draft obligations.

More than other CPS units, the hospital units incorporated

Women's Summer Service Unit, Howard, Rhode Island, 1944. Credit: MCC Collection, Archives of the Mennonite Church, Goshen, Indiana.

women into the structure of CPS witness and service. At the 1943 Goshen Training School, Edna Ramseyer, a faculty member from Bluffton College who was especially interested in seeing women demonstrate their peace convictions, proposed that they be allowed to work in mental hospitals. The idea took hold among the sixteen women attending the school. They organized themselves as the "C.O. Girls," or COGs. Included in their statement of purpose was a strong desire "to give expression to and to develop convictions on peace and war . . . [;] to assume our responsibility in supporting the stand taken by the young men . . . [; and] to relieve human need because that work is consistent with our stand as Christians."[64]

This was one of the beginning moments of what after the war came to be the Mennonite Voluntary Service program. Before the end of the summer, Ramseyer met with MCC officials to advocate more opportunities for women in the CPS structure. While MCC agreed, it is not clear whether its policymakers did so to improve the morale of the male CPSers or because they really wanted to create new opportunities for women.[65]

Some women found positions in hospital work because they

went there with husbands. Of the first twenty-five CPS men to arrive at the Marlboro hospital in November 1942, eight were accom-
panied by their wives. All those wives soon had jobs at the hospital,
and eventually fifty-eight CPS-related women worked there. According to a 1944 survey, 25 percent of COs in mental hospital
work had spouses working in the same institutions.[66] The women
came with a variety of skills, from registered nursing to office
work. Nor were the women only wives and girlfriends of men in service. Marlboro and similar units attracted young Mennonite wom-
en eager to offer service analogous to CPS.

The Mennonite COGs were a distinct group: women who volunteered for summer service in the years 1944 through 1946 at
hospitals where MCC had mental health units. In summer 1944,
sixty-one women worked alongside CPS units at Ypsilanti, Michigan; Marlboro, New Jersey; and Howard, Rhode Island. In summer
1945, seventy-eight COGs volunteered at a variety of hospitals,
and in 1946 the number was sixty. Approximately 300 women
from the three historic peace churches volunteered for this kind of
service in psychiatric hospitals. Many of the Mennonite women
also participated either in the CPS Relief Training or in "Christianity and Psychiatry" schools at those hospitals, preparing themselves further for new forms of service and new careers.[67]

CPS AS SCHOOL

In December 1940, even before President Roosevelt authorized the CPS system, NSBRO agreed that any alternative service arrangement should include an educational program designed to
develop the resources of a democratic culture. Translated into
Mennonite terms, that meant efforts to educate CPSers for a more
vital understanding of Mennonite peace principles and Mennonite ecumenicity.

In most MCC-sponsored CPS camps there were extensive educational programs. Mennonite leaders hoped that the schools' influence would ripple out much farther. In August 1941, MCC began appointing an educational director for each camp, and in October 1942, named a national educational secretary. Albert Gaeddert correctly observed that the church had never had such opportunity to reach "four thousand of its young men in an educational
program."[68]

Here was a moment for church leaders not only to nurture individuals' religious and character development but also to social-

ize a rising generation into a refurbished idealism. CPS could become a churchwide teach-in, a place to inculcate the Anabaptist
vision, an opportunity to refashion the identity of Mennonite
youth. MCC, explaining its objectives in a *Manual for Educational
Directors* published in 1942, expressed a twofold idealism among
Mennonite intellectuals. CPS should prepare young people to go
out into the world with postwar activism. But it should also educate them to come back from that world ready to fortify and sustain their rural communities. MCC's educational program for
CPSers may have been ambivalent and paradoxical toward the
world, but it was surely ambitious.[69]

To meet its lofty goals, from 1942 to 1944 MCC published six
small booklets with the series title Mennonites and Their Heritage. The idea was a set of core courses for the entire educational
program. But what exactly was the core? Robert Kreider, a young
recruit at Colorado Springs, wanted a curriculum that would accommodate the roughly one-fourth of the campers who were not
Mennonite. His idea was that each denomination's campers
should explore the best of his own religious heritage. By so doing,
campers of the various denominations would "discover common
bases for cooperation." Kreider considered Mennonites' attitudes
toward non-Mennonite fellow campers to be less than "healthy";
indeed they showed "religious bigotry." The ecumenism of his proposal would "bridge the cleavage between Mennonites and non-
Mennonites."[70]

Harold Bender responded to the GC Kreider with a different
design, a different core. His response was a more MC one, and it
suggested the limits of interdenominational cooperation and education in the CPS program. Mennonites might have to work with
other groups. But the core education should not be one of "interdenominational syncretism"; it should be "distinctively Mennonite." Bender thought Kreider's proposal had too much of the
"FOR and similar points of view." So he encouraged Henry Fast to
help Kreider understand that if "our Mennonite boys have a natural and wholesome protective reaction to the pressures and influences from non-Mennonite boys," that reaction was "religiously
and sociologically sound."[71]

As one might guess, Bender's position prevailed. He was at the
center of Mennonite machinery, with power to define the ideological core. When Bender wrote in an introduction to each pamphlet
that the goal for the core courses was "to contribute to a greater
appreciation of the church and its splendid heritage of faith and

CPS men and spouses at a Training School at Union Grove, Wisconsin, June 1944. Credit: MCC Collection, Archives of the Mennonite Church, Goshen, Indiana.

life," he meant the Mennonite churches.

The pamphlets were inter-Mennonite—three by MC authors Bender, Guy F. Hershberger, and Edward Yoder; two by GCs, C. Henry Smith and E. G. Kaufman; and one by an MB, P. C. Hiebert. Except for not giving voice to smaller groups, they represented Mennonite syncretism with an interpretation that emphasized commonality of history and of faith.[72] This was true even though that inter-Mennonite perspective was a down payment on the future more than a portrayal of the past.

As time went on, specialized schools were established at various units. By 1945 CPSers could attend Relief Training Schools seeking to prepare people for overseas work; Farm and Community Schools wanting to equip people for returning to their rural villages; Christian Workers' Schools to prepare for churchly vocations; Psychiatry and Christian Service Schools for future mental-hospital work; and many more. While these schools were attached to particular CPS units, many CPSers wishing to attend particular ones could gain transfers to the units offering the programs they wanted.[73]

It is hard to measure the impact of the regular educational program conducted in virtually every unit plus the specialized schools. Usually attendance for the core curriculum was compul-

Basketball team at Colorado Springs CPS Unit. Credit: MCC Collection, Archives of the Mennonite Church, Goshen, Indiana.

sory; other courses and schools were optional. One damper on participation in various camp activities was that marriages and financial problems led many CPS men to take part-time outside jobs.[74] And there were other diversions. A year after the formal educational program began at Grottoes, it was cut back to two evenings per week to give "the majority . . . ample time for athletics."[75]

Yet the impact of the educational program was significant. A questionnaire administered in March 1946 to 20 percent of the men still in camps or already discharged yielded good evidence that CPS helped bring an intellectual reorientation. Sixty-six percent of those tested responded that CPS had increased their appreciation of the Mennonite heritage; 81 percent replied that their understanding of nonresistance had grown stronger. Sixty-seven percent thought their denominations' futures would benefit from the inter-Mennonite nature of MCC's CPS program.[76]

MENNONITES IN MILITARY SERVICE

The story of Mennonites in World War II is not only about alternative service. In fact, from 1940 to 1947 more Mennonites went into one or another form of military service than into CPS. At war's end Howard Charles, a CPSer who later would be a respected Bible scholar, conducted a census and in 1949 Guy F. Hershberger updated the figures for the MCs' Peace Problems Committee.[77]

WORLD WAR II DRAFT CLASSIFICATIONS, ALL U.S. MENNONITES AND AMISH
(percentages based on the total in only the three categories indicated[78])

Classification	Number	Percent of total
I-A (regular military service)	3876	39.5
I-AO (noncombatant military service)	1397	14.2
IV-E (Civilian Public Service)	4536	46.2

Thus, 5273 Mennonite men, or 53.7 percent of draftees in the three key categories, chose military service. Their story remains marginal to Mennonite memory. No doubt due to a Mennonite ideological bias, there is little research published on them. Indeed the marginality of the story reflects a marginalization of persons who defied the official denominational stance.[79]

The statistics show denominational variations.[80]

DISTRIBUTION OF MENNONITE AND AMISH MEN IN THREE KEY CLASSIFICATIONS
(percentages based on the total in only the three categories indicated[81])

Denomination	Percent I-A	Percent I-AO	Percent IV-E
Mennonite Church	29.9	10.6	59.5
GC Mennonites	57.7	15.6	26.6
Mennonite Brethren	31.5	31.9	36.4
Menn. Breth. in Christ	78.5	16.7	4.8
Old Order Amish	2.9	3.5	93.5
Conservative Amish Menn.	13.8	9.7	76.3
Brethren in Christ	25.9	22.2	51.8

Ch. of God in Christ, Menn.	5.0	1.5	93.5
Defenseless Mennonite	54.8	34.9	10.2
Krimmer Menn. Brethren	48.1	15.5	36.3
Evangelical Menn. Breth.	14.6	26.6	58.8
Old Order Mennonite	0.0	0.0	100.0

Except for a few conservative groups, the figures offered no Mennonite denomination much comfort. In virtually every denomination, church leaders were troubled. In 1947 H. S. Bender estimated that the formal disciplines of two-thirds of all Mennonite congregations had made military service a matter for excommunication.[82] Yet even many young men in good standing had gone willingly.

Charles's questionnaire revealed four principal factors in the choices. Ranked in order, they were (1) community influences, (2) family influences, (3) financial considerations, and (4) the absence of peace teaching in local congregations. Mennonites clearly were not encased in an ideological straitjacket which automatically passed on the theology and practice of nonresistance.[83]

Education and occupation seem to have related to the choices. Men with only grade school and those with college educations more often selected CPS. In between, those who stopped after high school tended more often to select some form of military service. The grade school numbers probably reflected traditionalism, ruralism, and isolation; other statistics showed that rural Mennonites selected CPS more than did urban ones. By the 1940s high schools were more apt to serve large enough districts that they mixed Mennonite young people with many other groups. On the other hand, Mennonite colleges were centers of advocacy for CPS and for peace principles. Apparently their students responded.[84]

It is harder to correlate draft responses with theology. For every example there is a contrary one. Groups who were culturally more conservative certainly sent lower percentages of men to either form of military service. Yet congregations and conferences with strict and clearly defined policies to discipline soldiers often fared little better than did more lax ones. MC-affiliated conferences generally opposed noncombatancy as strongly as they opposed regular military service. The Southwest Pennsylvania Conference immediately excommunicated all members accepting either. Yet its proportion of draftees in military service, 57.9 percent, was the highest of any MC conference. Virginia Conference was theologically akin to the Southwest Conference, adamant toward military service, and inclined to fundamentalism—but its percentage was 40.5 percent. The percentage for the Illinois Conference, considered far more liberal, was 54.9.[85]

The denominations differed overall, but with some regional variation. Among GC Mennonites in the Pacific Coast Conference 68.2 percent went into CPS; in the same region the percentage for the Mennonite Brethren was 37.[86] In eastern Pennsylvania the Franconia (MC) and the Eastern District (GC) Conferences covered more or less the same territories, ever since they had parted ways in the Oberholtzer schism of 1847. But among Franconia men 35.3 percent selected I-A, 14.3 percent chose I-AO, and 50.4 percent joined CPS—compared to Eastern District percentages of 85.8 choosing I-A, 6.4 percent selecting CPS, and the others choosing noncombatancy.[87]

In a given community, responses to conscription among congregations suggest both similarities and differences in the textures of denominational traditions. In Hillsboro, Kansas, GC and MB meetinghouses were located two blocks apart. Of the 19 inducted from the GCs, 12 (63 percent) went into CPS. Of the 44 sons drafted from the MB church, 20 (45 percent) went into CPS. In Reedley, California, the GC and MB meetinghouses were also a block apart—but there the percentages were virtually identical. The two congregations' military percentages were also the same, except that more GCs going into military service chose the I-A position, whereas more MBs selected noncombatancy. From around Nappanee, Indiana, all of the Old Order Amish chose CPS, as did 21 of 27 from the MC congregation. But 16 of the 20 drafted from the GC church chose I-A.[88]

The biggest erosion of nonresistance was among the GCs. With a decentralized congregational polity, that denomination did not establish conference positions on church discipline for military service. And congregational policy was generally lax. Western GC conferences, more of whose people were of Russian-empire background, sent lower percentages into the military than did older, more acculturated congregations in the East. Pennsylvania and Ohio GCs led the way into the military.[89] An irony of the GC denomination is that it provided many leaders for CPS but disproportionately fewer men. Perhaps their Mennonite theological capital had eroded, but pragmatically their administrative skill and creativity were considerable.

In contrast to the plethora of services the church rendered in the CPS camps, at the outset there was virtually no program for men in military service. As late as 1945 Walter Dyck, a GC minister in Beatrice, Nebraska, complained that his denomination had done "more spiritually and materially" for the COs than for I-A's and I-AO's.[90] Many regional conferences, denominational headquarters, or inter-Mennonite agencies were slow to act. The larger denominations—MC, GC, and MB—left any pastoring of or contact with their military persons to the district conferences. The Kansas-Missouri MC conference appointed a Committee for the Spiritual Welfare of Men in Government Service while its Illinois coun terpart corresponded with its men in the military.[91]

More often, however, such contact was left to congregations and families. Arthur Nafziger of the Hopedale, Illinois, GC congregation was a faithful lay correspondent. Of fifteen men drafted from his congregation, thirteen chose I-A and one chose CPS. His correspondence suggests that those in military service certainly tried in their own way to be religious.[92]

Paul Springer was a correspondent who was one of a relatively few Mennonites who entered CPS, then transferred into the military. Springer realized that many people back home probably thought he did not "have any religious convictions left any more," but he disagreed. True, it was hard to express those convictions in the service, but "the more you stand against, the stronger [you] grow." Working in the medical corps, he felt "more and more convinced that this is where I belong." He attended chapel services faithfully even if he thought them a bit too militaristic. For another of Nafziger's correspondents—Lee Litwiller, who served at Naples, Corsica, and Rome—the war brought the excitement of visiting historic sites such as the Coliseum and the St. Sebastian catacombs. But the experience of a third, Herbert Nafziger, was quite different. Serving in France, he reported "ruin and death. Many dead Germans and horses. This surely makes a hard man of you."[93]

Paul Springer was not alone in leaving CPS, nor was he the only one to feel that military service, either noncombatant or regular, was more appropriate. After the war one CPSer who had transferred to noncombatancy noted that CPS had not rendered "the beneficial public service" he had wanted to give. Another recalled that in the army, more than in CPS, he had been able to "witness to the saving power of Christ."[94]

Collectively, churches varied in their responses to the men who had entered the military. In 1944 the Pacific District Conference of the MBs decided to collect money to aid all returning young men regardless of whether they were returning from alternative service or the military. The next year P. C. Hiebert rationalized the conference's implied support of military service by saying that the church had not sufficiently taught "the way of peace," so it should meet all the men, whether returning from alternative service or the military, with "Christian charity and love."[95]

In one of the oldest Mennonite communities, the territory north of Philadelphia, the Eastern District Conference (GC) and the Franconia Conference (MC) took divergent routes. In the spring of 1946 the Franconia Conference chose exclusion, saying, "Ministers are admonished to contact those members who took military service when they return, to try to win them to the Faith. They shall be asked to relinquish all connections with the Veterans organization and if called again for service must promise to take the Nonresistant position."[96]

With a very different tone and position, the Deep Run congregation of the Eastern District Conference resolved "that we express our praise and gratitude to Almighty God, who has so wonderfully preserved our young men from bodily harm and death during these past years of bloodshed, and that we heartily welcome back each and every one of them into the fellowship and work of our congregation."[97]

The Deep Run language expressed hardly any repentance for military service. Other GC congregations admitted collective guilt but refused to discipline individuals. In the East Swamp congregation, also of the Eastern District and a neighbor to Deep Run, Pastor Abe Schultz asked the entire congregation to acknowledge their collective failure to follow Christ's teachings—rather than ask the returned military men for a special confession.[98] More than a thousand miles away in Kansas, at a 1945 business meeting, the Tabor Mennonite Church near Goessel also decided that rather than hold the servicemen guilty of moral failure it would acknowledge the congregation's collective failure without disciplining individuals. H. B. Schmidt, Tabor's pastor in 1945, wrote that the decision "pulled the church together and moved them in the right direction. 'We have all done wrong—we all sin. We must forgive . . . [the men] as Jesus forgave them.' " He thought that nothing in his fourteen years as Tabor's pastor had united the congregation quite like that one decision in 1945.[99]

MC conferences varied in their responses. All began with the assumption that military service required church discipline,[100] but some chose to act more explicitly on that assumption than did others. In May 1945 the Virginia Conference declared that all who had entered the armed forces "shall be considered as by their own choice to have forfeited their fellowship in the church." Their return to full fellowship would require "repentance and confession"; however, the conference's tough position did not minimize its attempt to seek restoration. Somewhat differently, the Illinois, Indiana-Michigan, and Missouri-Kansas (later South Central) conferences put more blame on the ministry. Calling for more faithful teaching of nonresistance, they counseled patience and, again, restoration. Their somewhat softer statements did not exactly exonerate the men but made a different kind of reentry more possible.[101]

In Harper County, Kansas, the MC congregation kept combatants on the church rolls during the war. Then in 1946 Bishop Gideon Yoder called a public meeting to decide on their continuing membership. Although he assured the veterans that he maintained "the highest appreciation" for them, he announced that the church required a "public confession." Not all were willing, but at least eight made the confession and returned to full membership.[102]

When members who had gone into the military returned to the Oak Grove MC congregation in Ohio, the congregation presented them with a set of questions which it had agreed on in October 1945. "Do you confess that you believe in the peace principles as believed and practiced by the Mennonite Church?" it asked. "Are you sorry that you have violated these principles, and do you promise to be faithful in promoting and living out the same?" Few of the ex-servicemen were willing to answer yes and sign. Ten years later, in 1955, the congregation said it was willing to accept back into full membership all who had served and regarded the 1945 statement as excessively rigid.[103]

In January 1944 the editor of *Gospel Herald* expressed a hope that when the war was over many who served in the military "will be glad to denounce war and to return to the fellowship of the church." If they did "not return to the teachings and the fellowship of the church," he lamented, there would "be a very heavy loss to the church of potential membership.[104]

Such fear of loss was prophetic. In 1949 the MCs' Peace Problems Committee investigated how its military veterans of World War II stood with their church. It found that about 32 percent in its sample of 1,330 MC persons who had joined the armed forces were currently MC members. The remaining 68 percent were either in other denominations or unchurched. Of the 1,330 young men in the sample, the net loss to the MC had been about 900. In Virginia only 12 out of 68 had returned to MC congregations, in Lancaster 17 out of 104, and in Ohio 59 out of 181. In the more open Illinois Conference 69 out of 83 veterans were in good standing.[105]

There is no comparative data for other Mennonite groups, but in all Mennonite denominations there were few who joined the military and then came back to positions of denominational influence. To a large extent, CPS was the source of the next generation of leaders. In the coming decades the church favored ex-CPSers, and they favored the church. Most who had opted for military service, some of them no doubt marginal before they went, certainly ended up largely on the edges following their wartime experiences. It was one thing to accept veterans back into the pews. It was another to put them into positions of respect and authority where they might be role models and visible reminders of Mennonites' failure to be consistent about their most distinctive belief and practice.[106]

In seeking to understand why so many men went into the military, perceptive observers quickly recognized that they could not necessarily blame lax church discipline. Already in 1943 Harold S. Bender observed that statistics disproved that explanation. To the Peace Problems Committee he noted that in the same regional conference with strict discipline, one congregation might have 80 percent in CPS and the next one 80 percent in the military.[107]

Robert Kreider and Howard Charles offered a richer interpretation. They focused on environmental factors that shaped responses to conscription. In 1942 Kreider described four such factors—church, home, community, and other associations. Kreider thought that inadvertently or consciously some congregations had nurtured young men's disposition to enter the military. One way was by a general reduction in teachings on nonconformity. Only subsequently did they find that nonresistance did not stand well alone, without other kinds of nonconformity. Another way came from Mennonite mobility and the spreading of congregations over vast distances. Such spreading isolated many groups geographically and weakened their conferences' educational and other activities until the Mennonite identity of many outlying congregations seemed to be fraying. A third problem was that ministers took training in a variety of schools with differing theological orientations. Kreider thought that some of ministers were offering "a dogmatic, militaristic theological system incompatible and foreign to orthodox Mennonite theology and practice."[108]

Kreider's 1942 study was preliminary, but in 1945 a more thorough study by Howard Charles pointed to similar conclusions. The choices revealed the degree to which "the external barriers of psychological, sociological, and economic community isolation have already largely disappeared." To stem the influences, the only resources left were "inner spiritual" ones. The war experience raised questions of whether Mennonites were "going to resist successfully the tide of secularism of which militarism is a part."[109]

IMPACT OF CPS

The findings of Kreider and Charles along with other experiences of Mennonites in World War II suggest that two kinds of acculturation were underway. The number selecting military service hints at how far the Mennonite cultural order had already frayed and how much Mennonites had adapted to American ways. Yet wartime also offered Mennonites a chance for more purposeful adaptation. More than any other time in the twentieth century, church leaders were able to reorient Mennonite identity and activism.

Toward the end of CPS, administrator Albert Gaeddert was confident that the experience was transforming the church. "The seeds have been sown," he mused to a friend in 1945, "and there ought to be fruits, some of which should be nearly a hundredfold. We are living in such an interesting period, which has so many challenges to it; one almost fears that one will grow old too quickly."[110] From early on, scholarly assessments of CPS have agreed in such salutary assessments.[111] CPS altered the contours of the American Mennonite experience. Its idealism filtered back into Mennonite communities.

When CPS leaders returned to their home congregations, they brought a variety of characteristics. Empowering an emerging generation of leaders were not only a broadening of social and religious sensibilities; a new power came also from self-confidence, administrative experience, and political savvy they had gained in running the CPS system. Historians and sociologists distinguish between traditional and innovative leadership.[112] CPS required the innovative kind. Young Mennonite men thrust into positions as the camps' directors, business managers, and educational directors found and developed the resources to do a creditable job.

They managed thousands of dollars and hundreds of persons, and they negotiated intricate political, community, business, and church relationships. Following the war these skills, linked to the new religious guidepost, flowed into Mennonite church institutions and many diverse enterprises.

In 1946 William Yoder, a CPSer still in a Florida camp, already sensed something of the psychic impact of this entire service system. Writing in *Box 96*, the Mulberry Camp's paper, he argued that Mennonites' history of persecutions had created a wariness toward culture and an "inferiority" that easily counseled withdrawal. CPS showed how misplaced such inferiority was.[113]

At a twenty-fifth anniversary celebration of CPS, Boyd Nelson spoke of many ex-CPSers who had gone on to higher education and then into the professions, exhibiting "a good deal of self-respect." In 1941 Mennonite intellectuals had possessed self-respect, but by 1945 countless CPSers had caught it also. "From this experience has come a turning of the church's eyes out from its internal problems," Nelson thought, and a movement from being fearful and defensive to being "more positive," and to a "positive Christian response to human need."[114]

What Nelson was noting was observable in many ways. In the 1920s and 1930s fundamentalist fears had left Mennonite intellectuals under suspicion and at the margins of the church. By 1955 a host of younger intellectuals, partly schooled in CPS, occupied positions of influence. In 1935 a smoldering fundamentalism had choked almost all Mennonite theologizing. By 1955 the search for an Anabaptist theology was displacing the motifs of fundamentalism. In 1941 there was no Mennonite seminary. By 1955 there were three. In 1935 most Mennonites were wary of interchurch dialogue. Except in GC circles, to enter conversation even with other historic peace churches was suspect. By 1955 young Mennonite intellectuals in Europe were organizing meetings known as the Puidoux Conferences, and those meetings put them in conversation with noted mainline church leaders on questions of peace.[115] In 1935 many Mennonites were wary of dialogue not only with other Christians but also with fellow Mennonites. In the postwar years an inter-Mennonite renaissance flourished.[116]

Not wishing to see these new directions lost, by the end of the war CPS managers were aggressively arguing for a way to continue CPS. Elmer Ediger, CPS educational director during the latter years of the war, thought a program of voluntary service was the best way to guarantee the gains of CPS. The church needed

many members who will go out as leaven, as a good neighbor, as servants of the Master. A period of service and training, such as the Voluntary Service Program should give new zeal, new insight for the program of the church at home and abroad. Aren't these some of the factors which led us to want the "CPS experience" for the next generation of young people?[117]

CPSer Harry Martens preferred the metaphor of commencement for the conclusion of CPS. As men graduated from CPS he hoped their return to the churches would commence a life of service and work of national importance not only for former CPS men but also for the Mennonite denominations. So instead of a "setting of the [CPS] sun," there would be "the rising of the sun for a more real peace testimony."[118] Writing five years after the war Guy Hershberger was persuaded that CPS had stimulated "a new social consciousness, and a new sense of social responsibility."[119]

CONCLUSION

James Juhnke has noted the double impact of wars on American Mennonites. They both accelerate and brake the drift of Mennonites into American culture. They sharpen the sense of civic responsibility but also the sense of civic alienation. They focus and diffuse Mennonite identity. They fragment and revitalize Mennonites.[120]

World War II was hardly an exception. It reinforced long established patterns of deference to the state. By granting special privileges to the historic peace churches, the state marginalized them, and Mennonites responded by being "*die Stillen im Lande.*" Yet World War II also accelerated the movement into American society. The war made clear that Mennonite cultural unity was fractured. It reinforced a need for more deliberate mechanisms to insure that a measure of "separation from the world" might continue. Following the war an expanded set of conscious attempts were made to stem the Americanizing drift.

But the war also gave Mennonites greater ideological particularity. CPS helped link orthodoxy to social compassion. Now the church could be more socially active while remaining theologically conservative. Servant activism became the core of an ideologically revitalized Mennonite identity. CPS gave shape and character to ideals of benevolence and service, passed those ideals on to the next generation, and nurtured new self-confidence and sense of self-worth. It connected Mennonites to each other as no previous event in the twentieth century had done. CPS fashioned new institutions to channel a missional and service activism.

BALANCING SEPARATION
AND ENGAGEMENT

On June 27, 1946, Paul Comly French, the NSBRO director, record-ed in his diary a long entry about the day's discussions with Har-old S. Bender. The conversation centered on the future of peace-time conscription and alternative service and included what French thought was a surprising assertion by Bender. Bender had said that the Mennonites were developing their own school system and "formulating plans for their own economic order," so that (as French interpreted Bender) they "would be able to withdraw from life."[1]

It was not the first time French deduced such an intention from a prominent Mennonite leader's comments. In a diary entry of 1944 he recorded a conversation among himself, Colonel Lewis Kosch of Selective Service, and Orie O. Miller, in which Miller had suggested that if after the war the government would institute a peacetime draft which Mennonites could not accept, "two-thirds of the Mennonites would leave the U.S. and migrate."[2] And in 1945 he recorded that Joe Weaver, a Mennonite working in the National Service Board for Religious Objectors office, had told him that "there may be many thousands of Mennonites leaving this country."[3]

It would be easy to suggest that such Mennonite comments were simply smart politics—overstatement to establish a negotiat-ing position for future conscription discussions. They may have been that, but among some leaders the war's end also brought a genuine sense of unease. Thus the comments were surely parts of a much larger conversation between cultural resistance and engagement. Emigration did not emerge as a serious strategy. What did emerge were various institutional forms developed during the war and immediate postwar years to buffer contacts between Mennonites and American culture. A rapid development of Mennonite private schools, Mennonite Mutual Aid, the Mennonite Community movement and other rural revitalization interests—all these were new forms for continuing a degree of separation.

If Orie Miller and Harold Bender were talking to French about strategies for maintaining some form of Mennonite separatism, they were at the same time directing a new form of global engagement—MCC peacetime service to the victims of World War II. By the end of 1947 more than 470 Mennonite volunteers were helping relieve the devastation and wartime impoverishment of eighteen countries in the Middle East, Europe, and Asia. In addition to their volunteer labor, between the end of the war and December 1946, North American Mennonites donated more than $2 million worth of food and clothing and other relief supplies. That was part of a Mennonite outpouring of $12 million in cash and in kind for relief work during the decade of the 1940s.[4] In addition, MCC was offering assistance to roughly ten thousand Mennonite refugees from Poland and the Soviet Union.[5]

The various efforts were an increase in social and compassionate engagement that helped the ongoing transformation of American Mennonites from a parochial and withdrawn people to a people of global involvement and service.[6] Relief activism nurtured the larger process of reshaping Mennonite identity around service and voluntarism.

Among GCs the beginning in January 1946 of *Mennonite Life*, a magazine published from Bethel College in Kansas, was a signal of more social and cultural activism in the future. A continual theme in the magazine's early years was the question of why Mennonites had become quietistic and withdrawn. In the first issue's editorial—"Active or Passive Christianity"—Bethel historian Cornelius Krahn anticipated the magazine's answer. "Sometimes their withdrawal may have resulted in being an end in itself and have become a matter of self-preservation. . . . Too often it anchored in a quiet, peaceful port instead of doing its mission on the high sea."[7] Counterposed to the passive image that Krahn deplored, Robert Kreider, first MCCer admitted into postwar Germany, evoked another: that Mennonites, by "rebuilding . . . missions, schools, hospitals, [and] church-centered communities," should build "bridges of love and reconciliation."[8]

POSTWAR CHANGE

The searches for separation and engagement were appropriate to Mennonite social reality in the immediate postwar era. Precisely because of World War II, American Mennonites were more closely integrated not only into the national culture but into a global culture as well. For the majority of Mennonite men who had done military service, the experience speeded integration into American culture. Somewhat differently, CPS too was an integrating experience—but also a separating one. During their period of service many CPS men also traveled to distant places, resettled into new locations, and gained training and work experience that would propel them into urban-related vocations. In 1964 Paul Peachey, a young Mennonite sociologist, termed World War II a "watershed [divide]. . . in Mennonite city attitudes and relations."[9]

The changes that the war required of the civilian population filtered into the smaller Mennonite world. In 1943 Paul Mininger, later president of Goshen College, reflected on the changes in Goshen and Elkhart, Indiana. While the trend of Mennonite men finding work in the factories of the cities and towns had begun much earlier, Mininger thought that wartime gas rationing had induced many families to move to such areas. "Among these folk," Mininger thought, "there is a lack of familiarity with the ways of the world. They are unable to make the proper readjustments, and many of their children are being lost to the church." In addition to families becoming disoriented, Mininger feared for single women finding work in factories, restaurants, and stores. A number of them seemed to be "losing out in their church life and also in their moral life." Some were marrying "non-Mennonite men who are not Christian. . . ." Some were even "marrying soldier boys."[10]

Observers who did not necessarily deplore the postwar social changes also commented on the shifts in the Mennonite world. In 1963 Peachey observed that "metropolitan tentacles reached out to engulf erstwhile rural communities. In sum, Mennonites entered the city, and it can be said with some legitimacy, the city entered Mennonites."[11] Writing five years earlier, J. Lawrence Burkholder, an instructor at Goshen College, suggested that the "capitalistic spirit" of the urban centers was "invading" rural communities, including Mennonite ones, and turning agriculture into a "highly organized way of life" to fit the needs of capitalism. Mennonites, showing a proclivity for business and manufacturing, were taking on the "habits and conceptual framework of the petty bourgeoisie."[12]

In fact, such commentators seem to have exaggerated the breakdown of Mennonite communities. To be sure, in the war and postwar years the demographic revolution in the nation affected Mennonites. Some Mennonites moved into towns and cities. Others found new vocations that were more urban than rural. Nonetheless, the surprising fact of the Mennonite postwar period is its stability and continuity with the prewar period.

URBANIZATION

The incomplete demographic data available for the years before 1970 has been summarized best by Paul Peachey and Leland Harder. Between 1940 and 1960, while showing movement into the city, Mennonite Church (MC) membership remained overwhelming rural. In Peachey's survey of MCs, "city" meant a community with a population of 10,000 or more.[13]

MC Urbanization, 1940-1960

	Mennonite Church Membership	City Membership	Percent City
1940	56,487	3,514	06.2
1945	57,334	4,569	08.0
1950	64,591	5,618	08.7
1955	71,675	7,412	10.3
1960	73,576	8,187	11.1

A similar survey of GC Mennonites for 1950 and 1959 by Leland Harder used three classifications: country (outside of an incorporated town); town (up to 2,500 inhabitants); and city (population more than 2,500). Even with urban defined as more than 2,500, GC Mennonites in the United States remained overwhelming rural.[14]

GC Rural-Urban Residence, 1950, 1959

	Country	Town	City
1950	14,300 (41%)	12,719 (36.5%)	7,761 (22.5%)
1959	14,335 (40.5%)	12,532 (35.4%)	8,495 (24.1%)

Correlating the GC population of 1960 with the U.S. census of 1950, Harder pointed to the overwhelming rural quality. The U.S. population for the same regional subdivisions where Mennonites lived was 64 percent urban.[15]

The most complete demographic data available is in The Church Member Profile administered in 1972 to 174 congregations in five of the generally more progressive Mennonite denominations: MC (Mennonite Church); GC (General Conference Mennonite Church); MB (Mennonite Brethren Church); BIC (Brethren in Christ); EMC (Evangelical Mennonite Church). The survey included both U.S. and Canadian congregations, and used four demographic classifications: Rural Farm (three acres or more); Rural Nonfarm (residence on less than three acres outside of village or in a town of under 2,500 inhabitants); Small City (2,500-24,999); and Large City (25,000 or more).[16] Here are its findings, in percentages.

GC Rural-Urban Residence of Five Mennonite Groups, 1972

Place of residence	MC	GC	MB	BIC	EMC	All five groups
Rural Farm	38	33	25	32	31	34
Rural Nonfarm	36	28	19	18	30	31
Small City	14	16	20	16	24	16
Large City	12	23	36	33	15	19
	100	100	100	99	100	100

In 1972 only the Mennonite Brethren were urban. Furthermore, the changes from the 1950 and 1959-1960 surveys for the Mennonite Church and the General Conference Mennonite Church remained gradual, not dramatic.

MEN'S OCCUPATIONS

Some scholars suggest that the more accurate index of urbanization's impact is not residential changes but vocational shifts. Even without change in geography, vocational changes introduce urban life and urban family patterns. A 1950 census conducted by the Mennonite Research Foundation and covering employed men ages 18-65 in four Midwestern regional MC conferences—the Indiana-Michigan, Illinois, Iowa-Nebraska, and South Central (Kansas, Oklahoma, Missouri) Conferences—showed remarkable vocational stability. The numbers are percentages.[17]

Men's Occupations in MC Midwestern Conferences

	1940	1950
Farming	66.7	62.6
Industrial Labor	14.5	18.8

Clerical	1.5	.9
Executive Management	2.7	5.3
Teachers	2.1	2.4
Doctors	.2	.3
Other Professions	3.3	.8
Miscellaneous	8.8	8.4
	99.8	99.5

A different tabulation of the same 1950 census but including the Lancaster (primarily Pennsylvania), Indiana-Michigan, Illinois, Iowa-Nebraska, and Pacific Coast (primarily Oregon) Conferences, all MC, demonstrated a national picture not much different from that of the agricultural heartland. In these conferences, 66.4 percent of all employed and retired men were in farm and farm-related occupations.[18]

GC occupational change seems more dramatic, yet the categories are so varied and broad that the data hardly point to strong conclusions. In 1957 J. Lloyd Spaulding, an economist at Bethel College, compared farming occupations with nonfarming ones in seven very rural midwestern GC Mennonite congregations, showing change in the ten years just previous. The data, brought together in table form by Leland Harder, is for family heads.[19]

Family Heads' Occupations in Seven Rural
Midwestern GC Congregations:
Farming Compared to Nonfarming, 1946 and 1956

		1946		1956	
Congregation	*Occupation*	*Number*	*Percent*	*Number*	*Percent*
Bethel Mennonite,	Farming	67	70.5	49	43.3
Inman, Kan.	Nonfarming	28	29.5	94	65.7
	Total	95	100.0	143	100.0
Tabor Mennonite,	Farming	97	67.8	84	48.6
Newton, Kan.	Nonfarming	46	32.2	89	51.4
	Total	143	100.0	173	100.0
Walton Mennonite,	Farming	20	66.7	15	39.5
Walton, Kan.	Nonfarming	10	33.3	23	60.5
	Total	30	100.0	38	100.0

First Mennonite,	Farming	36	32.4	25	20.8
Hillsboro, Kan.	Nonfarming	75	67.6	95	79.2
	Total	111	100.0	120	100.0
New Hopedale Menn.	Farming	52	73.2	49	55.7
Meno, Okla.	Nonfarming	19	26.8	39	44.3
	Total	71	100.0	88	100.0
First Mennonite,	Farming	70	74.5	59	62.1
Beatrice, Neb.	Nonfarming	24	25.5	36	37.9
	Total	94	100.0	95	100.0
Bethesda Mennonite,	Farming	192	56.5	228	˙54.2
Henderson, Neb.	Nonfarming	148	43.5	193	45.8
	Total	340	100.0	421	100.0

WOMEN'S OCCUPATIONS

According to the 1950 census, MC women generally married and worked in the household. Eighty-seven percent of the adult women surveyed in the five conferences were either married or widowed. In the Pacific Coast Conference 4.7 percent of the married women worked outside of the home, in the rest 3.2 percent or fewer. Among women working outside of the home, whether married or unmarried, the majority in all conferences, from 51.9 percent (Illinois) to 76.9 percent (Lancaster), worked at tasks considered "unskilled." From 13.2 percent (Lancaster) to 30.2 percent (Illinois) of the women worked as professionals. The rest were in the undefined middle category of skilled labor.[20]

In other respects, with small variations, the Mennonite social profile resembled American patterns. A Mennonite Research Foundation study based on the 1950 census and on a 1951 study of Mennonite incomes and charitable giving suggested that the increase in Mennonite wealth closely followed national trends.[21] In 1950 the average marriage age for MCs was 21.7 while the national average was 21.3. On that score, Mennonite women were closer to the national figure than were men. In 1960 more GC women were married (71.9) than the national average (67.4).[22]

Meanwhile Mennonite professional families were like their American counterparts in that they tended to defer childbirth into their thirties—while farm couples tended to begin families in their early twenties. Among all Mennonites the birthrate was more than necessary for replacement. While precise birthrates are difficult to calculate, among Mennonites as among most Americans, rural families were more fertile.[23]

Continuing stability of some MC communities around 1950 is suggested by a study of Ohio Mennonites' mobility. Outside of some newer urban congregations, between 59.6 and 88.9 percent of the persons surveyed were at least second-generation Ohioans. Congregations clustered in Holmes County and around Smithville, Columbiana, Kidron, and Archbold all had at least second generation memberships of more than 70 percent.[24]

The social profile of Mennonites maintaining their rural locations and agriculturally related vocations was a testimony to the enduring past. Complementing that past were the intensive efforts of an earnest few who worked during the war and immediate postwar years to revitalize rural communities and make them more attractive to Mennonite youth. Beginning with the sociological recovery of mutual aid traditions and with concerns about Mennonites entering into the labor movement, the search particularly among the MCs intensified for alternative structures that would deflect the encroaching and intrusive elements of American culture.

RENEWED FORMS OF SEPARATION

Schools

Mennonite-sponsored secondary schools in the United States were not new in the 1940s. In 1868, at Wadsworth, Ohio, GC Mennonites established the first Mennonite secondary school in North America. Following their arrival in the 1870s Russian Mennonite immigrants created eight such schools between 1879 and 1902— in Minnesota, Nebraska, and Kansas.

Yet the entire period from the 1860s to 1900 did not match an explosion of new secondary schools that occurred during the 1940s. MC Mennonite communities took the lead by establishing schools in Lancaster, Pennsylvania (1942); Culp, Arkansas (1944); Johnstown, Pennsylvania (1944); Kalona, Iowa (1945); Belleville, Pennsylvania (1945); Salem, Oregon (1945); and Kitchener, Ontario (1945). In Kansas and farther west, new secondary schools, with one exception, came from conferences with roots in Russia, and sometimes with different conferences cooperating. One school at Meade, Kansas (1945), was sponsored by EMB and GC congregations; another at Elbing, Kansas (1946), by GC churches; and one at Hutchinson, Kansas (1948), by GC, KMB, and MB. Again in Lustre, Montana (1947), GC, MB, and KMB Mennonites worked together, while in Reedley, California (1944), MB and KMB did so.[25]

The growth of secondary schools during the 1940s was impressive yet completely dwarfed by rapid building of primary schools. Again, the MC Mennonites took the lead. In 1925 they opened a school in Dover, Delaware, then others in Greenwood and Cheswold, Delaware, in 1928 and 1933.

A really rapid expansion began in 1938—from Virginia in the East to Oregon in the West. By 1949 communities and congregations affiliated with MC or Amish Mennonite conferences had begun 52 primary schools.[26] During the 1949-1950 school year 2,924 students were enrolled in 54 such schools. Many were quite small:

MC and Amish Mennonite Elementary Schools, 1949-1950[27]
37 schools with fewer than 50 students
10 schools with 50 to 100
7 schools with more than 100

Certainly World War II was the immediate catalyst for the rapid school expansion, for it heightened the sense of American cultural intrusion and the need for stronger forms of separation. In graphic terms the war brought home the necessity for more effective means for teaching and passing the values of the church to the next generation.

Church schools were one response to so many draftees' accepting military service. Some in the Mennonite world vaguely blamed "environmental factors," but others were more specific. Silas Hertzler, longtime professor of education at Goshen College, put the fault squarely on schools. "Even though alternative service was readily available," he wrote in 1949, "as a result of attending public schools, and thereby absorbing the typical militaristic nationalism of the country, during the recent war 53.6 percent of the American Mennonite boys disregarded Mennonite principles and accepted some form of military service."[28] Hertzler was not alone. Already in 1943 MCC Peace Section had expressed concern about the "developing militaristic pattern in our secondary public schools" and had tried to counter the pattern by publishing a high school civilian service handbook.[29]

But the schools developed from other, more persistent reasons. Mennonite youth no longer grew up so much in the protected boundaries of Mennonite culture. Church-related youth activities and institutions which sprang up in the 1920s and 1930s were responses to the emergence of youth as a distinctive subculture. The Mennonite secondary-school movement certainly recognized the power of "peer pressure" in a more age-sectored population. In a 1958 "Apology for the Church-Related Secondary School Movement in the Mennonite Church" Ross Bender, then principal of Rockway Mennonite High School in Ontario, cited rising group or "gang" pressures as one reason for private schools.[30]

The most persistent chronicler of school developments during the 1940s was Silas Hertzler. For him the issues were even broader. He reasoned that the need for Christian schools increased as the "secularism, pragmatism, and materialism" of American society grew. Schools had formerly lived off society's accumulated Christian capital; now that capital was exhausted. A more obvious secularism "surreptitiously permeated" the attitude of so many Mennonites that they were ignoring "the danger of non separation."[31]

The founders of the Kalona, Iowa, school agreed. According to them, a reason for establishing their school was that their children sat under "thirty-five or forty hours per week of secular teaching" over against only two or three hours of religious instruction at church.[32]

Although the ultimate goal surely was nurture, the Mennonite school movement was designed also to retain control. Explaining the need for a school, Noah Good, leader for many years in the Lancaster Mennonite High School, remarked that "the public high school is run by someone over whom we have no control."[33] Donovan Smucker, a progressive among Mennonite thinkers, agreed. "Powerful secular and monolithic forces are now knocking on the doors of the public school system asking for entrance," he noted in 1943. "Already many doors have been opened, letting in these ominous agents of the New Order."[34]

To fear the state-controlled high school was justified. A study based on the 1950 Mennonite family census data for Ohio revealed that the largest drift away from the denomination was persons whose schooling stopped at some point in high school. Remaining in the church were 89.3 percent of those who attended college and 87 percent who did not attend school beyond the eighth grade. Of those stopping with high school, 83.2 percent stayed.[35]

For Harold Bender, Christian schools were a matter both of cultural maintenance and of mission. Mennonitism as a distinctive faith spoke to the "needs of the world." Indeed, the world "cries out for what we have to give." That faith, formerly preserved by distinctive language, geographic isolation, and folkways, could now be passed on better through a comprehensive educational system. If effective, that system would simultaneously strengthen the convictions of Mennonite communities, empower their building of a distinctively Christian culture, and more aggressively witness its ideals to American society. Withdrawal and engagement were complementary rather than oppositional.[36]

Mennonite Mutual Aid and Community Preservation

The sociological recovery that aimed to renew mutual aid and to revitalize traditional communities flourished in the immediate postwar era, even if only rather briefly. The recovery aimed at rural preservation and reintegration of Mennonites returning from CPS and other wartime dislocations into their home communities. Its most visible elements were Mennonite Mutual Aid and the Mennonite Community movement.

Mennonite Mutual Aid (MMA) was legally incorporated on July 19, 1945, as an MC entity. That beginning marked a new kind of community assistance. In 1944 a special MC conference had authorized forming an organization to provide investment opportunities. The idea was to make money available for church purposes yet provide an appropriate return. Driving the creation of MMA at that time was a combination of an old problem and a new wartime need. The old problem was how to provide some alternative to commercial insurance to protect against property loss and hardships due to sickness or death. The new need was to make it financially possible for CPS persons to return to their home communities. To provide sufficient vocational opportunities in largely rural Mennonite settings would require a redirection of investment from corporate stocks and bonds to church programs.[37]

During the first two years, MMA invested more than $78,000 in loans to sixty-four individuals. Almost all the loans were to former CPS men. $39,000 was agriculturally related. Other large loans went for home purchases and business investments.[38]

By 1949 the Mennonite Mutual Aid corporation was shifting from CPS rehabilitation and community investment to more concern about sharing losses—both property losses and medical, disability, and burial expenses. If direct aid for rural communities was no longer at the forefront, the net effect of the new system still offered support for small Mennonite communities. Protection against high medical costs without sacrificing the profits to external health insurance had its own reward. The more than $300,000 in assets MMA held by 1949 suggests how successful it was at garnering Mennonite capital for church use.[39]

Meanwhile among GCs a Board of Mutual Aid met for the first time in December 1945. Established at the June 1945 sessions of the GC general conference, the Board's purposes were vocational counseling, job and business information exchange and referral, loans for education and for home purchases, and venture capital for those beginning farming, businesses, or colonies. Returning CPS men were the Board's "primary concern." Like the MCs' committee, the GC Board also transformed itself by 1950 into a more general mutual aid agency to provide various kinds of help.[40]

These Mennonite aid organizations might be thought of as a Mennonite form of postwar conversion. While much of the larger culture was redirecting its investment from production of war materials to providing civilian goods, so in similar fashion the new Mennonite aid organizations redirected Mennonite capital from the nation's corporate and industrial sectors to Mennonite communities. Instead of permitting their wealth to flow into urban centers, Mennonites were setting aside at least a portion to help small communities enlarge their agricultural and business opportunities—especially for returning draftees. Another purpose was educational opportunities for those whose schooling had been interrupted by the war—a sort of Mennonite version of the nation's "GI Bill" for veterans.[41]

The Mennonite Community Movement

In 1942, at a Mennonite scholars' conference on "cultural problems," Melvin Gingerich, then on the Bethel College faculty, read a paper on "Is There a Need for a Mennonite Rural Life Publication?"[42] The question was rhetorical. Since the late 1930s Guy F. Hershberger and J. Winfield Fretz had been developing ideas about preserving the rural-based Mennonite community (soon using the idea of "small" community perhaps more than "rural"). Gingerich supported their ideas. But in 1942 Mennonites were preoccupied with the fundamentalist-modernist debate and with the CPS system and other war-related matters.

However, once the war was over some folks acted on Gingerich's 1942 aspiration. In October 1945, at a meeting ironically in Chicago, a few MC leaders—all nonfarm—formed the Men-

nonite Community Association. On the initial board of directors
were Clayton Keener, Guy Hershberger, John L. Yoder, A. J. Metzler,
Harold S. Bender, Ivan Miller, and Paul Erb. In 1947 the Association began publishing an attractive, slick-paper magazine, *The
Mennonite Community*. In its first issue, using the word "visions,"
the magazine's creators wrote that they hoped to foster "stronger
Mennonite communities, both rural and semi-urban," and "the
preservation, in these communities of Mennonite principles and
the Mennonite way of life." In other words, they aimed for "the kind
of living which God intends."[43]

In the issue's lead article, Hershberger spelled out the Mennonite Community vision. Mennonite communities—small, Christian, and rural—were like many other small communities, yet different. Finding ways to maintain them represented not just sociological fear of the city but a means to protect values cultivated in
face-to-face village life. Only when Mennonite life and Mennonite
faith were fully integrated could each survive. The Mennonite
Community Association wished to invite young people, particularly ex-CPSers, to a new adventure in community-building.[44]

The Mennonite Community movement was part of a larger
discussion about the role and position of Mennonites in American
society. Did the continuation of Mennonite faith require continual reinforcement of semi-separatist ways? During the 1950s the
most persistent critic of Mennonite withdrawal strategies was
J. Lawrence Burkholder. A dissertation he wrote at Princeton University in 1958—"The Problem of Social Responsibility from the
Perspective of the Mennonite Church"—was a clarion call for
greater Mennonite involvement in the world and a greater assumption of responsibility for national and international structures. According to Burkholder the search for rural and segregated
communities represented a "romantic tendency." But much more
problematic than romanticism was a perversion of theology. The
Mennonite Community movement and the related forms of separation ran the danger "of identifying the Kingdom of God with a
particular cultural expression." It brought "Christianity and
'soilism' in close proximity," too close for Burkholder.[45]

However intriguing the Mennonite Community vision—sociologically, historically, and theologically—it did not draw a large
following. The Association had problems keeping its magazine going, and in 1949 the MCs' Mennonite Publishing House took it
over. Five years later the publishing house merged the *Mennonite
Community* journal with the *Christian Monitor* to form a new pe-

riodical, *Christian Living*. While the new one covered some Mennonite Community concerns, its focus was more the Christian family. That change surely suggested that a transformation was at work in American and Mennonite life. With increasing diffusion, the family—not the community—became the focus for carrying the values of the past into the future.[46]

INTENSIFIED FORMS OF ENGAGEMENT

If the Mennonite school movement, the Mennonite Community movement, and the reinvigoration of Mennonite mutual aid were all means of insuring the survival of Mennonites as a distinctive and separate people, other forces in the postwar period were carrying Mennonites into farflung corners of the world and new relationships beyond Mennonite community boundaries. The activism that CPS had nurtured was now channeled into voluntary service and an altruistic vigor that redefined Mennonite people as a "servant people." A servant and missional activism that engaged Mennonites in more energetic witness, not withdrawal, became the core of a refurbished Mennonite identity. If activism was the center of the new ideological identity, self-confidence was a close ally.

Voluntary Service

The movement for a structured program of Mennonite Voluntary Service (popularly called "VS") began during World War II. It was partly a response of Mennonite communities searching for alternatives to participation in Civilian Defense projects during the war. It was also a way to provide service opportunities for women similar to CPS for men. An MCC form of VS began at the 1943 Relief Training School in Goshen, with Edna Ramseyer's call for just such opportunities for women.[47]

Soon Mennonite denominations emulated the MCC program. In 1944 the MCs opened a summer unit attached to Mennonite missions in Chicago. By mid-1948 the GCs had nine summer projects going.[48] Often the denominational and MCC agencies overlapped. The MBs opened units in the summer of 1949 under MCC auspices, but then MCC turned the units over for denominational administration.[49]

During 1949, five years after the Mennonite VS beginning, 507 individuals volunteered time in the various programs. More than 100 were volunteers serving at least a year. The other 404 were in summer or other short-term assignments.[50] The first year-long assignments began in 1946. The numbers both of long-term and of short-term volunteers grew steadily in the coming decades. Between 1944 and 1962, 2,754 people volunteered for summer service with MCC and another 1,765 gave a year or more.[51]

For many VSers, the experience was much like CPS. Early VSers found great meaning in "positive service." Virgil Vogt, an MC Mennonite working with VS and Student Services and an early leader in the intentional community movement, called VS a "living parable." He thought it would challenge both "the accepted patterns of mediocrity in our church life . . . [and] the irresponsible individualism which characterizes most of our decision making."[52]

VS was also a way to continue many of the distinctive elements of the wartime experience, including group living, leadership training, personal sacrifice, and bearing witness to compassion and reconciliation. Irvin Horst understood the way VS embodied the new idealism of the church. Writing to VSers he touched some of the deepest veins of the Mennonite soul. "One of the secrets of voluntary service," he reflected, was "the seeming paradox of being both quiet and 'loud,' both humble and courageous, both doing and speaking."[53]

A 1965 project commissioned by the Institute of Mennonite Studies termed the postwar voluntary service "the most influential of the renewal movements in the Mennonite church."[54] It would be hard to argue with the conclusion. VS continued the idealism generated through wartime service. What Hershberger defined in 1944 as "a new social consciousness and a new sense of responsibility" became visible in the postwar world in many forms, but particularly in VS. In many ways VS did become the peacetime equivalent of CPS.

If voluntary service fulfilled a renewed Mennonite social conscience and missional impulse, there were also other precedents and pressures behind the programs' beginnings. In Henry, Illinois, at the outset of World War II, a minister of a nonpacifist denomination told a young man going into CPS that "you have attracted our attention, but what we are going to watch is what you are going to do after this is over to prove that you have something."[55]

Whether or not the minister or anyone else was watching, Mennonites in the postwar period felt such eyes on them. In early 1946, as compulsory service was winding down, Wilton E. Hartzler of the Greystone Park CPS unit echoed that Illinois minister. Writing in the *CPS Bulletin* he noted that the interest of CPS men and church leaders in a peacetime VS program was "conclusive evidence" that the Mennonite church was finally moving into "the activist non-resistant, 'faith-service' programs that it so long needed." Hartzler saw voluntary service as necessary to preserve nonresistance, maintain the possibility of alternative service in any future war, and "prove ourselves now."[56]

Hartzler thought that it was one thing to do CPS during war. But to prove that active service was more than a cowardly response to wartime demands, Mennonites needed to do truly voluntary service. From another quarter, the GCs' Western District Conference agreed. In 1950 its delegates passed a resolution urging their churches to supply VS workers "from among their boys of draft age AT LEAST in the ratio that obtains in the case of those drafted."[57]

Mennonite Central Committee

Nothing illustrated the new servant-activism better than the wartime and postwar expansion of MCC work. Into 1940 MCC worked only in the Soviet Union, Brazil, and Paraguay (mainly resettling Mennonites from the Soviet Union). Between 1940 and 1944, it expanded into seven more countries or territories— England, France, Poland, India, China, Egypt, and Puerto Rico. Then came the real explosion. Between 1945 and 1949 MCC entered seventeen more countries, more than in any comparable time in history. Six were European nations devastated by the war: The Netherlands, Italy, Austria, Belgium, West Germany, and Hungary. The expansion into Asia and into Africa was partly to aid war sufferers in Japan, Indonesia, Taiwan, and Ethiopia. In South America, resettlement of Mennonite war refugees accounted for some of the new countries—Uruguay and Argentina. Most workers in this rapid expansion were volunteers. In the Middle East the efforts began as refugee assistance during the war, as MCC assigned people to Egypt to work, particularly with Yugoslavian refugees, under the United Nations Relief and Rehabilitation Administration (UNRRA). In Ethiopia MCC helped in hospital and clinical care. On the Indian subcontinent Mennonite relief workers assisted the movement of more than one million Hindu Sikhs from Pakistan to India and of Muslims from India to Pakistan, as both countries moved toward independence from British colonial rule.[58]

Mennonites gave both to those in their own household of

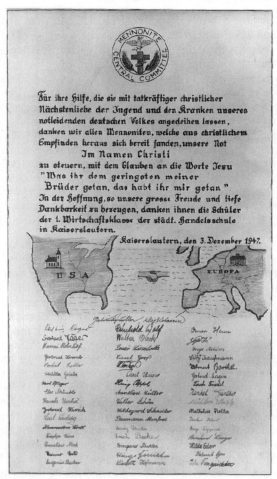

Thank-you note from Kaiserslautern, Germany, to Mennonite Central Committee, 1947.
Translation: "For the help that you gave, in Christian brotherly love, to the young people and the sick of our suffering German nation, we thank all the Mennonites who because of Christian convictions were ready to lighten our need 'In the Name of Christ,' believing the words of Jesus, 'Whatsoever ye do unto one of these the least my brethren, you have done it also unto me.' Wishing to express our great joy and deep thankfulness, the pupils of the first administration class of the City Business School in Kaiserslautern thank you." Kaiserslautern, 3 December 1947.

faith and to others. In Pakistan their relief supplies went primarily to Muslims, in Hungary primarily to Jews. In Europe—where MCC worked closely with the Red Cross, the Council of Relief Agencies Licensed for Operation in Germany (CRALOG), and UNRRA—the ethnic, political, and religious identity of the recipients was irrelevant. Need was need and could not be compromised by political or cultural categories. The distribution of canned meat, canned vegetables, canned fruit, powdered milk, used clothing, shoes, and bedding—all done "In the Name of Christ"—recognized no boundaries. In The Netherlands, early in the relief efforts a commotion broke out at an MCC distribution center because someone identified one person waiting in line as a former collaborator with the Nazis. Some in line insisted that such a person should not be given aid. But Peter Dyck, the MCCer in charge, made it clear that Mennonites had not come to Holland "to sort out the good guys from the bad."[59]

However ecumenical MCC was becoming, the tragedy of fellow Mennonites caught in the war's dislocations still touched a deep sense of kinship. Thus the outpouring of generosity was partly linked to traumas of coreligionists. Among the millions of refugees displaced by the war, Mennonite refugees from the Soviet Union and Poland found their way into various parts of western and central Europe and the Scandinavian countries. The agreements that the victorious allies reached at the historic meeting of the winning countries' heads of state at Yalta were that all refugees and displaced persons should be returned as quickly as possible to their own countries. Most refugees were eager to return. But Soviet Mennonite refugees were not, and Mennonites from Poland and Prussia were barred from doing so.

Probably no one will ever know how many Mennonites were among the many, many refugees who fled westward from the Ukraine with the retreating German armies. The usual figure is thirty-five thousand. In any case, roughly twelve thousand Mennonite refugees reached Germany. The other twenty-three thousand presumably died during the westward flight or were captured and repatriated by Russian officials. Most of those returning to the Soviet Union were forced back during the spring and summer of 1945. In addition to the twelve thousand from the Ukraine, Mennonites displaced from Danzig (Gdansk) and elsewhere in Prussia and Poland found their way into occupied Germany, Austria, Denmark, and The Netherlands. These numbered about eight-six hundred, for a total of more than twenty thousand Mennonite refugees in western Europe.[60]

Following the victory of the Allies, Germany was divided into four occupation zones—British, French, U.S., and Russian. The capital city Berlin, deep inside the Russian zone, was similarly divided. At the conclusion of the war, many of the Mennonite refugees were in the Russian zones, which both in Berlin and in Germany at large lay easternmost. Fearing repatriation to the Soviet Union, Mennonites desperately sought to cross from the Russian zones into those ruled by the western powers. A strange but effective Mennonite grapevine developed which allowed many of the twelve thousand to find each other. Many reunions occurred in UNRRA camps in the Munich area (under Allied control) or in bombed-out buildings of the Viktoria Luise Platz in Berlin's American sector.[61]

The first of these refugees' contact with Westerners was in the summer of 1945. Dutch Mennonites at Maastrict on the German/ Netherlands border found thirty-three survivors out of 614 Mennonites who had left the Chortitza colony in the Ukraine with the retreating German armies in the fall of 1943. Also in July 1945, letters from refugees in the American zone of Berlin reached MCC offices. Thereafter Cornelius F. Klassen, director of MCC in Europe, and Robert Kreider, the American Mennonite representative in CRALOG, became the first authorized MCC persons to make contact with Mennonite refugees in the Berlin area. Klassen visited Berlin in December 1945 and Kreider in April 1946. The two joined others in working to keep refugees from being deported. MCC's direct relief to refugees in Berlin intensified when Peter Dyck, then directing MCC relief efforts in The Netherlands, arrived in the German city on June 12, 1946. His spouse, Elfrieda Dyck, soon followed, and the two began their work in the Viktoria Luise Platz. At that time they served roughly 120 persons, but the number soon grew to twelve hundred.[62]

As was the case with CRALOG, MCC could hardly work except by cooperating with Allied military authorities, for the authorities were Germany's effective government. U.S. military commanders found buildings and MCC supplied the rest. A refugee community emerged with a temporary structure that included schooling, a hospital, religious services, choirs, and all the maintenance associated with sustaining a growing community. From June 1946 to the end of January 1947, the refugees were a small settlement living in the less-damaged American sector of a devastated Berlin.

Then events unfolded which came to be understood as a modern-day Exodus. The story captured the American Mennonite imagination as did nothing else in the entire drama of postwar relief. In Berlin the Mennonite refugees were in a tiny island surrounded by the Russian zone of occupation. Daily they lived with fear of being deported back to the Soviet Union. Their ultimate safety would be assured only if they could cross the Russian zone around Berlin and get to one of the western-controlled zones. But crossing Russian-controlled territory meant the risk of being picked up under the terms of the policy agreed to at Yalta. Nonetheless, on Friday, January 31, 1947, more than eleven hundred Mennonites from Russia managed to get out of Berlin and cross into the American zone of Germany. To them and their American coreligionists, their success was a special act of God. It may have been that. But if so, God apparently used U.S. military commanders as he had used Cyrus in the Old Testament. The truth was, the U.S. military—apparently ignoring the Yalta accords—had unilaterally changed the ground rules to limit radically the eligibility of former Soviet citizens to be forcibly returned.[63]

Mennonites of Poland suffered with equal pathos. In Poland the Germans' September 1, 1939, invasion soon brought them victory. For the next five years, Mennonites of Danzig and the lower Vistula Delta region suffered little damage or economic difficulty. Some volunteered and served in the German army. But as Germany's fortunes reversed, during the last seven months of the war Poland's German population suffered enormous losses. Just as the Nazis had inflicted suffering on the Soviet people, so advancing Soviet troops now retaliated. One result: panic and flight among German-speaking peoples, including Mennonites. Bruno Ewert, one of the elders of the Mennonites in northern Poland and Prussia at the outset of the war, estimated that one quarter of his people were lost or killed in those final months. A quarter of them found haven in Denmark, while the rest fled to the western zones of Germany.[64]

American Mennonites took deep interest in the tragedy of the displaced Mennonites of the Soviet Union and Poland and in Mennonites' condition in western Europe. As more information became available, the North American Mennonite press gave more and more space to the plight of the refugees and other European Mennonites. In some periodicals nearly every issue told of deprivation among European populations in general and Mennonite refugees in particular. An MCC press release of May 1945 noted that in Holland many people were living on only half the number of calories considered the daily minimum. The "almost unbearable priva-

Peter J. and Elfrieda Klassen Dyck in Bremerhaven, West Germany, 1948. Credit: MCC Collection, Archives of the Mennonite Church.

tions" of the Hollanders would draw many relief agencies' attention. But North American Mennonites should show "particular concern" since, at least when the war began, 100,000 of the Dutch people were fellow Mennonites.[65]

Nothing so dramatically indicated the American interest in the well-being and experiences of the Russian, Danzig, and Polish Mennonites as a speaking tour by Peter and Elfrieda Dyck in the fall of 1947.

After the dramatic departure from Berlin through the Soviet zone, the Dycks and 2,303 refugees from various camps went to the German port of Bremerhaven and boarded a ship named *Volendam* for the South American country Paraguay, whose government had agreed to accept the group. In August 1947, having delivered the refugees, the Dycks returned to North America.

Thereupon they embarked on what is surely the most remarkable itinerant tour in North American Mennonite history. Between late August and late October they told the story and showed movie films, which they themselves had made, to about forty-five thousand people in the United States and sixty thousand in Canada. Many of the meetings were three hours or even longer as Peter, a master storyteller, led his audiences through the tragic withdrawal from the Soviet Union, the escape from Berlin, the transport to South America, and the refugees' eventual resettlement in Paraguay and Argentina.[66]

The Dycks told the story in schools, churches, country pavilions, and retreat centers. For many Mennonites it was the first time they viewed a film in a religious service. One reason that meetings took place in nonchurch settings was that many congregations forbade the showing of films in their meetinghouses. But whatever the locations, the pathos and heroism of the story transcended such cultural prohibitions.

The first meeting was in a meadow on a poultry farm near Morgantown, Pennsylvania. Estimates put the audience anywhere from five thousand to ten thousand. The meeting's organizers collected an offering in milk buckets from a neighboring farm. At another meeting, in Rosemary, Alberta, the Dycks arrived several hours late—but the audience, gathered in a large tent erected for the occasion, had patiently waited. The meeting did not close until after midnight. Through 108 meetings the tour raised more than $80,000 to help settle refugees in South America.[67]

That money was only one example of Mennonite generosity for postwar relief. Across North America communities and congregations responded in different ways, but virtually every congregation participated. Late in the summer of 1945, Mennonite and Church of the Brethren farmers of Goessel, Moundridge, and Hesston, Kansas, contributed ten thousand bushels of wheat ground into flour for distribution by the Brethren Service Committee.[68] That was part of a much larger shipment. By December 1945 twenty-eight carloads of flour and wheat were in transit and another thirty were in the planning stages.[69]

At Whitewater, Kansas, congregations spent several Saturdays in January 1946 processing 5,400 cans of meat for European shipment.[70] At Wayland, Iowa, the Eicher Mennonite Church processed 1,028 cans of meat and 300 pounds of lard.[71] In the fall of 1945, the various Mennonite congregations of Mountain Lake, Minnesota, prepared more than fifteen tons of canned food.[72] In December 1945 the churches of Pandora and Bluffton, Ohio, sent two carloads of cattle.[73] In March 1946 some communities raised cash contributions through relief sales. In early 1946, Mennonites in and around Goshen, Indiana, raised $9,300 toward sending three carloads of rolled oats; those at Wellman, Iowa, raised $4,200; and the Pratum, Oregon, GC congregation's mission society held a sale which raised $350 for foodstuffs.[74]

MCC collection centers gathered used clothing, which women's societies mended and fixed for reuse. Some congregations made soap. The foodstuffs, soap, and clothing were gathered in regional MCC collection centers and forwarded. One such depot was at Newton, Kansas; in March 1945 it shipped twenty tons of used clothing. By the following December it had an additional 220 bales of clothing, each bale weighing 116 pounds, thus adding almost thirteen more tons.[75] In Reedley, California, MCC packed eighty-five tons of raisins in forty-pound steel buckets for shipment to needy people.[76]

The cumulative totals from these various relief efforts are indeed significant. Some of the monies flowed through the MC Mennonite Relief Committee (MRC), but by far the most went to MCC.[77]

Combined MCC and MRC Relief Contributions, 1949-1950

Year	Cash	Gifts in Kind	Total
1945	$260,890	$369,893	$630,729
1946	728,603	1,948,285	2,676,888
1947	775,191	2,136,154	2,911,345
1948	719,670	1,777,584	2,497,254
1949	439,375	1,304,870	1,744,245
1950	227,544	874,881	1,102,425

Beyond these monies for direct relief, American Mennonites also contributed liberally for refugees' resettlement. In the United States those contributions were handled by the Mennonite Aid Section in MCC. Before 1950 most costs of moving Soviet and Polish Mennonite refugees to South America were covered by the International Refugee Organization, a United Nations-related agency. Even so, more monies were needed and contributions to Mennonite Aid for resettlement assistance were in addition to contributions for relief.[78]

MCC Contributions via the Mennonite Aid Section

1945	$930
1946	791
1947	553,913
1948	477,065
1949	371,837
1950	236,267

By the end of 1949 MCC had contributed to resettling more than 11,000 refugees. The largest number to any single country—5,699 to Canada—had been handled by the Canadian Colonization Board, an independent Mennonite agency that worked closely with MCC. U.S. Mennonites had been more directly involved in the resettlement of 4,749 to Paraguay, 42 to Uruguay, and 161 to the United States.[79] The financial contributions to MCC alone for relief and resettlement totaled just under $13,000,000. It was indeed a down payment on a more active service and missional calling.

Missional Activism

Paralleling the global reach of MCC's program of postwar relief and reconstruction was an expansion of missional activity. The decade from 1945 to 1955 was a most explosive one for Mennonite missions outside of North America. The MCs' Board of Missions and Charities founded new work in seventeen different countries. During the same decade the Eastern Mennonite Board of Missions and Charities (a board of the MCs' Lancaster Conference) ventured into Luxembourg, Honduras, Ethiopia, and Somalia. GC Mennonites thrust outward by establishing new missions in Japan, Taiwan, and Colombia and by joining with other Mennonites for mission activity in Paraguay and Uruguay. The Mennonite Brethren began new mission programs in Brazil, Colombia, Japan, Germany, and Austria. The Conservative Mennonites moved into Costa Rica, the Krimmer Mennonite Brethren into Peru, the Church of God in Christ, Mennonites (Holdemans) into Haiti, the Evangelical Mennonite Church into the Dominican Re-

Mennonite student group who went to Europe in the summer of 1947 to do voluntary work. Credit: Mennonite Library and Archives, Bethel College, North Newton, Kansas.

public, and the Beachy Amish into Germany. Regional mission boards, particularly among the MCs, began other overseas mission projects. The year 1957 found 638 Mennonite missionaries active in 28 different countries plus 214 MCC workers in stations around the globe. By 1965 the numbers were 930 missionaries in 42 different countries—plus, in that year, 453 persons in foreign MCC or voluntary-service work in 39 countries.[80]

MCC's and mission boards' activities often converged. Mission programs brought in MCC programs, and MCC's relief work brought Mennonite missionaries. In Taiwan, Ethiopia, India, Vietnam, Japan, Hong Kong, Jordan, Uruguay, Puerto Rico, and Belize, MCC relief and development efforts preceded the establishment of Mennonite congregations.[81]

Yet the agencies were of different kinds, and their interests were also distinct. Mission agencies, at least, frequently were somewhat disturbed that young people seemed more interested in social efforts than in mission. Joseph (J. D.) Graber, longtime executive secretary of the MCs' Board of Missions and Charities, spoke the sentiments of other mission agencies when he expressed gratitude for the "heightened social consciousness" but also concern lest "this degenerate into a mere social service." Helping the suffering in the name of Christ was good if it also opened opportunities for the proclamation of the faith.[82]

The globalizing impact on Mennonite peoples has yet to be fully understood. By 1970 there were over five thousand MCC alumni. Some had served short terms. For instance, in the immediate postwar years 958 Mennonites participated in two- to three-month assignments helping with UNRRA livestock shipment to various countries. Overall, the majority of MCC volunteers, long-term or short-term, worked in assignments overseas. Many were young people who came with relatively little experience. MCC, missions, and other agencies of volunteer service opened up new worlds. Many volunteers found new self-identities in distant places and quite a few returned to some kind of foreign work after an initial two or three short-term assignments.[83]

The total number of Mennonite overseas missionaries and service volunteers for the postwar period remains untabulated. But international connections had dramatically grown. By 1970 there was hardly a Mennonite congregation without someone who had international experience.

Mennonite Economic Development Associates

In 1953 a new organization, Mennonite Economic Development Associates (MEDA), formed and began a different kind of Mennonite international activity. Its strategy was to blend compassion with investment, by offering grants and loans for long-term economic development instead of charity for immediate needs.

MEDA was the brainchild of North American businessmen wanting to add a new dimension to the assistance MCC was providing for resettlement of Russian and Prussian refugees in South America. MCC had picked up the relocation costs and bought land for these displaced persons, but was not ready to extend large-scale capital. In the 1940s MCC conceived of itself more as a relief agency than as a development one.

Charter members of the new organization included Ed. J. Peters of Wasco, California; Erie J. Sauder of Archbold, Ohio; Edward G. Snyder of Preston, Ontario; Ivan Miller of Corry, Pennsylvania; Orie O. Miller of Akron, Pennsylvania; Howard Yoder of Wooster, Ohio; Cornelius A. DeFehr of Winnipeg, Manitoba; Henry Martens of Reedley, California; and Sylvanus Lugbill and Ceaphus Schrock, both of Archbold, Ohio. The ten were among the more successful of Mennonite businessmen. They each pledged an initial $5,000 towards venture capital for the further economic development of the Mennonite colonies in Paraguay.

When MEDA organized in 1953 to assist economic development, it had few concrete examples to follow. Such help was not yet part of the charitable programs of most private voluntary agencies. The U.S. and Canadian governments were only beginning such aid. In 1948 President Truman initiated the Point IV Program; the Canadian International Development Agency (CIDA) came later. So MEDA was pioneering new thinking.

MEDA's early projects in Paraguay included establishment of dairy farms, cattle breeding, a tannery, a shoe factory, a foundry, a bottling plant, rice plantations, and a program for farm credit. The dairying ventures succeeded so well that the Mennonite colonies, although located in the undeveloped Chaco region, became major producers of dairy products for all of Paraguay.[84]

Mennonite Mental Health Services

The creation of what ultimately came to be known as Mennonite Mental Health was an expression of the new service idealism and self-confidence. A natural outgrowth of the experience of many CPS men in mental health was the establishment of Mennonite-sponsored hospitals and care facilities. Starting with the annual meeting of December 1944, MCC began moving toward a permanent program. In 1945 a Mental Health Hospital Study Committee composed of P. C. Hiebert, H. S. Bender, and Robert Kreider recommended that MCC continue a program of voluntary-service units in state mental institutions and that young Mennonite doctors and students aspiring to medicine "be encouraged to specialize in the field of psychiatry"—clearly a "neglected area of Christian service."[85]

By the fall of 1946 MCC was prepared to change its use of a farm at Leitersburg, Maryland, which it had bought for one of the experimental farm-community CPS units. It now made the farm the site of its first psychiatric care facility. A leader in the mental health effort was Elmer Ediger, then working in the MCC offices in Akron. In bringing the recommendation to both MCC and the MCC Mutual Aid Section, Ediger rhapsodized on the possibilities. "With the administering of electric shock, which is now the standard treatment for many mental illnesses, and high Christian standards, it is to be expected that marvels could be accomplished." Like the expectations of CPS, the idealism assumed that this set of "growing edge" institutions would be "experimental not only for our own constituency but for all society." Thus, with their own institutions, Mennonites did not think of themselves as "withdrawing" as Paul Comly French had interpreted them, but of assuming social responsibility in their own way. What made Ediger's confidence curious was that Mennonites were entering this new and highly specialized medical field without a single trained psychiatrist. Out of CPS work they of course did have an outstanding record as caregivers in mental hospitals.[86]

Mennonite psychiatrists or not, the mental hospital program began. In fall 1946, MCC approved the opening of Brook Lane Farm at Leitersburg and also agreed to cooperate with the Pacific District Conference of the Mennonite Brethren to open a hospital on the West Coast. In March 1948, the Lancaster Conference (MC) voted to open a mental hospital as its own project. By 1952 all three hospitals were fully operational. In 1954 Prairie View Hospital opened at Newton, Kansas, becoming the fourth such Mennonite facility.[87]

Mennonite Disaster Service workers in Udall, Kansas, 1955. Credit: *Mennonite Weekly Review*, courtesy of Mennonite Library and Archives, Bethel College, North Newton, Kansas.

Mennonite Disaster Service

In the summer of 1950, a Sunday school class of young married couples from the Pennsylvania (now Whitestone) Mennonite Church (MC) at Hesston, Kansas, meeting at a picnic, initiated still a different kind of activism. Many of those present had participated in CPS during World War II. They inquired of each other how they might contribute to society and continue the service CPS represented. Living in an area frequented by tornadoes, floods, and droughts, the class members struck on a way to make their Christianity intensely practical. After conferring with one another for a few more weeks they and another Hesston congregation formed a Mennonite Service Organization (MSO) to mobilize in case of disaster. They enumerated the skills and tools they could bring to an emergency.

Nothing much happened until floods hit Kansas in May 1951. Wichita, Great Bend, Marion, Florence, Topeka, and Kansas City called for help. The threatened or ravaged communities needed people to fill sandbags, patrol dikes, make sandwiches, and assist in cleanup and reconstruction. In the first two weeks, at least 120

men and women volunteered. From four different Mennonite conferences in Kansas and Nebraska, they came to cook, paint, hang
wallpaper, and work together in still other ways. They wore arm
bands identifying themselves as members of the "MSO." The city
officer in Great Bend, under whose supervision some of them
worked, affectionately called them the "Mighty Soaked Outfit."
Others nicknamed them the "Midnight Service Organization."[88]

Nearly a year later, in March 1952, tornadoes swept through
White County, Arkansas. Again the Kansas congregations organized a formal assistance program. Emerging was the idea and
structure for what came to be Mennonite Disaster Service (MDS)—
an affiliate of MCC. The idea was one whose time had come. In other states and regions Mennonites quickly followed suit. Soon volunteers in many parts of the U.S. were organized to respond to natural disasters. By 1976, when MDS celebrated its twenty-fifth anniversary, MDS involved more than nineteen hundred Mennonite
and Brethren in Christ congregations divided into 270 zones, 52
units, and five regions. The only paid staff was the executive director in Akron. The rest of the organization worked (and works) exclusively on a volunteer basis. Yet the record of this vast, decentralized organization, as its historian Katie Funk Wiebe has written, "reads like a roll call of national disasters. Name the disaster
and you'll find MDS was there."[89] Sources cited in n. 88.

Organizing for natural disasters, like so many other forms of
doing good, also raised peculiarly Mennonite questions of conscience. Beginning with World War II, preparing for emergencies
by identifying emergency personnel networks and standby emergency supplies became closely linked with the wartime nation's
Civilian Defense system. Could or should nonresistant Mennonites be a part of that system? Because the Civilian Defense (or, as
called in the 1950s, "Civil" Defense) command structure could be
integrated into the military system, MDS officials worried about
possible conflicts of conscience. Although MDS wished not to be
organizationally identified as part of the Civil Defense system, it
did encourage individuals with particular skills, particularly "am-
ateur radio operators, firefighters, medical and nursing personnel," to declare their willingness to cooperate with recognized governmental and private disaster agencies such as Civil Defense and
the Red Cross.[90]

CONCLUSION

The demise of the Mennonite Community movement and the ever-expanding ministries of relief, compassion, and voluntary service signaled a changing Mennonite identity. The question of how Mennonites should relate to culture remained a major issue, to be sure. But now being Mennonite had less and less to do with the practice of nonconformity visually defined, with speaking German, with being rural, and with many behavioral taboos that defined the boundaries between Mennonites and the larger culture. More and more, ideology, servant activism, and voluntarism were replacing cultural markers as the central carriers of Mennonite peoplehood. What sociologists refer to as abstract symbols or symbolic factors were replacing concrete and specific signs.[91]

In the vanguard of the new change was a younger generation schooled in CPS and postwar voluntary service and building on the mid-twentieth-century intellectual reconstruction of Mennonite history. That generation was moving the church toward a more clearly defined theology of service and a more globally engaged missional identity.

If the younger generation had new opportunities following World War II, an older generation of "brokers" had opened the way. Robert Kreider wrote that Orie Miller symbolized the groping of Mennonite people from "parochialism and isolation into a world of involvement and service to society."[92] The comment could apply to many farsighted leaders of Miller's generation. Confronted by the needs of Mennonites in the new Soviet Union, by the realities of a severe economic depression in the United States, and by the largest conscription system in U.S. history, those earlier leaders had set in motion the institutions and idealism that freed Kreider's generation for expanded activism.

In a special way MCC, the organization founded in 1920 and for many years led so ably by Orie Miller, symbolized the transformation of American Mennonite identity. Global in scope, integrative in its linking together of word and deed, and inter-Mennonite in its composition, its service was to a bruised humanity regardless of ideology, class, religion, or ethnicity. Servant activism "In the Name of Christ" was the most prominent symbol of this changing identity.

CHAPTER
9

MENNONITISM AND EVANGELICALISM

On May 14, 1949, a small group of scholars convened a seminar at the Goshen College Biblical Seminary which apparently was the first inter-Mennonite gathering devoted explicitly to examining Anabaptist theology. Mennonite scholars involved in the historical recovery of the Anabaptist Vision had always meant to refashion Mennonite theology, yet they had not attempted to theologize in a systematic way about the implications of sixteenth-century Anabaptism for the contemporary church.

In an editorial in *MQR* Harold S. Bender himself, who was prominent at the seminar, supported the effort to articulate the tradition's theology more self-consciously. Some "modern descendants of the Anabaptists" were "no longer . . . in living connection with their theological ancestry," he wrote. Some Mennonites were so involved "in modern theological trends, whether fundamentalist and pietistic or otherwise[,] that they have lost their center of orientation."[1]

If Bender was concerned that his church was losing its center, a variety of voices from various Mennonite denominations agreed. In 1959 Sanford C. Yoder, a lifelong moderately progressive MC leader, observed that his people had entered "an altogether different relationship with the society in which we live." They were, he said, "no longer the deliberate, quietly moving people . . . [they] once were."[2] In 1962 John R. Mumaw, an eastern conservative who was moderator of the MC's general conference, warned ominously of "winds of change" across his church. Some changes perhaps came "by the process of revolution," others from "disintegration" or "infiltration," and still others from "imaginative leadership, or bold prophetic projection"; but together, the changes were confusing. Meanwhile in 1951 the MBs' Board of Reference and Counsel (BORAC) delivered a report whose first section was "A Frank Analysis of our Spiritual State."[3]

With changes in a few particulars, the BORAC report might have been offered at any Mennonite conference. During recent years, it said, new "educational opportunities" and "economic advantages" had brought "revolutionizing changes," changes which created a pluralism that now threatened the security and health of church polity, doctrine, and ethics. To be sure, the MB church had been "preserved from . . . serious inroads of rank modernism." Yet the report identified four main threats to its doctrinal integrity: (1) lack of "clearly defined Scriptural guidance"; (2) "indefiniteness and difference" in interpretation; (3) "an absence of unity"; and (4) "a hesitancy in accepting defined statements . . . about being a separated people from the world."[4]

Separation from the world was surely a concern also of conservatives like MC bishop Sanford (S. G.) Shetler in western Pennsylvania. In 1957, lamenting that what had been "middle-of-the-road policy" a generation earlier was now dismissed as "radical conservatism," Shetler described the state of the church by using the metaphors of "progress" and "drift."[5]

For Mennonites to have multiple theologies was not new. Since the sixteenth century, Anabaptists and their successors had cared more about fashioning disciplined communities of believers than about articulating theological systems, even looking on formal theologies with suspicion and mistrust. Usually their theology had been implicit rather than very explicit. Anabaptist Vision scholar Robert Friedmann made that pattern a virtue, part of the genius of the Anabaptists. Anabaptists, he wrote in a 1973 book, had considered theology "rather a stumbling block to . . . discipleship and no real help in man's earthly predicament."[6] That attitude had allowed more than a little theological pluralism, as Anabaptists borrowed from Protestants, Catholics, mystics, and others.[7]

By the 1950s Mennonite thinkers widely considered that such borrowing, or what Bender called "outside influences," weakened the faith. A major theme of a landmark book by Friedmann in 1949, *Mennonite Piety Through the Centuries*, was that Pietism had corroded pristine Anabaptism and Mennonitism.[8] Countering such borrowing was one reason to work at a distinctive Mennonite theology.

The Goshen seminar was only the opening moment in the theological recovery and articulation of the Anabaptist tradition. In 1955 GC Mennonites held a study conference to consider the nature and function of the believers' church. Stated one way or another, that theme was central to much of the Mennonite theological activity of the 1950s. Clearer doctrines of the church, its authority, and its doctrine might apply the brakes to theological acculturation. For the three largest progressive denominations (MC, GC, MB), the 1950s were an appropriate time for such search and clarification. New mission and other activist thrusts following the war, and Mennonites' greater movement into various social and economic sectors of American society, had set Mennonite congregations and denominations sailing in various theological currents and swirls.

The scholars who met in Goshen and their counterparts among the MBs and GCs formed only one of various movements which sought to position Mennonites for the coming decades. Others were hammering out different strategies. In virtually all Mennonite denominations, revivalism and evangelical alliances and theologies attracted their shares of attention.

MENNONITES, REVIVALISM, EVANGELISM

Missionary and evangelizing activity had been central to Mennonite theologizing since the sixteenth century, albeit in tension with—and often overwhelmed by—the equally strong idea of being a people apart. But as Mennonites felt more at home in the world and as the boundaries of Mennonite society became more permeable, the search for better forms of evangelism intensified.

In the 1950s and 1960s a very visible strategy was mass evangelism in the form of great revival crusades. To be sure, other strategies persisted. Examples include a call in 1952 by the GC Evangelism Committee to bring in new people through the Sunday school,[9] or in the MB denomination from 1963 to 1973 a largely unsuccessful "Decade of Enlargement" campaign to double membership.[10] But the 1950s were the heyday of great interdenominational crusades. The Baptist mass evangelist Billy Graham had led the way in 1949 when he pitched a huge tent outside of Los Angeles, and some Mennonites followed suit.

Historically, Mennonites in America had largely remained aloof from two earlier waves of revivalism, the colonial "Great Awakening" and then the so-called "Second Great Awakening" early in the nineteenth century. In what may be termed revivalism's third wave—that of the late nineteenth and early twentieth centuries, led by the great revivalistic preacher Dwight L. Moody and others—they had become more involved. About that time, both in North America and in the Russian empire, some new more revivalistic Mennonite denominations had formed, such as the Mennonite Brethren in Christ and the Mennonite Brethren. Meanwhile the large MC church generally accepted mild forms of revivalism.[11] So by the 1950s most Mennonite groups were more or less sympathetic to revivalism. Yet many could also agree with Harold Bender, who observed in 1956 that the "movement for evangelistic activization" often came with "significant side effects and related changes" that produced "a significantly different Mennonitism."[12]

Even so, on June 3, 1951, Mennonite mass revivalism entered a new phase, for on that day George R. Brunk II and his brother Lawrence pitched a revival tent on East Chestnut Street in Lancaster, Pennsylvania. Sons of the outspoken Mennonite bishop and editor George R. Brunk I, the brothers had grown up in the confines of the Virginia Mennonites' conservative tradition. By 1951 George II had attended Eastern Mennonite College, William and Mary College, and Union Theological Seminary in Richmond. Lawrence had prospered in business and farming. Since 1946 the two had engaged in various kinds of evangelistic activities.

The first Brunk tent had twenty-five hundred seats, and the Lancaster revival went on for seven weeks. The brothers attracted such crowds that they put up a second tent. Reportedly on July 22, the last night, fifteen thousand people—mostly Mennonite—attended. Then a week later, at the invitation of the MC Franconia Conference's bishops, the Brunk brothers began a similar crusade in that other old, populous historic, eastern Pennsylvania Mennonite community. From July 29 to September 3, they preached and sang nightly. For the Franconia crusade they added a third tent, with six thousand more seats. Powerful microphones allowed them to address ten thousand people at a time.

Before 1951 ended, the brothers held two more protracted series—from September 9-October 14 at the Martins Mennonite Church near Orrville in eastern Ohio; and October 10-November 25 back in Lancaster County, Pennsylvania, this time at rural Manheim.

Everywhere the crowds were large. In Franconia people attended on weekday evenings, and some ten thousand or twelve

Brunk Revival Crusade in the Franconia Conference (MC) 1951. Standing: George R. Brunk II. Credit: Mennonite Library and Archives of Eastern Pennsylvania, Harleysville, Pennsylvania.

thousand on weekends. On one Sunday in the large, old, traditional Franconia MC congregation, more than 130 persons committed or rededicated themselves to be Christians. In the whole Franconia-area crusade there were reportedly 850 such commitments, 250 of them first-time faith decisions, including spectacular ones from some local rowdies known as "Franconia Cowboys." Soon erstwhile "Cowboys" were calling themselves "Franconia Christian Workers."[13]

The Franconia congregation enjoyed a membership gain of 55 in one year. And a gain of 177 in the whole Franconia Conference became the largest yearly increase on record 1945-1970. Observers credited the Brunk revival.[14]

Even while trying to preserve the "old-time religion," the Brunk campaigns of the 1950s introduced modern techniques. Multicolored banners with various slogans hung across the tent stages. Campaign organizers advertised in newspapers and on radio and flooded the targeted community with promotional leaflets.[15] In a spirited defense of the Brunk revivals, Clayton (C. F.) Yake, editor of the MC Mennonites' main paper for youth, saw revolution. The Brunk revival "movement," he wrote, was revolutionary "in magnitude, ... in purpose, ... in its services and techniques," and in its "daring." He thought "it attacks our traditionalism where it lacks vitality" and "breaks down conventionalities and formalism."[16]

Alongside the Brunk successes came a spate of calls to be more aggressive in evangelism.[17] One call was to get laypersons more involved, as in a Christian Laymen's Tent Evangelism organization. In 1952 Howard Hammer, a Mennonite evangelist from Ohio, used that organization to begin tent campaigns in the Midwest.[18] In other cases ministers such as Andrew Jantzi, a preacher in the Conservative Amish Mennonite Church, began their own tent-revival meetings.

Among MBs also, revival activity moved toward greater professionalism. In 1952 such activity was not so very different from earlier times, with most MB congregations holding revival meetings for a week or two annually or semiannually (plus annual missionary conferences, expository Bible conferences, and Christian workers conferences). In 1954 their U.S. Conference elected a three-person board of evangelism and in 1957 appointed Waldo Wiebe, a longtime pastor, to be "conference evangelist."[19] MBs were moving away from the pattern of multiple lay evangelists.

Meanwhile the Brunks' success grew. In 1952 they held major campaigns at Johnstown, Pennsylvania; at Waterloo, Ontario; at Goshen, Indiana; and at Morgantown, Pennsylvania.

As the revival activity increased, so also did the assessments and concerns. Strong voices asked whether this kind of evangelism was congruent with traditional Mennonite theology. In 1953 the MCs' General Council expressed concerns that parts of the MC church were not giving enough support to the revival efforts, and that "denominational pride" might keep MCs from assimilating some of the people won. A few weeks later a conference on evangelism at Goshen College raised different concerns. Conferees were troubled by more and more appeals to primary- and junior-age children, by certain of the evangelistic methods, and by evangelists' emphasizing a "crisis commitment of faith in Christ" without calling for "full discipleship."[20]

Soon *Gospel Herald* editor Erb seemed to give weight to what a later analyst, Bluffton College professor Dale Dickey, has labeled a "counter-movement."[21] In an editorial entitled "Evangelism for Full Discipleship," Erb sharply questioned whether the "honest search for truth" which discipleship demands is not "something very different from a revivalistic intoxication that sends the addict

reeling from one evangelistic meeting to another . . . . If those
things do not make the attendant a biblical Christian their influence is shallow and in the long run harmful."[22]

Some MBs also expressed Erb's concern. In 1952 the MBs'
Christian Leader carried three articles about being sure that revival activity led to permanent renewal of the church.[23] Reuben
Baerg, president of the Pacific Bible Institute, cautioned readers to
"discriminate between a revival of mere psychological impulse or
one born and generated by the holy spirit." The wrong kind could
be merely a "superficial gusto which hoists the banner of evangelism only to grieve the spirit of God."[24]

During the 1950s and early '60s, the Brunks carried their "revival fires" (as the inside history of the Brunk revivals has called
them) not only to their own Swiss-origin MC Mennonite communities but also to communities of GC and MB "Russian" Mennonites.
Often all of an area's Mennonite congregations cooperated to
sponsor the campaigns. In some cases, Billy Graham fashion, the
campaigns were communitywide, with churches other than Mennonite cooperating.[25]

Nonetheless, with time the crusades' impact diminished,
both among MCs and among GCs and MBs. Like a meteorite, the
Brunk revivals burned brightly, but then about 1955 and 1956
they began to fade. In 1957 and 1958 they were still visible, but
mainly in western Canada. Also among MBs, during the 1950s and
1960s revival meetings diminished. MB revivals became more and
more sporadic rather than regular, and occurred in selected congregations rather than as standard practice.

Historian William McLoughlin has argued that revival movements occur during periods of "critical disjunctions in our self-
understandings." He suggested that outbursts of intense religiosity come with broader "cultural transformations" in American
life.[26] Surely the Mennonite revivals of the early 1950s are an example. The postwar times were a transforming period. Everywhere,
as Mennonites moved with the economic and cultural shifts of the
larger culture, there were signs of disjunction.

It is not clear that Mennonites needed revival then any more
than at other times in the twentieth century. Surely the revivals
brought real repentance. But in a religiously based culture, they
could also be a stylized form to legitimize changes which people
did not know how to stop. Perhaps for some Mennonites the litanies of purgation were ways to prepare themselves for—and maybe
even accelerate—such changes. Much as George Brunk used mod-

Mennonites meeting with Billy Graham, 1961. Left to right: Dwight Wiebe, John (J. C.) Wenger, Billy Graham, Charles Hoeflich. Credit: Philadelphia National Bank, courtesy of Archives of the Mennonite Church, Goshen, Indiana.

ern techniques to sustain the "old-time religion," so his hearers could sustain new changes by invoking time-honored religious incantations.[27]

MENNONITES AND EVANGELICALS

A somewhat different though related dynamic was Mennonite interest in postwar American Evangelicals. George Marsden, leading historian of American Fundamentalism and Evangelicalism, has written of the postwar Evangelicals as representing the fourth stage in the evolution of the Fundamentalist-and-Evangelical movement. (His first three stages were nineteenth-century Evangelical expansion; early-twentieth-century Fundamentalist controversies; and, from the mid-1920s to about 1940, withdrawal and regrouping.) By Marsden's analysis the fourth phase began when some Evangelicals abandoned sectarian withdrawal to move more into America's mainstream. Scholars have

called this segment "establishment Evangelicals," referring especially to those institutionalized in the National Association of
Evangelicals (organized 1942), Youth for Christ (1944), Fuller
Theological Seminary (1947), World Vision (1950), and the magazine *Christianity Today* (1956).[28]

After World War II some Mennonites became more and more
involved with these organizations—for example, with the National
Association of Evangelicals, or NAE. The two largest Mennonite
bodies, the MC and the GC, never did join. Nonetheless, some GC
congregations joined, and GC agencies established various relationships with some NAE agencies even as they did the same with
the more "liberal" and mainstream National Council of Churches
(NCC).[29] In the MC, leaders such as Guy F. Hershberger and Myron
Augsburger worked with some NAE leaders, especially those like
Carl F. H. Henry who were open to Mennonite views on peace and
social questions.[30]

Some Mennonite denominations joined. Among the first was
the small Evangelical Mennonite Brethren (EMB), in 1945.[31] That
same year the MB denomination joined, with impetus from its
Board of Foreign Missions which saw certain practical advantages
in membership.[32]

In 1950 the MBs terminated their membership, over a question of how the NAE president expressed an active anticommunism. (MBs did not object to anticommunism, but rather to political entanglement.) Yet even as they withdrew they pledged continued financial support,[33] and the NAE still accepted their delegates at its annual conventions and elected some MBs to its various boards, even its board of administration. And later, in 1968,
the MBs rejoined. Serving as an unofficial delegate to the 1966
NAE convention, Marvin Hein, a prominent MB who was pastor of
the large Hillsboro, Kansas, congregation, "felt somewhat uncomfortable." Yet he said that his "positive impressions" far out-
weighed his negative ones and that surely Mennonites and
Brethren in Christ were making an impact on NAE thinking. Indeed a Brethren in Christ leader, Arthur Climenhaga, served as the
NAE's executive secretary.[34]

Not surprisingly, the main impact of which Hein wrote was an
attempt to convince Evangelicals of New Testament nonresistance. From the 1950s onward MC evangelist, educator, and pastor Myron Augsburger was an influential Mennonite voice in the
NAE. After attending the 1962 convention he decided that the
NAE was more likely than the NCC or the World Council of Church-

es to take a strong position against violence.[35] Nonetheless, an interdenominational seminar on "Evangelicals in Social Action Peace Witness," held at Eastern Mennonite College and Seminary in the Vietnam-war context of 1967, seemed to show that at best the relationship between Mennonites and the NAE remained uneasy.[36]

Some Mennonites made connections farther to the right on the Evangelical-Fundamentalist spectrum. As it opened in 1955, the MB Seminary had two faculty members who were graduates of Dallas Theological Seminary. *Zion's Tidings*, journal of the small Ohio-Indiana-Illinois-based Evangelical Mennonite Church, endorsed Bob Jones of the highly Fundamentalistic Bob Jones University. Jones and another prominent Fundamentalist, John R. Rice, spoke in the denomination's congregations. A 1957 survey showed that students from EM Church congregations strongly preferred conservative Protestant colleges—especially Taylor or Fort Wayne Bible College in Indiana, Moody Bible Institute, Wheaton College, and Bob Jones University—over Mennonite ones. Partly the students objected to Mennonite cultural "encrustations" such as dress restrictions, but they were also moving away from core Mennonite understandings like nonresistance.[37]

Stan Nussbaum, the Evangelical Mennonite Church's historian, has observed that "the 'evangelical' family makes no doctrinal demands which EMC is not prepared to meet and has no basic concerns which EMC does not share."[38] In 1975 the denomination's General Administrative Board restricted inter-Mennonite associations and participation to four agencies—MCC, Mennonite Disaster Service, Council of Overseas Mission Board Secretaries, and Africa Inter-Mennonite Mission. It put no such restrictions on NAE connections, and in 1974 and 1975 the EMC gave more money per capita to NAE than did any other member denomination.[39]

For another small group, the Mennonite Brethren in Christ (MBC), the name Mennonite just carried too much stigma; and so in 1947, in a clear choice between Evangelical and Mennonite identification, parts of the MBC renamed themselves the United Missionary Church. In fact the stigma came from the very items that distinguished Mennonites from Evangelicals—nonresistance, nonconformity, and separatism.[40] Missionary Church people apparently saw such emphases as ethnic tribalism rather than as biblical faithfulness.[41]

MENNONITES AND CONSERVATISM

In the 1950s some Mennonites were struggling to hold on to the past. The decade was a time of trial for the Church of God in Christ, Mennonite, or "Holdemans" (a small group who emphasized crisis conversion while maintaining plain dress and other restrictions). Young men had returned from CPS with expanded experiences. In 1946 the denomination's conference had questioned some earlier rulings. Also between 1948 and 1969 a bureaucratic revolution was in progress with an increase in the small denomination's boards and agencies from twenty-one to forty-one. The church emphasized mission, and its missionaries became involved in new medical, educational, and agricultural activities. At home, some members were joining economic cooperatives, business partnerships, and other relationships with people of different religious persuasions. Longtime isolationist patterns were under strain. Moreover, 1945-1949 brought the deaths of eight of twelve strong leaders who before the war had regulated much of Holdeman life.[42]

With such changes brewing it was easy for younger leaders such as C. M. Penner, son of a prominent Holdeman minister, to see the changes as wrong. In 1950 Penner presented the church's conference with a list of activities which he thought showed "decay." They included four-part singing, birthday parties, large wedding dinners, laxness in upholding avoidance regulations, and other matters. When the conference's responses did not suit them, he and others withdrew. Some were expelled. Some of the alienated formed dissident Holdeman congregations, while others joined different Mennonite denominations or other Protestant groups. Amid conflicting pressures for change and conservation, it was not easy to find consensus about what constituted the "true church."[43]

The largest Mennonite group, the MCs, had a long and strong doctrine of nonconformity, which had served as a protective shroud for resisting change and maintaining tradition. Narrowed under the influence of Mennonite fundamentalism, the nonconformity doctrine still invoked intense MC dialogue during the 1950s.

In Virginia's Shenandoah Valley, Eastern Mennonite College lay in territory where the nonconformity doctrine was strong. Yet in 1950 two student orators suggested that the doctrine was difficult to defend. J. Richard Burkholder, soon a missionary in Brazil and later a professor at Goshen College, argued that (1) nonconformity was "an entirely negative approach to life and by itself incomplete"; (2) it had degenerated into legalism with little regenerative power; (3) distorted ideas of separation had devolved into "asceticism" and into an isolationism not in keeping with the great commission; and (4) the narrowing of nonconformity was causing Mennonites to apply it only to restricted segments of life.[44] Daniel Hertzler, who eventually would be editor of the *Gospel Herald*, likened the nonconformity doctrine to ecclesiastical walls designed to reinforce isolationism.[45]

Hertzler and Burkholder hoped to redefine nonconformity. Hertzler wanted it to change and "blossom forth as transformity."[46] Burkholder emphasized that a nonconformity properly understood implied "dynamic discipleship"—a "true Anabaptism" which had the virtues of both modernists and fundamentalists, and, more importantly, which accepted personal regeneration and practiced the moral teachings of Jesus.[47]

At more official levels, MC leaders reconceptualized nonconformity and hoped to revitalize it. Such ideas appeared especially in two documents: a book by John (J. C.) Wenger, *Separated unto God* (1951), commissioned by the MCs' general conference as early as 1944; and a statement of that conference in 1955 entitled "Declaration of Commitment in Respect to Christian Separation and Nonconformity to the World."[48] Both documents broadened the concept of nonconformity. They still emphasized attire—the central preoccupation in previous decades—but now attire became only one element in a larger pattern of restraint, responsibility, simplicity, and separation. Nonconformity properly understood covered courtship and marriage, organizational affiliation, recreational patterns, speech, worship patterns, commercial connections, mutual aid, and relationships to the state. Following the 1955 statement, various MC agencies held forty-four nonconformity conferences across the church.

Similar attempts continued but revitalization of traditional nonconformity failed. More and more, MC women cut their hair and left off the prayer covering, and both men and women put on jewelry. Younger males all but abandoned the straight coat. As an essential element in the identity of MC Mennonites, nonconformity was evaporating.

By the early 1960s a senior figure like John R. Mumaw, president of Eastern Mennonite College and one who had always practiced nonconformity in attire, was counseling change. In a concluding address to the MCs' general conference in 1961 he suggested that "we should not dwell too long on our image of the past."[49] In fact, by then the MC denomination's leaders were already acting out that advice.[50]

In the next decade visual nonconformity became more the exception than the rule, particularly among the younger generations. In 1973 Conrad Brunk, a young scholar from Virginia and son of revivalist George Brunk II, observed that "the Mennonite Church seems to be swiftly losing its last external vestiges of nonconformity. To a large extent we have melted into the mainstream of American cultural life."[51]

Much the same happened also to the Mennonite-related Brethren in Christ, except that their movement away from dress restrictions was more deliberate. During the 1950s, as part of a larger revision of doctrine, an official review and study committee moved to delete codes of attire. In the interests of greater evangelism, the BIC set aside some historic restrictions on grounds that they were unnecessary cultural impediments.[52]

Meanwhile prewar issues such as millennialism continued, but now the texture was different. In 1952 at Elkhart, Indiana, the MC church held a Prophecy Conference explicitly to air opposing views.[53] *Gospel Herald* editor Erb seemed happy that people spoke freely.[54] Apparently some of the earlier dogmatism was receding.

In 1955 the managers of an annual Mennonite lecture series, the Conrad Grebel Lectures, chose to have Erb speak on millennialism. Subsequently published as *The Alpha and the Omega*, Erb's addresses steered a middle course and chided those who pursued "the profitless argument between different schools of thought."[55] Quoting a warning from the prominent Protestant theologian Reinhold Niebuhr that "it is unwise for Christians to claim any knowledge of either the furniture of heaven or the temperature of hell," Erb called for humility.[56] Not all Mennonites adopted Erb's moderation, yet most of their discussions of millennialism were more moderate after World War II than before.

MENNONITES AND CHURCH-PLANTING

If differences in theology and interchurch connections caused some disagreement among post-World War II Mennonites, those same Mennonites were almost unanimous on the importance of establishing new congregations. For sixteenth-century Anabaptists the impulse to plant congregations in villages and towns had been central. However, intense persecution and consequent social withdrawal had quickly subverted that drive. For centuries Mennonites and Amish found it difficult to break out of the cultural barriers that developed from that withdrawal.[57] Into the late twentieth century some Mennonites were still struggling to find the cultural and theological posture that would let them plant new congregations outside of traditional Mennonite population pockets.

Even so, in many Mennonite congregations and conferences an upsurge in church planting following World War II became an important part of a larger, revitalized missional activism. In a history of the GCs' Western District Conference (covering Kansas and adjacent areas), David A. Haury has tallied twenty-eight new congregations which joined the conference between 1942 and 1979. Most grew out of Mennonite migration to cities. In the 1950s urban church-planting came to dominate the conference's Home Missions Committee.[58] Despite the congregations' connection with ethnic Mennonites' migration, the new congregations were more successful than older ones at including members whose backgrounds were other than Mennonite.[59]

Meanwhile, the MB Southern District Conference, geographically more or less parallel to the GCs' Western District, moved in a similar direction. In 1950s its committees on evangelism and home missions were still promoting traditional evangelistic services in traditional congregations, but they also accepted a mandate from conference to supervise and direct the establishment of new congregations. By 1955 the committees had helped bring forth three such congregations.[60] That was only a start. According to the conference's historian, 1956-1972 was a time when "establishing new churches [took] priority." In those sixteen years the conference began sixteen more new congregations, mostly in cities of medium or larger size.[61]

At the eastern end of the continent in the postwar years, the MCs' Lancaster Conference continued time-honored traditions of church extension. Like other MC district bodies, the conference pursued a strategy of "colonization," that is, having several families move into a given community. The communities might be close to or more distant from the Lancaster heartland. Usually they were smaller towns, yet the Lancastrians went also to New York City. Already in the 1940s young people had been active in urban tract distribution, street meetings, and raising money to support city missions. In 1949, in New York City, a Lancaster-sponsored congregation began whose start was in literature distribution dating back to 1943. By 1960 the Lancastrians had begun four more congregations, small ones to be sure, in the New York City area.[62]

New York City was only the beginning. Between 1951 and 1963 the Lancaster Conference began three new congregations in Harrisburg. By 1952 street meetings which its people had begun in Baltimore in 1949 developed into another congregation. I-W service by Lancaster Conference young people brought the formation of congregations in Boston, Massachusetts; New Haven, Connecticut; and Portland, Maine. Traditional evangelism plus I-W service produced two congregations in the Washington, D.C., area.

Between 1934 and 1980 the Lancaster Conference started more than 150 new congregations. Not all of them survived, but the number testifies to a strong commitment to church planting and the fact that a culturally conservative conference was able to reach people often thought to be difficult to bring into Mennonite circles. A. Grace Wenger, historian of the conference and its mission board, correlated the church planting with efforts also to connect the church more directly to the needs of the urban poor. The soil for some of the new congregations was daycare centers, Headstart programs, and other efforts for preschool children. No doubt the turn to cities made it easier to see such needs.[63]

If the new, more urban strategies of church planting reflected Mennonite migration and the needs of the city, they also reflected currents that were running in Mennonite theology. In a history of GC home missions, Lois Barrett has astutely observed that as their mid-twentieth-century historical renaissance helped Mennonites discover their own urban beginnings, they found it easier to think of the city as an appropriate arena for their witness.[64]

MENNONITES AND ANABAPTISM

Amidst all of these competing theological movements and loyalties, the scholars who gathered at Goshen in May 1949 to discuss Anabaptist theology hoped that focusing on Anabaptism's theological center would also provide new focus for Mennonite denominations. A second meeting which brought the faculties of the GCs' Mennonite Biblical Seminary in Chicago and the MCs' seminary at Goshen together for about the same purpose took place in April 1950, at the Mennonite Biblical Seminary.

Already in the opening address of the Goshen conference, Bethel College historian Cornelius Krahn foretold the nature of the coming discussions. He said the pervasive theme or *leitmotiv* of Anabaptism had centered around the "ecclesia—the church or the body of believers." That concept was to Anabaptism what "faith alone" was to Lutheranism and the sovereignty of God to Calvinism. "Anabaptist theology," said Krahn, "is *ecclesiocentric.*" Whatever their truth for sixteenth-century Anabaptism, his words spoke to a twentieth-century church in rapid social change. "In our individualistic age," Krahn said, Anabaptism's emphasis on the church body "has been somewhat neglected."[65]

What followed in both gatherings were variations on that theme. Robert Friedmann emphasized Anabaptism's new kind of order and discipline, using concepts such as discipleship, obedience, *Gemeinde* or brotherhood, and concrete Christianity. He presented the Anabaptists as having been preoccupied with the gospel's social aspects, or the idea that "there is no way to God without the brother." Anabaptists' aim, he said, had been "restitution of the eternal order of God's kingdom—as far as this is possible for frail human beings."[66]

Harold S. Bender made the case that the church and discipleship were inextricably linked. He argued further that Anabaptist discipleship was different from that of a Thomas à Kempis, who had not made enough critique of the existing social order, or that of Reformation Spiritualists, who had seen the need for a new kind of organization but had shrunk from its implementation.[67] Erland Waltner emphasized an Anabaptist ecclesiological revolution that had made the church a visible and voluntary body with entrance requirements different from those in the state-church tradition.[68]

Alongside the search for a clearer definitions of Anabaptist theology came changes in most Mennonites' congregational and conference structures. Among the MCs, already in 1948, a Reorganization Study Committee was moving the church toward a more bureaucratic, hierarchical, and concentrated organization. The Committee proposed a General Council for the denomination through which "all reports, recommendations, and problems" would pass before going to the MCs' general conference. In that council the executive, composed of elected members rather than of bishops, would streamline administrative matters. Very likely, district conferences would lose some autonomy.[69] A half-decade later, by 1955 and 1956, the smaller Conservative Mennonite Church moved to enlarge and elect its executive committee.[70]

The "recovery" of Anabaptism raised ideals about church which in turn posed many questions about congregational structures and conference polities. Mennonites found themselves caught with an ideology of a "brotherhood" church radically different from the same Protestant neighbors whose church forms and appearances they were borrowing. Hence, disjunctions. Even while they affirmed the essential unity of clergy and laity, progressive Mennonite groups were moving toward professional clergies. Even while they affirmed the principle of congregational autonomy, they continued building church bureaucracies. And fearing sectarianism, they cautiously entered into ecumenical relationships. More than usual the tensions, which Mennonite sociologist Leland Harder termed "disequilibrium" (between mission and separation and between activism and withdrawal), required careful thought.[71] Two questions stood out: first, the role and place of the church as a visible entity in the world; second, how to structure both congregations and conferences.

The typical forum for theologizing about such issues became the churchwide study conference. Between 1953 and 1961 the GCs' binational general conference sponsored five such meetings, and the Mennonite Brethren staged three binational ones (1956, 1958, 1959). Regional conferences and church agencies also sponsored study conferences. For instance, in 1955 the Ministerial Committee of the MC denomination sponsored a Study Conference on Church Organization and Administration. After surveying some regional conferences, John L. Horst, ordained minister of the main MC congregation at Scottdale, Pennsylvania, summarized his church's changing trends: (1) greater role for the laity in conference governance; (2) more precise definition of objectives and use of executive committees; (3) transfer of bishop functions to ministers or the appointment of a bishop for each congregation—both patterns implying greater autonomy for the congregation and less bishop power; (4) movement toward one salaried, seminary-trained minister.[72]

But despite general agreement on congregational authority and on equality of laity and clergy, the meanings of such principles needed interpretation. Goshen seminary teacher Howard Charles concluded that in the New Testament church "the pattern of organization . . . was not uniform."[73] Nor did sociologist Paul Peachey find a uniform pattern in Mennonite church organization through history. Anabaptists, he pointed out, had taught that the "church is not dependent for her essential existence on a continuity of external organization." It was the Catholic tradition which had confused "external form and the inner essence."[74]

Both Charles and Peachey spoke of inner essence, but of course such talk did not answer questions of how the church perpetuates itself in visible, social form. Peachey thought that clearly sixteenth-century Swiss and Dutch Anabaptists had "consistently thought in congregational terms."[75] He believed that, for Mennonites, building central institutions signaled loss of vitality. The institutions might appear "to stabilize church life" for a time, but they would not "stem the tide of spiritual decline";[76] paradoxically, they only accelerated the drift.[77]

Meanwhile, among the MBs a Board of Reference and Counsel report in 1951 addressed similar concerns. But unlike Peachey, the Board thought a hierarchical system might combat encroaching pluralism and an erosion of solidarity. Formerly in MB polity both congregational and denominational leaders emerged from *within* congregations. Now a newer system of recruiting pastors from professional training schools often concentrated leadership in persons who were really outsiders to the congregations. Moreover, in 1951 the MB general conference noted that its pastors were being trained in many different seminaries and Bible institutes—Lutheran, Baptist, Pentecostal, Presbyterian, and interdenominational.[78]

The new pastoral system and the strong tradition of congregational autonomy introduced a new pluralism that threatened an equally strong sense of "brotherhood" which implied authority and consensus in the wider church. The Board of Reference and Counsel's strategy for retaining the wider consensus was a recommendation to create a churchwide Board of Elders to safeguard doctrine and polity.[79] Such a board should have more than only advisory powers. The 1951 general conference submitted that far-reaching proposal to the regional conferences, and they all rejected it. In other culturally-adapting Mennonite conferences, similar attempts to renew Mennonite separatism through revitalized structures of authority would also prove difficult.

Among GC Mennonites a 1955 Study Conference on the Believers' Church addressed similar issues. With their strong tradition of rejecting formalized and controlled religious culture and insisting instead on a radical congregationalism, GCs had earlier negotiated some of the changes now in progress among other Mennonite denominations. For instance, already in the 1940s GCs had largely shifted from multiple, lay pastors to the single, paid pastor, whereas MCs and MBs were doing so in the 1950s and 1960s. But in the process of adapting, old truths had become blurred. Defining the tasks of the conference, Elmer Ediger, then the administrator of Prairie View Hospital, thought it necessary to go back to the basic distinctions between a "believers church" and a *volkskirche*. While Ediger thought some "strong brotherhood characteristics" still survived and were evidence of believers church, there were also "wholesale deviations."[80]

Others thought that one of the main deviations was the erosion of discipline in the life of both congregation and conference. Addressing the conference, church historian Cornelius (C. J.) Dyck reflected on a variety of factors which had undermined discipline in some parts of the church, but none more significantly than the emphasis on individualism.[81]

Meanwhile the GCs balanced their calls for more "brotherhood" with equally strong calls for congregational autonomy. Bethel College president E. G. Kaufman, ever the defender of the GCs' progressive tradition, insisted that the newer theologies should not undermine autonomy and localism.[82]

In one way or another, most of the 1950s-era study conferences had official approval from their denominations. A forum that had no formal standing but profoundly influenced all of the discussions about the place of the church in the world were the meetings and writings of what came to be known as the "Concern" movement (a label which came from the name of a pamphlet series the movement produced). In April 1952, in Amsterdam, Holland, seven young American Mennonite intellectuals—Irvin B. Horst, John W. Miller, Paul Peachey, Calvin Redekop, David A. Shank, Orley Swartzentruber, and John Howard Yoder—met for a two-week theological retreat. They were mainly MCs and all were graduates of either Goshen or Eastern Mennonite College. More to the point, they were a new generation. Eventually all would take up graduate study and earn doctorates.

For the moment the seven represented a generation set apart by youthful, idealistic work for the postwar social reconstruction of Europe. After their nurture in parochial Mennonite environments, their European experience brought them into direct conversation with the ideological debates of a Western culture darkened by the shadows of Auschwitz and Hiroshima.

At the retreat, the seven spent most of their time discussing the place of Mennonites in such a modern world. Common to their concerns was what Yoder later came to describe as the gap between the "Anabaptist vision and Mennonite reality."[83] Paul Peachey feared that Mennonites were taking up the Protestant Re-

First meeting of Concern group in Amsterdam, 1952. Left to right: Irvin Horst, Orley Swartzentruber, John W. Miller, Paul Peachey, David Shank, John H. Yoder, Calvin W. Redekop. Credit: John H. Yoder Collection, Archives of the Mennonite Church, Goshen, Indiana.

formers' attitudes toward the world. He defined those attitudes as "assimilative rather than prophetic, responsible rather than catalytic," and said they connected the church with the incongruities of the status quo. Now was the time to help the Christian church disentangle itself from worldly culture. Now was the moment for a fresh articulation of the Christian social ethic.[84]

John H. Yoder's contribution to the discussions—a paper entitled "The Anabaptist Dissent: The Logic of the Place of the Disciple in Society"—outlined what the Christian social ethic might be. He called on the church to be frankly sectarian; its central error, he argued, was to make itself the "guarantor of morale and cohesion for the social order."[85] The central characteristic of a sect was that it refused "to assume responsibility for the moral structure of non-Christian society."[86] Christians who assumed such responsibility made a fatal compromise, for by subordinating the love norm of ethics to a realism which presumably understood the invincibility of evil, they ended up justifying "relativism and opportunism."[87] With such an analysis Yoder was both addressing the Mennonite world and responding to the dominant strain in American Protestant ethical thought of the day—the teachings of theologian Reinhold Niebuhr.

Orley Swartzentruber's contribution to the discussion made

it clear that he did not consider the Mennonite church in North America to be the bearer of that appropriate ethic. While Anabaptism had shown an "utter disregard for the sociological unity of the corpus christianum," American Mennonitism was "a self-conscious sociological reality"—a "Corpus Mennonitarium." The change had come unconsciously, from Mennonites' conservatism and naïveté. The Mennonite church's strength lay not in theological or intellectual acumen but in its sociological institutions. But Mennonites' concern for self-preservation caused them unwittingly to generate a new corpus christianum, albeit with a Mennonite cast.[88]

A number of the Concern seven and their sympathizers were soon in some conflict with established leaders of the Mennonite church, particularly of the MC. It would be easy to suggest that the conflict was nothing more than normal tension between generations. Early in the dialogue Yoder invoked that possibility. Writing to John C. Wenger and Harold S. Bender in the summer of 1954 he alluded to the generational crisis in the MC church following World War I. But Yoder saw a difference. In the 1920s, the young leaders (many of whom also had come together in European reconstruction work) had taken the more liberal viewpoints. Now the youthful protesters were defending a historic Anabaptism against Protestant-like compromisers. The Concern group thought that much of what transpired 1925-1950 under the name of the Anabaptist renaissance had really been a "protestant orthodoxy with nonresistance and nonconformity appended."[89]

In his letter to Bender, Yoder invoked an image of sons doing battle with fathers. Pointedly, he reminded Bender that "in the process of growing up I have put together an interest in Anabaptism, which you gave me, an MCC experience to which you were instrumental in assigning me, and theological study to which you directed me." The result, Yoder insisted, was "a more logical fruition of your own convictions than you yourself realize."[90] But despite the sons-versus-fathers image, generational conflict hardly explains the Concern movement and its impact. At stake was the consuming Mennonite intellectual enterprise of the twentieth century: searching for an appropriate Mennonite response to modernity. The Concern response was an important chapter in that search.

Although the Concern movement challenged the assumptions of the institutional renaissance and the sociological recovery, it really was less important for its critique than for the new definitions it proposed. The Concern thinkers rejected a church with institutional structures dominated by top-down committees and budget controllers. In August of 1952—meeting with Orie O. Miller and other members of the Mennonite Central Committee in Europe—Yoder, Horst, Peachey, and Redekop observed how decision making was centralized and pyramided.[91] The Concern group based its institutional critique on historical and theological issues. Established leaders such as Bender tended to see institution-building as consonant with historic Mennonitism. By contrast, Concern people saw church institutions as creating a Mennonite corpus christianum.[92]

By the mid-1950s Concern writers were likening their views on institutionalism to the efforts of the Swiss Anabaptists to break with the sixteenth-century Reformer Ulrich Zwingli. In 1954 Yoder wrote that the distinctive Anabaptist position in the Reformation had not been one of doctrine, ethics, or church discipline. Those matters were only symptomatic. The real disagreement was that "the reformers were driven by the necessity . . . of managing a social ecclesiastical organization in the interests of its survival."[93]

In 1957 in a similar vein Paul Peachey suggested that MC opposition to the Concern group's anti-institutional position was like Zwinglian and Lutheran reactions to Anabaptism. "Anabaptism," he wrote, had "indeed degenerated into a denomination."[94] Such a view was ominous. If the Constantinianization of Christianity and the subsequent Mennonitization of Anabaptism were similar, then the question of how to respond was acute. The charge that there was a corpus mennonitarium required action similar to the Anabaptists' revolt against the corpus christianum.

Yet the Concern movement hardly contemplated alternatives as radical as those of the sixteenth-century Anabaptists. Rendering a prophetic witness and calling for a renewal of congregational life was different from calling for a schism. The Concern people wanted also to be ecumenical. Moreover, while articulating a sectarian theology, they rejected a sociological sectarianism.

Concern resistance to such sectarianism came partly from Paul Peachey's analysis of the original Swiss Anabaptists' strong urbanism and diversity of occupation and class. In a scholarly article in 1954, Peachey challenged earlier interpretations that suggested that from its inception Anabaptism had stood for cultural withdrawal. According to Peachey, any cultural negativism among Anabaptists had grown from their forcible exclusion rather than voluntarily.[95] Moreover, the voluntary cultural withdrawal of the twentieth century was of a different order, for now it was a new Constantinianism. It reduced free and authentic religious choice.

The Concern position invited structural integration into the larger society combined with ideological separatism. Structural pluralism created the Mennonite version of the corpus christianum. Ideological pluralism was necessary for biblical faithfulness.

ALTERNATIVE VOICES

Precisely as Concern people were articulating their answers to questions of engagement and withdrawal, other voices were offering different answers. Already in 1958 J. Lawrence Burkholder of Goshen College and soon the Harvard Divinity faculty, and Gordon Kaufman, son of E. G. and on the Vanderbilt University divinity faculty, were forceful advocates for more activist Mennonite strategies.

A 1958 *Concern* piece by Kaufman on "Nonresistance and Responsibility" suggested that Yoder's position left Mennonites removed "from . . . the deepest problems of society"[96] and therefore involved a compromise equal to that in any attempt to make the Christian ethic normative for the political order. Christians should not indulge in a *"dichotomy of condemnation"* by which they proudly distanced themselves from the world. Instead, Kaufman called for a *"dichotomy of understanding"* which recognized how much Mennonites were implicated in society's structures and which witnessed to the integrity of God's presence and unity in the world. Kaufman thought that Yoder's formula destroyed the "very unity of God."[97]

Also in 1958, J. Lawrence Burkholder submitted a doctoral dissertation at Princeton University, "The Problem of Social Responsibility from the Perspective of the Mennonite Church." For Burkholder neither the Mennonite Community movement nor the Concern group offered adequate answers. Both were romantic confusions of the kingdom of God with particular cultural expressions. Both had arisen from a "nondialectic quality of Mennonite theologizing," a quality that assumed Christ's teaching and authority were for church and not world.[98] That assumption blunted all sense of Mennonite responsibility for the world.

If the community movement had been a means for retreat, the Concern movement could be understood as a more sophisticated one. To make the gospel speak to both church and world did not mean Mennonites must sell out their cultural program. But they would have to recognize that Christians could seek the "goals of brotherhood, peace and mutuality" only under "conditions of compromise." Like it or not, Mennonites were part of the world system. Injustice and opportunistic use of power implicated them. They had better avoid "perfectionist illusions."[99]

These efforts to translate Anabaptism into a workable theology for twentieth-century Mennonites hinted at the difficulty of vesting the tradition with appropriate social meaning. Earlier, Fundamentalism and liberalism as intellectual and cultural responses to modernity had each attracted Mennonites, albeit not in the same numbers. They were responses of ossification or accommodation. Caught in the conflict between these warring systems, Mennonites found that the rediscovery of a distinctive past offered them opportunity to escape the ideological impasse.

But if the Anabaptist renaissance offered Mennonites a third-way escape from impasse, it still did not let them escape ideological conflict. Conflicting understandings about who the sixteenth-century Anabaptists had been and their meaning for twentieth-century Mennonites fractured the effort to translate the historical renaissance into twentieth-century theology.

CHAPTER
10

NEW CONSCRIPTION AND NEW FORMS
OF PEACE THEOLOGY

In November 1950 eighty-seven delegates and visitors gathered at the Westminster Hotel at Winona Lake in northern Indiana for the most representative American Mennonite peace discussions ever convened. Many years later Robert Kreider noted that "it was a little awesome seeing so many of the patriarchs of the church there together."[1] Representatives came from thirteen different denominations and sixteen institutions and organizations.

The year 1950 was an appropriate time for Mennonites to refocus their peace identity. Convening at mid-century, the Winona assembly met five years after the end of World War II and at the beginning of the Korean War and a new conscription system.

The concluding document of the conference was widely disseminated. Entitled "Declaration of Christian Faith and Commitment" and signed by sixty-two church leaders, it remained for decades the most prominent of inter-Mennonite peace statements. If the needs of the moment called forth a new document, that statement nonetheless reaffirmed more than it reformulated. More than pointing in new directions, which it scarcely did, the document consolidated a consensus. It both reaffirmed two-kingdom theology and acknowledged an "obligation to witness to the powers that be of the righteousness which God requires of all men, even in government." During the 1950s convictions about the obligation to witness would become even more prominent.[2]

But if Winona Lake looked like a consensus around established ideas for peace, the consensus was fragile at best. The year

1948 had already exposed cracks in the Mennonite peace witness. Writing in the *Gospel Herald*, Orie O. Miller, surely a key shaper of the consensus, questioned whether "our emphasis on quietism, non-activism in politics, [and] group exclusiveness, stifled among us those whom God might use in a prophetic role to governments and peoples."[3] The GC periodical *The Mennonite* revealed a persistent search for more active witness. By various means—ranging from offering instructions on how to secure information from Washington, through emphasizing the need to lay Mennonite concerns before the U.S. Congress,[4] to fostering a vigorous new debate on conscription—the discussion made clear that, politically, some Mennonites were on the move. Between June 1948 and September 1949 no fewer than seven articles appeared in *The Mennonite* on whether, whatever the nation's plan of conscription, Mennonites should move from cooperation to noncooperation.[5]

While no Mennonite conference in the late 1940s and 1950s was willing to take the radical-confrontation approach that noncooperation implied, the discussion was an omen of things to come. Amid this new spirit of political activism, Jesse Smucker, editor of *The* Mennonite, obviously harking back to an earlier age of optimism, asked his readers to remember that "salvation does not come by slow social reformation as we believed in the past generation. It comes through flashing judgments."[6]

A different kind of pressure on conscription was evident at the 1948 meeting of the MBs' general conference. The convention adopted a resolution accepting noncombatancy in the medical corps—albeit with a proviso that the church should seek to have its noncombatant members exempted from taking the military oath. The resolution was advanced by recent Russian immigrants who had done such military medical service during World War I in Russia but under Red Cross jurisdiction. In particular Benjamin B. Janz, a leader of the 1920s' immigrants to Canada, insisted adamantly that such an arrangement could be worked out with the U.S. military.[7]

A full six years later, in 1954, with the aid of MCC officials, Orlando Harms and John B. Toews conversed with various Pentagon officials in hopes of securing such an exemption. But the military's position was firm: anyone serving in the military had to take the military oath. In a quick political lesson, Toews and Harms learned the true purpose of the U.S. Medical Corps. It was, they reported at the 1954 MB general conference, "not that of saving lives." Rather it was that of "removing every obstacle which so easily is created through wounded and suffering soldiers in the pursuit of the army's assignment to destroy the enemy."[8]

On hearing the report, the convention rescinded the 1948 resolution that had accepted noncombatancy. But the damage was done. The church had legitimized a restricted form of noncombatancy. An uninformed and ill-advised resolution, the conference learned, could be interpreted by its members and government officials "as an acceptance by the Conference of . . . noncombatant service."[9]

In the years following the Winona Lake conference, other events and interests would further challenge the seemingly shared consensus. The new conscription system, the civil-rights movement, and a more ecumenical dialogue over peace theology all called into question the adequacy of the 1950 statement.

THE POSTWAR CONSCRIPTION SYSTEM: I-W

In March 1948, only a year after the last CPS men were released from World War II service, U.S. president Harry S Truman asked for another conscription system. He and his advisers thought tensions between the West and the Soviet Union over the Balkans and Central Europe plus growing fears of worldwide communist subversion required a new draft.

The officials offered a conscription bill that restricted conscientious objection only to persons who "by religious training and belief" were "opposed to participation in war in any form." However, the bill also provided for total deferment of conscientious objectors, with no requirement of alternative service. No doubt the particular formula of restriction and deferment seemed an easy way for the government to weed out a variety of objectors. On the one hand were those who based their objections on more general moral and humanitarian grounds. On the other hand were those (selective objectors) who might conscientiously object and refuse to fight in some wars but participate in others considered more just.[10]

In what is surely a Mennonite paradox, some Mennonite leaders were not sure they wanted total deferment with no need to do alternative service. For people still anxious to prove their citizenship, who had just recently begun ambitious programs of voluntary service, deferment looked too easy. Historian Perry Bush has noted that in an April 1948 meeting the MCC Peace Section concluded that it wished to "clarify our willingness to do constructive service."[11] MCC officials need not have worried. In Congress the total-deferment idea quickly died. By early 1952 it was clear that such deferment of conscientious objectors was politically unacceptable.

In 1951 Mennonite leaders agreed on objectives they wished to secure in any new conscription system and circulated the goals under the title "Guiding Principles on Alternatives to Military Service." Mennonite representatives appearing before Congress followed the document, and often even Selective Service administrators did so as well. The principles included four requests. These were (1) that a new conscription system permit clearly nonmilitary service; (2) that the new system be placed under civilian control, rather than being part of the military; (3) that the remuneration and length of service be comparable to military service; (4) that religious groups have the right to establish programs for the nonwork hours of men in alternative service.[12]

A revised conscription bill, passed in 1951, together with subsequent administrative rulings provided nearly everything MCC had asked for. The law and the rulings established what became known as the "I-W" program. ("I-W" was pronounced and often written "1-W," the "I" being a Roman numeral and "I-W" being the Selective Service classification for men working wrong. Those eligible were classified I-O until they were working as conscientious objectors). The system, agreed to by both the government and the pacifist community, allowed men whose draft boards awarded them the I–W classification to perform two years of civilian alternative service in a public or other nonprofit agency. Categories of civilian work approved included service in the U.S. in hospitals, mental hospitals, church-related organizations, and public service agencies. The categories also allowed overseas work, for instance administering relief in approving programs. A good example of approved church-related agencies, both at home and abroad, was MCC. Theoretically the local draft board had authority to place a man (the law drafted only males); in practice, however, the boards generally were happy to let draftees find their own positions. From 1952 to 1974, the years the program was in effect, approximately 15,000 Mennonite men performed I-W service.[13]

Three forms of service emerged as the dominant alternatives. They were (1) PAX Service, which took single men to overseas assignments under either MCC or the GC Mission Board, with the men given only expenses plus $10 per month of discretionary money;[14] (2) Voluntary Service, or VS, as established by MCC and various Mennonite denominational agencies (at least at first VS usually was some form of social service and it virtually always included the experience of living in a group, commonly called the "VS unit"); and (3) I-W earning service, which allowed the draftee to keep whatever wages he earned from the employing private or public agency.

In 1951 and 1952, MCC and Mennonite denominational ófficials were generally pleased with the new system. MCC expanded its VS and PAX programs and established a I-W services department. At the outset of the program, Paul Erb, editor of the MCs' *Gospel Herald*, predicted that "every I-W will be a lay evangelist, extending the front line of Christian witness."[15] A 1954 survey of Mennonite and Brethren in Christ men in I-W service found that 80 percent agreed that their situations did indeed offer "a good opportunity" for such witness.[16]

However, the degree to which the men translated opportunity into action remained a point of concern and even contention. In 1953, questions to a small sample of 30 I-W men in various places evoked widely differing responses on whether the service was "kingdom of God work."[17]

One basis for the early optimism was the percentage of young men seeking the I-W position. While there is no comprehensive draft census for the entire 1952-1974 period, available numbers all point to a substantial increase in conscientious objection compared to the years of World War II. Among GCs the difference between 1944 and 1954 was especially striking.

Percentages of GC Mennonite Men in Different Draft Categories, 1944 and 1954 (all U.S. regions)

Classification	1944 Percent & (Number)		1954 Percent & (Number)	
I-A (regular military service)	55	(1435)	42	(717)
I-AO (noncombatant military service)	18	(474)	11	(194)
IV-E or I-W (civilian alternative svc.)	27	(711)	47	(819)

Meanwhile among MCs a draft census among district conferences in 1954 showed a range from 73 percent of Illinois Conference draftees in I-W service to 96 percent or higher in districts such as Lancaster, Franconia, and some smaller ones.[18] It is not clear how much the higher overall percentage was due to more effective peace teaching, how much to a war that seemed more ambiguous and less popular than World War II, and how much to a more liberal alternative-service system, especially one that provided pay.

From late 1952, when the first COs were drafted, the number of men called up or volunteering increased rapidly. By the end of 1953 almost 5,000 men were in I-W service—3,500, or roughly 70 percent of them Mennonites and Brethren in Christ [BIC]).[19] By late 1954, with the release of the first I-W men, the numbers began to drop. By 1956 they reached a plateau of about 1,600 Mennonites and BICs.[20] By late 1953 Mennonite and BIC I-Ws were working in at least 200 different settings scattered across 16 foreign countries and 26 U.S. states and the District of Columbia.[21]

By 1957 there were approximately 1,500 agencies employing I-W men. But if the I-W people scattered, they also clustered, especially in various urban centers. An MCC census of December 1953 identified the concentrations. Some examples were Denver with 198 men; Chicago, 97; Cleveland, 142; Indianapolis, 140; Topeka, 129; Norristown, Pennsylvania, 118.[22]

With the alternatives of PAX, VS, and I-W earning service, plus the myriad of employers certified for accepting conscripts, I-W men facing service had a remarkable range of choices. But both congregations and their young men were often confused. In 1956, four years into the new draft, the GCs' Board of Christian Service, with oversight of I-W and VS programs, noted that many young people were "quite unaware" about the various alternatives. Such lack of awareness was all the more troubling because virtually every church official responsible for I-W programs wanted young men to choose VS rather than the much more individualistic and less-supervised earning service.[23] It would have been hard to find a Mennonite leader who did not hope that the young people would be attracted to the more sacrificial form of service.

By insisting that they not repeat the CPS pattern of becoming the government's agents, the churches had gained flexibility for the individual CO. But they had also vastly reduced their ability to guide and control. What emerged was in effect a two-track system. Some young men fulfilled their draft obligation on stipends similar to what CPS men had received, while others received the going wages for their kinds of work. While wage-earning service was the most popular alternative among the draft-age men, in all Mennonite groups it was the least attractive to church officials. Draftees who retained their wages had an automatic economic independence, which could become leverage for greater social and cultural freedom. In that pattern Albert Gaeddert correctly noted an absence of "that which binds a man to his church."[24]

Yet the majority—including some young men very loyal to the church—chose earning service rather than PAX or VS. An MCC census in July 1954 revealed how overwhelming was that choice.[25]

Institutional Settings of I-W Workers from
MCC-Related Churches, 1954

Setting	Percent of Total
Mental Hospitals	43.3
General Hospitals and Sanitaria	39.2
Foreign Service (PAX, etc.)	3.9
Homes for Delinquent/Retarded Children	3.4
Public Welfare (migrant and Indian work)	2.9
Schools	2.5
Old People's Homes	1.7
Dairy Herd Improvement Association	1.3
Other (including conference and church work)	1.8

Two years later a government census of 1956, covering all I-W men and not only Mennonites and Brethren in Christ, found 87 percent in mental or general hospitals, 8 percent in foreign assignments, and 5 percent working in agencies of the U.S. government.[26] Those percentages did not change much over time. About 80 percent of all who accepted I-W service worked in hospital settings for wages.

For most young men the I-W years created radical changes in the structures, routines, and locations of their lives. For many it was the transfer from village to urban America, from living in the more protected morality of the home community to living in the larger world and having to fashion one's own moral code. I-W meant freedom for self-determination. For almost all it was a period of discontinuity, both from what preceded and what would follow. It was an interim, an interval from more lasting pursuits. As such it was a convenient time for social and cultural experimentation.

The dislocation of thousands of young Mennonite men often resulted in choices and behaviors that I-W planners back in Mennonite centers such as Akron, Elkhart, Newton, and Hillsboro found wanting. Church officials' early enthusiasm quickly turned to concern. The young men were good workers on the job, but many of their independent choices for living arrangements and entertainment raised the churches' eyebrows.

At virtually every meeting in which denominational and MCC officials dealt with the I-W program there was a litany of concerns about I-W men's religious condition and interests. Phrases from a meeting in Chicago in September of 1953 echoed the litanies in many other settings:

> Some men have lost the urge for Christian service. . . . Some men are "growing" spiritually, others are not. . . . Some men are saving quite a bit of money but seem unwilling to use any for the promotion of the spiritual welfare of themselves and others. . . . Some men are not interested in hearing their home pastors. . . . Many are more interested in sports than in spiritual activities. . . . Where opportunity exists many attend Mennonite churches in the locality of their place of service, while some are attending other churches. [But] some are not going to church. . . . On the average, I-W men are not "dedicated" like voluntary service workers . . . . I-W service is "just another job" to many, while others have a real "sense of mission". . . . A few persons have come into the service with bad habits, and a few are developing bad habits since coming into service. . . . There is a general impression that "wages" is the chief concern of the larger number of men in I-W service. . . . More men should be encouraged to go into church-operated voluntary service. . . . Too many men do not have a real purpose in life."[27]

The Denver I-W Story

The entire I-W system, both strengths and weaknesses, was mirrored in Denver as well as anywhere. Sometimes referred to as the "I-W capital," Denver always had one of the largest I-W concentrations. Furthermore the men who gravitated there were as ecumenically and geographically diverse as in any I-W center. In 1956 seven different Mennonite denominations were included in the Denver I-W population.[28] As for geography, in 1959 Edgar Stoesz, MCC VS and I-W Office representative, was surprised to discover that 30 percent of the men in Denver were from east of the Mississippi—indeed that he met more men there from Lancaster County and Indiana than from Kansas and Colorado.[29]

Much earlier, by the summer of 1953, more than 200 I-W men had found their way to Denver. Eight hospitals and sanitariums

Mennonite Church and Mennonite Brethren I-W basketball teams in Denver, c. 1958. Credit: Wallace Goertzen, Henderson, Nebraska.

plus various other kinds of institutions employed them. Rose Memorial Hospital was the largest single employer of I-Ws, with 83. While the numbers in Denver dipped in the late 1950s they climbed again to nearly 250 by 1964; and in the late 1960s, during the height (or depth) of the Vietnam draft calls, there were more than 300 I-W men in Denver with MCC connections: 152 MCs; 48 from the Church of God in Christ, Mennonite (or Holdemans); 48 GCs; 44 Old Order Amish; 16 MBs; 13 Beachy Amish; 6 Conservative Mennonites; and a smattering of others.[30]

What attracted the men to Denver? Perhaps it was the relatively high wages and the recreational possibilities of the mile-high city. No doubt for Easterners some other attractions were that it was near the mountains and far from home. In any case, for church officials trying to maintain church standards the problems of the "Denver Marines," as they were often dubbed, seemed greater than just about anywhere else.

A 1958 report on the Denver unit by two denominational officials, Dwight Wiebe of the MBs and Arlo Kasper of the GCs, tallied 58 out of 130 Mennonite I-W men attending church at least half their Sundays off duty.[31] After MCC's Edgar Stoesz visited Denver a year later, he reported that 50 percent of the men were responsive to the church program—but "the other 50 percent are obviously using I-W as a time to get away from home at best and some to actually run from the church." He asked, "Can we afford to allow this to continue?"[32]

Visiting the same year, 1959, GC leaders Albert Gaeddert, H. B. Schmidt, and Fred Unruh decided that the most pressing problem was not the "minority of strongly negative men" but rather a greater number who were "indifferent, unchallenged, and poorly motivated." The men were meeting a government obligation, the GC leaders observed, "but in no way [did the men] give witness in their work or life of a real love for humanity."[33]

According to the three GC leaders, the problem seemed to grow from the ease with which Mennonite draftees could secure CO status. Under the current system, they were getting that status without being able "to give even a reasonably good" answer as to why they were in service.[34] A different delegation who visited in 1959—Bishop John E. Lapp of the Franconia Conference and Esko Loewen, a former CPSer who was now a GC minister in Kansas—repeated a claim from a minister-member of the Denver I-W Council: "Up to 75 percent of the I-Ws fail to have a basic understanding of what their position means." And, said their report, that was true regardless of which Mennonite groups the men came from.[35]

Local Mennonite pastors gave contradictory assessments about the religiosity of the area's I-W workers. According to an MCC report filed in 1960, area pastors had suggested that 50 percent of the married attended church but that probably 75 percent of the unmarried never did.[36] Yet in 1964 E. M. Yost, an MC pastor in Denver, calculated that 65 percent of the I-Ws were involved in Mennonite church activities. Furthermore Yost thought that the Denver I-W program had been "distorted" by negative attitudes coming from "those few men" who behaved badly.[37]

If the pastors gave mixed reports, so did Denver I-W workers themselves. They had their own paper, *The Denver Post-Mortem*, and some of its writers decried the easy attraction to alcohol, cheap movies, cigarettes, and other young male vices. They wondered whether the service being given was "Genuine or Counterfeit."[38] One of the men, Ralph Lehman, thought the problem was not so much a counterfeit faith as a lethargic one. Too many of those in service "passively sit back, refuse to accept unit responsibilities."[39] But another I-W man, Chester Flickinger, thought that some rebellion might refurbish their Mennonite identity. Taken back home, it could reform Mennonite views that "are a bit stereotyped and probably haven't changed much since [the] Reformation."[40]

In their frustration with I-W behavior as they perceived it, leaders in denominational offices tried to limit the numbers going to Denver.[41] They agreed that each applicant seeking placement in Denver should have his pastor's recommendation and attend four orientation sessions before being allowed to go. To enforce the agreement, the local Mennonite officials convinced Selective Service in Colorado to release the recalcitrants for transfer.

Historian Perry Bush has observed, quite correctly, that with this help from government, the I-W administrators now had a mechanism to "forcefully apply their COs to the task of Christian service whether or not the men themselves shared this motivation." However, if in their frustration local church leaders in Denver and officials in denominational offices did not see the incongruity of their position, MCC leaders did, and stopped the plan.[42]

If the Denver I-W men displeased their churches, they certainly more than pleased their employers. Virtually all work-related reports coming into MCC, whether through visiting pastors and denominational officials or more directly from hospital administrators, were highly favorable. If the Mennonite families, churches, and communities were not always instilling deep convictions against youth vices, they surely were instilling the work ethic. In 1959 a Mr. Lindee, hospital administrator at the Colorado General Hospital, told a visiting MCC delegation that in his seven years of employing hundreds of I-W workers, only one had required dismissal. It was "an exceptionally satisfactory record."[43] In 1964 Leota F. Pekrul, Personnel Officer at the University of Colorado Medical Center, observed that in her institution some departments refused to fill positions until a I-W assignee was available. She considered that the I-W workers were "unusually conscientious and . . . displayed a high degree of patient sensitivity," and that their stability and dependability were important assets to the hospital program. Whatever their lack of social restraint in the eyes of church officials, Pekrul saw them as having "a highly developed sense of responsibility." To her, they were "clean-cut, wholesome and moral young people."[44]

Around the country other I-W employers reported the same. At least in hospital settings, the I-Ws worked with diligence, sincerity, and compassion to earn the commendation of their superiors.[45] No doubt employers were effusive partly because hospitals typically paid low wages for orderlies and other menials and accordingly attracted marginal workers. In any case, judged by the perfectionist ethic of Mennonite communities, many were failing. Judged by the expectations of medical institutions they passed with high marks.

Gaining Churchly Influence

The Denver story had parallels in other units. What the stories made clear to denominational and MCC officials was that the churches should establish better control over the whole I-W system.

Control was difficult, however. A decentralized system which allowed young men to find their own employment and quickly become financially independent naturally made for autonomy. The kind of cohesive units that CPS had developed were hard to achieve. The new system, with its independent living and varied schedules, led to virtually no common meetings at some single urban location. At an MCC meeting one participant noted all too correctly that "all outward controls are fully removed. . . . We will not be able to set up another outward control system. . . . We will now need to see if we cannot help . . . [the I-W man] develop his inner discipline."[46] Even more troubling were the findings of an MCC-sponsored evaluation conference in 1957. The ease with which young men could acquire the I-W status, the conferees concluded, "may actually neutralize peace convictions."[47]

That fear, that the I-W program might actually be detrimental to the peace witness, appeared in the MCC periodical *The I-W Mirror*. Under the title "Can CO's Survive Tolerance?" John W. Miller, now a Goshen College professor, noted that so long as the CO position had "cost even a little it served by itself to screen out the carnal Christian." But now young men no longer felt the pressure to enter the military that Mennonite boys had felt in World War II. That fact, plus the financial comfort that a CO could now enjoy, made for a situation in which "Pharisaism often runs rampant." Miller feared that the situation raised "a great question mark over all the seeming advancement we have made in the past fifty years."[48] Daniel Miller, a Kansas Amishman at an August 1955 meeting of the Amish Christian Fellowship in Goshen, agreed. "Is the present I-W setup making spiritual softies out of us?" he asked. His question was rhetorical. For him and for others, the answer was clear.[49]

The favorite remedy of church officials during the entire I-W era was the pastoral visit—whether organized by local district conferences, denominational offices, or MCC. But the visits were occasional at best. And they had their own problems. Typical was an experience of William Keeney, a former CPSer, on such a visit to I-W sites in Michigan in March of 1954. Most of the I-W persons were unavailable. They had changed home addresses without notifying denominational offices, their work schedules had changed, they were away on unexpected leaves, or they had little interest in visiting with a Mennonite representative. With those whom he saw, "the contact . . . was rather superficial." His conclusion: "One is again impressed by the individuality and isolation of this service."[50]

If I-W men were to have discipline, it had to be inner. By the mid-1950s the MCs in particular were persuaded that nurturing such inner discipline would happen best on a denominational basis rather than through MCC's inter-Mennonite program. Largely at the initiative of the MCs' Mennonite Relief and Service Committee (MRSC), discussions began for less-centralized administration. The idea was to link the I-W workers into specific congregations, into a city's VS units, and into specific district and denominational missions and young people's or women's organizations. Such ties, MRSC believed, offered the best hope for increasing I-W people's loyalty to church standards. MCC might still be responsible for discussion with government and it might still have a I-W Coordination Committee composed of denominational representatives. It might still perform various services for smaller denominations. What actually emerged, however, was not exactly what MRSC proposed. Instead, for the most part, MRSC assumed responsibility for MC men and women and MCC worked with the rest.[51] More decentralization did come in 1960 when MCC transferred coordination responsibility from itself to that I-W Coordinating Committee. Now each denomination was clearly responsible for its own program.

Already by 1956 MC leaders thought decentralization had brought improvement. As staff for the MCs' Peace Problems Committee, Paul Peachey visited numerous units that summer and found the effect "wholesome." A 1957 MC study said that decentralization was offering "psychological advantages."[52] However, in 1962 the GCs' general conference observed that nothing much had changed. Delegates of differing kinds expressed unease about the I-W men's peace witness. Was it "really the kind of alternative to military service we want it to be, and that it ought to be?"[53]

Decentralization or not, the problems seen by church leaders would not go away. In 1967 Wilfred J. Unruh, staff member for the GC Board of Christian Service, virtually read I-W earning service out of the church's peace witness. It might fulfill the draft obligation, but it lacked essential elements of the church's peace witness. Besides a lack of church control, the system's minimal requirement of forty hours of service per week stood in contrast to the timeless quality of peace and witness service. And the financial benefit from earning service violated still another essential element of a peace witness. In response to Unruh's evaluation, the GC Board adopted the position that although I-W earning service was legitimate as government service, it could no longer receive church support.[54]

In 1970 the inter-Mennonite I-W Coordinating Board formally disbanded.[55] Similarly in 1971 the Mennonite Church (MC) folded its remaining I-W administrative structure.[56] While the draft continued to 1974, such disbanding was de facto withdrawal of inter-Mennonite support for the I-W system.

Conservative Groups and I-W Service

Some of the conservative groups—particularly the Church of God in Christ, Mennonite (the so-called Holdeman church) and the Old Order Amish—navigated differently than the progressive churches through the perils of I-W. The Holdemans did so partly by limiting their young men to a few locations. In 1960 they had nearly 100 men in I-W service, all at six places.

The church made the choices, and did so with care. For example, while most Holdeman members lived in the western half of the country, Grove State Hospital at Catonsville, Maryland, became one of their important I-W centers. A Holdeman minister had worked there during CPS service. As conscription revived, he renewed contact with the hospital and began recruiting Holdeman young men. The church rented "The Junction," a rooming house that both accommodated up to twenty Holdeman young men and had a meeting room for their religious services. And it provided a continual pastoral presence. Rotating ministers came and each spent about six weeks with the unit. The Holdeman denomination used that plan in all its I-W centers.[57] As MCC and I-W Coordinating Committee representatives visited various units, they invariably had favorable comments on the piety and the strength of witness of some of the conservative groups' units—Holdeman, Beachy Amish, and Conservative Mennonite.[58]

As for the Old Order Amish, few if any previous events in American history brought them the kind of structural change I-W did. In 1966 they formed what later took the name "Old Order Amish Steering Committee." Initially made up of Indiana Amish bishops meeting on October 20, 1966, at the Graber School building in Allen County near Fort Wayne, the group soon included bishops from other regions and became a national organization. The problem which evoked such organization as the Amish elders described it, was that their people "were following too closely in the steps of the Mennonites which is undermining our Amish way of life."[59]

Like their more liberal cousins, the Amish had generally accepted the current conscription system, and their young had gone off dutifully to the same sites as other I-W men. However, some Amish called for refusal to cooperate with the I-W system. In late 1953 and early 1954 *The Budget* of Sugarcreek, Ohio (the most widely circulating newspaper for mainly Amish readers), carried on a brief discussion about the possibility of noncooperation.[60] Some argued that the entire I-W system could have been avoided had the Amish established and carried out their own system of Voluntary Service following World War II.[61] Andrew S. Kinsinger, first chairman of the Steering Committee, saw the irony of a people who would not let their children attend high schools now sending their sons to alternative service in faraway cities.[62]

Even more than other MCC-related youth, Amish young men went into hospital service, for pay. In an Amish listing of October 1953 and January-February 1954, 368 of 370 Amishmen were in such work. The other two were in VS.[63] Unfortunately, before long the bishops concluded that although their young men went into service with "good intentions," they had too much "idol time" (*sic*) and became "involved with amusements" and with "nurses or in other ways were led astray." So when a man's term of service was over, he might be either married to an "outsider" or otherwise not inclined to return to his Amish community.[64]

In response, Amish leaders moved on several fronts. Pathway Publishers, an Amish publishing house in Ontario, initiated a monthly periodical called the *Ambassador of Peace*, to nurture the I-W men's nonresistant faith.[65] More significantly, the leaders requested Selective Service to let Amish young men fulfill their two years of service on specially operated farms in Amish communities, provided the draftee was opposed to engaging in "public works" and was in good standing with his congregation. Meeting with Selective Service Director Hershey on February 8, 1967, the Amish leaders found him thinking of ordinary farm deferments rather than the specially run farms. Hershey even promised to make a careful review of farm deferment requests which local draft boards rejected.[66] No doubt the ability of the Amish to work out a private understanding reflected Hershey's longtime fascination with the plain peoples' integrity. In a somewhat improbable relationship, committee chairman Kinsinger later remarked that he "became rather fond of" General Hershey.[67]

On their side the Amish tried to safeguard their new and fragile understanding with Hershey. They requested farm deferment only for young men whose lives were impeccable; indeed, they found it prudent to restrict the request only to those who had never worked in small factories or shops. Requesting a farm deferment for one who claimed in principle to be opposed to "public works" only to find that he had a record of off-farm work would be embarrassing.[68]

Moreover, the farm deferments were only a temporary solution. Over the next year the Amish and Selective Service negotiated a more permanent plan. An Amish farmer agreeing to hire a I–W man would legally turn over his farm to the Steering Committee for the duration of the CO's employment. The "Church Farms" would then be the kind of agencies Selective Service could legally approve to hire I-W men. In essence the solution was like an Amish proposal at the outset to set up a special Amish "agricultural service." At any given time up to about 100 Amish young men worked under the plan, thus fulfilling their draft obligation under the direction of the Steering Committee.[69]

Assessing the I-W Experience

The behavioral problems of I-W became an easy focus for denominational officials. To be sure there were problems with maintaining church regulations. But a larger problem of postwar stresses on traditional Mennonite understandings and behavior easily found focus on the I-W men. During the 1950s urbanization, geographical dispersion, changes in church practices, and altered meanings of the doctrine and practice of nonconformity were all underway in the American Mennonite world. In some ways these changes were only most evident in the I-W units. As it detached young people from traditional communities, often by locating them in new urban environments, the I-W program naturally became the focus of concern and discussion among church leaders who sensed the shifting ground.

Some observers were not so quick to indict the I-W people but focused on home congregations. In the late 1950s one unidentified I-W man wrote to MCC that "I am getting tired of the church pointing its fingers at I-W. Everything you see in I-W you see in the home churches. . . . To attempt to deal with the I-W problem without regard to its source is like . . . smashing the thermometer if you don't like the temperature."[70] Paul Holdeman, Western Area I-W Director for the Church of God in Christ, Mennonite, thought much the same. He reflected that during CPS it had been easy to hold the government responsible for the shortcomings of the system. But the I-W program showed whether Mennonites had "taught 'The Way' first in the structure of the home and then in the structure of the church."[71] Joseph Stoll, editor of an Amish educational journal and a frequent writer in the *Ambassador of Peace*, concurred. He thought the behavioral problems were the result of the sponsoring churches' neglect. Such neglect now carried a high "price tag."[72]

The church was culpable. Visiting at a meeting of the GC Board of Christian Service in 1958, six years into the I-W program, MB I-W Coordinator Dwight Wiebe lamented that the churches had not made clear what they expected of I-W service. Only 70 percent of all Mennonite pastors reported the names of men in service to conference offices. Ties between men in service and existing church programs remained marginal at best. H. B. Schmidt, a GC I-W coordinator, concurred. The "weakest link," he said, was orientation.[73]

In fact, even more was at stake. Raymond Wilson, a Quaker leader, said that the Korean War had "crept up" on the pacifist community.[74] Coming so soon on the heels of World War II, it had found a pacifist community generally unprepared. Zelle Larson, historian of conscientious objection in the early 1950s, has corroborated that view. "Some pacifists were tired after five years of wartime exertions," he has written. "Others coming out of Civilian Public Service camps and prisons were busy reestablishing their 'civilian' lives."[75]

Maybe Mennonites were among the tired. Perhaps any generation can only supervise one project as stupendous as CPS. In any case the Mennonite churches were not willing to be involved as they had been in CPS.[76] They did not commit the same large resources. As unwelcome stepchildren, men in I-W earning service (the overwhelming majority in I-W) never found the favor with church officials that CPS men had enjoyed and VS people now had. One mother wrote the MCs' I-W office asking, but also nudging, "Are not the boys in I-W earning service worth as much attention as those in VS?"[77] While every church official would have answered yes, in reality those in earning service were not the favorites.

If the church was tired and turning to other interests, the system as designed by the government also rendered the church irrelevant. Each young man facing conscription was free to negotiate his own placement. It was an exceedingly comfortable plan for people seeking CO status. The church did not need to protect the rights of conscientious objectors, so the decisions were left to the young more than under previous conscription systems.[78]

MENNONITES AND THE CIVIL-RIGHTS MOVEMENT

Although often preoccupied with their own status and problems, Mennonites were not wholly strangers to the concerns and struggles of others, including African-Americans and other racial minorities. The historic U.S. Supreme Court ruling for integration of schools, *Brown* v. *Board of Education of Topeka, Kansas* (1954), began a new phase of the modern civil-rights movement.

A history of Mennonite missions among American Native peoples dates back to the 1880s when the GCs began contact with the Arapaho and the 1890s when the MBs began working among the Comanche.[79] Mennonite work with Hispanic groups began substantially later. The first Hispanic congregation—the Lawndale Mennonite Church (MC)—began in 1934 in the Chicago area. Mennonite Brethren began working at Mission, Texas, in 1937.[80]

Contact between Mennonites and African-Americans began in the colonial period and was most persistent in the Shenandoah Valley of Virginia, where Mennonites in the eighteenth century planted communities in an area with some slaves. Virginia Mennonites offered at least a mild witness against slaveholding at least as early as writings by Peter Burkholder (1783-1846), a bishop and the first prominent leader of the settlement. And during the nineteenth century, Mennonites did not divide over slavery as did many denominations.[81]

While Virginia Mennonites began mission work among mountain-dwelling whites much earlier, during the 1930s they be-

Martin Luther King Jr. at Goshen College, 1960. Left to right: Willard H. Smith, Guy F. Hershberger, King. Credit: *Elkhart* (Indiana) *Truth,* courtesy of Archives of the Mennonite Church, Goshen, Indiana.

gan religious work among the local African-American population. Other district conferences had begun earlier. Seemingly the earliest African-American members of a Mennonite congregation were Robert and Mary Elizabeth Carter and son Cloyd, who joined the Lauver Mennonite Church (MC) at Cocolamus in Juniata County, Pennsylvania, in 1897. In the Lancaster area the first African-American accepted into a Mennonite congregation was in 1917. In 1938 MC Mennonites opened a mission for African-Americans in nearby Reading. The earliest attempt to establish an African-American Mennonite congregation began in 1886 when the Krimmer Mennonite Brethren opened a mission work in Elk Park, North Carolina. African-American congregations among other Mennonites emerged only after World War II.[82]

The long efforts notwithstanding, the number of African-American Mennonites remained small. As the civil-rights movement began there were roughly 150 African-American Mennonites in North Carolina and 200 in thirteen MC congregations scattered from Pennsylvania to California.[83]

It was hardly the numbers in their own congregations that captivated some Mennonites' interest in the civil-rights movement. Rather, it was mainly Martin Luther King's theology and strategy of nonviolence. Here was a social movement that embodied qualities close to Mennonite thinking. In fact King frequently used language somewhat like Mennonite discourse on nonresistance:

> Agape is not a weak, passive love. It is love in action. Agape is love seeking to preserve and create community. . . . Agape is a willingness to sacrifice in the interests of mutuality. Agape . . . doesn't stop at the first mile, but it goes the second mile to restore community. It is a willingness to forgive, not seven times but seventy times seven to restore community.[84]

With the language of "agape," "love," "community," "sacrifice," "second mile," and "forgive," it is no surprise that Mennonites were soon visiting the South to dialogue with King and to look closely at the work of his organization, the Southern Christian Leadership Conference (SCLC). MCC Peace Section sponsored study visits to the South in 1956, 1957, 1958, and 1960. During those years Guy F. Hershberger attended some executive meetings of the SCLC. In 1961 MCC began a VS unit in Atlanta to work toward racial reconciliation.[85] Various denominational agencies also sent delegations out to study. Invariably their reports encouraged Mennonites to identify with the civil-rights movement. Following a 1957 visit, Paul Peachey reported to *Gospel Herald* readers that while the movement had been influenced by Gandhi, "the motivation is the intense Christian faith of the Negroes themselves. The leaders are the ministers. The rallying places are the churches and the strategy conferences are the prayer meetings."[86]

Three years later Hershberger offered a similar assessment of King. "However much we find it necessary to disagree with him on points of theology (and this we must do), he must nevertheless be recognized as a Christian pacifist who sincerely seeks to follow Christ."[87]

The first official response to the new racial awareness was a statement "The Way of Christian Love in Race Relations" adopted by the Mennonite Church in 1955. The statement, originally drafted by Hershberger for a Christian Race Relations Conference held earlier that year, linked Christian nonresistance with current racial struggles. "To refuse participation in warfare demands that Christians likewise rise above the practices of discrimination and coercion in other areas, such as race relations."[88] Ervin Stutzman,

Voluntary Service workers at Gulfport, Mississippi, 1946. Credit: Mennonite
Library and Archives, Bethel College, North Newton, Kansas.

who has recently interpreted the evolution of MC peace theology
and practice, correctly observed that strategically the linkage
"provided a strong impetus toward Mennonite social activism."[89]

That linkage was perhaps most visible at a GC VS unit in Gulf-
port, Mississippi. In the spring of 1945, with World War II ending,
MCC opened a new CPS public health unit just outside North Gulf-
port, an incorporated community mainly of poor blacks next to
Gulfport, which was white and segregated. In late 1946 the unit,
first known as Camp Bernard, later Camp Landon, became the
MCC's first postwar VS project. In 1953 responsibility passed from
MCC to the GCs.

From its inception the small CPS and VS community worked
to provide recreational facilities, social programs, and religious instruction for both African-Americans and whites. In the early
years Orlo Kaufman, one of the long-term volunteers, hoped they
could maintain a balance between the two races and that "slowly
steps be taken to bring about better understanding and mutual
concern through some form of interracial meetings."[90] But working with both groups soon proved untenable, so the work with
whites ended. In the words of David Haury, author of a history of

Mennonite work at Gulfport, "the segregated South had . . . produced a segregated Voluntary Service Unit."[91]

In many parts of the South, the informal defense of segregation became ever more vigilant following the 1954 Supreme Court decision. VSers known for their friendship with African-Americans became objects of public scorn, were denied services, and even received threats. In 1968 Camp Landon received a bomb threat for hosting an integrated dinner promoting the preschool program Headstart. Still the VSers continued to press their work of crossing the racial barriers and seeking racial reconciliation. After a Camp Landon choral group sang in both the African-American and the white wards of the local hospital, one observer noted, "They are Mennonites. They don't draw any race lines."[92] It was an example of what Haury called the unit's "quiet demonstration" at Gulfport. With time the workers won grudging community favor and support. Never in the headlines, and largely free from the activism and demonstrations occurring in much of the South, Camp Landon remained a "presence and witness" throughout the turbulent 1950s and '60s.[93]

A situation that made perhaps the greatest impact of any on Mennonite thinking about the civil-rights movement was a community that emerged around the Mennonite Biblical Seminary between 1945 and 1958, when the seminary was situated in Woodlawn, a south-side Chicago neighborhood near the University of Chicago. Already in the late 1940s a biracial Mennonite congregation had developed; now, along with its neighborhood, the congregation became more African-American.

A host of young academics and spouses, many headed for leadership in the church, attended either the seminary or the nearby university and received a firsthand education about America's racial stresses. Some examples: Leo Driedger, Cornelius J. Dyck, Delton and Marian Franz, Leland and Bertha Fast Harder, J. Howard Kauffman, Robert Kreider, Elmer Neufeld, Betty Jean Pannabecker, Calvin Redekop, and Leola Schulz.[94]

On more than one occasion the GC Board of Christian Service, led partly by people with Chicago experience, asked what the civil-rights movement might mean for traditional Mennonite nonresistance. As early as 1957 it inquired, "Are nonresistance and nonviolence (as witnessed in the South today) basically opposed?"[95] A year later they felt "a tension . . . in carrying out responsibilities as Christian citizens." The tension revolved around the question of "how passive is nonresistance? Does nonviolence connote a 'pushy political strategy' for the sake of one's own cause? What positive forms can Christian nonresistance take?"[96]

In the late 1950s Vincent Harding, a young African-American pursuing a Ph.D. in American history at the University of Chicago, joined the congregation and became an associate pastor. He was a most eloquent speaker and writer with the tone of a strong but gentle prophet. Before long he and his wife, Rosemarie, an African-American Goshen College graduate, became the point persons for Mennonites on racial issues. "The expert, Vincent Harding" was what Guy F. Hershberger came to call him.[97] His counsel was sought; his impassioned speeches drew response. In 1961 the Hardings opened an MCC VS unit in Atlanta.

Harding was drawn to Mennonites because they seemed potentially to have all of the right stuff for the civil-rights struggle. With their tradition of VS and the underused men in I-W service, and increasingly with congregations in major urban centers, the Mennonites, he thought, were well poised for the work.[98] In 1959 at a "Mennonite Seminar on Race Relations" at Woodlawn, he asked: If the attendees were "ministers of reconciliation," then "dare we ask what our task is. . . ? We are peacemakers, do we dare ask what our task is?" His answer was just as forthright: "It is to go into the midst of the battle." But Harding knew that Mennonites were tempted to make nonresistance "synonymous with sitting on our hands and closing our eyes and turning our backs on injustice and hatred and violence among men."[99]

In 1959 Harding also remarked that the "still prevalent idea of a culturally chosen Mennonite people has been as deeply prejudicial and divisive in our lives as any racial segregation and bias."[100] That indictment was much like one Paul Peachey had expressed in 1955, at the first major Mennonite gathering to discuss racial questions—a conference on "Christian Race Relations" sponsored by the MCs' Committee on Economic and Social Relations, held at Goshen, Indiana. Mennonites, said Peachey, still had a strong "we-consciousness"; therefore they had "successfully . . . resisted the 'melting-pot' process of Americanization" and retained European cultural and nationality characteristics. Such strong sense of particularity, Peachey suggested, seemed to leave Mennonites poorly suited to help either the American majority or African-Americans to move toward integration.[101]

Later the advocates of a broader cultural pluralism would argue just the opposite—that a sense of particularity might foster a more diverse and pluralistic American culture. But in the 1950s

Mennonites tended to see their marginality as a handicap rather than an asset for breaking down discrimination.

By 1967 Vincent Harding, then a professor at Spellman College in Atlanta, seemed to put less hope in Mennonites. In a riveting address to the 1967 Mennonite World Conference in Amsterdam, Holland, he called on them to hear the voices pleading for revolutionary action to end injustice. Mennonites had a long history of "seeking justice for ourselves" but often they had cared "very little about the worlds of color and revolution" and the cries from those worlds for justice. Even now, Mennonites were participating in the "violence of the status quo." Harding's message was a dramatic call for the peace people to rethink the limits and relevance of their ideal for revolutionary times.[102]

REASSESSING NONRESISTANCE

If in his 1967 World Conference address Harding called for reassessment of Mennonite nonresistance and a search for active peacemaking, that reassessment had in fact been underway for some time. Remembering the compromises of World War II, troubled by the I-W system, feeling the agony of African-Americans, and conversing in more ecumenical circles, some leading Mennonites already in the 1950s were busy rethinking old habits and thinking in new ways about peacemaking and about their relationships to American culture.

One of the major rethinkers was J. Lawrence Burkholder. He had grown up in the Lancaster Conference (MC) but somewhat peripherally, living outside its main area and being son of a professor in a small non-Mennonite college. Thereafter he attended Goshen College and the Lutheran Theological Seminary at Gettysburg, Pennsylvania, pastored a small Mennonite congregation in upstate New York, and served in China under Mennonite agencies and as a relief administrator for the United Nations. Then in the 1950s Burkholder studied at the Princeton Theological Seminary. He was especially impressed with the ethical dilemmas of wielding power in a situation such as China's and with Niebuhrian ethics at Princeton. His various experiences instilled doubt about the adequacy of the Mennonite sectarian and absolutist ethic. So by 1958 Burkholder was calling for Mennonites to extend their doctrine of the lordship of Christ from the boundaries of the church to include the world.[103]

For too long, Burkholder argued, Mennonites' social ethics

had been circumscribed by the boundaries of their small sectarian world. Christian ethics needed to take into account the responsibility of the church to the world as well as to itself. In so doing it could not accept the perfectionism of pure agape love, but would have to settle for a different standard, justice. To pursue social justice, Burkholder called for more engagement and less fear of the compromises that working in the world inevitably brings. The way of traditional Mennonite nonresistance was too disengaged to serve well as a comprehensive ethical norm.[104]

Such a turn in Mennonite ethics did not suit Burkholder's old Goshen College teachers Guy F. Hershberger and Harold S. Bender. In a display of their own kind of power, they blocked the usual channels for publishing a Mennonite dissertation. As Burkholder later wrote,

> At that time Mennonite scholars were busy articulating a sectarian ethic for the Mennonite community. Social idealism seldom reached beyond church sponsored relief work. Furthermore, justice was given no place in the Mennonite glossary. Non-violent resistance was considered "unbiblical." Hence I was reproved and the typed thesis, having been rejected for publication, turned brown in the dusty shelves of libraries.[105]

For a few years Burkholder did teach at Goshen College, but not surprisingly he left in 1960 for a professorship at Harvard Divinity School. Then in 1971 he returned to Goshen College as its president. Finally in 1989 a research agency connected with the joint MC-GC Associated Mennonite Biblical Seminaries published his dissertation.[106]

That Hershberger was not prepared in 1958 to endorse Burkholder is not surprising. That same year Herald Press published *The Way of the Cross in Human Relations*—Hershberger's most comprehensive statement on Mennonite nonresistance since the 1944 publication of his classic *War, Peace, and Nonresistance.* In 1958, as in the entire corpus of his writing, Hershberger was not calling for an ethic of withdrawal. He reasoned that Mennonite social ethics had social relevance. The church, which he liked to call the "colony of heaven," was a social entity. Therefore it had social significance beyond the personal ethics which fundamentalism espoused. On the other hand Hershberger believed that the church was not called to the doctrine of social responsibility which people

Mennonite delegation at the 1962 Puidoux Conference. Left to right: John H. Yoder, Gordon Kaufman, A. H. A. Bekker, H. Kossen, William Keeney. Credit: MCC Collection, Archives of the Mennonite Church, Goshen, Indiana.

like Reinhold Niebuhr and John C. Bennett, and to some extent Mennonites J. Lawrence Burkholder and Gordon Kaufman, were calling for. In Hershberger's mind, the beginning point of social-responsibility ethics was the needs of the social order. So when social problems seemed intractable, its proponents were always tempted to adjust the hard teachings of Jesus.

Instead, Christian ethics should begin with discipleship—faithfulness to Jesus. And in fact, being faithful was the Christian way to social relevance. For Hershberger, at least from 1944 on, the "curative mission" that good Christians brought to the world was its own form of engagement.[107]

If Hershberger's *The Way of the Cross in Human Relations* was a response to various challenges about the irrelevancy of a perfectionist ethic, other Mennonites also were becoming part of a dialogue with European state churches, the World Council of Churches, Reinhold Niebuhr, and other advocates of the church assuming more responsibility for society's order. That dialogue began already in the early 1950s in Europe, between the peace churches and the established churches. From 1951 to 1953 Albert Meyer, John H. Yoder, Paul Peachey, and Irvin Horst, all MCC workers in Europe, participated in preparing two documents—"War Is Contrary to the Will of God" (1951) and "Peace Is the Will of God" (1953)—which the World Council of Churches incorporated into its own documents and publications.[108]

In 1953 at an ecumenical gathering in The Netherlands on "Modern Theological Thought and the Criticism of Nonresistance," John H. Yoder, also an MCC worker in Europe and a student of Karl Barth, offered a sharp contrast between Niebuhrian and Mennonite ethics. Yoder felt that while there was much in Niebuhr that Mennonites could embrace, especially his belief in the "absolute normativeness of the law of love of the kingdom of God," there was also a fundamental problem. The starting point for Niebuhr's ethics was the human predicament; for Mennonites it was God's revelation. That made all the difference.[109]

The most concentrated dialogue between the established churches and the historic peace churches continued in what became to be known as the Puidoux Conferences. Held successively at Puidoux, Switzerland (1955); Iserlohn, Germany (1957); Bièvres, France (1960); and Oud Poelgeest, The Netherlands (1962), those conferences let Mennonite scholars interact with many church leaders from eastern and western Europe plus a scattering from other parts of the globe. The rubric of all four conferences was "The Lordship of Christ over Church and State." That title pointed in the very direction Mennonite peace theology was heading.

At the first conference Yoder read a major paper, "The Theological Basis of the Christian Witness to the State" (later enlarged and published as *The Christian Witness to the State*). While not edging away from the dualism of sectarian ethics, Yoder opened the door for greater Mennonite witness in public affairs. By no means did he adopt the posture of J. Lawrence Burkholder or Gordon Kaufman, but neither was his message one of political withdrawal. Yoder defined a duality—but a duality of response, not of orders. He argued that the moral law included even the state, and so it also was obligated to say yes to God. Still it would not say yes in the same way the church should say yes. Since the lordship of Christ extended over both realms, both could be held accountable, yet not in the same way.[110]

In America too, younger Mennonite scholars were moving Mennonites toward engagement. In 1956 the Mennonite Church (MC) held a conference on "Nonresistance and Political Responsibility," and in 1957 MCC sponsored one on "Christian Responsibility and the State."

At the 1957 conference Elmer Neufeld, then a doctoral student at the University of Chicago, paraphrased Princeton ethicist Paul Lehman, who had asked whether " 'the community of the holy' (of a select ethnic group) has [not] persisted and distorted 'the holy community,' doing so by a kind of pharisaic perfectionism."[111] Neufeld argued that whether or not Mennonites believed it, they lived in a political universe and their actions had political relevance. His was only one voice expressing a new understanding of the dynamic relations between church and state, religion and culture, the political and the nonpolitical. Categories that separated and compartmentalized also distorted. The state, politics, and culture were not necessarily in the "perfection of Christ" but neither were they outside of the reign of God. Neufeld spent the bulk of his essay defining the principles that might guide Christian responsibility in the political order.[112]

With the twin concepts "lordship of Christ" and "Christian Witness to the State," what sociologists Leo Driedger and Donald B. Kraybill have called "a new canopy" now covered Mennonite thought about the state. So for many Mennonites political activity —national or international—took on new legitimacy. As Driedger and Kraybill have suggested, now Mennonites could "have their theological cake and eat it too."[113] Since the state would obviously not accept lordship as defined by Mennonites, the ground remained for political disengagement. However, insofar as the state was under the new sacred canopy, Mennonites could also emphasize the obligation to witness.

Nonetheless, during the 1950s and even the early 1960s the boundaries of that witness remained fairly traditional. An older generation continued to advise caution and restraint, and their voice carried the day. Harold Bender hesitantly embraced Neufeld's position, even while noting that "the implicit meaning of his conclusions must be quite radical."[114] But he did not accept the position of Edgar Metzler, a Kitchener, Ontario, pastor.

Earlier, in 1948-1949, GCs had carried almost the whole burden of advocating resistance to the conscription system itself. But now in 1959 Metzler, who undoubtedly had been socialized by his earlier work with the National Service Board for Religious Objectors, called for such noncooperation. For him it was a way of witnessing to the state. Until Mennonites were prepared to sanction civil disobedience and to refuse to participate in the compulsory conscription system, their witness was only "fine sentiments" (as one member of Congress described Mennonites' congressional testimony). For Metzler the I-W program, devoid of "moral nerve, . . . is not a witness against conscription." Instead, it "is part and parcel of the compulsory system of conscription."[115]

Almost instantly Bender responded in the *Gospel Herald*. One could not biblically resist the state "to witness to the truth or against an evil." Resistance was legitimate only when the state compelled an "act which is clearly forbidden in Scripture."[116] Bender's position clearly won this skirmish in the Mennonite battle over the acceptability of noncooperation and civil disobedience. But a decade later the noncooperators were the new exemplars of virtue and devotion. Of course by then the 1960s had created their own logic.

CHAPTER
11

EXPANDING INTER-MENNONITE RELATIONSHIPS

In 1938 Clifford (M. C.) Lehman, a leading but rather independent-minded missionary and intellectual in the Mennonite Church, conversed with the Bluffton College trustees about a vacancy in the Bluffton president's office. On hearing the news Harold Bender wrote to Sanford Yoder, Goshen College president and executive secretary of the MCs' main board of missions, that "Lehman has made another unfortunate move."[1]

In the late 1930s the thought of a prominent MC scholar going to a GC school troubled Bender. Indeed, given the history of MC dissidents finding haven at Bluffton, it naturally troubled quite a few MC leaders. Mistrust and even suspicion between Mennonite groups was common into the early 1940s and beyond. An editorial several years earlier in *The Mennonite* called on Mennonites to cease their petty arguments over all sorts of little differences. Once the fathers had "quibbled over doctrines." In the 1930s they could easily find each other's piety wanting because of "the shape of the hat or the cut of the garment." Given the proclivities for division it was hard for Mennonites to tell the world that they stood "for more than these." It was time to "forget the differences."[2]

Twenty years after Bender thought it unfortunate for an MC to go to Bluffton, the MC and GC denominations linked their respective seminaries in a process that ultimately turned the two into one school. If some things never change, other things change rapidly. Inter-Mennonite relationships in the post-World War II era is a story of rapid rapprochement, affiliation, and even merger.

For centuries Mennonites were often unaware of the existence of other groups. Divided by multiple beginnings in the sixteenth century, by the relative isolation of the seventeenth and eighteenth centuries, and by the schismatic history of the nineteenth century, Mennonite groups easily became largely negative or even polemic toward each other. During the nineteenth century, as modernity impinged and schisms multiplied, it was common to suggest that an infectious disease—*Täuferkrankheit*, or "Mennonite sickness"—was rampant. But if the nineteenth century was the century of schisms, the twentieth is the century of inter-Mennonite activity.

In America inter-Mennonitism began its renaissance before 1940. In the decades before World War II there were three important inter-Mennonite movements. They included the 1913-1936 triennial meetings of an All-Mennonite Convention; beginning in 1920, the development of Mennonite Central Committee; and between 1916 and 1927 the merger of three Amish Mennonite (progressive, as contrasted to Old Order) district conferences with Mennonite Church (MC) district conferences.[3]

However, the takeoff point for inter-Mennonite cooperation was the World War II experience. Inter-Mennonitism grew rapidly from the cooperation required of denominational leaders to manage the Civilian Public Service system and from the fraternity that developed among men in the camps. In 1957 Harold S. Bender wrote that "World War II gave the greatest impetus to inter-Mennonite co-operation." He offered no evidence to measure "greatest" against the force of other inter-Mennonite impulses, but sometimes the truth is so compelling that measurement is scarcely necessary.[4]

INTER-MENNONITE VOLUNTARY ASSOCIATIONS

The war was the springboard for a vast new network of inter-Mennonite agencies as well as for expanding the familiarity that facilitated the merger of different denominational groups. Paul Kraybill, long-term MC denominational and Mennonite World Conference executive, referred in a 1974 study to 69 inter-Mennonite agencies, associations, and voluntary societies that had begun between 1941 and 1974. Many were organizational spinoffs from MCC: Voluntary Service (1946); Menno Travel Service (1947); Mennonite Mental Health Services (1947); European Trainee Program (1950); I-W Services (1950); Mennonite Disaster Service (1955); Mennonite Indemnity (1957). In addition to such organizations, by 1976 fifteen congregations had also chosen to affiliate with at least two different Mennonite denominations. By Kraybill's calculations only three inter-Mennonite agencies predated 1941.[5]

The growth of the inter-Mennonite associations reflected various social realities. Interest in mass media promoted the establishment of a radio program, The Calvary Hour (1936); Mennonite Writers' Fellowship (1951); Mennonite Publishers' Fellowship (1960); Inter-Mennonite Media Group (1967); and Mennonite Council on Mass Communications (1968). Growth in Mennonite affluence resulted in associations for management and distribution of Mennonite wealth: Schowalter Foundation (1953); Mennonite Foundation, Inc. (1953); and Mennonite Economic Development Associates (1954). Other organizations were means to keep in touch with the thinking and activity of fellow Mennonite denominations, institutions, and activities. They included Council of Mennonite Colleges (1946); Council of Mennonite Seminaries (1958); Mennonite Camping Association (1960); Mennonite Chaplains' Service (1962); and Council of [conference] Moderators and Secretaries (1973). Still others reflected new occupational groupings that came as Mennonites left the farm and rather often became professionals: Mennonite Nurses Association (1942); Mennonite Medical Association (1948); Mennonite Teachers' Association (1951); and Association of Mennonite Social Workers (1959).[6]

These many voluntary networks spanned the schisms of the past and frequently rendered the denominational differences almost inconsequential. The associations existed (and exist) at least partly to express or explore more fully the commonalities of the larger Mennonite tradition. Whatever their purposes, they became a new form of gathering for work, play, worship, and conversation.[7] The largest—Mennonite Central Committee, Mennonite Disaster Service, Mennonite Relief Sale committees, and others—become subcommunities of work and engagement stretching over time. For many people they have become a sort of primary community. After natural catastrophes Mennonite Disaster Service volunteers from various Mennonite and sometimes other denominations work together for weeks and even months, in cleanup and reconstruction of homes and business. Women quilting for the relief sales shape their weekly schedule around their groups' quilting times.

Today there are associations, conferences, and networks for Mennonite retirees, young adults, farmers, social workers, historians, nurses, editors, pilots, peacemakers, and many other social groups. Some may not take up much of their members' time, but even they often provide effective symbols of personal identity. For instance, some Mennonite businesspeople feel that Mennonite Economic Development Associates has significantly influenced their work and the texture of their lives. For physicians, nurses, and other health care professionals, the Mennonite Medical Association provides a network of colleagues, friendship, and ethical discernment.

A different kind of Mennonite ecumenical activity involved the merger or affiliation of various Mennonite denominations and others groping toward new relationships with different denominations. As with the formation of voluntary associations, such activity matured and its pace quickened in the decades following World War II.

THE CENTRAL CONFERENCE-GENERAL CONFERENCE MERGER

On February 18, 1946, the first post-World War II merger of Mennonite denominations culminated when the Central Conference (CC) officially joined the General Conference (GC) church. The CC was a collection of congregations, chiefly located in Illinois, that had followed Bishop Joseph Stuckey out of the Amish during the mid-to-late nineteenth century. In 1908 they formally organized as an independent conference with twelve congregations. Although independent, from 1872 onward Stuckey and other CC leaders had considerable contact with GC and other Mennonites. Thus about 1930, when specific steps began toward merger with the GC, that inter-Mennonite movement already had a long, if informal, history.[8]

In 1929 and 1930 both the CCs' and the GCs' central conferences established comity committees to explore greater cooperation. Early in 1930 the two groups met to consider collaboration in publications, evangelism, and missions.[9] The first clear result of their work was an agreement to merge the two denominations' periodicals—*The Christian Evangel* (CC) and *The Mennonite* (GC).[10] During 1934 and 1935 the two pages were published as one periodical; however, in January 1936 they resumed separately.

Until the joint publication, all the discussion suggested that what was driving the merger movement was an urge for Mennonite cooperation. However, the resumption of separate periodicals suggested another driving force: depression economics. By temporarily merging, the two journals avoided having to suspend publication, as happened with some other denominational papers.[11]

Nonetheless, the end of joint publication reflected more than economic upturn. In the first issue of the revived *Christian Evangel*, editor William B. Weaver noted that "the time was not for this kind of union" because some members of the smaller Central Conference feared that to "merge" would in effect be to "submerge."[12] Others feared that merger would undermine the close connections among congregations in central Illinois and perhaps even limit the future effectiveness of those key congregations.[13]

If 1936 was not the time, by 1941 the merger movement had grown to the point that the two groups once again began steps that led to the 1946 merger. By January 1945, CC leaders concluded that the risks were small, especially since the GC denomination had a polity which would let the CC conference function more or less like a district body, continuing its various mission and benevolent activities and maintaining its own publications.

Yet the freedom to continue past activities was not a positive reason to join. Propelling the merger were new experiences and a new moral ecology facing small Mennonite groups in the 1940s. Now the anticipated gains of merger were erasing some old inter-Mennonite distinctions that were no longer intelligible, especially to the next generation. Moreover the merger seemed to add the strength of numbers in a world increasingly full of challenges, to broaden mission activity, and to remove "any sense of inferiority" that too often seemed to plague small Mennonite groups.[14]

THE EVANGELICAL MENNONITE CONFERENCE-EVANGELICAL MENNONITE BRETHREN CONFERENCE AFFILIATION

The Evangelical Mennonite Brethren Conference (EMB) and the Evangelical Mennonite Conference (EMC) were two small groups which each lived through the 1940s with an uncertain Mennonite identity. In 1953 they came together to establish the Conference of Evangelical Mennonites (CEM). Nine years later they decided to resume their separate ways. Thereafter their Mennonite identities became even more frayed.

Unlike the CC-GC union, the EMB-EMC affiliation brought together groups which were ethnically dissimilar and geographically

separated. Like the Central Conference, the EMC's roots were in
the Amish parting of ways in the late 1800s. In 1865, under leadership of Amish bishop Henry Egly, it had withdrawn from other Amish over questions of church discipline, church membership, and,
most deeply, the significance of a clear experience of conversion.
Originally known as the "Egly Amish," during World War I the
group renamed itself the "Defenseless Mennonite Church" and
later, in 1948, changed its name to the "Evangelical Mennonite
Church." By contrast, the EMB conference began in 1889 among
recent Russian Mennonite immigrant congregations in Nebraska
and Minnesota. Its founders deplored laxity of church discipline
in existing conferences and wanted to adopt some American denominational practices such as Sunday schools. Like the EMC
they too groped for an appropriate name. Originally known as the
Conference of United Mennonite Brethren of North America, they
subsequently took the name "Defenseless Mennonite Brethren in
Christ of North America." Then in 1937 they renamed themselves
the Evangelical Mennonite Brethren Conference.[15]

Beyond the similarity of seeking an appropriate identity, the
two small denominations represented different ethnic streams—
the EMC predominantly Swiss and south German, the EMB
Dutch-Russian. EMC congregations were primarily in Ohio, Indiana, and Illinois. The EMBs were scattered across the western
United States and Canada.

The history of contact, cooperation, and even merger discussions between the EMB and the EMC dates back at least to the decade 1921-1931, when their two denominational periodicals were
published as one. As with the CC-GC discussions, the period before World War II was not productive for merger talks. But in 1947
a Joint Unity Committee started exploring a merger that could
constitute a home for all "evangelical Mennonites" uncomfortable
with what the committee considered to be liberalism in other
Mennonite groups.[16] In 1950-1951 the EMB and EMC conferences
met jointly. In January 1953 their periodicals—*Zion's Tidings*
(EMC) and *Gospel Tidings* (EMB)—began joint publication as *The
Evangelical Mennonite*. In June 1953 the two bodies met to inaugurate the Evangelical Mennonite Conference.

Yet the enthusiasm for merger was short-lived. By 1957 John
R. Dick, longtime leader of the EMB conference, likened the two
conferences to an elderly couple unable to make the adjustment
to a new marriage. In an article entitled "Too Old to Marry?" published in their joint journal, he noted that such a union after many

years of independence required "compromises, adjustments, and some heartaches."[17] His piece was the death knell for an affiliation fragile from the very start. In September 1962 both groups amicably dissolved the union.

The demise of the affiliation surely reflected the groups' differing ethnic, historical, and geographical realities. Moreover they had tried to affiliate around the Mennonite elements in their identities even though neither group was very sure about its Mennonitism. For both groups, Mennonite and Evangelical were intrinsic but seemingly rather incompatible elements of their identities. To merge with either a more clearly Evangelical group or another Mennonite group was to accentuate one element of this fragile combination. Stan Nussbaum, historian of the EMC, observed that "a merger with any denomination would therefore mean that EMC would have to become either more 'Mennonite' or less 'Mennonite,' and the EMC membership is not agreed on which it wants to be."[18] That dilemma was also the story of the EMBs in the 1960s. Much later, in 1987, the EMBs resolved the dilemma by removing Mennonite from their self-description and renaming themselves the Fellowship of Evangelical Bible Churches.

THE MENNONITE BRETHREN-KRIMMER MENNONITE BRETHREN MERGER

Unlike the case of the EMB and the EMC, a merger of the Krimmer Mennonite Brethren and the Mennonite Brethren in 1960 brought together two groups whose histories were intertwined. They shared the language and culture common to Mennonites who had immigrated from the Russian empire. Both emerged during the religious ferment in the empire's southern regions in the mid-nineteenth century.

The MB movement originated in the Molotschna colony in the Ukraine in 1860. The KMB birth was in the Crimea in 1869. They both chose the name *Brüdergemeinde* (brotherhood church). The KMBs were soon called Krimmer (German for "Crimean") to distinguish them from the Molotschna group. The name confusion and the need to distinguish on the basis of geography suggests similarity of religious outlook. At the outset both understood themselves as reform movements demanding a more rigorous piety than practiced in the larger Mennonite community. Thereafter their evolving theologies fastened on many of the same concerns. Moreover the two groups immigrated to North America about the same time

(1870s) and located near each other in central and western Kansas, Nebraska, South Dakota, North Dakota, northern Saskatchewan, and central California.[19]

The original KMB constitution included the phrase that the church "stands ready to unite with any conference of Mennonite churches where such union can be achieved agreeable to both parties."[20] In North America from the 1890s onward that ecumenical spirit fostered a pattern of inter-Mennonite discussions.[21] In such a discussion in 1938, the KMB conference noted that its church needed to "remain guarded against the various churches and sects."[22]

In so saying, the conferees recognized a vulnerability which many small denominations shared. Small groups might retain an internal unity. However, since they lacked the full complement of denominational activity and institutions, they tended to form missional and educational links with other groups to the point of threat to their own traditions. The sense of that problem, no doubt made stronger by the experiences of World War II, set the stage for the 1949-1960 discussions that resulted in the merger with the Mennonite Brethren.

The same sense of being overwhelmed by alien ideologies and groups was the beginning point of a 1949 merger overture by the MB Executive Committee to the KMB conference. The committee noted that "contending for the faith" was becoming increasingly difficult "in view of the ever-growing apostasy which has already engulfed entire denominations" and of the "persistent encroachments of aggressive cults and other spiritual movements." Numbers might offer protection against the forces who threatened to "obliterate our spiritual heritage." The invitation also noted the commonalities of history and theology, plus the advantages that merger might bring to missions and educational programs. But the striking need articulated in this overture was mutual protection.[23]

The KMBs were hesitant. Logistical issues required careful planning. Long discussions followed about the form of merger—whether the KMB would continue as a newly created district conference within the MB structure or be amalgamated into existing district conferences. Within KMB congregations and between differing congregations, opinions differed on the wisdom and necessity of merger.[24]

However, a key fact was that the Gnadenau congregation in Kansas, the first immigrant congregation and the mother church of the KMB conference, was not divided or hesitant. Uneasy with the discussions' pace, Gnadenau proceeded on its own. As of July 1954 it began common worship services with an MB congregation at Lehigh, Kansas.

While at first the two congregations kept their separate identities, the direction was clear. In the fall of 1954 Gnadenau officially joined the MB conference. The decision was a congregational one, but in effect it foreclosed the denominational question as well. With the historic center of the denomination now MB, all that remained was some logistics—and time. In 1960 the MBs' general conference met to celebrate the denomination's centennial; the highlight of the event was the formal MB-KMB merger.[25]

DIALOGUE BETWEEN THE MENNONITE CHURCH AND THE GENERAL CONFERENCE MENNONITE CHURCH

The 1950s and 1960s were also decades for different kinds of inter-Mennonite dialogue. In 1960 leaders of both the MC and the GC denominations asked for reconsideration of the Mennonites' divisive past. In an article in the *Gospel Herald*, Harold Bender identified twenty-five schisms among the people who then constituted the MC denomination and pointed to schisms as the failure of the church. Too frequently, he wrote, the divisions were caused by individuals or small groups of leaders determined "to have their own way." Other schisms grew out of differing "methods of work, or strictness of discipline or cultural change." He claimed that not a single division had occurred over "significant doctrinal" questions.[26] Edmund (E. G.) Kaufman, longtime president of Bethel, concurred. Kaufman thought the divisions of the past could be explained on the basis of "sociological factors" and the absence of a "hermeneutic that is biblically orientated." Add to that a "good dose of American individualism" and a church with "no central authority," and division was inevitable.[27]

The year 1960 marked the centennial for the GCs as well as for the MBs. Part of their celebration was a 1960 study conference on "Christian Unity in Faith and Witness" held at Donnellson, Iowa. Even earlier, in 1959, at Donnellson, Iowa, the GCs' general conference passed a resolution noting that a major objective in the GC birth a century earlier had been to seek the "union of all Mennonites." Now, said the conference, it was time to "review, extend, deepen, and make firm inter-Mennonite cooperation" in a number of areas.[28]

At the Donnellson meeting William Klassen, a professor at the GCs' Mennonite Biblical Seminary, suggested that the conference take those instructions one step farther. As a precursor for more effective cooperation, Klassen thought, perhaps the conference should send a confessional letter to both the MC and the MB churches "penitently admitting that our church life has not always exemplified Christ's spirit." More pointedly he asked that the letter to the MBs recognize that "we share in the guilt of their withdrawal" in Russia in 1860.[29] At the gathering for an MB centennial in 1960, Erland Waltner, president of the GC denomination, offered such a letter of greeting and penitence, and the MB delegates responded in kind.[30]

In 1965 the GC and MC conferences each established an Interchurch Relations Committee to explore further Mennonite cooperation. In forming their committee MCs recognized the degree to which Mennonites were now also aligned with a variety of non-Mennonite denominations. The question of interchurch dialogue was not simply a question of how to relate to other Mennonite groups.[31]

In 1965 both of the newly established Interchurch Relations Committees wrote to the MBs suggesting greater dialogue. The MBs responded by noting that while such conversations might certainly offer worthwhile "instruction, admonition, encouragement, and new insights," the "consensus of our brotherhood . . . is not such that we could engage actively in meetings and discussions having to do with mergers or other bold steps to achieve church unity organically."[32] The KMB merger notwithstanding, that position was consistent with MB practice. Historian John A. Toews has correctly observed that MBs were "reluctant to extend the hand of fellowship to members in other Mennonite conferences, whether it be for worship or for work."[33]

The resolution that established the GC Interchurch Relations Committee came at least partly from a request passed at the 1965 sessions of the Eastern District Conference. That regional conference, the result of the 1847 separatist movement that subsequently helped give rise to the General Conference denomination, now passed a resolution calling for the GCs' executive committee to work toward "joining with" the MC church.[34] In response, in 1965 the GCs' general conference called for aggressive steps to achieve a more "adequate understanding, experience and expression of 'oneness in Christ.' "[35]

That call evoked favorable editorial responses from the MCs'

Gospel Herald. Editor John Drescher thought Mennonites were "overdue for a call to unity."[36] It was time to face the differences that separated the two largest Mennonite groups and engage in open dialogue. But other MC voices were not as interested. James Goering, an instructor at Bridgewater College in Virginia, responding to Drescher from the vantage of the Virginia Conference, counseled caution. Goering thought the MC approach to the authority of Scripture and the office of the ministry promoted more uniformity than did the interpretive freedom and congregational autonomy practiced among the GCs.[37]

The MC Interchurch Relations Committee was partly a product of pressures from a growing number of new Mennonite congregations seeking dual GC and MC affiliation. But it also began from broader interests, a fact suggested by a series of papers presented to MC general conference sessions between 1967 and 1971.[38] A 1967 paper—"The Challenge of the Divided State of American Protestantism"—sought to define how a Mennonite church might appropriately relate to both the "ecumenical" and the "conservative evangelical" camps in American Protestantism. Beyond deploring the polarization, the committee recognized that it was important to have conversation with and learn from elements in both camps. That position only reflected the reality that throughout the 1960s MC church relationships ran in differing directions. Seventeen MC church officials served variously in departments and on committees of the "ecumenical" National Council of Churches, while two were similarly involved with the National Association for Evangelicals.[39]

No doubt numerous impulses stimulated the MC rethinking of relationships in the American environment. John H. Yoder, an influential member of the MCs' Interchurch Relations Committee and author of a number of its reports, thought that the previous generation of leaders had invested too much effort leading American Mennonites "into the cultural and educational mainstream of magisterial Protestantism." In materials circulated within the committee he articulated a theme common to the earlier Concern movement—that MC scholars too often pursued advanced theological studies in universities of "Calvinistic or American liberal mainstream traditions" or in European state-church institutions. The result was not only extensive theological borrowing but also the training of "magisterial-pastoral" leaders. In identifying with the Reformed tradition, the Mennonites had cut themselves off from conversation with groups in the Wesleyan and holiness traditions. For Yoder, such contacts had held considerable promise.[40]

The committee's interest in Mennonite relationships was more theological than organizational. A 1967 paper titled "Christian Unity in a Divided Mennonitism" noted the difficulty of pursuing unity among religious communities not united by a hierarchically defined common doctrinal system or by organizational relationships based on administrative efficiency. Mennonite unity needed to permit theological latitude so long as there was "far-reaching agreement" and a "brotherhood" polity which provided accountability for differences and variation. The committee specifically named the Hutterian Brethren, the Society of Brothers, the Apostolic Christians, the Plymouth Brethren, and the Church of the Brethren as possible groups for further collaboration.[41]

The GCs and MCs came to these discussions of interchurch relationships with their differing histories. For GCs, inter-Mennonite ecumenicity had always been a central and cherished goal. So lack of evidence that the two groups were moving toward closer union frustrated the GCs' Interchurch Relations Committee. Their report to the 1971 conference began by declaring that "the high expectations of inter-Mennonite cooperation . . . between our General Conference and the Mennonite Church have receded considerably."[42] That comment reflected a hesitancy on the part of the MCs. They held to a concept of church that was more cautious about individualism, more inclined toward a common discipline, and more appreciative of centralized church authority as a means for maintaining the right fellowship.

So the MCs explored multilateral relationships both in and outside the Mennonite denominational family. In 1967 alone the MC committee engaged in discussions with the Covenant Church, the Brethren in Christ, the Church of the Brethren, and various Baptist groups.[43] The GCs also held casual discussions with some non-Mennonite denominations. Yet their primary interests, as their church's executive secretary Heinz Janzen wrote to a fellow church leader, was an "aggressive courtship" with the MCs.[44]

Whether or not the GC-MC discussions moved toward organizational merger, for GCs and MCs those discussions were driven by some of the same needs as those of the smaller groups, especially the need to preserve identity. A 1969 joint meeting of the two committees recognized that "unless a strong Anabaptist commitment can coalesce, Mennonite identity will further disintegrate."[45]

COOPERATION IN SEMINARY EDUCATION

The inter-Mennonite event which perhaps did most to co-alesce that common Mennonite identity and to shape subsequent MC-GC relationships occurred in 1958: the linking of Mennonite Biblical Seminary (GC) and Goshen Biblical Seminary (MC) to form the Associated Mennonite Biblical Seminaries (AMBS).

The story behind the affiliation of the two institutions is quite a commentary on Mennonite relationships during much of the twentieth century. Mennonite Biblical Seminary was successor to a series of GC institutions: *Christliche Bildungs-Anstalt der Mennoniten Gemeinschaft*, more commonly known as "Wadsworth Institute" (1868-1878); Mennonite Seminary (1914-1921), a division of Bluffton College; and Witmarsum Theological Seminary (1921-1931), a continuation of Mennonite Seminary as an institution affiliated with but organizationally separate from Bluffton College. In 1913 discussions leading to the establishment of Mennonite Seminary had involved unofficial representatives from five Mennonite groups: GC, MC, Mennonite Brethren in Christ; the ("Egly") Defenseless Mennonite Church; and the Central Conference of Mennonites. Yet in reality Mennonite-Witmarsum Seminary had always been a GC and Central Conference school with some students attending from other groups.[46]

Efforts throughout the 1930s and early 1940s to reopen a GC seminary focused on affiliation with some established institution. Many GC officials persistently favored Bethany Seminary in Chicago, a Church of the Brethren school. But conservatives who worried that Bethany was not "organized on fundamental principles of faith" repeatedly blocked such a move.[47] In the summer of 1945 the end of the war and the prospect of faculty and students being freed from CPS spurred hurried action to open the school that September. The Bethany connection, if not entirely satisfactory, was the only plausible way to begin. Thus began Mennonite Biblical Seminary (MBS), in Chicago

Virtually parallel to MBS's beginning were developments at Goshen, Indiana. In 1944 Harold S. Bender became dean of the Goshen Bible School, which in 1946 was renamed Goshen Biblical Seminary (GBS). Also in 1946 that seminary moved to the standard three-year Bachelor of Divinity degree based on work beyond the four-year college degree.

In 1944, as Bender became dean, he used his inaugural address to define the kind of distinctive theological education he hoped to fashion. Such education would be biblical "with the word of God the standard of its teaching, the guide to its method, and the light to its future course." But Bender immediately connected the meaning of being biblical to his persistent idea of discipleship as "the essence of Christianity." In this context biblical study meant translation into practice—or praxis, to use a contemporary term. The praxis Bender was looking for was a prophetic kind. While the church always needed the prophetic voice, the modern world with its "relentless pressure to overthrow the sovereignty of God" needed it especially. Bender left no doubt that he hoped the Goshen Biblical Seminary would train Mennonites for the task.[48]

At Chicago Donovan Smucker, MBS faculty member, thought that if the new seminary could not be a "creative third alternative," then it "had no future."[49] Already in 1943 he had outlined what he thought a Mennonite seminary's theological center should be. "We are a bibliocentric people," he wrote, "and the liberal seminary is simply not Bible-centered. On the other hand, a brittle fundamentalism does not foster faith. Mennonitism is a curious mixture, a radical proposal which combines what I am calling an enlightened fundamentalism with an ethical passion."[50]

But the chance for either MBS or GBS to achieve Smucker's and Bender's ideas of the prophetic role was diminished by the smallness of either denomination and their paucity of intellectual resources. So it was not surprising that discussions about forms of affiliation began soon following the post-World War II reconstruction of each school.

Relationships between the GCs' and the MCs' seminaries were cordial from the mid-1940s onward. Various cooperative seminars and summer schools reflected the ease with which the faculty moved between the two denominational settings. Intellectuals from both denominations as well as from other Mennonite groups had been meeting since 1941 under what came to be known as the Conference on Mennonite Cultural [or sometimes "Cultural and Educational"] Problems. Its discussions plus extensive contacts in the CPS system no doubt enhanced the ease of working together.

In 1954-1955 joint GBS-MBS summer schools evoked possibilities for closer relationships. The participants in the 1954 summer sessions, faculty and students alike, felt so comfortable that they initiated discussions about greater cooperation. Between 1954 and 1956 a group of MC and GC leaders produced a workable proposal to link GBS and MBS and yet insure the autonomy and denominational distinctiveness of each.

Goshen Biblical Seminary and Mennonite Biblical Seminary administrative joint meeting, c. 1958. Left to right: Erland Waltner, Samuel F. Pannabecker, Harold S. Bender, Paul Mininger. Credit: Mennonite Library and Archives, Bethel College.

More difficult to resolve than ideological, administrative, and curricular issues was geography—the question of location. A compromise proposal called for a joint academic program built at two locations close to each other. Under the arrangement GBS would remain in Goshen and MBS would move from Chicago to Elkhart, about ten miles from Goshen. Together the two schools would sponsor an Institute of Mennonite Studies, thus binding themselves in the scholarship of Anabaptist-Mennonite history and theology. So in 1958 Mennonite Biblical Seminary opened a new campus in Elkhart. The association between MBS and GBS matured. In 1964 they appointed a joint academic dean, and in 1969 GBS relocated to the Elkhart site. For practical purposes, except for some church relations, the two seminaries were one.

Organizational cooperation was natural, given the increasingly interwoven relationships and comfort between the two groups. Ideologically the transfer of MBS to Elkhart was a tacit move toward the Bender-Hershberger, or "Goshen school," formulation of Mennonite identity. As the means to define their identity amidst their own drift into American culture, GC Mennonites were embracing the possibilities of Harold Bender's more community-oriented orthodoxy rather than the more individualistic interpretations of some scholars, such as the now-deceased C. Henry Smith, of their own denomination.[51]

Mennonite Brethren Biblical Seminary faculty, c. 1965. Left to right: D. Edmond Hiebert, Henry Harder, Waldo Hiebert, John B. Toews, Rueben Baerg, Abram J. Klassen. Credit: Center for Mennonite Brethren Studies, Fresno.

MENNONITE BRETHREN SEMINARY

Meanwhile, in 1955, the Mennonite Brethren opened their own seminary in Fresno, California—the Mennonite Brethren Biblical Seminary (MBBS). In its opening decade the MB school took its cue not from an "Anabaptist Vision" but from American fundamentalism.

However, that was to change. In the mid-1960s a new generation of leadership came to both the seminary and to Fresno Pacific College, the adjacent MB liberal-arts institution. Under the leadership of John B. Toews, new seminary president, and Arthur J. Wiebe, college president, both institutions recruited younger faculty more conscious of their Anabaptist roots and more interested in the identity-redefinition which scholarship had brought to the

MCs and GCs. New institutional mission statements committed the schools to a more clearly Mennonite identity. A document prepared in 1964, titled "A Mennonite Brethren Seminary," declared that "the Seminary holds to the Anabaptist view of the Church. . . . The Seminary is committed to teach, live and exemplify the life of the true church."[52]

During the late 1960s and the '70s the new seminary faculty became involved in various conference-wide activities that moved the MB denomination toward a reconsideration of its Anabaptist roots. The same development nurtured inter-Mennonite associations. Moreover, closely allied with the seminary (and with some new conference agencies of like mind) was the work of historian John A. Toews, especially a major book, *A History of the Mennonite Brethren Church*, published in 1975.

Toews provided new ways for MBs to interpret the past and look to the future. While recognizing that various theological influences were present at the MB creation in 1860, he offered a fresh and more definitive answer to the MB debate about their ideological parentage. For him, 1860 had brought a rebirth of Anabaptism. He thought that the taproot of the MB church was to be found in the convictions of Conrad Grebel and Menno Simons rather than in those of Eduard Wuest and other European Pietists and Evangelicals.[53]

The rediscovery of a beginning nourished by Mennonite traditions encouraged a more self-conscious embrace of the Anabaptist tradition. The same rediscovery nurtured a growing participation in the networks that link Mennonite peoples together.[54]

CONCLUSION

As they built associational networks, pursued denominational mergers, and established closer working relationships, Mennonites were participants in patterns common to American religion. Princeton University sociologist Robert Wuthnow has pointed out that a postwar growth of special-purpose organizations was part of a restructuring of American Protestantism. Samuel McCrea Cavert, a former Executive Secretary of the World Council of Churches, has described the post-World War II period as one of "ecumenical advance." Creation of the World Council of Churches in 1948 and the beginnings of the National Council of the Churches of Christ in 1951 were key parts of that advance. While the immediate postwar period brought an upsurge of piety, religionists of all kinds felt beleaguered by the Second World War and its after-math. In the face of new horrors and destructive impulses, Christian unity of whatever kind possible seemed necessary. Creation of the National Association of Evangelicals in 1942 was an earlier response to the same associational need.[55]

The story of inter-Mennonite cooperation and merger, while reflecting the concerns of the beleaguered, displayed new confidences and opportunities as well. After the Central Conference merger with the GCs in 1946, Raymond Hartzler, a Central Conference leader who was an important player in the merger, noted that "our group's sense of Mennonite geography, our circle of acquaintance, our knowledge of Mennonite missions and other kingdom service, have all been enlarged; and we have found it to be for our good."[56] The same could be said for much of the inter-Mennonite movement. Not only did it enlarge; it also provided new opportunities.

Inter-Mennonite cooperation, whether through the voluntary associational network or through the easier interface of denominational communities, also has helped persons gain a sense of the richness and multicolored tapestry of the whole Mennonite house. Cooperation permits smaller constituent groups and individuals to feel part of something that transcends the limits of individual or group history. The inter-Mennonite community provides many of its people with belonging and meaning that can be spacious, imaginative, and enduring.

CHAPTER

12

THE OLD ORDERS

History has a way of playing tricks. The old and discarded can become fashionable. What seems marginal reemerges with new significance. The story of Amish and Old Order Mennonites in American culture during the twentieth century is stranger than fiction. In a culture organized around the future, they preserve the past. In a society infatuated with modernisms, they are our most successful anti-modernists. In a society that celebrates individualism, even radical individualism, they choose conformity and community. In a society where fashions glitter, their plain dress stands out in stark contrast. And yet they have become cultural heroes. Hollywood now pays attention to the Amish and their plain attire attracts the attention of fashion designers. Their quilts, originally made from stitching pieces of unused cloth together with a frugality uncommon in a culture of abundance, have become an art form with examples hanging in prestigious museums from New York to San Francisco.

In a culture nearly choking on consumption, the Old Orders maintain a frugal and self-sufficient lifestyle. In 1971 an Amish farmer with fourteen children—twelve still living at home—reported out-of-pocket expenses of $4,700 for the family.[1] And this family no doubt was well housed and well clothed and ate better than most Americans.

The ancestors of modern-day Amish were hunted down and killed for their heretical ways. Today the Old Order Amish descendants of those martyrs are hunted down and photographed by long-range cameras roaming the back roads of Amish communities. By 1965 roughly two million tourists annually visited Lancaster County, Pennsylvania, a major Amish population center. The tourists come for various attractions but primarily to visit Amish country.[2] The Amish interest the visitors because they are an antidote to much of modern American culture. They point toward a different kind of order. In modernity's lament for lost community there are few better teachers of how to sustain and enrich a communal order than these marginal people. In a world of impersonal relationships and intermediary agents and institutions, they sustain direct and face-to-face contacts.

At one level antimodernism characterizes the culture of the Old Order Amish and Old Order Mennonites. Ever since the late nineteenth century, Old Order peoples have resisted much of modern culture, including rapid and automatic technological change; the mass popular and entertainment media; urbanization; and all but the smallest-scale industrialization.

At another level sociologist Donald B. Kraybill's term "negotiation" is better than "antimodern" to capture the Old Order attitude towards modernity. Old Order people have consciously and determinedly negotiated between their own values and traditions and the demands of modernity. So while they have resisted certain modern forms they have also accepted others. They read by gas lanterns and ride in horse-drawn buggies, yet their machine shops have the latest in hydraulic pressure and some of their dairies use state-of-the-art equipment. Their buggies are a dated form of transportation, but they may include molded fiberglass parts, hydraulic brakes, and solar panels for recharging the lantern batteries.[3] The Old Order peoples are rich and unique in their ability to balance change and stability, tradition and adaptation.[4]

In 1693 in Europe, a schism separated Amish from Mennonites. But after the late-seventeenth- to mid-nineteenth-century migrations of both groups to North America, there was little difference that ordinary Americans would have noticed between the two peoples. Those groups called "Old Order Amish" and "Old Order Mennonite" became separate and distinguishable from other Mennonites only in the late nineteenth century. In contrast to other Amish and Mennonites, who were more willing to adapt to the growing industrial, urban, and national culture, the Old Orders made stronger and more conscious decisions to resist or at least control modern intrusiveness and change.[5]

The Old Order Amish emerged out of a series of Amish-wide conferences from 1862 to 1878 which sought to regulate change and reconcile the differing Amish traditions with each other. Slightly later, between 1872 and 1902, the majority of what became the Old Order Mennonites withdrew from other Mennonite groups in Indiana, Ohio, Pennsylvania, Ontario, and Virginia.[6]

The Old Order Mennonites, while sharing many similarities with the Old Order Amish, are simultaneously different. Sociologist Donald Kraybill has identified them and the Beachy Amish as a "transitional" group between the Old Order Amish and the progressive Mennonites. Often Old Order Mennonites mark their boundaries less sharply. They maintain restraints on technology, but somewhat less strictly than do the Old Order Amish. Many Old Order Mennonites drive cars. Old Order Mennonites and Beachy Amish are more likely to use the English language instead of a Germanic dialect.[7]

OLD ORDER GROWTH AND RETENTION

Analysis of the Old Order Mennonite and Amish populations and their shifts is somewhat hazardous because the groups do not collect demographic data and systematize it as do more acculturated groups. They have never been much interested in gathering national statistics. Local communities print family listings, but these are not brought together systematically. Population figures sometimes include only church members, sometimes members and children. So estimates vary considerably.

Two estimates from 1966 suggest the problems. John A. Hostetler, surely the dean of Amish-studies scholars, put their numbers at 49,371. James Landing, a geographer at Pennsylvania State University, calculated 63,900. Much later Steven Nolt, a younger scholar, suggested 40,010 as the appropriate figure for 1966. Nolt contrasted the 40,010 of 1966 with a population of 16,930 in 1936. Assuming the accuracy of his figures, Nolt observed that whereas in 1936 the Old Orders constituted 14 percent of the total Amish and Mennonite population, in 1966 they were 23 percent.[8]

Proliferation of Amish settlements during recent years parallels the population growth. Amish historian David Luthy has tracked the establishment of Amish settlements from the earliest ones through 1992. Their establishment during our period—the middle third of the twentieth century—is significant in comparison with the earlier periods but is dwarfed when compared with what happened later.

*Establishment of Amish Settlements in the United States
(that still survived in 1992)*[9]

Date of Establishment	Number
Before 1920	25
1920-1929	4
1930-1939	0
1940-1949	6
1950-1959	12
1960-1969	23
1970-1979	57
1980-1989	60

While the number of settlements has grown dramatically, Luthy and also a 1978 study by geographer William Crowley[10] have indicated that the concentrations remain in a cluster of core states: Pennsylvania; Indiana; Ohio; and more recently, Missouri, Wisconsin, and Michigan.

Among the Old Order Mennonites the pattern of establishing new settlements seems not as pronounced. After 1927 the Groffdale-affiliated Old Orders did begin new ones in different parts of Pennsylvania. They first moved outside of the state in 1970 to begin a community in Morgan County, Missouri.[11] Like the Old Order Amish, the Old Order Mennonites accelerated the founding of settlements during the 1970s and 1980s.[12]

Whatever population figures one uses, it is clear that there has been a remarkable upswing in the Old Order Amish population. Since the Old Orders engage in virtually no formal proselytizing, the growth is almost entirely biological. The Old Order peoples remain rural and continue to have large families. In 1952, from a study of an Amish community in Pennsylvania, John A. Hostetler suggested that the average was between seven and eight children. A 1962 study of sixty-six Amish families at Dover, Delaware, found an average of 7.1 children.[13]

A second variable in Amish population is rate of retention. After studying the Old Order Amish in Elkhart and Lagrange counties of northern Indiana, sociologist Thomas Meyers of Goshen College noted that retention increased dramatically if persons born into Amish homes in the 1930s are compared with those born in the 1940s. Of those born in the 1930s, 21 percent opted out of the community. Of those born in the 1940s, only 10 percent did so.[14]

However, Judith Nagata, studying an Amish community in Illinois, found dramatically higher rates of defection. The Grainville (a pseudonym) Amish settlement was established in 1936. In a survey of 26 families whose child-bearing was completed by 1966, Nagata found that the rate of children's eventual defection was 51.05 percent. The primary reasons for defecting were interests in nonagricultural vocations, wanting mechanized farming, or acquiring prohibited material goods. Yet even with the high loss, Grainville's Old Order Amish population grew from 532 in 1940 to 772 in 1965.[15]

Amish who leave have tended to join other Christian churches. According to Nagata's informants in the Grainville area, every Amish person who left had done so. The vast majority at Grainville and elsewhere stay within the Amish and Mennonite family. In 1966 in the Grainville area they could choose especially among three alternatives—MC, Conservative Mennonite, or Beachy Amish Mennonite. In all three Grainville congregations the memberships were almost entirely ex-Amish. In the MC, 190 of 212 members were ex-Amish; in the Conservative, 171 of 173; and in the Beachy, 100 percent. The MC congregation, formed in 1936, and the Beachy congregation, formed in 1958, were both schisms from the Old Order Amish.[16]

This pattern of reaffiliation within the Amish and Mennonite family of churches fits what Mennonite sociologists describe as an acculturation ladder that exists among Mennonite denominational groups. People unhappy with the restrictions in one Amish or Mennonite subculture can move into another that more adequately reflects their changing interests.[17] Nagata noted that in most Old Order Amish communities in existence for at least fifty years, Mennonite congregations also exist and provide such alternatives.[18]

OLD ORDER STRUCTURE AND ORGANIZATION

Descriptions of Amish are historically complicated, partly by the absence of centralized structure and therefore lack of imposed authority other than congregational. Amish polity has always been radically congregational. What other Amish congregations do surely has influence, but in the end the local congregation makes the important decisions that affect its people's lives and values.

Beyond kinship networks, Old Order Amish life is structured

through three social groupings. These are church districts, settlements, and affiliation.[19] The church district is the smallest unit. Its number is circumscribed by the number of people who can realistically gather in a farm home for the Sunday morning service. In older communities districts typically each include from 125 to 175 people (adult members and children), in newer communities about 100. Densely populated settlements include quite a number of districts. District functions, in addition to worship, include rites such as baptisms, marriages, and funerals, plus—very importantly—church discipline. Each district is a self-governing unit; however, since Amish typically meet for Sunday worship services only on alternative Sundays, members of one district have ample opportunity to worship in another on the free Sunday. In that and other ways, there is considerable communication and even influence across district lines.[20]

In the Old Order Amish scheme, the church districts are the most immediate and regulative units. Each has its set of rules, the *Ordnung*, which codifies the values and prescribes and proscribes what is acceptable and unacceptable behavior. A person who breaks the rules must make public confessions. Those who do not confess, or whose confessions are unsatisfactory, are placed under the *Meidung* ("shunning"—a prescribed and systematic social ostracism). Church discipline happens in the district, not subject to review by any other body. Most who leave the Amish are youths who have never become church members and therefore are not candidates for the Meidung. Members who leave generally have been placed under the Meidung, even if temporarily.[21]

In settlements with multiple districts, the boundaries of those districts are geographical. In 1974 there were 426 Old Order Amish districts in the United States. Ohio led the way with 136, followed closely by Pennsylvania with 104 and Indiana with 91. By comparison, in 1971 the more progressive Beachy Amish had 55 congregations with a membership of 4,024. (The Beachy are quite plain and Amish in attire but allow such basic conveniences as electricity, telephones, and automobiles, often have a more Protestant understanding of salvation, and have organized missions.) More than 60 percent of the Old Order members resided in Pennsylvania, Ohio, and Indiana.[22]

An affiliation is a collection of church districts that share a common discipline. In a single settlement there may be various affiliations that reflect differing standards. Some observe very strict disciplines and others somewhat less strict. Therefore affiliations are groupings that can be thought of as existing along a slightly more liberal to very conservative continuum of discipline. Settlements are the entire collection of Amish in a given area regardless of differences in disciplines.[23]

Among Old Order Amish, the formation of the national Old Order Amish Steering Committee in 1966 provided the first formalized and continuing centralized structure for discussion and decision-making.[24] The committee began in response to the I-W system but through the years has become a forum for Amish communities to address a range of issues common to their peculiar values and aspirations. Although a national committee, it has taken pains to insure that it remain entirely representative of the local churches. Election and removal procedures for committee members are designed to insure accurate representation of congregational interests. The committee has stated its mission as being "to uphold the principles, religion and customs of the Old Order Amish as they were handed down to us and in a way that the Oldest of the Old Order can cooperate and benefit as much as possible."[25]

The main Old Order Mennonite fellowships, while culturally similar to the Amish, are organizationally closer to the more acculturated Mennonites, especially the MCs, with whom they share a common history. For instance, both the Groffdale and the Weaverland groups are organized as conferences. They each hold semiannual meetings and for each the highest authority is conference decisions.[26]

As for Old Order Amish life and outlook, in spite of growing numbers, decentralized church governance, and even numerous twentieth-century schisms, there is a shared center. While the boundaries (like those in the Mennonite world) shift, there is a convictional center to the Amish communities of whatever variety. Those central convictions shape and unite Old Order Amish, whatever their affiliation.

THE SHARED CENTER

The starting point for understanding these Old Orders is that they are *not* relics from the premodern world. They are not old-fashioned because history passed them by. They are old-fashioned because of conscious choices. They are old-fashioned because they have deliberately devised mechanisms to impede social change. They have wrestled with the meaning of the modern world and have decided to reject much of it. They have chosen deliberately to confront the commonly acknowledged "acids of modernity" in different fashion from most people.

The articulated theology of the Old Orders and that of modernizing Mennonites share much in common. Central to both is the notion of the kingdom of God being incarnated in human forms in all ages of history. Both begin with the assumption that the kingdom of God as realized in partial, earthly form should be recognizable and distinguishable from the kingdoms of this world —and that the church, not secular structures, is God's main agent for bringing forth and demonstrating God's kingdom. What is different is how Old Orders and their modernizing cousins try to embody those ideas.

The Old Orders take literally the biblical injunctions to be a separate people. "Be not conformed to this world: but be ye transformed by the renewing of your mind, that ye may prove what is that good, and acceptable, and perfect, will of God" (Rom. 12:2). "Be ye not unequally yoked together with unbelievers: for what fellowship hath righteousness with unrighteousness? and what communion hath light with darkness?" (2 Cor. 6:14.) Another biblical passage frequently invoked for understanding the imperative of separatism is this one: "But ye are a chosen generation, a royal priesthood, an holy nation, a peculiar people . . ." (1 Pet. 2:9). Whereas some religious communities, including various Mennonites, define those prescriptions primarily in religious terms or in selective ways, the Amish give them technical, psychological, and sociological as well as religious meaning.

For the Amish the doctrine of the radical separation between the church and the world means that the boundaries are clearly drawn. Contact between the believing community and nonbelievers is to be carefully controlled. Believers should not dress or behave like the world. Business relationships and other kinds of associative activity with the outside world are regulated.[27] For those unwilling to live by the rule of separation, the Old Orders have historically used shunning and if necessary excommunication as means of preserving the faithful community.[28]

However, separation is not an end in itself. Separation is required for Amish society to create the kind of redemptive community and yieldedness to God which is the heart of Amish understandings of Christian faith. A community can be redemptive only when it becomes a loving community which practices the *Ordnung,* or the community rules, designed to insure the surrender of the self. Self-surrender rather than self-assertion is the goal of the community.

In Old Order culture the concept is embedded in the word *Gelassenheit*. Gelassenheit is a letting go of self, a submission before God, a surrendering or giving oneself to God. Both Mennonites and Amish believe that the submission of the individual to God is best nurtured among a community of likeminded individuals. For the Old Orders the concept of yielding oneself to God is impossible without the counterpart of fully yielding oneself to God's community on earth. Yieldedness practiced in individual or subjective terms is too easily seduced by the desires of the self. Only in a community that regulates the entirety of life can Jesus' followers achieve some measure of authentic and complete yieldedness. The less complete the community the less likely will yieldedness be complete.[29]

The concept of yieldedness finds further expression in the formal egalitarianism of Old Order communities. Old Order communities eschew hierarchy. Ministers are selected from the congregation. They possess no formal education. Virtually no one in the Old Orders has an education beyond the eighth grade. Church regulations are designed to maintain conformity and equality.[30]

Yieldedness turns the American search for self-fulfillment upside down. Old Order people find fulfillment in the well-being of their community more than in the exaltation of the self. Therefore one readily forgoes personal advancement to enhance the communal. One cultivates the arts of deference, listening, and humility. The denial of luxuries is part of yieldedness. Plain standards of dress, home, transport, and work are all means of cultivating yieldedness and resisting self-aggrandizement.[31]

Humility is closely related to yieldedness. Even leaders should be humble and restrained. Charismatic, aggressive, voluble, and emotional leadership is foreign to Amish communities. Moderation and conservatism are essential qualities for Amish and Old Order Mennonite folks, including leaders.

OLD ORDER DIVERSITY

To the untrained eye the Old Order groups look alike and equally anachronistic. Yet even among Amish there are enough differences to make the Amish resemble one of their quilts with variously different patches sewn together. All Old Order Amish ride in buggies but the style of buggy varies considerable. They all dress plainly, but subtle distinctions such as the men's wearing two, one, or no suspenders point to differences. They all sing from the same ancient German hymnbook (*The Ausbund*) but the pace varies. The speed of their singing is often an index of tradition and innovation.[32]

The differences are partly the side-effects of distances which separate communities from each other. They are also a consequence of the continuing impulse toward fragmentation. Of the many Amish gradations and schisms, John A. Hostetler has noted three major divisions in the twentieth century:[33]

1927	Beachy Amish Mennonite Church
1956	Nonconference Conservative Mennonites
1966	New Order Amish

The Beachy Amish beginnings, which occurred in Somerset County, Pennsylvania, soon attracted followers in other Pennsylvania counties and over several decades in Indiana, Ontario, and Kansas.[34] By 1960 established Beachy congregations existed in eight different states. From the beginning the Beachy were willing to accept greater technological innovation. A number of their congregations emerged closely on the heels of the CPS experience when young men returning to Amish communities wanted to acquire automobiles. Also during the 1940s they readily engaged in mission activity. Another catalyst for the migration of Old Order Amish into the Beachy Amish was acceptance during the 1950s and 1960s of the tent evangelism of Mennonite revivalists such as Andrew Jantzi, George Brunk II, and Myron Augsburger. David Miller, an Old Order Amish revivalist from Oklahoma, who already in the late 1940s frequented various Old Order communities, joined the Beachy in 1957.[35]

Old Order Amish shun formal organization beyond the church district and the affiliation. Mennonites usually organize themselves into conferences. The Beachy Amish identify themselves as a *fellowship*. In Amish terms a fellowship implies a set of congregations who agree on religious issues yet in a manner not as binding as an affiliation, which requires a common discipline. For the Beachy Amish, typical conference features—executive committee, moderator, central offices, official records—are a violation of congregational autonomy. Yet the Beachy do have a rather full set of institutional networks that tie congregations together. Perhaps the most important one, at least according to Elmer

Yoder, Beachy historian, was the formation of an Amish Mennonite Aid organization in 1955.[36]

The group that emerged in 1956, calling themselves the Non-
conference Conservative Mennonites, consists of former Beachy
Amish and Mennonite Church (MC) individuals who, according to
Hostetler, gathered around common concerns about the "drift towards worldliness" in both groups. They were unwilling to accept
church organizational forms of Mennonitism, yet neither did they
conform to all the restrictions of the Beachy Amish.[37]

The story of the New Order Amish involves many strands of
activity and religious innovation. During the 1950s, in Ohio's
Holmes County, with its large Amish concentration, some congregations moved to soften shunning. If a member who had been excommunicated for violating the standards later joined a nonresistant and plain church, not necessarily the person's former one,
then fellowship between the errant individual and those in the
person's former congregation could be restored.[38]

To some Old Order people, especially in eastern Ohio, such
laxity was unacceptable. So a less flexible group, led by bishop Andrew Weaver, withdrew. They wanted to preserve a stricter form of
shunning, but more generally they wanted to maintain tighter
boundaries. They also objected to some adjustments their fellow
Old Orders were making in household and farm technology. Some
groups from other areas, particularly Lagrange County, Indiana,
became their allies and in some cases even relocated to Ohio.

Meanwhile a series of Amish Mission Conferences in the early
1950s brought yet a different kind of pressure. Technically the
movement was started by Russell Maniaci, a Catholic who had
converted to the Amish faith. Apparently it also grew from seeds
nurtured by Amish men returning with new service and missionary idealism from CPS, I-W, and PAX. One participant in the mission movement, Harvey Graber, described it as an attempt by Amish to breath new life into a conservatism gone "reactionary."
Graber depicted that conservatism as "more concerned with conformity to a past way of life than with nonconformity to the present world."[39]

The first Amish Mission Conference was a three-day event
held in 1950 on the farm of Jonas Gingerich near Kalona, Iowa. It
attracted more than 150 persons daily and led to two more conferences in 1951 and 1952, the first at Nottawa, Michigan, and the
second near Goshen, Indiana. After the 1952 conference the mission proponents formed a Missions Interests Committee with rep-

resentatives from Kansas, Ohio, Indiana, and Iowa. Two more conferences followed in 1953 and 1955.

Also, from 1951 to 1958 the movement produced a new publication, the *Amish Mission Endeavor*. The paper began to report on mission activity of Mennonite-related groups and thus to encourage Amish missions. But its demise after so few years suggests that it had not been able to find a niche in Amish life. During the *Endeavor* years Amish opposition to both the conferences and the publication solidified, mainly around three concerns: (1) the original leader of the mission movement, Russell Maniaci, was a nonethnic Amishman; (2) the sessions were conducted in English instead of the Pennsylvania-German dialect common to Amish communities; (3) some conference speakers were from other Mennonite groups. Graber correctly realized that something more was at work. He understood the mission movement as "an awakening." But to many other Amish it signaled a "trend toward worldliness."[40]

Still other sources of tension in Old Order communities during the 1950s were inroads of religious subjectivism and the Calvinistic doctrine of "eternal security." Amish typically warned against the pride of being certain that one had gained God's eternal favor. Now, no doubt under the influence of widening American contacts, some Old Order members insisted that Christians could and should gain assurance of their salvation both in this life and in the next.

An active proponent of that idea, David A. Miller of Thomas, Oklahoma, preached in many Amish communities. Speaking in barns, houses, and the outdoors, he attracted large numbers. In 1952, after he spoke in Lancaster County, Pennsylvania, for a week and a half, local Amish there excommunicated him.[41] Amish-studies scholar Gertrude Huntington, who was researching Ohio Amish at the time, has recounted that Miller's "influence was sweeping the central Ohio community." In the summer of 1953 in Holmes County he preached two and three times a day, always at a different place. Sometimes in barns and broiler houses upwards of 800 Old Order people attended a single service, quite in contrast to normal gatherings in Amish homes. Moreover, Huntington observed, (as with Mennonites) the revivals offered "emotional outlets" for the Amish. Whereas the Amish religious calendar was "rhythmic and orderly" and emotional responses were "regulated," Miller provided "excitement." So intriguing was this more expressive style of preaching that children began to play "Dave Miller" for hours, gesturing and preaching in "vivid imitation."[42]

Those who sympathized with Miller and his "new" gospel found allies among Amish who were calling for other changes. Some wanted to accept more new technology. Others called for stronger morality and emphasis on family. Some moved from temperate use of tobacco and alcohol to abstinence. Others sought to curb the teenage license ("sowing of wild oats") that some Amish communities notoriously tolerated.

Eventually such differences accumulated until they forced a division. It occurred in 1966, with the change-minded becoming known as the "New Order" Amish. In Lancaster County about 100 families took the new path, as did numerous families in Holmes County, Ohio. In some other places similar movements took the name "Amish Brotherhood." The New Order communities remain close to the Old Order. While generally exercising greater freedom in farm technology, they continue using traditional horse-drawn buggies. Even while they remain more open to some new religious insights and practices, they cherish and hold to the strengths of the old ways.[43]

The Old Order Mennonites, although less numerous than their Amish counterparts, have suffered similar fractures. In 1927 the Old Order community in Lancaster County, Pennsylvania, divided when the Groffdale Conference, also called Wenger Mennonites, withdrew to protest growing acculturation among the Weaverland Mennonites. The Weaverland group had accepted automobiles, although it insisted that the whole car, including the chrome, be painted black—hence a common nickname, "Black Bumper Mennonites." The Groffdale group continued with horses and buggies, although they tend to speak of "teams" and "carriages" so that their nickname is "Team Mennonites." Both groups consider the differences important. However, they remain closely allied,[44] for after all, among Mennonites and Amish organizational division is often not so much a matter of deeply divided spirit as a means of conflict resolution. Unlike the Old Order Amish, the Old Order Mennonites worship in church buildings—or more correctly in traditional parlance, "meetinghouses." For decades the same five buildings in the Lancaster area have served congregations of both groups.[45]

Since its beginnings in 1927 the Groffdale Conference has experienced several further schisms. In 1946 a tiny group soon known as the Reidenbach Mennonites broke away after arguing that when the conference had let its young men serve in the CPS

system it had given de facto support to the war system. A very conservative group, they also forbade their members from working in
places that mixed them with other peoples. Thus they limited
themselves vocationally to mainly farming and carpentry. Other
"Team Mennonite" split-away bodies—the Paul Wenger group in
Virginia and the Harvey Nolt group in Pennsylvania—remain tiny
and are further examples of Mennonite schisms to reinforce cultural restriction.[46]

In many other places the Old Orders have developed gradations of adaptation and resistance to American culture. All maintain considerable separation from the world and hold separatism
as an ideal. Nonetheless there is room for variation in translating
the doctrine into practice. For all, separatism needs to be visible.
Cognitive or symbolic forms of separation, as practiced by some of
their Mennonite cousins, are not adequate.

CHANGE AND ADAPTATION IN AMISH ECONOMIC LIFE

The image of the Old Orders as standing still is a caricature
delightful to fast-changing moderns, but it does grasp the reality
of change and continuity in Amish life. Changes there are, in many
forms. But the Old Order peoples regulate change by one overwhelming consideration: how will the changes affect their community? Changes which seem overwhelming and irresistible to
most moderns do not overwhelm the Old Order folks; instead
change must yield to the imperatives of community preservation
and family life. Change and preservation work in a dialectical and
intriguing fashion. When change is required to preserve the past,
then the Old Orders readily change.

Farming has long been the central occupation of Old Order
communities. Farming honors Old Order values of communal
work and the dignity of the human-nature relationship. Central
also to the Old Orders' farming is the way it involves entire families. Old Order people use farming methods that keep the family
working together and dependent on each other for the farm's success.

Furthermore, in rural society it has also seemed easier, albeit
less and less so, to stop the encroachments of the larger culture. In
the early 1970s, Edward Weaver, editor of the Weaverland Mennonite Conference publication *Home Messenger*, asked, "Can we, as
a plain church retain our non-conformity and non-resistant doctrines as we come more in contact with the world around us[?] It

seems a lot harder to retain a plain church when the members leave the farm for the factory."[47]

In seeking to maintain their rural ways, the Old Orders have had to develop adaptive strategies to meet changes in national and even international agricultural production. The inventory of tools and farm machinery used by Old Order Amishmen from the 1920s to 1960s has changed significantly. Today quite a few Old Order farms have at least semi-modern mechanical equipment. This includes tractors, combines or harvesters, mechanical corn pickers, gas-fired corn driers, milking machines, mechanical saws, mechanical brooderhouse feeders, and many more mechanical devices—often adapted from electrical to gasoline or diesel power. Often the Old Orders allow tractors only to power belt-driven machines, not for field work; or if they do allow them in the fields, very often they do not allow rubber tires, apparently both to keep their application limited and to prevent their use for road transportation. Nonetheless, technology itself is not wrong. Old Order people adapt and use much of it. The technology to be avoided is that which readily permits one to wander outside of the community.[48]

Farming by family units is also done to set the next generation up in farming. A study by John A. Hostetler and some colleagues from Temple University has documented that farming units are an important way Old Order Amish parents help their children stay Amish. Published in 1980, that study considered Amish farmers in Lancaster County who were landholders and who had married between 1962 and 1972. It found that among such persons, 76 percent who owned farms obtained them from relatives. The study also included siblings of persons who had married during those ten years. Of all the siblings, 98 percent of those established on farms stayed Amish compared to 87 percent of the nonfarmers. Thus the retention rate was high for the nonfarmers, but even higher for the farmers—indeed enough higher to suggest a correlation between getting established on farms and remaining Amish.[49]

Historically, Amish farmers have diversified as a hedge against price fluctuations and animal diseases and as a means to insure profitability. Also, diversification has made for self-sufficiency. Into the 1960s the typical Amish farm kept a balance between livestock and field crops. The animal stock often included hogs, cows, horses, and poultry, and the farm grew grains and grasses for their feed.

However, as specialization became more common in Ameri-

can agriculture, Amish farmers also began more and more to concentrate their resources. Studying selected Amish farms in Illinois
in 1971, sociologist Victor Stoltzfus noted a concentration on livestock operations. Livestock production is profitable and it is
labor-intensive, hence can put the family to work. Moreover its activities vary less by season than do field crops, so it keeps the family working year-round. And in an economy of inflating land prices,
farmers can expand livestock operations without necessarily having to find more acreage.[50]

Historically also, the Amish have depended heavily on their
own communities' resources to finance expansion of their farms.
That is, they have borrowed from one another rather than from
commercial lending institutions. But a study of Lancaster County
Old Orders found their ability to do so was diminishing already in
the early 1940s, even though, in researcher Walter Kollmorgen's
words, they "pooled more effectively [than in other communities]
to make the economic ladder to land ownership a reality."[51]

However, since the 1940s, as farming operations have became
more expensive and new machinery has required larger investments, Amish farmers have increasingly turned to commercial
loans. Stoltzfus found that in 1971, even in a rather small community, the Old Order Amish had outstanding commercial loans of
$1.3 million. But he also found that if the Amish community was
no longer able to finance its people's investments, it did assume
collective responsibility for the loans. Fellow Amishmen refi-
nanced loans rather than have one of their members default.[52] At
least in some cases the reputation for community integrity per
mitted Old Orders to negotiate loans on better terms than those
extended to other clients. In similar vein, Nagata found that at
Grainville the bank manager often extended loans to Amish without requiring collateral. The bank considered the backing of Amish mutual aid to be as good a guarantee as collateral.[53]

Nagata also found that in Grainville, even with commercial
loans available and even while the total acreage owned by Amish
had expanded from 1930 to 1965, the average size of individual
farms had gotten smaller. Apparently birth and retention rates
had outrun the economic ability to purchase land.

Total Acreage, and Decline in Average Size
of Amish Land Holdings in an Illinois Community
1930-1965

Date	Total Amish-Owned Acres	Average Size of Holdings
1930	14,539	100.90
1952	25,755	91.80
1965	20,287	76.55

Another consequence of land pressures is an increase in farm tenancy among Old Order Amish. Especially for young Amishmen hoping to get into farming, working for a nearby farmer or leasing land becomes an interim arrangement and in some cases permanent. Still another consequence has been a steady drift of Amish to other work. A 1973 study of Amish in Geauga, Ashtabula, and Trumbull counties in northeastern Ohio found that of 791 male heads of households surveyed, only 28 percent (223) worked in farming. Twenty-four percent (190) were factory workers, and the researcher estimated that another one-fourth worked in home businesses or cottage industries.[54] (The researcher did not list carpentry and other construction, which are common trades among Amish in some communities.)

Such cottage industries became more or less necessary as the skills and services necessary for Old Order lifestyles disappeared in the larger economy. At one time Old Order people went to the village blacksmith to get their horses shod. They bought their buggies, harnesses, and farm machinery from the same dealers as everyone else. In more recent decades, they have had to develop their own blacksmith shops and to fashion various goods no longer available in the general market. Hence Old Orders have faced both the need and the opportunities to develop cottage industries of their own. Also, some of their cottage industries repair or recreate old things or new items in old styles. For instance many communities have furniture-building and clock-repair shops.[55] Not only have the industries strengthened their home communities; they have also, as one Old Order Mennonite has observed, created more interdependence between settlements.[56]

Such adaptations have brought many results. They have altered values associated with a self-sufficient farming community. Increasingly time and labor are calculated in monetary terms. Reciprocal labor—neighbor helping neighbor—is not as easy when tied to a business clock as when it follows the rhythms of agriculture. To be sure, mutual aid in times of distress seems not to have declined, but apparently assisting one another on a regular basis is a casualty of the new economic realities. To the degree that Old Order women have remained farther removed from the "wage system," their capacity for reciprocity is greater.[57]

Meanwhile, if time-related values have been altered, other ones seem to persist. That study of northeastern Ohio Amish indicated no significant cultural differences between the church districts where farmers predominated and those whose earners were mostly factory workers. There were differences between some districts. But the differences were about appropriate uses of farm technology, not about broader cultural issues.[58]

Even so, some Old Order people caught in the vocational transition have felt the changes keenly. Some young families have not easily reconciled the tensions between "outside" work and the old values. In 1971 one young Amishman writing in *Family Life*, an Amish periodical published in Ontario, recounted that when his parents had not been able to buy him a farm he borrowed the money and hoped to pay it off by also working at a recreational vehicle factory. "But," he wrote, "our conscience kept telling us that we might be doing wrong by building worldly trailers, which would be used mostly on pleasure trips[,] to pay off our farm. Then, too, there was dirty and vain talk, with men and women working together, with jesting and profanity going on every day."[59]

Clearly the young man felt dissonance between his values and his work. And for the past century scholars, at least, have wondered about the long-term effect of such dissonance on the integrity of formerly isolated communities.[60]

AMISH CONFLICT WITH THE STATE

In the United States there is a long history of Amish conflict with government at its several levels. Conflict over conscription dates back to the Revolutionary War. While that conflict remains a central marker dividing Amish religious practices and the obligations of American citizenship, other and newer forms of conflict have arisen in the twentieth century.[61] Since the 1930s, as the state expanded its domain and range of activities the conflicts between the enlarging state and the self-sufficient and politically aloof Amish became more numerous. Apart from the military draft, the most significant tensions were over schools and social security taxes.

CONFLICT OVER EDUCATION

Before the 1920s the Old Order Amish had very little conflict with public schooling. As long as the schools were rural, locally controlled, and permeated with American Protestant values, public schools were acceptable. Into the early-twentieth century some Amishmen even served on local school boards. Then the consolidation of school districts and extension of formal school requirements up to age sixteen set the stage for conflict between the state and various minority communities, including the Amish. The Amish resisted both developments. Their determination to retain control over their children's education and to end formal schooling at the eighth grade was not due to hostility to education. Rather it came from a clear reading of the different intents of various kinds of education. Amish education reinforced values learned in family and church. Since the function of education was to pass on time-tested truths, the personification of those truths in the instructor was more important than state certification or current pedagogy. By contrast public education, particularly when detached from local communities, was becoming attuned to the nation's cultural needs. In the 1970s Joseph Stoll, an Amish educator, correctly observed that as Amish and American lifestyles increasingly diverged "the modern child lives in a different world from the children of our plain groups."[62]

Sociologist Donald B. Kraybill has argued that the Amish "intuitively grasped that modern schools are social separators that fragment both social structure and human consciousness." One-room schools rooted in the values of their own particularistic communities are indeed very different from schools certified by state or national standards. Earlier than many contemporary theorists of pluralism, the Amish realized that cultural and religious pluralism cannot reproduce itself without the institutional arrangements designed to preserve differences.[63]

The impact of these changes in public schooling came at different times to various Amish communities. But virtually all the communities shared one response—creation of private schools. The first Amish parochial school, the Apple Grove School near Dover, Delaware, opened in 1925 as authorities consolidated the seventh and eight grades into the local high school. In the next decades Amish in some communities in other states followed suit. Schools emerged in Pennsylvania in 1938 and in Ohio and Indiana in 1948. Since school consolidation typically began at the

high school rather than the elementary level, some Amish communities could wait.[64]

Decade-by-Decade Establishment of Old Order Amish Schools

1920s	1
1930s	3
1940s	9
1950s	46
1960s	148
1970s	173

By 1982 a directory of Old Order-operated schools in Canada and
the United States identified 569 Amish and 144 Mennonite
ones.[65]

However, the creation of alternative schools could hardly forestall conflict with state authorities. Conflict over high school attendance broke out in Pennsylvania in 1937. Attendance was
compulsory, normally until age seventeen, although there was a
provision that allowed Amish children to receive farmwork permits and thereby leave off formal schooling at fifteen. In September 1937, a School Committee or "Delegation" of sixteen representatives from the sixteen Amish church districts and Old Order
Mennonite groups in Lancaster County met in the home of Amish
leader Stephen F. Stoltzfus of Bird-in-Hand.[66]

Some of the representatives, including Stoltzfus, wanted to
resist the compulsory attendance law; others wished to negotiate
a settlement. A temporary and even ingenious solution was to
have the young people repeat the eighth grade until they would
turn fifteen and could get the farmwork permits; thus they would
not have to attend high school. Some school districts allowed that
solution; others refused. The situation resulted in countless ar-
rests of parents and their imprisonment in the county jail. Since
friends and businessmen paid the necessary fines, those stays
were short. The war years lent a reprieve, as state officials were preoccupied with other tasks. Thereafter, in 1949, the Pennsylvania
Assembly passed legislation which made getting the work permits
more difficult.

In the fall of 1949, more than two dozen Amish fathers were
arrested for keeping their fourteen-year-olds at home. The next fall
authorities denied 98 percent of the requests for work permits
which Lancaster County Amish filed. Thereon thirty-six fathers

Amish men leaving prison, 1949. Credit: *Lancaster New Era*, photo by Ed Sachs.

were arrested; thirty-one of them, arguing that they were innocent, spent several days in jail until non-Amish benefactors bailed them out. Not until 1955 was the matter resolved. In that year the state of Pennsylvania relented to the point of revising its school code to let Amish children withdraw after the eighth grade and attend Amish vocational schools. In practice the revision meant that Amish children could work on their families' farms, keep journals of their activities and learnings, and meet with uncertified teachers for three hours per week for certain required subjects.[67]

Other issues remained, and in 1957 the Amish in Pennsylvania established a statewide school committee to deal further with authorities. One issue in the late 1950s involved heating systems in Amish schools. The matter became so troublesome that the Amish had to deal not only with state building inspectors but with the state's secretary of education and its attorney general. Church regulations called for a heating stove in the one-room school, while state required that the heater be in a separate building or else in the basement and encased in a chamber capable of containing any fire for up to four hours. For some time neither side would compromise. Then, once again, the state yielded—either to the logic of the Amish system, to nostalgia for the one-room school, or to both. Andrew Kinsinger, the first man to chair the Amish committee, recorded that he found that the state's chief inspector was "secretly rather sympathetic with the Amish views." Another inspector, with tears in his eyes, remarked, "If I only had a school like this to send my children and grandchildren to, I would of [sic] been most happy."[68]

Amish schoolchildren scurrying into cornfields at Hazelton, Iowa, 1965. Credit: Photo by THOMAS DEFEO, courtesy of *The Des Moines Register.*

Just as Pennsylvania was finding solutions, other states were moving toward open conflict. In 1965 a situation in Iowa attracted national attention; moreover, it set the stage for the U.S. Supreme Court to rule on the educational rights of Amish and other minority groups.

In eastern Iowa's Buchanan County the issue of consolidating the Hazelton and Oelwein school districts was up for a vote. After officials assured the Amish that their two one-room schools would be preserved, the Amish voted for consolidation. By doing so, they made some non-Amish opponents of consolidation furious—furious that once the Amish enjoyed protection for their own traditional schools they would not help others win the same protection. Besieged by angry citizens, local officials summoned some Amish before a justice of the peace who found them guilty of conducting schools with uncertified teachers. Thereupon some Amish parents refused to pay their fines. In turn, their opponents began to call for liens against their property—a real threat. The conflict escalated to the point that in November local school officials tried to pick up Amish children from their farms and one-room schools and take them to the consolidated schools. The effort boomeranged. Soon national news media were broadcasting pictures of Amish children scurrying into cornfields and other refuges with local officials in pursuit. Of course such visual images brought national sympathy for the Amish. Iowa's governor, Harold E. Hughes, intervened and stopped efforts to catch the Amish children and forcibly transport them. Anonymous donors paid the outstanding fines. Anonymous foundations agreed, for the next two years, to pay the salaries of certified teachers for the Amish schools. Meanwhile the parties were to work toward a permanent solution.[69] The solution, reached in 1967, was that Amish who had been in the state ten years or more would be exempt from the state's educational code.[70]

An even more historic outcome was that the Iowa fracas set in motion the formation of a National Committee for Amish Religious Freedom. Made up of non-Amish, the committee organized with Reverend William C. Lindholm, a Lutheran pastor from Michigan, as its first chair. Other members included prominent Christian and Jewish leaders as well as concerned academics and lawyers. At issue were questions not only of Amish rights or privileges but also of religious and cultural pluralism and the place of nonconforming minorities in American society.[71]

Soon the new Amish-freedom committee was immersed in what would become the most historic legal case of all: *State of Wisconsin, Petitioner v. Jonas Yoder et al.* The climax was a U.S. Supreme Court ruling in 1972. Jonas Yoder was among a small group of Amish who began migrating into Green County in southern Wisconsin in 1963. In March 1969 three fathers in the group were found guilty of violating the state's compulsory attendance laws. In condemning them, the county court acknowledged that its decision infringed on Amish religious liberty. But it reasoned that the more important consideration was the state's duty to assure the children their education.[72] In response, the Amish-freedom committee's attorney, William Ball of Harrisburg, Pennsylvania, appealed to the district court. He lost. An appeal to the Wisconsin State Supreme Court was successful. But the state of Wisconsin chose not to accept the verdict, and took the issue to the U.S. Supreme Court.

On May 15, 1972, the highest court ruled unanimously that Amish children were not obliged to attend high school. Chief Jus-

tice Warren Burger supported the Amish position that "enforcement of the State's requirement of compulsory formal education
after the eighth grade would gravely endanger if not destroy the
free exercise of respondents' religious beliefs."[73]

Legal commentators considered *Wisconsin* v. *Yoder* a landmark case. Leo Pfeffer, a New York City attorney and a constitu-
tional scholar, termed it a key step in establishing the principle
that freedom of religion "is a specially 'preferred' right."[74] However,
the Amish saw the matter differently. They were not much interested in landmark cases and legal precedents. To them, the case
ended in victory for their ability to preserve their communities.
The Supreme Court had affirmed their right to nurture their children with their own values, letting them educate for their own
kind of life.

Conflict over Social Security

After education, the major matter of recent controversy and
confrontation between the Amish and government has been social security. Many people have objected to paying social security
taxes. But the Amish objected not only to the taxes but also to receiving the system's benefits. To them the taxes were irritating,
but the benefits were potentially destructive. The conflict surfaced
first in 1955 when legislation extended the social security system
to cover self-employed persons, including farmers. By then the system was twenty years old, but the Amish had not participated.

Now three Amish bishops—David Fisher of Pennsylvania, Neil
Hershberger of Ohio, and Henry Miller of Indiana—repeatedly met
with U.S. government officials to seek Amish exemption. Their
plea was simple. "We want no state or Federal aid or financial assistance."[75] The Amish had a long history of avoiding any kind of
commercial insurance; by the same token, they wanted no part of
governmental insurance.[76]

The conversations between Amish and government offered ri-
val conceptions of social welfare. The nation's social welfare policies reflected the atomization of society and the need to provide
protections for people who could depend neither on themselves
nor on their families and their local communities. By contrast,
into the 1960s Amish communities had little unemployment, few
single mothers, and virtually no elderly persons living singly. In
short, they had few cases in which their people's lives were threatened by absence of support systems. Furthermore, for the Amish

to accept governmental assistance might cause their own tradition of mutual aid to wither. And mutual aid was more than a support system. Inherent in it was a quality of care and compassion that was integral to their understanding of Christian community.[77]

Three years of discussions produced no agreement. So in 1958 the U.S. Internal Revenue Service (IRS) began seizing property of the Amish. By the 1960s it did so from more than 130 Amish households who had refused to pay the tax. Many seizures attracted considerable public notice, but none more than a case of IRS agents unhitching the horses of a Valentine Byler of New Wilmington, Pennsylvania, as he plowed his fields. Deprived of his livelihood, Byler sued Washington for damages. For Amish, such a step was rare, since they considered suing a violation of their nonresistance. Eventually, faced with Amish displeasure, Byler withdrew his suit. But public reaction to the Byler and other seizures prompted the IRS to suspend such confiscations.[78]

Then the Commissioner of the IRS, Mortimer M. Caplan, proposed a compromise. Meeting with Amish bishops in September 1961, he suggested that the Amish pay the required social security taxes but at retirement receive only exactly what they had paid in. In effect the Amish would receive no government gratuities. But the Amish leaders resisted. To them, Caplan was still asking for participation in public insurance.[79]

Meanwhile during the early 1960s national legislators from regions with sizable Amish populations introduced more than a dozen bills seeking exemption for the Amish. Finally a proposal succeeded. In 1965 Congress passed a new law which granted exemption to any religious group which opposed paying social security taxes for reasons of conscience.[80]

Conclusion to Amish-State Conflicts

By the late 1960s the Amish could point with some satisfaction to having carved out a recognized and acceptable niche for themselves with governments at various levels. In 1971 their national Steering Committee, reflecting in somewhat fractured syntax on its past conflicts and present status, observed,

We have come to the point where the Old Order Amish are recognized and respected by our Federal Government, giving us as much authority to take care of our own people and children if we are organized and capable of doing so. Through Parochial Schools for the school age children and through the Steering Committee for the draft age boys and through the Social Security exemption for farmers as well as many other problems which arise from time to time.[81]

CONCLUSION

The Old Orders cross history, tradition, and faith in a set of interlocking relationships that puts them in a category with other small, segregated, and virtually impermeable communities. The impermeability makes it difficult for interested outsiders to join. Segregated as they are, they sometimes seem distant even from their closest Mennonite cousins.

Nonetheless the Old Orders have not been merely groups unto themselves. While they have few connections with North American Mennonites of Dutch-Russian descent, they are intimately connected with other Mennonites and Amish of Swiss-and-south-German descent. Through interconnections formed by kinship and community networks, the Old Orders help populate and flavor many congregations whose roots are in the Swiss-and-south-German immigrations. Among the more conservative of such Mennonites and Amish the Old Orders are a retardant to change.

Unlike popular stereotypes suggest, Old Orders are not static in history. They modulate change by a concern for preserving their communities. In the whole Amish and Mennonite family, they have been most skillful at refining mechanisms to insure that their distinctive cultures will persist. In so doing, these most tradition-minded members of the Amish and Mennonite family have become the most visible in the national culture. A generation ago, they were almost social castoffs. By 1970 they were fast becoming folk heroes. Surely that change says more about America than it does about the Old Orders.

CHAPTER

13

MENNONITES AND THE VIETNAM WAR

In a landmark survey of American religious history, scholar Sydney Alhstrom defined the 1960s with its election of a Roman Catholic president and other changes as a time which ended the Puritan quadricentennium and marked a new stage in American religion.[1] And indeed the 1960s did seem to bring an ever-stronger religious pluralism, plus new perspectives such as African-American, feminist, and liberation theologies. For Ahlstrom the net result was that "dissensus was more visible than consensus."[2]

For Mennonites the 1960s hardly unraveled four hundred years of Anabaptist-Mennonite history, but they did challenge a fragile consensus. That was the consensus built at mid-century around the "Anabaptist Vision," CPS, and the resulting "servant activism." In the 1960s and early '70s a new unease, already present in the '50s, intensified. Along with American society, Mennonites found themselves polarizing: hawk versus dove; law-abider versus protester; youth versus age; counterculture versus establishment; activist versus quietist. Frustration, fears, and the underside of America as shown in violence in city ghettos and on distant battlefields, penetrated not just American suburbs but also Mennonite homes and congregations.

MCC IN VIETNAM
While the 1960s faced Mennonites with many conundrums, none touched their identity and their relationship to the larger culture as deeply as did the Vietnam War. Wars have been cata-

lysts for major shifts in Mennonite thinking; the Vietnam War was no exception. A statement from the 1966 MCC annual meeting began by noting that "Vietnam continues to trouble the Mennonite conscience." It was, the press release observed, one of Mennonites' "most perplexing dilemmas." Already for some years MCC had defined the U.S. military prosecution of the war as both illegal and indecent. But even more distressing, the U.S. government considered MCC's work in Vietnam to be an ally of its war efforts. MCCers who went to Vietnam to alleviate "wretchedness and hopelessness" and to assist in economic, health, and community development found that the military took "obvious pleasure" MCC's work.[3]

MCC had entered Vietnam in 1954, with much the same motives that were taking its workers to other places. There were people in Vietnam who were suffering and needy—so MCC went there "In the Name of Christ."

In the decision to go there was nothing incongruous. But 1954 was also the year in which forces under the Vietnamese leader Ho Chi Minh defeated the French, long the colonial overlords of Vietnam and other parts of Indochina, at a place called Dien Bien Phu. Thereafter the United States in effect replaced the French in the Vietnam War. To many Vietnamese the shift from French to American was no great change: different people, a different language, and still foreigners.

As it entered Vietnam, MCC was the only North American Protestant relief organization to work there. Its workers were the typical volunteers, going out with much more idealism than understanding of the local culture. Few if any went consciously to help the United States "contain" communism, but some MCC workers were comfortable with the regime the United States called South Vietnam. Others thought the best hope for Vietnam's future lay with the parties arrayed against the United States and its allies.[4] But whatever the MCCers thought, they were among the foreigners.

In Vietnam, in keeping with a worldwide policy of linking its work with local Christian communities, MCC joined hands with Christian and Missionary Alliance (CMA) missionaries and the church of those missionaries' handiwork—the Vietnam Evangelical Church, or Tin Lanh. Also, MCC did much of its work in cooperation with the Eastern Mennonite Board of Missions and Charities (EMBMC, agency of the MCs' Lancaster Conference), which was working in the southern Vietnam region around Saigon. In the early years MCC mainly did direct medical work plus distribute food and material aid, mostly to orphanages, homes for the blind, children's hospitals, and similar institutions. In November 1954 one shipment alone brought one hundred thousand pounds of corn meal.[5] Starting in 1960 MCC moved into agricultural and community development as well.[6]

Still another kind of MCC work was to resettle Vietnamese refugees, in a program with at least some similarities to a later, official U.S. effort known as "pacification." A diplomatic conference at Geneva, Switzerland, and the resulting "Geneva Accords" that followed the French defeat in 1954 divided Vietnam quite artificially into two "regroupment zones." Western nations soon called the zones "North Vietnam" and "South Vietnam," as if they were separate nations. According to the Accords, civilians could change zones. About nine hundred thousand refugees moved from the northern to the southern sector. Thereafter MCC assisted some of them. In so doing MCC worked more and more with what Americans called the South Vietnamese government.[7]

Vietnam offered all the difficulties of working in a third-world economy ravaged by military conflict. In such situations a mixture of deep poverty plus the influx of foreign money and goods has often profoundly corrupted the local societies. Vietnam was no exception. In that context the MCC decision to work through the Tin Lanh created its own set of problems.

The workers distributed MCC's material aid largely through that church, sending relief supplies to their final destinations via its network of congregations and individuals. Consequently church leaders were able to set priorities different from MCC's, and to keep materials for themselves and Tin Lanh members.[8] In 1964, MCC gave special assistance for families who were flood victims; but local church leaders emphasized church reconstruction and pastor support. Paul Longacre, director of MCC–Vietnam, complained that many of the leaders were all too "obsessed with [their] . . . citadels of brick and mortar."[9]

Of course MCCers set out to work through nonresistance and without political involvement, but that was not easy. For instance, as they began medical work they resolved not to become a medical service for military patients. Yet with time a Mennonite-run clinic at Nhatrang developed a cooperative arrangement with a nearby U.S. military hospital. Patients with acute problems and those needing specialized surgery were sent to the military hospital. Less acute cases and those needing post-operative care would be

Hospital at Nhatrang, built by MCC, 1961. Left to right: Pastor Tin, Dr. J. B. Dick, Pastor Huyen, Pastor Huong, Pastor Thai. Credit: MCC Collection, Archives of the Mennonite Church, Goshen, Indiana.

handled by the Mennonite clinic. Meanwhile an MCC program of refugee assistance accepted commodities and supplies from the U.S. Agency for International Development (USAID) which, although a civilian aid agency, had close ties to the U.S. military effort. Given the difficulty of movement, MCC workers accepted military transport. Similarly, they used the U.S. Army's postal service and shopped at its commissaries. In outlying sections, when military action came dangerously close to villages where MCCers lived, they occasionally took refuge in U.S. military camps and fortified buildings. By 1966, Doug Hostetter, a worker who was articulate and troubled by such entanglements, recorded in his diary that the U.S. military felt "our work is very important in the winning of this war."[10] Mennonites were perilously close to the U.S. military, even as they did good "In the Name of Christ."

As so often with aid, MCC supplies also nurtured dependency. In "Occasional Bulletins" that began in 1965 and frequently reflected the dilemmas of MCC's Vietnam work, Longacre asked whether MCC's material abundance was fostering an "unable-to-do-anything concept" within the Tin Lanh. Compared to MCC work, the Tin Lanh's own relief effort seemed so meager. The net result was to encourage the Vietnamese widow to look to Westerners rather than to give her mite. So Longacre began to ask if MCC was not partially defeating its own purpose, and whether it ought to withdraw.[11]

Medical work produced similar dependence. By 1965 MCC had operated a medical clinic in Nhatrang for six years, hoping (at least at first) that with time local people would take it over and even supply their own personnel and funding. After six years that change had not come, nor did it seem within reach.[12]

Relations with the Tin Lanh continued to be difficult. In 1966 Earl Martin, who shared Hostetter's mood, feared that the Tin Lanh's preoccupation with institutional survival might compromise MCC's ability to promote the "revolutionary, international, universal essence of the Gospel." Furthermore the Tin Lanh was such a small minority that its very smallness could limit MCC's ability to identify with the "interests and concerns of all peoples."[13] A further problem was that most CMA missionaries strongly supported American foreign policy in Asia and specifically the military effort in Vietnam. MCC dissent from such support hampered relationships not only with the CMA but also with other religious groups with whom MCC began cooperating in 1966.[14]

On January 1, 1966, the shape and nature of MCC's Vietnam work changed dramatically. On that date MCC joined Lutheran World Relief and an interdenominational Protestant agency, Church World Service, to form Vietnam Christian Service (VNCS). Initially MCC carried the administrative responsibility for VNCS work. VNCS also had relationships with the World Relief Commission of the National Association of Evangelicals and with the Tin Lanh. In fact by 1966 there were numerous voluntary agencies working in Vietnam to alleviate suffering and assist in development—all of them authorized by the South Vietnamese government (SVG). Although the agencies were nongovernmental, they worked mostly through governmental contracts. In 1969 their Vietnam budgets totaled $13,265,983, with half the money coming from various governments. Four million dollars were U.S. government monies. That level of support made it obvious that U.S. officials appreciated the agencies' work and considered it at least compatible with and at most a help to the military effort.[15] Moreover, agencies looked to the South Vietnamese government for operating privileges—visas for personnel, duty-free entry for supplies and equipment, etc. And the SVG expected something in return.[16]

VNCS sought to continue MCC's style with a "services-centered" approach rather than an "institutional" program emphasizing large-scale material aid. It tried to promote self-help rather than long-term assistance.[17] It hoped also to stay close to the Vietnamese people and thereby keep an identity separate from the military and USAID.[18]

However, as Longacre aptly noted, "people are easier to identi-

fy than materials." Americans just did not look like Vietnamese.
And in October 1967 Earl Martin protested to the VNCS's Saigon
office that its workers were going on site with too little training in
language and culture. "Is the slinging about of commodities becoming more important than working closely with the people
we've come here to serve?" he asked pointedly.[19] Furthermore,
some elements of the VNCS coalition did not want their program
to appear "pacifist."[20] But apparently the South Vietnam government did not consider VNCS to be too pacifist. In 1967 South Vietnam awarded VNCS director Paul Leatherman, a Mennonite, its
Order of Merit of the Republic of Vietnam.[21]

In 1968 the Vietnamese forces who opposed the United States
and its southern allies launched a devastating set of attacks—the
"Tet offensive." The battles created a great many new refugees and
worsened existing problems. Society in southern Vietnam polar-
ized ever more, and religious agencies felt the strains. Doug
Hostetter, working in a place called Tam Ky, observed that any
neutral ground there soon seemed "almost, if not completely
gone." Now the workers could administer God's love only "to people who live in 'good areas.' " Of course the U.S. military determined those areas.[22] And Tet made ever more clear that the conflict in Vietnam was political and cultural as much as military. If
the United States was to defeat the perceived enemy, it would need
to build a client state with stable social structures through im-
provements in agriculture, education, medical care, and community formation—exactly the social services that the voluntary
agencies provided.[23]

Both U.S. government officials and observant Vietnamese saw
the connection.[24] A Vietnamese professor told Earl Martin that
"what these humanitarian agencies may not realize is that the real
effect of their presence here is . . . [to obscure] the destructive nature of the total American intervention."[25]

As a way to be nonpartisan and keep its own identity, MCC
tried persistently to establish contact with America's "enemies"—that is, with the Democratic Republic of Vietnam (DRVN, or
"North Vietnam") and with the Provisional Revolutionary Government (PRG, the political arm of the forces usually called "Viet
Cong") in the South. From 1967 to the end of the war in 1975, MCC
had sporadic contact and distributed relief supplies valued at approximately $275,000 to people on the "other side."[26]

Atlee Beechy, a Goshen College professor with considerable
practical experience in peace advocacy and relief administration,

Earl Martin in Quang Ngai, 1967. Credit: Lance Woodruff, courtesy of MCC Collection, Archives of the Mennonite Church, Goshen, Indiana.

was chief among those who carried out such efforts. The contacts began in 1966 and 1967.[27] Between August 1970 and March 1971 Beechy held discussions with DRVN and PRG representatives in Paris, Prague, Berlin, Oslo, Stockholm, New Delhi, and Vientiane. According to Beechy, the conversations were to "witness to our faith and to our concern for peace" and to explore additional ways for MCC to assist all of Vietnam's peoples.[28] Beechy believed that without those efforts the Vietnam program "would have been a serious distortion of the biblical imperative of feeding the hungry and carrying out the reconciling ministry."[29]

Various MCC-related persons made such contacts also in Vietnam. But how could they overcome their American identities? In 1975, when it was clear that U.S. and so-called South Vietnamese forces were near defeat, Earl and Pat Martin tried to get assurance from the victors that they could stay on in their village, Quang Ngai. As they later recalled, they wanted to demonstrate that they "were a different kind of American, that the motive for our presence was somehow purer, more honorable."[30] But to their dismay they learned that even after they had lived in the village for several years, villagers thought of them as agents of the U.S. Central Intelligence Agency (CIA).[31] Such, in Vietnam, were the conundrums of being both American and a pacifist Christian.

One way to work at the conundrum was to make contacts and

try to deliver aid across the "enemy" lines. Another was to be a conduit of truth to the American government and the American people.

As the war was building up in 1965 and 1966, Longacre's reports from Vietnam directly contradicted what the American people were hearing from their government in Washington. In May 1966, he wrote about "ulcerating conditions," a "general war-weariness," and economic inflation brought on by the American presence. Military victory, he was sure, would "take a long time."[32] Early in 1968 William T. Snyder, MCC's chief executive who had just visited Vietnam during the Tet offensive, reported flatly that the U.S. "military effort . . . cannot succeed; that is something the American public is not being told."[33]

With such information and convictions, by November of 1966 various Mennonite groups and individuals had forwarded at least five major letters of concern and protest to U.S. President Lyndon Johnson. These included a May 1965 letter from the GC Board of Christian Social Concerns; a summer 1965 communique from the GC and the MC general conference sessions; a June 1966 letter from MCC to Johnson; a February 1966 letter, with special Vietnam issues of the *Gospel Herald* and *The Mennonite* enclosed, to all U.S. senators and congresspersons; and a letter from Paul Peachey conveyed to Johnson via private channels.[34]

A year later in October 1967, James Metzler, an MCCer in Vietnam, wrote an open letter to Johnson in which he compared himself to being "like one of the Germans who could hardly believe what he saw Hitler doing to the Jews."[35] Also in late 1967 the chairman of MCC, Christian (C. N.) Hostetter, Jr., wrote a strong letter to Johnson emphasizing that MCC workers on the field were sure that the United States was pursuing a "self-defeating" policy and that the "remedies only make the disease worse."[36] At about the same time, Eastern Board missionaries wrote a "Letter to American Christians" that expressed a similar view along with dismay at seeing the Christian church "being tied to the destruction of this land."[37]

Yet such protests to American officials did little to resolve the ambiguities Mennonites faced in Vietnam. A Vietnamese peasant once asked, "Why did they have to choose my country for the war?" To many Vietnamese it was indeed America's war, not theirs. And to carry an American identity was to be implicated.[38] In 1976 Earl Martin concluded that "Mennonite missionaries over the past eighteen years have been active agents of American imperialism in

Vietnam. . . ."[39] Paul Longacre expressed the problem more as a dilemma.[40] A dilemma it surely was.

CONFLICT OVER VIETNAM IN PUBLICATIONS AND INSTITUTIONS

In varying degrees the conundrum of Vietnam also affected many Mennonites who never left North America. The debate about Vietnam troubled congregations, conference offices, church institutions, and denominational periodicals. In the end that debate and the whole climate of the 1960s stimulated Mennonites to rethink their relationships to government and even to revisit the meaning of Jesus and his incarnation.

Nowhere was the debate more intense than in the official GC paper *The Mennonite*. As President Johnson was escalating the war in 1965, Maynard Shelly, editor from 1961 to 1971, was pensive. He perceived that America's Vietnam policies faced Mennonites with questions of church and state, proper conceptions of patriotism, the meaning of nonresistance, and the whole panoply of Mennonite peace understandings. But he also sensed that Vietnam might stop Mennonites' cultural drift and restore some of their "boldness." Mennonites, he wrote, had made "timidity . . . a way of life." By timidity Shelly meant complacency, the ease of thinking the familiar and comfortable. Boldness required a willingness to risk job, theology, status, and much more.[41] In 1968 Shelly was still asking: "Is a quiet, passive witness enough? Should not Christians do more to stem the tide of war?" Perhaps Mennonites were now at a new frontier of their thought and would "give attention to the political problems of peace."[42]

Meanwhile in Shelly's paper in 1966, Vincent Harding, the African-American historian, prophet, and at that time active Mennonite, was even more imperative. "We have," he wrote, "a choice to make. It is now thrust before us with every bomb that falls in Vietnam, with every patriotic speech that rings out in our communities. . . . Christ's or Caesar's—whose people are we?"[43] Here was two-kingdom Mennonite theology in bolder garb.

A few months later, again in *The Mennonite*, Harding pointedly presented the United States as an aggressor corrupted by its militarism and a leader who exceeded the law. To him, the nation's path was all too much like Germany's a quarter century earlier. He suggested that Mennonites should at least consider draft resistance and peace missions to Vietnam and China.[44]

Bethel College student ringing the campus bell during an anti-Vietnam War demonstration. Credit: Mennonite Library and Archives, Bethel College, North Newton, Kansas.

Responses to such statements revealed sharp cleavage in Mennonite thinking, both about the war's legitimacy and about appropriate Mennonite responses. From Bluffton, Ohio, one man argued that "unwary Mennonites" were being "drawn into an unholy alliance with the revolutionary force"; for Mennonites to join peace demonstrations was "hypocritical" because those activities were promoted by communists.[45] But a very different correspondent hoped that conference leaders had not "slipped to the point where they are offering only token resistance to militarism and war."[46] As time passed *The Mennonite* published many statements which essentially repeated those two positions. Many of the communications really asked the same question that other Americans were raising about the war.[47]

In January 1966, at the behest of the GC and MC Peace and Social Concerns Committees, *The Mennonite* and the *Gospel Herald* collaborated to produce similar issues on Vietnam. The purpose was to create "a congregational action manual on the war in Vietnam" and to "equip readers in the United States and Canada to witness to their governments."[48] To do so, the two papers offered the perspective of Mennonites working in Vietnam and ran articles which challenged American explanations of the war.[49]

One article by prominent Mennonite theologian John H. Yoder, entitled "Our Witness to Government," expressed the newer, more activist peace theology which Yoder had helped to fashion in the 1950s. Yoder argued that Mennonites had the right and even an obligation to address government. Since Christ was Lord of history, Mennonites did well to remind national leaders of their limited place. Also, Mennonites should speak to government because of love for the neighbor, because "we reject idolatry," and because national leaders generally considered themselves to be Christians. After all, Christians were supposed to counsel and if necessary even reprimand fellow Christians who were in error.[50]

Yet the concrete forms of witness for which the January 1966 numbers of *The Mennonite* and the *Gospel Herald* called were hardly different from what some Mennonites had been practicing for the last decade. These included joining in groups who worked for peace, becoming more informed and then sharing the enlarged insight with others, writing to government urging changes in public policy, and supporting MCC's kind of work. Distribution of the two issues—and of 3,000 extra copies—included sending a copy of *The Mennonite* to every U.S. Senator and one of the *Gospel Herald* to every member of the House of Representatives.[51]

Meanwhile on various college and university campuses, Mennonite students engaged in different kinds of antiwar activity. At Newton, Kansas, for Veterans Day, 1966, Bethel College students announced a three-mile "Repentance Walk and Mail" which was to end with depositing letters at the town's post office. However, community pressure and even threats of violence induced the students to abbreviate the event. Three years later the Bethel College Peace Club cooperated with a national "Vietnam Moratorium Committee." Quite successfully, the national committee carried out a stoppage of classes on many U.S. campuses, replacing them with seminars and other events to build opposition to the war. At Bethel, students and faculty staged a four-day rally and vigil which included ringing the campus bell once for each of the 40,000

American casualties in Vietnam and a march of more than twenty miles to Wichita.[52]

In 1966 Goshen College hosted a two-day conference with leaders of the Indiana University chapter of the antiwar Students for a Democratic Society (SDS)—among them SDS national chairman Clark Kissinger. Apparently Kissinger found a reflective response. At least he wrote back to Goshen students saying that "no other meeting with a student group has reminded us so forcefully of the values that must underlie our politics in SDS."[53]

In November 1969 roughly 525 Mennonite students and Voluntary Service workers participated in a peace march at Washington, D.C. Delton Franz, newly appointed as director of MCC's office in Washington, was sure that "something is 'blowin' in the wind' across the Mennonite college landscape."[54] The wind was indeed blowing, and not only at colleges. By summer 1966 MCC Peace Section was actively discussing the need for a Washington office. Behind the discussion was some Mennonites' growing interest in more effective witness to the state. At meetings in November 1965 the MC and the GC Peace and Social Concerns Committees had prodded for such action. Each committee urged the central board of its respective denomination plus MCC to consider such an office.[55] In 1967 such urgings gained strength as Mennonites repeatedly went to Washington to testify regarding bills for revising the military draft.[56]

In 1968 the MCC Washington office opened. Guy F. Hershberger defined it as a means for "the Mennonite peace witness to make an impact on Washington."[57] But it was also part of a larger shift—from testifying almost exclusively to protect Mennonites' own draft exemption and other interests to speaking out on behalf of many peoples and against many injustices.

By 1968 MCC was also looking for other ways to be more active in international conflict resolution. As of January 1968 it appointed a Canadian Mennonite journalist and church leader, Frank Epp, to a newly created, half-time post: Director of Studies in International Conflict. Epp's first project was a case study on "Vietnam and the Church." He aimed to find guidelines for the church to follow to help forestall such conflicts or intervene more effectively.[58]

In the GC denomination a December 1, 1967, meeting of its Council of Boards took a more radical stance on the war than any Mennonite body had ever taken. The Council called for sending medical aid to "war victims in North Vietnam"—even though it expected that to do so might bring "accusations and propaganda maneuvering." Even more controversially, the Council endorsed tax resistance. At issue was a federal excise tax on telephone use and a proposed surcharge on the U.S. income tax, both clearly marked as war taxes. The Council asked whether "the Christian who conscientiously objects to military service" should not also object to paying such taxes; and it urged "congregations and groups in congregations" to challenge whether the government could legally make them pay. Further, it requested congregations to give support, "emotionally and financially," to persons who got into trouble because they conscientiously refused.[59]

Some Mennonites found all the new activism quite troubling. In its first issue of 1966, the fundamentalist *The Sword and Trumpet* took a Mennonite position that was rooted in a high doctrine of separation and premillennial eschatology. Like all other wars, it editorialized, this war was wrong. Yet it was not the church's job to sit in judgment on national actions. Separation of church and state meant that the two worked in "distinctive spheres, with neither reaching across with a heavy hand into the affairs of the other." The journal's editors reasoned further that since the church had failed really to build a true community of faith, it was in no position to instruct government. And eschatologically, "Vietnam is but one skirmish in the 'wars and rumors of war' associated with the decline of the church and with the ascendancy of Antichrist."[60]

Taking much the same position were for instance J. Otis Yoder, moderator of the Virginia (MC) Conference and a consulting editor of *The Sword and Trumpet*, and, from western Pennsylvania, Sanford (S. G.) Shetler, an MC bishop and editor of a like-minded periodical called *Guidelines for Today*. In 1966 Yoder repeatedly protested to the MCs' Peace and Social Concerns Committee that the committee and other activists should not speak as if they represented the whole denomination. He feared that such "political actionism" would abandon "biblical non-resistance" and replace it with the outlook of "the beatnik pacifists."[61] Meanwhile Shetler was sure that as the antiwar activists were "COLLABORATING WITH A FIFTH COLUMN OF LEFTISTS AND COMMUNISTS TO DISARM [THE] U.S. MILITARILY, THEY ARE ALSO TRYING TO DISARM [THE] U.S. SPIRITUALLY."[62]

To quite an extent people such as J. Otis Yoder and S. G. Shetler were expressing a viewpoint often heard among MCs in the 1920s and 1930s. To be sure, there was a difference: now their opponents really were more activist. But as in the 1920s and 1930s, MC church leaders in the 1960s were anxious lest the differences seriously divide the church. A call put out by a Mennonite congregation (both MC- and GC-affiliated) at Boston, Massachusetts, asked for a special emergency antiwar conference. The call worried Bishop John E. Lapp of the Franconia (MC) Conference, among others.[63]

In response to such fears, the Committee on Peace and Social Concerns brought the leading antagonists together into a new study of church-state relations. Specifically, the group was to take up "the question of 'one morality' or 'dual morality' as it relates to the Christian, the church and the world-state." That is, could Christians ask the state to act more according to Christian ethics? Or should they reason that states had to operate by an ethics different from that of the church?[64]

DRAFT RESISTANCE OR COOPERATION?

In a peace church with long traditions both of nonconformity and of resisting military service, the draft resisters of the Vietnam era were an anomaly. They were a divisive element, dissidents in an already-dissenting tradition. In World War I, of about 2,000 Mennonites conscripted, nearly 10 percent had been court-martialed for resistance or at least noncooperation in the military camps. During World War II, with its alternative service system acceptable to most Mennonites, the proportion of draft resisters was far less. The data is incomplete, but apparently fewer than ten Mennonites and Amish went to prison—and several of them only because of mistakes in classification. After the war, under a new conscription law passed in 1948, several more Mennonites were jailed.[65] Nonetheless Vietnam-era resisters, as historians Melissa Miller and Phil Shenk have correctly observed, "tapped a geyser of emotion, criticism, and bewilderment" among many Mennonites.[66]

MC and GC

One starting point in the story of Vietnam-era Mennonite resisters was a long conversation in a coffee shop in Elkhart, Indiana in early summer 1969. In the shop's nondescript surroundings Doug Baker, Jon Lind, and Devon Leu—three current or recent students at Goshen College—frequently met and talked of the anguish the war and other injustices brought to their souls. On that evening in 1969, they pondered how to get the Mennonite church to take a resisting position.[67] Soon, in August at Turner, Oregon, there would be a meeting of the MCs' general conference, now renamed General Assembly. The resisters traveled to Oregon, to share their anguish with the church. The distance symbolized the journey that the MC church was about to take.

Living in a tent colony adjacent to the conference site and wearing garbs that *The Sword and Trumpet*'s editor termed "hippie," the resisters offered images quite in contrast to the larger assembly's cultural correctness.[68] More to the point, they arrived with a statement requesting that their church look on their position of noncooperation with Selective Service as a proper expression of Christian conscience and of the Mennonite tradition, and that it support persons who took that position. They doubted that the church would agree. However, to their surprise some church authorities immediately agreed to process their statement. Among those especially receptive were John A. Lapp, a historian at Eastern Mennonite College in his mid-thirties, member of the MC Peace and Social Concerns Committee, and secretary of the MCC Peace Section; Paul Mininger, president of Goshen College; John E. Lapp, prominent bishop in the Franconia Conference and father of the younger Lapp; and George R. Brunk II, evangelist, leader in the conservative Virginia Conference, son of *The Sword and Trumpet*'s founder, and himself an important assistant editor of that journal.[69] Whatever Brunk's views of political activism, he surely understood dissent and fidelity to one's convictions.

After a committee of the youthful protesters and church leaders refined the statement, it did not reject the mainline MC preference for alternative service. It thus maintained continuity with churchwide statements on the draft made in 1937 and 1951. But it did acknowledge that the Selective Service system was an integral part of the military and an agency whose "only purpose" was to "channel men into various vocations related directly or indirectly to killing." Moreover since the channeling involved coercion, it was at odds with Mennonites' concept of Christian vocation. So the statement declared that noncooperation was also a valid and "legitimate witness." Even more, it pledged the resources of the church to assist the young men choosing this option.[70]

Not since the American revolution nearly two centuries previous had a Mennonite conference gone on record endorsing noncooperation with an American military draft. Not all delegates approved. Critics reasoned that, at the least, such a radical departure should not have come until there had been longer and more intensive discussions by appropriate church bodies. Despite Brunk's role, the conservative *The Sword and Trumpet* lamented the church's alignment "with the whole unsavory war resisters movement."[71] The principle of nonresistance, well established in political circles as legitimate, might now "come into disrepute with officials."[72] In other words, *The Sword and Trumpet*'s editor was afraid that the church was jeopardizing alternative service. And he was not alone. Draft resisters often encountered that argument among Mennonite families and friends.[73]

GC Mennonites played out a similar scene in October 1969, at sessions of the Western District Conference. That conference also passed a resolution recognizing an individual's "total noncooperation with Selective Service" as a valid Christian position. However, it narrowly defeated an accompanying resolution in support of war protests. *The Mennonite* reported the developments under the headline "Mennonite ghetto faces eviction." Its article said that "the old rent—a simple C.O. position—was not going to cover the witness of the Mennonite church." The new rent would be more costly.[74]

MCC

In the next month, November 1969, in Chicago, MCC conducted a "Conscience and Conscription Conference." There, Doug Baker later noted, attendees in blue jeans and beards outnumbered "straights." Baker sensed further that conference leaders clearly favored the noncooperation position and perhaps even thought of it as "the ideal response."[75] A year later David Toews of Winnipeg attended a similar MCC conference and observed that more than half the participants were under thirty years of age. He dubbed the experience "how to be a radical in one easy weekend."[76]

Whether or not such conferences were truly radical, MCC Peace Section's executive secretary John A. Lapp began the Chicago sessions with questions that, for Mennonites, were both old and new. "Can a peace church live with conscription? If so, how?" Since 1940 Mennonites had indeed assumed they could, but "if not, what do we do?" What kind of alternative service gave an adequate witness? What responsibilities did the church have toward young men who accepted this or that option? The church had long been asking such questions. But now a new generation, uneasy with the alternative service both of World War II and of I-W service, was raising them anew.[77]

In Chicago J. Richard Burkholder, a Goshen College instructor in Christian ethics, and James C. Juhnke, a Bethel College historian, delivered the principal papers. They could hardly have made more clear that new Mennonite winds were blowing.

Burkholder noted that back in 1944 Guy F. Hershberger had written that the conscription system was a part of the military program and "a tool which lends itself to the evil purposes and methods of totalitarian states." However, in 1959 Harold Bender had discussed the effectiveness of refusing to register with Selective Service and had argued that "conscription is merely the command of the state to do work." Thus, by implication, Bender had treated conscription as morally neutral, at least technically. Using Bender's position somewhat as a foil, Burkholder noted that Bender had tended to expand the discussion from "conscience" alone to effectiveness, or consequences. For Burkholder, if Mennonites were evaluating the *consequences* of their responses to conscription, that fact made a huge difference. It meant that they could no longer ignore the political relevance of their responses. No longer could they give the typical, dualistic answer that since the state existed outside the perfection of Christ it was natural and acceptable that its ethics be sub-Christian.[78]

Borrowing a concept from the American peace activist A. J. Muste, Burkholder also raised questions about the Christian's "vocation." Why did Christians who sought to live by God's will so readily accept the government's disruption of their vocation? Why did they grant the state the right to determine one's calling and work? Traditionally, Mennonites had answered with a "second mile philosophy"—saying that even under the state's compulsion they would transform their service into work for God's kingdom. But could Mennonites so easily equate the two miles with two years of service? Granted, two years of jail time could be just as disruptive to a Christian's vocation, and Burkholder suggested that Mennonites might once again choose a different response, migration. But his main point was less to advise on how to deal with conscription than it was to clarify the forms and degrees of civil disobedience permissible in Mennonite thought. Now Mennonites were weighing civil disobedience in terms of its biblical faithfulness and its impact on the entire conscription system.[79]

The other major speaker, James Juhnke, depicted Mennonites as having compromised their fundamental positions to gain a bit of security and acceptance in American culture. The roots of the compromise went back to Mennonite cooperation with conscription in World War I. A few had gone to Canada and thereby "resisted through the time-honored Mennonite response of migration or flight."[80] But on their churches' advice, most Mennonite men had accepted conscription and gone to the military camps. There they had found "no escape from some compromise with the military establishment." From their traumas and the general scorn that Mennonites received for being slackers rather than good citizens, the search was on for a more acceptable civic identity. Partly to be more acceptable, Mennonites had then engaged in a new, altruistic activism and also in a "sacrifice of silence in the new idolatrous identification of God and country."[81] And when by World War II Mennonites had carved out an exemption system for themselves, they had done so at the price of muting any prophetic witness. To be sure, American society had become more tolerant of conscientious objectors. But in turn Mennonites had become more tolerant of American militarism.[82]

For Juhnke the responses to conscription and militarism were the defining elements in the American Mennonite identity. They had replaced adult baptism as the element that set Mennonites apart from the rest of the world. The "compromise of silence" and the willing retreat into a "favored position" on conscription were telltale signs of an eroded Mennonite identity. The "grateful silence was justified through a theological stance of nonprophetic dualistic separation of church and state." The compromise was not the dualism itself but its nonprophetic character.[83]

Thus Juhnke reasoned that Mennonite draft resistance was now an appropriate and even necessary corrective. The resisters were the rightful heirs to the long tradition of "nonconforming discipleship." They were breaking down the "old consensus" and projecting a "new vision the Mennonite church should recognize." To be sure, some compromise would always be present. But if Mennonites could not escape all compromise, they still needed to keep a "prophetic tension with the world"—a tension true to the past and necessary for revitalizing the future.[84]

As the Chicago conference closed, its findings committee repudiated the alternative service system as it existed. The committee found particularly objectionable the provision that allowed I-W draftees to earn civilian wages. Alternative service had "become so routine as no longer to call for a serious moral decision of discipleship"—and "so routine as to have largely lost its symbolic value in witnessing against war." The findings went on to affirm military noncooperation and to embrace the noncooperators for giving "new vitality to their commitment to radical discipleship and to their witness against war." Conferences and congregations were encouraged to "nourish them in their faith" and to provide financial support "in event of prosecution, imprisonment and other costs of discipleship."[85]

Soon after the conference, MCC Peace Section adopted and published a pamphlet entitled *The Draft Should Be Abolished* (May 1970). Its text repeated the arguments that the draft was intrinsically part of the military system. It presented Mennonites as wanting to preserve democratic rights as well as to oppose militarism. Conscription was a "system of involuntary servitude" and operated inequitably. Even the special privileges it gave to historic peace churches were inequitable. The pamphlet's conclusion called for a "reorientation of national values from war to peace, from regimentation to freedom, from militarism to humanity." The whole pamphlet was partly in keeping and partly at odds with Mennonite traditions of peacemaking. Opposing conscription was in line with Mennonites' history. Attacking the system's special privileges was not.[86]

Draft Census

Even in the 1960s and 1970s only a few Mennonites, even young ones, actively opposed conscription. The data vary. A 1973 MCC census found 10 Mennonite noncooperators (3 GC and 7 MC) who had been prosecuted; 17 not yet prosecuted, with the particulars of their cases unclear; and 9 who had gone as refugees to Canada, plus one to Ireland.[87] That study found 37, but another spoke of "more than four dozen" young Mennonite men who had tried some form of noncooperation.[88]

Whatever the total, what is most striking is the gap between Mennonite rhetoric and the small number who truly resisted conscription. The statistics of how many Mennonites cooperated with conscription are also uncertain, but clearly the proportion who accepted conscientious objector classification and went into alternative service increased during the 1950s and 1960s. Unofficial MCC records suggest that during the 1950s and '60s approximately 30 to 40 percent of GC and MC young men and about half of MB conscripted youths entered military service.[89] Another MCC statement indicates that whereas 51.8 percent of drafted Mennonites choose the CO position in 1960, 63.3 percent did so in 1970.[90]

The increase in conscientious objection may have reflected a post-World War II recommitment to Anabaptist theology, but it surely also mirrored a broader American disillusionment with the particular war in Vietnam. Moreover the numbers still suggested that quite a few persons from the larger Mennonite groups were going into military service; and the percentages from some of the smaller ones such as the Evangelical Mennonites and the Evangelical Mennonite Brethren were surely no less. By comparison, 37 or 48+ noncooperators were few indeed.

MB and EMB

Many Mennonites were far less willing than the draft resisters or the MCC conferences to move toward civil disobedience. For some the prophetic voice felt like a loss of patriotism. In 1969 the Evangelical Mennonite Brethren (EMB) church withdrew from MCC partly on grounds that MCC was moving toward "a more social action program."[91] The decision reflected a general loosening of that small denomination's Mennonite identity and a gradual drift toward Protestant evangelicalism. With that drift the EMBs were becoming comfortable enough with American militarism that between 1965 and 1972, 47 percent of their drafted members went into combat duty. In World War II and the Korean War the comparable statistics had been only 14.6 and 21 percent.[92]

The Mennonite Brethren, a larger group with considerable evangelicalism in the Mennonite-Evangelical mix, also reassessed its relationship to political society and political protest during the 1960s. At the triennial sessions of the MBs' North American conference in November 1966, delegates passed a "Statement on Political Involvement." Initially drafted by two young professors at Pacific College, Peter Klassen and John Redekop, then refined by a leading, older church figure, historian John A. Toews, the resolution called MBs toward a more engaged and prophetic political witness. The historic MB posture toward government had been a combination of nonparticipation, loyalty, and professions of patriotism in return for military exemption. But current social and political complexities called for more, and the paper suggested a position analogous to John H. Yoder's middle axioms. As the "Cross-Bearing Community" the church should always guard its relationship to the "Sword-Bearing Authority"—and do so by observing three principles: selectivity, being redemptive, and being prophetic. Of course Christians could be involved only in spheres which did not require them to suspend Christian ethics—mostly spheres of benevolence such as public education, health, and welfare. The prophetic principle required that Christians "judge all social institutions and political structures in the light of Christ's teaching." In the immediate context the church had to raise "a vote of protest against racial discrimination, social injustice, economic exploitation, and political corruption."[93]

The MB proposals pointed in directions the larger Mennonite bodies were going. They looked toward political activism, even a variety which was oppositional and prophetic. Yet their 1969 conference (despite an overall motto of "Christian Responsibility in a World of Unrest") also showed the limits of MB political activism. Two young delegates from Shafter, California, brought a resolution which called the delegates to protest the Vietnam war vigorously and to reshape the church. Posturing themselves in the Anabaptists' historic antiwar tradition, the students called for four actions. MBs should (1) "denounce" U.S. participation in the war and support political candidates committed to a peace platform; (2) declare the U.S. Selective Service "immoral" and pledge "unreserved support to draft resisters"; (3) recognize that silence in the face of major questions of injustice was "correctly interpreted as approval of the status quo"; and (4) consider that any call for a more "workable society" had to begin by refashioning the church into an honest, open, and communal entity.[94]

The 1969 MB conference rejected the students' statement on the procedural grounds that it had not come through the appropriate channels. Such far-reaching resolutions, conferees reasoned, required more discernment. But the real objections were not procedural. The conference passed a counter-resolution which its Board of Reference and Counsel (BORAC) hastily composed, a resolution which showed that conference leaders intended to hold the line against supporting draft resistance. The statement reaffirmed historic understandings, saying that war and violence were "incompatible with the nature and calling of the Church" and that the church was called to the ministry of reconciliation and thus to promote peace and good will in all relationships. But at the same time, it said, Christians were to be "subject to the powers that be" so long as they, the Christians, did not have to compromise their loyalty to Christ. And it still advocated alternative service as the way for MBs to be both reconcilers and obedient.[95]

BORAC committed itself to further study of the issues the
youthful protesters had raised. But then it decided not to bring a
resolution to the next conference, in 1972.[96] By 1975, under
BORAC auspices, John A. Toews authored a pamphlet entitled *Our
Ministry of Reconciliation in a Broken World*. In it Toews broadened the MB understanding of peacemaking from war to all forms
of international, national, industrial, economic, and racial conflicts. But he omitted any mention of the draft crisis which had
precipitated the 1969 discussion. By the time the pamphlet appeared, the Vietnam war and active conscription were passing as
pressing issues.[97]

In 1972 the MBs' North American convention reaffirmed the
traditional MB approach to questions of political activity. A "Resolution on Proclamation of the Gospel and Christian Social Responsibility" supported the idea of witnessing against injustices
in the socioeconomic order but emphasized that such witness always needed to be linked to evangelism. Proclamation and social
action or political witness, when biblically understood, were in-
separable.[98] In discussions leading up to the 1972 resolution,
some BORAC members expressed concern about churches which
emphasized only proclamation.[99] The principle to be emphasized,
said member Victor Adrian, was "the *inseparability of proclamation and social action*." MBs were to be "100% for proclamation"
and "100% for social action."[100]

THE 1960s IMPACT ON MENNONITE THOUGHT

The ferment of the 1960s caused Mennonites to rethink not
only their responses to conscription but their very theology. For instance, in the *Mennonite Life* issue of January 1970, Bethel College faculty member William Keeney, in an article on "Conditions
for a Revolutionary Century," argued that the "flux and change of
history" are moments when God breaks through to "redeem and
renew." So, Keeney wrote, Christians should be open to revolutionary changes and seek to discern how God wanted to use them in
the work of "redemption and judgment."[101]

If that was not necessarily a formula for keeping Mennonites
comfortable, neither were two articles in the same issue by Alvin
Beachy, also a Bethel College faculty member. Beachy found civil
disobedience throughout the Bible. What else was Jesus' trium-
phal entry into Jerusalem? Such biblical resistance had come
with eschatological vision. Eschatological politics were politics of

hope, of radical breakthrough. But Mennonites, with an ethic of being the quiet of the land (*Stillen im Lande*), had confused God's activity with "harmony and order."[102] Beachy also pointed to Pilgram Marpeck, a sixteenth-century Anabaptist. When Marpeck had found conflict between subservience to the state and obedience to Christ, he too had chosen civil disobedience.[103]

The same issue of *Mennonite Life* carried hints of a new, more activist-minded historiography. The Anabaptist Vision writings of Bender and others had reconstructed a past that helped keep Mennonites safe from liberal doctrine and helped protect Mennonite communities. By contrast, the historical renaissance of the 1960s sought a past that would nurture Mennonites' entry into the public order and their working to reform not only Mennonite communities but American society. The new outlook portrayed past Mennonite activism (relief) as being self-serving and "compromised." True, the past activism had given Mennonites a niche of respect and toleration. But now it was time to replace such acceptance with efforts to engage the political powers so as to promote equality and justice. The time had come for a witness that was more pure and less activated by self-interest.[104]

By the mid-1970s J. R. Burkholder would offer a new version of Ludwig Keller's "old evangelical brotherhoods." Keller had linked Mennonites to a long line of dissenting, evangelical groups who during the entire Christian era of Western civilization had largely been marginal and often even underground. Once more, Burkholder linked Mennonites historically to diverse communities who had sustained the pacifist witness to their rulers—groups such as the Donatists of Augustine's time, the fifteenth-century Unity of Czech Brethren, and the Kimbanguist Church in Africa of the 1970s.[105]

Like Alvin Beachy, Burkholder was calling for engagement, not withdrawal. He wrote, "The temptation of our tradition has been that of withdrawal: escape to a realm of security, avoidance of the struggle with the world and the stage, the realm of the demonic." He conceded that such retreat was defensible when the issue was sheer survival. But rationalizations that presented retreat as "effort to build . . . a lighthouse" or "the beloved community set apart as an example" seemed "suspiciously self-serving." Burkholder suggested that sectarians all too often retreated into a "psychological and spiritual security" in which they no longer heard the pleas "of the poor widow."[106]

For those subscribing to the Burkholder, Juhnke, Keeney, and

Beachy interpretations of Mennonite past and present, it was easy to see the draft resisters and the civil protesters as the tradition's true, uncompromised heirs. Such people perceived a Mennonite drift into comfortable membership in American society. Against that drift, radical witness was all the more necessary if Mennonites were to preserve their historic psychological distance from the world and its values. In the dialectic between engagement and separation, and between integration and alienation, the protesters and the historical revisionists would help keep the delicate balance. Those who seemed most alienated from their people would unwittingly preserve the distinctive people.

The majority of Mennonites still held to the dualistic view of church and state and were not ready to espouse civil disobedience or draft resistance. Yet even they were drifting toward more engagement in American politics. By 1970 more and more of them approved church efforts to influence governmental policy. A 1972 survey of five Mennonite denominations revealed that roughly half the members polled thought such influence was indeed the church's business.[107]

Mennonites were inclined to defend their growing activism not so much from history or with arguments arising from American politics as from biblical exegesis. Mennonites had always tempered their understanding of history with the commitment to be a biblical people. In the end any change in theological understanding required a fresh reading of the Bible. Such new reading had begun already in the 1950s. It reached an apogee with the publication, in 1972, of John H. Yoder's *The Politics of Jesus*.[108]

Yoder's book both maintained and extended the Mennonite way of theologizing. Its theological and ethical framework was not substantially different from that of his earlier writings. However, compared to Guy F. Hershberger's and Yoder's own earlier redefinition of Mennonite nonresistance, the biblical exegesis was more systematic. Yoder argued strongly for the essentially political nature of Jesus. In so doing he seemed to imply that the metaphysical and pietistic Jesus of Mennonite life was a caricature. Nor did he offer much place for mystical conceptions. Jesus was "not just a moralist. . . ; not primarily a teacher of spirituality. . . ; not just a sacrificial lamb preparing for his immolation. . . . In his divinely mandated . . . prophethood, priesthood, and kingship, [Jesus was] the bearer of a new possibility of human, social, and therefore political relationships."[109]

According to Yoder, Jesus did not become human just to inspire devotional exercises and metaphysical speculations and cultic communities; he came to inaugurate a kingdom. His incarnation began a messianic community that broke the powers of darkness and inaugurated the eschatological age. Among other acts, that kingdom practiced the jubilee—remitting debts, returning property, and liberating slaves. In it were the seeds of an egalitarian society, a society that could and would redistribute wealth and resources.[110] And the kingdom rejected coercion and violence as ways to achieve these reforms.

The Politics of Jesus argued that in the new eschatological age, the ethics and life of Jesus were to be the standard. As Jesus' followers accepted that standard, they too could break the powers of darkness. Once those powers were broken, there could be a new social order. The kingdom was not "hidden." Rather, it became real —in "obedience, in pardon and [in] repentance."[111] Jesus empowered his followers to establish the messianic community in all times and places. The believers' behavior and their community could indeed " 'partake of' the same quality or nature as that of [their] Lord."[112]

By being both present and future, the eschatological age cut through the dichotomies of most post-Reformation theology. Yoder's book suggested that at least five choices needed rethinking. These were the choices (1) between the Jesus of history and the Jesus of dogma; (2) between the prophet and the institution; (3) between the catastrophic and the inner kingdom; (4) between the political and the sectarian; and (5) between the individual and the social.[113] In such points Yoder presented the doctrine of the messianic kingdom as the center of the New Testament and as offering the possibility of incarnation in the present age.

The idea of the church as a messianic witness evoked deep resonance with many Christians other than Mennonites. In the 1970s and 1980s Yoder's *Politics of Jesus* attracted more readers than did any other Mennonite theological writing. Christian ethicists and biblical scholars of many traditions cited Yoder's work. A decade after the book's appearance, the magazine *Christian Century* named Yoder as one of the "most influential" theologians in the United States.[114]

If Yoder's book was appealing beyond Mennonite circles, it also offered a powerful reminder to Mennonites who were rapidly losing their distinct sociology. Like Hershberger and Bender before him, Yoder still offered Mennonites a middle ground. That ground lay between being a marginal people, existing only on society's fringes, and becoming merely a part of a modern society which was adept at undermining prophetic sects by folding them into the approved, established order. Messianic communities should and could be powerful instruments of witness. If they were, they would keep their distinctive peoplehood.

EPILOGUE

In the United States during the late 1960s and early '70s, talk of "identity crises" became fashionable. Emerging from the world of psychiatry, no doubt especially from the work of Erik Erikson, the notion of individuals undergoing periodic identity crises and identity reformulations was expanded to include groups. Paul Peachey, Mennonite sociologist and one of the first to apply this language to Mennonites, wrote that such crises come when "old syntheses disintegrate for whatever reason, and new ones must be forged."[1]

For Peachey the signs of such an identity crisis among Mennonites were numerous. One of the most visible was a new schismatic movement in the MC denomination. There is a long tradition of congregations and ministers considering themselves to be part of the MC tradition yet standing aloof from any conference affiliation. In 1945 that was the situation of at least five congregations and 47 ministers. By 1966 the numbers were 64 and 138, respectively. According to Peachey most of these individuals and congregations were "typically to the 'right' of the parent group."[2] He thought that other signs of stress and crisis were a growing role of right-wing extremist groups (both political and religious), and the "more subtle and 'respectable' " upward mobility of Mennonite professional and businesspeople.[3]

Historian John A. Toews, writing in 1972 from the vantage point of being a longtime and highly respected leader in the MB community, thought that MBs also were "experiencing an identity crisis unprecedented in their history." This was a strong statement for a group whose birth in the Russian empire in 1860 had been most painful and uncertain, who had migrated in differing generations to North America, and whose identity had always wavered between Anabaptist-Mennonitism and either European Pietism or American evangelicalism. Yet most MB observers would have probably agreed with Toews.[4]

According to Toews the heart of the MB church's identity crisis was a seeming inability to integrate the concerns of its "left wing," oriented to social action, relief, service, and MCC-style activism, and its "right wing" elements, who wished to "restrict our concerns to evangelism" and traditional kinds of "mission." Heightening the identity crisis was the fact that the left wing generally identified more closely with the Mennonite world, while the right wing felt more at home with the National Association of Evangelicals and its kind.[5]

Similar fissures showed up in a survey of 3,591 individuals representing 200,000 Mennonites in Canada and the United States in five denominations who were among the most progressive in the Amish-Mennonite-Brethren in Christ family: the GCs, MBs, MCs, EMCs, and BICs. "Unresolved tensions" was the way the survey's researchers, Mennonite sociologists J. Howard Kauffman and Leland Harder, described those fissures. By their analysis, the main "unresolved tensions" were sectarianism versus ecumenicism; Anabaptism versus political participation (they obviously believed that Anabaptism had been nonpolitical, at least in the modern sense); personal piety versus social concerns; and the enigmatic impact of both fundamentalism and cultural assimilation.[6]

No doubt these identity-crisis assessments reflected the trauma the 1960s held for Mennonites and for many other Americans. For Mennonites, that decade seemed to set historic understandings of nonresistance against a more activist peacemaking; a leftist political and cultural critique against attitudes quite comfortable with support-America patriotism; and those wishing to be the *Stillen im Lande* (the quiet in the land) against those wanting to speak out with prophetic voice.

Mennonites in the 1960s surely were being tugged in differing directions. But that was not new. Mennonites living in the 1930s and entering the middle third of the twentieth century had also been pulled different ways. All the progressive Mennonite denominations had felt caught in the tensions between so-called liberals and fundamentalists. Certainly they were caught between cultural modernizers and cultural conservatives, between those wishing to retain cherished ways of dress, of language, and of authority, and those wanting newer freedoms and newer cultural forms.

So identity crisis was not exactly new in the 1960s. In the 1940s Mennonites' greatest intellectual achievement—Harold Bender's "Anabaptist Vision"—was a response to an identity crisis. Bender had sought an intellectual and ancestral home for a people bewildered by rapid social change.

And so, quite profoundly, American Mennonites entered the last third of the twentieth century much as they had entered its middle third. Once again they were unsure how to maintain their inheritance within modern American culture.

As Peachey wrote of Mennonite identity crisis in 1968, he correctly observed that such a crisis was common to all "Jewish and Christian groups in America." Its intellectual and cultural origins were in the eighteenth-century Enlightenment. But, Peachey thought, there was also a new element. This was the crisis of modernity, which now was penetrating Mennonite imaginations and communities. Like virtually all Christian and Jewish groups, Mennonites had "forged links between their faith and their cultural legacies." As intrusive modernity assaulted the cultural systems of different religious groups, disorientation set in.[7]

In common with the stories of other small ethnic and religious communities, the story of American Mennonites included both persistence and reformulation of the relations between faith and culture. But if the Mennonite story was like others, it also was different. From their beginnings in America, Mennonites had always lived with faith and surrounding culture in opposition. While American Mennonite theology was always malleable, its core had always included understandings that were foreign to America.

Always a gulf had existed between Mennonites and the American religious mainstream. Mennonites had never assumed that America was the new Garden of Eden. They had never seen the American state as the uniquely chosen instrument of God to advance history to its completion and perfection. They had never thought that the American nation was the chosen instrument to bring salvation to all of humanity.

The chasm between Mennonites and American society always hinged around conceptions of nationality and the role of the state in the unfolding of Christian history. At bottom, what distinguished Mennonites from America was their belief in nonresistance. Nonresistance (whether the passive or the more active version) has been the double entendre that has both cohered and dismembered Mennonite communities; it has both sustained and eroded a distinctive identity. In the Mennonite world it has been the source of both alienation and creativity. No other period in American Mennonite history has been as full of wars and rumors of war as the period from 1930 to 1970. Living through World War II, the Korean War, the Vietnam War, and the Cold War, Americans—including Mennonites—constantly were either preparing for the next war, engaged in war, or recovering from the last one. No wonder Mennonite identity became frayed.

Pressures also came from the Great Depression, fundamentalism, the postwar era's changing economic, educational, and spatial realities, and the civil-rights movement. Such pressures continually challenged inherited ways of thinking and acting. Visual nonconformity, a politically inactive nonresistance, nonsalaried multiple lay leadership, and leaders and conferences with authority and prescriptive power—all of which had long been hallmarks for Mennonites—gave way in the century's middle third.

The changes and identity-fractures were more far-reaching for the progressive Mennonites than for the Old Orders. Old Orders managed to maintain their traditions more intact. Already in the nineteenth century they had refined various mechanisms to resist modernity's intrusions. With their doctrines of separation so inventively refined, their identities remained more constant throughout the twentieth century. To the Old Order peoples, the term identity crisis scarcely applied.

Precisely as the progressive Mennonites lost many of the cultural symbols of their identity, they replaced those symbols with newer institutional, ideological, and activist ones and with inter-Mennonite networks which nurtured the persistence of a distinctive Mennonite community. The new symbols and networks were antidotes to the "acids of modernity" that threaten distinctive communities.

The middle decades of the twentieth century were good ones for institution-building. Mennonite educational institutions multiplied. Mission programs expanded. Social service institutions flourished as never before. During these same decades such institutions brought even more people into their orbits and became stronger carriers of Mennonite identity.

The inter-Mennonite movement diminished distance between ethnic traditions and denominational communities.

Kauffman and Harder's study of the five progressive denominations revealed far more denominational similarities than differences. At the same time that Mennonites participated more and more in the dominant American culture, they found each other and created new institutions and associations where they could embrace and fortify shared values.

The most important redefinition of Mennonitism and the most persuasive guarantor of continued Mennonite distinctiveness was the articulation of a new system of ideas. Harold Bender's Anabaptist Vision was an exceptional exercise in revising history. But it was much more. It was the crowning achievement of twentieth-century ideological reconstruction of Mennonite identity.

The Anabaptist Vision provided American Mennonites with a new sense of particularity and mission. It redefined Mennonite communities as messianic outposts empowered to forecast and anticipate the kingdom of God. It empowered Mennonites to a new "servant activism" that flowed out through agencies like MCC to the corners of the globe. It cast aside the notions of Mennonitism as something tribal or ethnic. Into the early 1970s[8] the Anabaptist Vision rhetoric joined with the recently developed global "servant activism" to provide Mennonites with an identity rooted in a particularistic past and a global present.

The twentieth-century Mennonite story offers an excellent example of how communities with their own special cultures and convictions can endure in modern America even under pressures to conform to larger national patterns. Since the mid-nineteenth century, many social scientists have assumed that modernization, urbanization, and global economics would force all particularities, including religious communities, to merge into the larger whole. The idea was that the community in the older sense was "breaking-up," suffering "erosion or eclipse," and in "decline."[9]

Scholars have thought that the change which sociologist Ferdinand Tonnies defined as moving from "Gemeinschaft to Gesellschaft"—that is, from community based on face-to-face personal relationships to larger, impersonal groupings held together more by contracts and other formal, functional relationships—would shape all other social realities. And they have thought that such change would engulf all peoples.

In recent decades many scholars have become suspicious of that grand, overarching explanation of Western history. To see all peoples as moving along the same straight path to modernization is to ignore the fact that some persistent and inventive peoples have kept their own particular characters. Some of those communities have not only achieved self-preservation; they have expanded. Mennonites are a case in point.

Above all, the story of Mennonites in America from 1930 to 1970 is one of moving from the margins of society to more participation in society's institutions, its culture, and its values. Yet Mennonites have also maintained their own discernible community. Among them the Old Order groups have worked hardest at preserving the spatial folk communities in which most Mennonites and Amish throughout history have lived. Progressive Mennonites have worked more at preserving community via new denominational structures, ideological formulas, and ecumenical alliances.

Into the 1970s both strategies worked. At least they helped Mennonites and Amish maintain an inner sense and self-identity of belonging to their own communities. And the Mennonite and Amish communities did not disappear into the larger American culture.

KEY TO ABBREVIATIONS
Used in notes and bibliography

LIBRARIES AND ARCHIVES

AMC   Archives of the Mennonite Church, Goshen, Indiana

CMBS-F Center for Mennonite Brethren Studies, Fresno, The Mennonite Brethren Biblical Seminary and Fresno Pacific College, Fresno, California

CMBS-H Center for Mennonite Brethren Studies, Hillsboro, Tabor College, Hillsboro, Kansas

EPMHL   Eastern Pennsylvania Mennonite Historical Library, Souderton, Pennsylvania

LMHS   Lancaster Mennonite Historical Society, Lancaster, Pennsylvania

MLA   Mennonite Library and Archives, Bethel College, North Newton Kansas

MHL   Mennonite Historical Library, Goshen College, Goshen, Indiana

PUBLISHED TITLES

CL   *Christian Leader*, periodical of the Mennonite Brethren church

GH   *Gospel Herald*, periodical of the Mennonite Church (MC)

JMS   *Journal of Mennonite Studies*, published at Winnipeg, Manitoba

ME   *The Mennonite Encyclopedia*

MHB   *Mennonite Historical Bulletin,* published in association with the AMC

ML   *Mennonite Life,* published at Bethel College, North Newton, Kansas

MQR   *The Mennonite Quarterly Review,* published under the auspices of Associated Mennonite Biblical Seminary, Goshen College, and the Mennonite Historical Society

MWR   *Mennonite Weekly Review,* an independent weekly published at Newton, Kansas

TM   *The Mennonite,* periodical of the General Conference Mennonite Church

SPECIFIC ARCHIVAL COLLECTIONS

Bender papers   Papers of Harold S. Bender, in AMC

Fast papers   Papers of Henry A. Fast, in MLA

NOTES

CHAPTER 1

1. For additional biographical information on these individuals see obituary of Kratz in *Year Book of the General Conference of the Mennonite Church of North America* (1941), 31-32; "Maxwell H. Kratz," *ME*, II, 233; John Umble, *Mennonite Pioneers* (Elkhart, Ind.: Mennonite Board of Missions and Charities, 1940), 137-152 (on Levi Mumaw); Wesley Prieb, *Peter C. Hiebert: "He Gave Them Bread"* (Hillsboro, Kan.: Center for Mennonite Brethren Studies—Hillsboro, 1990); Paul Erb, *Orie O. Miller: The Story of a Man and an Era* (Scottdale, Pa.: Herald Press, 1969); and *MQR* 38 (Apr. 1964), a Harold S. Bender memorial issue with a biography by J. C. Wenger. The *MQR* issue became the basis for John C. Wenger, et al., *Harold S. Bender: Educator, Historian, Churchman* (Scottdale, Pa.: Herald Press, 1964); a full biography of Bender sponsored by a "Harold S. Bender Life and Times Project" and written by Albert N. Keim of Eastern Mennonite University is forthcoming.

2. Minutes of the MCC Executive Committee, Jan. 18, 1930, b. 1, MCC Archives IX-5-1, AMC. The story of Mennonites in Moscow in 1930 is told in Frank Epp, *Mennonite Exodus: The Rescue and Resettlement of the Russian Mennonites Since the Communist Revolution* (Altona, Man.: Canadian Mennonite Relief and Immigration Council, 1962), 241.

3. MCC annually published a *Mennonite Central Committee Workbook* which details the myriad activities and benevolencies of its work around the world.

4. U.S. Bureau of the Census, *Census of Religious Bodies, 1936: Mennonite Bodies; Statistics, Denominational History, Doctrines and Organization* (Washington, D.C.: Government Printing Office, 1940), 5.

5. See Peter J. Klassen, *A Homeland for Strangers: An Introduction to Mennonites in Poland and Prussia* (Fresno, Calif.: Center for Mennonite Brethren Studies—Fresno, 1989); John B. Toews, *Czars, Soviets and Mennonites* (Newton, Kan.: Faith & Life Press, 1982); James Urry, *None but Saints: The Transformation of Mennonite Life in Russia, 1789-1889* (Winnipeg, Man.: Hyperion Press, 1989).

6. See James Juhnke, "Mennonite History and Self-Understanding: North American Mennonitism as a Bi-Polar Mosaic," in *Mennonite Identity: Historical and Contemporary Perspectives*, ed. Calvin Wall Redekop (Lanham, Md.: University Press of America, 1988), 83-99.

7. Statistics in the last several paragraphs are from: U.S. . . . , *Census of Religious Bodies, 1936*, 5.

8. The Anabaptist relationship to modernity has been the subject of an abundant historiography. The issue is part of the larger debate about the degree to which various sixteenth-century religious movements broke with the thought and structures of medieval faith and society. Among the works which present Anabaptism as a precursor of modernity are Roland Bainton, *Studies in the Reformation*, Collected

Papers in Church History vol. 2 (Boston: Beacon Press, 1963), 199; Ernst Troeltsch, *Protestantism and Progress: A Historical Study of the Relationship of Protestantism to the Modern World*, trans. W. Montgomery (Boston: Beacon Press, 1958), 48, 95-96, 104, 153, 174; and Jaroslav Pelikan, *Reformation of Church and Dogma (1300-1700)*, The Christian Tradition vol. 4 (Chicago: University of Chicago Press, 1984), 305.

9. James Stayer, *Anabaptists and the Sword* (Lawrence, Kan.: Coronado Press, 1972), 330.

10. On the social and political withdrawal following the Revolutionary War, see Richard K. MacMaster, *Land, Piety, Peoplehood: The Establishment of Mennonite Communities in America, 1683-1790*, The Mennonite Experience in America vol. 1 (Scottdale, Pa.: Herald Press, 1985); and Richard K. MacMaster with Samuel L. Horst and Robert F. Ulle, *Conscience in Crisis: Mennonites and Other Peace Churches in America, 1739-1789: Interpretation and Documents* (Scottdale, Pa.: Herald Press, 1979).

11. Robert Wiebe, *The Search for Order, 1877-1920* (New York: Hill and Wang, 1967), ch. 1. This paragraph and the following are adaptations from Paul Toews, "Dissolving the Boundaries and Strengthening the Nuclei," *CL* 45 (July 27, 1982), 6.

12. On the Jewish response to modernity, see Jacob Neusner, *Death and Birth of Judaism: The Impact of Christianity, Secularism and the Holocaust on Jewish Faith* (New York: Basic Books, 1987); for the Dutch Reformed, see James D. Bratt, *Dutch Calvinism in Modern America: A History of a Conservative Subculture* (Grand Rapids, Mich.: Eerdmans, 1984).

13. See John Higham, "Hanging Together: Divergent Unities in American History," *The Journal of American History* 61 (June 1974), 5-28; Higham suggested that in American society ideological and technical forms of unity have replaced primordial unity.

14. John A. Hostetler, *Amish Society* (3rd ed. Baltimore: Johns Hopkins University Press, 1980), 273-274. For further history, especially including the concept of *Ordnung*, see Paton Yoder, *Tradition and Transition: Amish Mennonites and Old Order Amish, 1800-1900* (Scottdale, Pa.: Herald Press, 1991); Theron F. Schlabach, *Peace, Faith, Nation: Mennonites and Amish in Nineteenth-Century America*, The Mennonite Experience in America vol. 2 (Scottdale, Pa.: Herald Press, 1988), 201-203, 207-220; James N. Gingerich, "Ordinance or Ordering: *Ordnung* and Amish Ministers Meetings, 1862-1878," *MQR* 60 (Apr. 1986), 180-99; and [JFB,] "Research Note: Ordnung," *MQR* 56 (Oct. 1982), 382-384.

15. Alvin J. Beachy, "The Amish Settlement in Somerset County, Pennsylvania," *MQR* 28 (Oct. 1954), 279-283; Alvin J. Beachy, "The Rise and Development of the Beachy Amish Mennonite Churches," *MQR* 29 (Apr. 1955), 118-119.

16. Sources in n. 15; Rufus Beachy to Moses Beachy, Dec. 11, 1926, b. 1, Moses Beachy papers, AMC.

17. On the theme of Amish and Mennonite humility, see Joseph C. Liechty, "Humility: The Foundation of Mennonite Religious Outlook in the 1860s," *MQR* 54 (Jan. 1980), 5-31; and Schlabach, *Peace, Faith, Nation*, 28-32, 95-105.

18. Beachy, "Rise and Development," 133; see also Elmer S. Yoder, *The Beachy Amish Mennonite Fellowship Churches* (Hartville, Ohio: Diakonia Ministries, 1987). In surveying the entire story of the Beachy Amish, Yoder concurred that the Somerset developments ought to be thought of as the beginning of the Beachy fellowship, but he noted that others have pointed to 1927 Lancaster County movements as that beginning.

19. See Emma Hurst, "Moses G. Horning and the Old Order Divisions in Pennsylvania," *MHB* 21 (Apr. 1960), 1-2, 4; and Robert Bates Graber, "The Sociocultural Differentiation of a Religious Sect: Schisms Among the Pennsylvania German Mennonites" (Ph.D. diss., University of Wisconsin-Milwaukee, 1979). The quotations are from "The Automobile Issue Among the Old Order Mennonites: 1920," a printing of the Kurtz letter in the *MHB* 27 (Oct. 1976), 5-6.

20. The literature that reflects on Mennonite denominationalizing is considerable, e.g.: Juhnke, *Vision, Doctrine, War: Mennonite Identity and Organization in America, 1890-1930*, The Mennonite Experience in America vol. 3 (Scottdale, Pa.: Herald Press, 1989); Rodney J. Sawatsky, "History and Ideology: American Mennonite Identity Definition Through History" (Ph.D. diss., Princeton University, 1977); Beulah Stauffer Hostetler, *American Mennonites and Protestant Movements: A Community Paradigm* (Scottdale, Pa.: Herald Press, 1987); and Theron F. Schlabach, "Reveille for *die Stillen im Lande*: A Stir Among Mennonites in the Late Nineteenth Century," *MQR* 51 (July 1977), 213-226. On the nature of American denominationalism, see Russell E. Richey, ed., *Denominationalism* (Nashville, Tenn.: Abingdon Press, 1977); and Sydney Mead, *The Lively Experiment: The Shaping of Christianity in America* (New York: Harper & Row, 1963).

21. Harold S. Bender, "Editorial" and "To the Youth of the Mennonite Church," *MQR* 1 (Jan. 1927), 1, iv.

22. For an extended discussion of the place of history in Mennonite identity, see Sawatsky, "History and Ideology."

23. Harold S. Bender to John Horsch, Nov. 19, 1929, corresp. 1929 A-H, Horsch papers, AMC.

24. Harold S. Bender, "The Anabaptist Vision," *Church History* 13 (Mar. 1944), 3-23.

25. U.S. . . . . , *Census of Religious Bodies, 1936*, 3.

26. Ibid.

CHAPTER 2

1. See MCC Exec. Comm. minutes, AMC: Jan. 18, 1930; Jan. 25, 1930; Apr. 26, 1930; Oct. 13, 1930.

2. See, e.g., Orlando Harms, *The Journey of a Church* (Hillsboro, Kan.: Center for Mennonite Brethren Studies—Hillsboro, 1987), 107. Harms noted that during the 1920s Hillsboro, Kan., paved and guttered its streets, purchased its first engine-operated fire equipment, and constructed a municipal waterworks. Hillsboro, a town of 1,600 persons who were largely Mennonite immigrants from the Russian empire or their offspring, was the home of several Mennonite Brethren institutions.

3. For a convenient sources, see Theron Schlabach, *Peace, Faith, Nation: Mennonite and Amish in Nineteenth-Century America*, The Mennonite Experience in America vol. 2 (Scottdale, Pa.: Herald Press, 1988), 117-127; for a full account and context see John L. Ruth, *Maintaining the Right Fellowship: A Narrative Account of Life in the Oldest Mennonite Community in North America* (Scottdale, Pa.: Herald Press, 1984), esp. chs. 8-10 (ch. 9 recounting the actual schism).

4. Ruth, *Maintaining the Right Fellowship*, 473.

5. Ibid., 477.

6. Ibid., 460-461, quoting an unidentified newspaper clipping.

7. Ibid., 462.

8. Ibid., 463.

9. Harms, *Journey of a Church* (n. 2), 152-154.

10. Various news briefs in *TM* 64 (Aug. 29, 1929), 1.

11. *Minutes and Reports of the 25th Session of the General Conference of the Mennonite Church of North America, August 20-28, 1929* (Hutchison, Kan.), 35.

12. Rachel Waltner Goossen, *Prairie Vision: A History of the Pleasant Valley Mennonite Church, 1888-1988* (Hillsboro, Kan.: Pleasant Valley Church, 1988), 55.

13. *Edward, Pilgrimage of a Mind: The Journal of Edward Yoder, 1931-1945*, ed. Ida Yoder (privately published, 1985), Sep. 11, 1939.

14. James O. Lehman, *Salem's First Century: Worship and Witness* (Kidron, Ohio: Salem Mennonite Church, 1986), 130.

15. James O. Lehman, *Sonnenberg, a Haven and a Heritage: A Sesquicenten-

nial History of the Swiss Mennonite Community of Southeastern Wayne County, Ohio (Kidron, Ohio: Kidron Community Council, Inc., 1969), 322-324, 52, 288-300; Lehman, *Salem's First Century*, 131-133.

16. Goossen, *Prairie Vision*, 42-43.

17. James O. Lehman, *Seedbed for Leadership: A Centennial History of the Pike Mennonite Church* (Elida, Ohio: Pike Mennonite Church, 1974), 54-56.

18. Ibid., 54-60.

19. Stanley E. Voth, ed., *Henderson Mennonites: From Holland to Henderson* (n.p.: Henderson Centennial Committee, 1975), 110.

20. James C. Olson, *History of Nebraska* (Lincoln: University of Nebraska Press, 1966), 284-291.

21. Voth, *Henderson Mennonites*, 138.

22. William Zornow, *Kansas: A History of the Jayhawk State* (Norman, Ok.: University of Oklahoma Press, 1957), 251-274.

23. Joseph S. Miller, *Beyond the Mystic Border: 100 Year History of the Whitestone Mennonite Church* (Hesston, Kan.: Whitestone Mennonite Church, 1985), 102.

24. *Edward, Pilgrimage* (n. 13), Sep. 6, 1934.

25. Ibid., June 22, 1932.

26. John D. Thiesen, *Prussian Roots, Kansas Branches: A History of the First Mennonite Church of Newton* (Newton, Kan.: First Mennonite Church, 1986), 54-58.

27. Harms, *Journey of a Church* (n. 2), 148.

28. Miller, *Beyond the Mystic Border*, 101.

29. Reedley Mennonite Brethren Congregational Records, CMBS-F. Figures for other congregations are from various MB district and general conference yearbooks.

30. Mary Miller, *A Pillar of Cloud: The Story of Hesston College, 1909-1959* (North Newton, Kan.: Mennonite Press, 1959), 97-105.

31. Ibid.; Justus G. Holsinger, *Upon This Rock: Remembering Together the 75-Year Story of the Hesston Mennonite Church* (Hesston, Kan.: Hesston Mennonite Church, 1984), 19.

32. Peter J. Wedel, *The Story of Bethel College*, ed. Edmund G. Kaufman (North Newton, Kan.: Bethel College, 1954), 332-333.

33. Wedel, *Story of Bethel College*, ch. 17; David A. Haury, *Prairie People: A History of the Western District Conference* (Newton, Kan.: Faith & Life Press, 1981), 232-241.

34. William Schmidt, "History of Tabor College" (M.A. thesis, University of Wichita, 1961), 82-84.

35. See, in *Tabor College Herald* n.s. 1: "Tabor College Bible and Mission School" (July 1931), 5; P. E. Schellenberg, "Editorial" (Sep, 1931), 6-8. See also: P. C. Hiebert, "Autobiography," Peter C. Hiebert papers, CMBS-H; Paul Toews, "Henry W. Lohrenz and Tabor College," *ML* 38 (Sep. 1983), 11-19.

36. Tabor College Faculty minutes, Dec. 3, 1930, CMBS-H; H. W. Lohrenz to R. C. Seibel, Feb. 27, 1933, f. 5, b. 16, H. W. Lohrenz papers, CMBS-F.

37. "Possible By-Products of the Depression," *GH* 25 (July 14, 1932), 315.

38. John H. Martin, "Disobedient People Responsible for Drought-Stricken Nation," *GH* 23 (Oct. 23, 1930), 651. For similar expressions see J. N. Kaufman, "Can We See the Hand of God in the Present Financial Depression," *GH* 24 (Mar. 3, 1932), 1058-1059; C. Z. Martin, "Some Scriptural Reasons for the Drought and Depression," *GH* 23 (Aug. 21, 1930), 452.

39. Daniel Kauffman, "Editorial: Why People Are Poor," *GH* 27 (Jan. 24, 1935), 917.

40. "Editorial," *TM* 47 (Aug. 4, 1932), 2.

41. *Edward, Pilgrimage* (n. 13), Jan. 1, 1933, Apr. 27, 1934.

42. "Meditations on the Unemployment Situation," *GH* 23 (Apr. 17, 1930), 1-2.

43. John A. Hostetler, *The Sociology of Mennonite Evangelism* (Scottdale, Pa.: Herald Press, 1954), 82a.

44. *Report of the Conservative Mennonite Conference, August 9-12, 1955*, copy in MHL.

45. John A. Toews, *A History of the Mennonite Brethren Church: Pilgrims and Pioneers*, ed. A. J. Klassen (Fresno, Calif.: Board of Christian Literature, General Conference of Mennonite Brethren Churches, 1975), 198-204.

46. Lois Barrett, *The Vision and the Reality: The Story of Home Missions in the General Conference Mennonite Church* (Newton, Kan.: Faith & Life Press, 1983), ch. 5.

47. Barrett, *Vision and Reality*, 89-94.

48. Theron Schlabach, *Gospel Versus Gospel: Mission and the Mennonite Church, 1863-1944* (Scottdale, Pa.: Herald Press, 1980), 238ff.

49. Ruth, *Maintaining the Right Fellowship* (n. 3), 485-486; Schlabach, *Gospel Versus Gospel*, 77. For a fuller discussion of MC racial attitudes, see Schlabach, 247-261.

50. Ruth, *Maintaining the Right Fellowship*, 486, provides an interesting discussion of how this worked in the Franconia Conference.

51. Goossen, *Prairie Vision* (n. 12), 48-49.

52. Harold S. Bender items in *ME*, IV, 1009-1010: "Young People's Conference"; "Young People's Institute"; and "Young People's Problems Committee." [MC] *Mennonite General Conference: Report . . . :* (1921), 18; (1923), 11; and (1919-1931), *passim*.

53. Erland Waltner, "Young People's Union," and Orlando Harms, "Youth Committee," in *ME*, IV, 1010-1011.

54. See Margaret Bendroth's review of literature on the history of evangelical women: "Fundamentalism and Femininity: The Reorientation of Women's Role in the 1920s," *Evangelical Studies Bulletin* 5 (Mar, 1988), 1-4.

55. J. K. Bixler, "Women's Spiritual Service in the Church," *GH* 21 (Jan. 17, 1929), 886.

56. Oscar Burkholder, "The Devotional Covering," *GH* 23 (Apr. 17, 1930), 67; see also Sharon Klingelsmith, "Women in the Mennonite Church, 1900-1930," *MQR* 54 (July 1980), 163-207.

57. Cited in Klingelsmith, ibid., 179.

58. Ibid., 163-207, describes the shift in control.

59. Arlene Yousey, *Strangers and Pilgrims: History of Lewis County Mennonites* (Croghan, N.Y.: privately published, 1987), 179-180.

60. Samuel Floyd Pannabecker, *Open Doors: A History of the General Conference Mennonite Church* (Newton, Kan.: Faith & Life Press, 1975), 288-291. See also Gladys V. Goering, *Women in Search of Mission: A History of the General Conference Mennonite Women's Organization* (Newton, Kan.: Faith & Life Press, 1980).

61. Sources listed in n. 60. See also Valerie G. Rempel, " 'She Hath Done What She Could:' The Development of the Women's Missionary Services in the Mennonite Brethren Churches of the United States" (M.A. thesis, Mennonite Brethren Biblical Seminary, 1992); ch. 2 covers 1920-1940.

62. Samuel Floyd Pannabecker, *Faith in Ferment: A History of the Central District Conference* (Newton, Kan.: Faith & Life Press, 1968), 305.

63. Pannabecker, *Open Doors*, 292.

64. Paul Whitmer, "The Future of the Mennonite Church: In the United States and Canada," *TM* 44 (Aug. 29, 1929), 5.

65. Paul Whitmer, "The Future of the Mennonite Church, Part II," *TM* 44 (Sep. 5, 1929), 5.

66. Noah Mack, "The Situation in American Mennonitism," *The Sword and Trumpet* 2 (Oct, 1930), 8.

67. Ibid.

CHAPTER 3

1. Guy F. Hershberger to Daniel A. Lehman, Dec. 2, 1927, f. 2, b. 1, Guy F. Hershberger papers, AMC.

2. See Norman F. Furniss, *The Fundamentalist Controversy, 1918-1931* (New Haven: Yale University Press, 1954); Stewart G. Cole, *The History of Fundamentalism* (New York: Richard B. Smith, 1931); Richard Hofstadter, *Anti-Intellectualism in American Life* (New York: Knopf, 1963); and H. Richard Niebuhr, "Fundamentalism," *Encyclopedia of the Social Sciences*, VI (New York: Macmillan, 1937); Ernest R. Sandeen, "Towards a Historical Interpretation of the Origins of Fundamentalism," *Church History* 36 (1976), 66-83; Sandeen, *The Roots of Fundamentalism* (Chicago: University of Chicago Press, 1970).

3. George R. Marsden, *Fundamentalism and American Culture: The Shaping of Twentieth-Century Evangelicalism, 1870-1925* (New York: Oxford University Press, 1980).

4. Fundamentalism with a capital "F" will refer to the historic movement in Protestantism. All other fundamentalisms—generic, Mennonite, etc.—will have the small "f." Capitalization of "modernism" will be similar.

5. Marsden, *Fundamentalism and American Culture*, vii-ix.

6. Ibid., vii-ix, 3-8. Other scholars make similar observations, e.g., this from Bradley J. Longfield in *The Presbyterian Controversy: Fundamentalists, Modernists, and Moderates* (New York: Oxford University Press, 1991), 224: "As members of the dominant cultural tradition in America, all of the major protagonists [J. Gresham Machen, Williams Jennings Bryan, Henry Sloane Coffin, Clarence E. Macartney, Charles R. Erdman and Robert E. Speer] in the Presbyterian controversy strove mightily not simply to defend their particular theological and ecclesiological views but also to maintain the influence of Christianity in the dramatically changed and rapidly changing culture of post-World War I America. But differing theological and cultural roots within the wider Protestant Anglo-Saxon tradition led to different understandings not only of the essence of Christianity but also of the role of Christianity in culture. How the church was to influence the culture and what that influence was to entail were crucial questions underlying the battles fought over ordination requirements, Princeton Seminary, and foreign missions."

7. See C. Norman Kraus, "American Mennonites and the Bible," *MQR* 41 (Oct. 1967), 309-329.

8. See Theron F. Schlabach, *Peace, Faith, Nation: Mennonites and Amish in Nineteenth-Century America*, The Mennonite Experience in America vol. 2 (Scottdale, Pa.: Herald Press, 1988), 107-108. However, by the early twentieth century, particularly among the MCs, a more systematic, doctrinal, and propositional approach was setting in. See the trilogy by Daniel Kauffman: Daniel Kauffman, *Manual of Bible Doctrines, Setting Forth the General Principles of the Plan of Salvation, Explaining . . . Ordinances . . . and . . . Restrictions . . .* (Elkhart, Ind.: Mennonite Publishing Co., 1898); Kauffman, ed., *Bible Doctrine . . .* (Scottdale, Pa.: Mennonite Publishing House, 1914); and Kauffman, ed., *Doctrines of the Bible: A Brief Discussion of the Teachings of God's Word* (Scottdale, Pa.: Herald Press, 1928).

9. See Theron Schlabach, *Gospel Versus Gospel: Mission and the Mennonite Church, 1863-1944* (Scottdale, Pa.: Herald Press, 1980), 127, 150, 275-276; Rodney J. Sawatsky, "The Influence of Fundamentalism on Mennonite Nonresistance, 1908-1944" (M.A. thesis, University of Minnesota, 1973).

10. Schlabach, *Gospel Versus Gospel*, 114.

11. Harold S. Bender to John H. Mosemann, Aug. 27, 1926, f. 6, b. 3, Bender papers.

12. Kenneth Cauthen, *The Impact of American Religious Liberalism* (New York: Harper & Row, 1962), 27-29.

13. For further biographical detail, see Abraham Warkentin and Melvin Gingerich, *Who's Who Among the Mennonites* (N. Newton, Kan.: Bethel College Press, 1944), 99.

14. John E. Hartzler, *Education Among the Mennonites of America* (Danvers, Ill.: Central Mennonite Publishing Board, 1925), 181.

15. See Harold S. Bender, "Outside Influences on Mennonite Thought," *ML* 10 (Jan. 1955), 45-58.

16. Daniel Kauffman to H. S. Bender, Feb. 2, 1929, f. 1, b. 3, Bender papers.

17. John C. Wenger, "Chiliasm," *ME*, I, 557-59; Beulah Hostetler, *American Mennonites and Protestant Movements* (Scottdale, Pa.: Herald Press, 1987), 204, 279; H. S. Bender to Abner G. Yoder, Nov. 5, 1928, f. 4, b. 4, Bender papers.

18. Bender to Kauffman, May 16, 1928, f. 1, b. 3, Bender papers.

19. Ibid.

20. Daniel Kauffman to John L. Stauffer, Feb. 5, 1932, Stauffer papers, Menno Simons Historical Library and Archives, Eastern Mennonite University, Harrisonburg, Va.

21. See, e.g., Allen Erb, prominent leader in the MCs' Kansas-Missouri Conference, to H. S. Bender, Aug. 1, 1934 (f. 12, b. 6, Bender papers) about disappointments that the college was not giving equal time to the premillenial position in its eschatological teaching.

22. See, e.g.: John L. Stauffer to Religious Welfare Committee, June 30, 1941; Chester K. Lehman to same, June 10, 1941; both in Stauffer papers.

23. Wenger, "Chiliasm," 558-559.

24. John A. Toews, *A History of the Mennonite Brethren Church: Pilgrims and Pioneers*, ed. A. J. Klassen (Fresno, Calif.: Board of Christian Literature of the General Conference of Mennonite Brethren Churches, 1975), 377-379.

25. Samuel F. Pannabecker, *Open Doors: A History of the General Conference Mennonite Church* (Newton, Kan.: Faith & Life Press, 1975), 172, notes that the language shift among GCs was made between 1920 and 1930. Toews, *A History of the Mennonite Brethren Church*, 324-326, describes the language transition in the MB congregations in the United States following World War II.

26. On Presbyterianism as a source for MC fundamentalism see extensive 1929 H. S. Bender-George R. Brunk corresp. on Princeton Seminary and the relationship of Calvinism, Arminianism, and Mennonitism, f. 6, b. 1; also Bender-J. Gresham Machen corresp., 1933-1935, f. 1, b. 10; Bender papers. Bender repeatedly affirmed Machen's work and among other efforts sought to bring him to Goshen for a speaking engagement. On MB-Baptist relationships see Howard Loewen, "Augustus H. Strong: Baptist Theologian for the Mennonite Brethren," in Paul Toews, ed., *Mennonites and Baptists: A Continuing Conversation* (Winnipeg, Man.: Kindred Press, 1993), 193-210.

27. On this pattern as an integral part of the fundamentalist movement in American Protestantism, see Joel A. Carpenter, "Fundamentalist Institutions and the Rise of Evangelical Protestantism, 1929-1942," *Church History* 49 (Mar. 1980), 62-75; Virginia Lieson Brereton, *Training God's Army: The American Bible School, 1880-1940* (Bloomington, Ind.: Indiana University Press, 1990).

28. John C. Wenger, *The Mennonites in Indiana and Michigan* (Scottdale, Pa.: Herald Press, 1961), 42-43.

29. John Horsch, *The Mennonite Church and Modernism* (Scottdale, Pa.: Mennonite Publishing House, 1924).

30. See James C. Juhnke, "Mennonite Church Theologies and Social Boundaries, 1920-1930—Loyalists, Liberals and Laxitarians," *ML* 38 (June, 1983), 18-24.

31. *Edward, Pilgrimage of a Mind: The Journal of Edward Yoder, 1931-1945*, ed. Ida Yoder (privately published, 1985), Apr. 9, 1931.

32. Theron F. Schlabach, "Reveille for *Die Stillen im Lande*: A Stir Among Mennonites in the Late Nineteenth Century," *MQR* 51 (July 1977), 226.

33. The elements of this interpretation are suggested elsewhere: C. Norman Kraus, "American Mennonites and the Bible, 1750-1950," *MQR* 41 (Oct. 1967), 309-329, notes the relationship of fundamentalism to the centralizing of authority; Rodney Sawatsky, "History and Ideology: American Mennonite Identity Definition

Through History" (Ph.D. diss., Princeton University, 1977), 114-15 and elsewhere, has shown the linkage of fundamentalist theology with cultural nonconformity and the centralization of authority; Beulah Hostetler, *American Mennonites and Protestant Movements: A Community Paradigm* (Scottdale, Pa.: Herald Press, 1987), chs. 6 and 7, suggests all three elements as the means by which the MCs' Franconia Conference kept fundamentalism at bay. Such are the explanations if fundamentalism is defined only in ideological terms; but an interpretation which considers fundamentalism to be a cultural as much as an ideological phenomenon suggests these elements were its enactment rather than the means to exclude it.

34. Melvin Gingerich, *Mennonite Attire Through Four Centuries* (Breinigsville, Pa.: The Pennsylvania German Society, 1970), 28, 148.

35. Ibid., 148.

36. Ibid., 28, 148.

37. Daniel Kauffman to John L. Stauffer, Dec. 17, 1932, Stauffer papers (n. 20).

38. Smucker to H. S. Bender, July 30, 1924, f. 4, b. 4, Bender papers.

39. Sanford C. Yoder, *The Days of My Years* (Scottdale, Pa.: Herald Press, 1959), 115.

40. Guy F. Hershberger, "Comments on Sawatsky's Thesis: 'The Influence of Fundamentalism on Mennonite Nonresistance, 1908-1944'" (unpublished paper), 55; b. 57, Hershberger papers, AMC.

41. John C. Wenger to H. S. Bender, Dec. 18, 1935, f. 6, b. 13, Bender papers.

42. Guy F. Hershberger, "The Times of Sanford Calvin Yoder: The Mennonite Church and the First Fifty Years of Goshen College," in *An Evening to Honor Sanford Calvin Yoder* (Goshen, Ind.: Goshen College, 1974), 7-40, is a remarkably candid exploration of the resistance to change in MC circles and the attendant costs.

43. J. B. Smith, "A Statement of Facts and an Appeal to the Mennonite Board of Education" (three-page circular, n.d., n. pagination), f. 6, b. 12, Bender papers.

44. See Leonard Gross' conversations with Elizabeth Bender—"Mennonite Leadership: Holding the Church Together," *Mennonite Historical Bulletin* 47 (Apr. 1986), 6.

45. Stauffer to Mosemann, Sep. 19, 1931, Stauffer papers (n. 20).

46. H. S. Bender to Daniel Kauffman, Mar. 14, 1933, f. 7, b. 8, Bender papers.

47. Brunk to H. S. Bender, June 16, 1920, f. 6, b. 1, Bender papers.

48. *Edward, Pilgrimage*, at Feb. 13, 1932; see also Sanford Yoder, *Days of My Years* (n. 39), 115.

49. *Minutes of the Virginia Mennonite Conference* (Harrisonburg, Va.: Virginia Mennonite Conference, 1950), 180-189.

50. *Mennonite General Conference: Report of the Sixteenth Mennonite General Conference Held Near Goshen, Indiana, August 28-30, 1929*, p. 29 (these reports hereafter cited as [MC] Menn. Gen. Conf. *Reports*, with dates and pages).

51. For an analysis of the composition and tenure of the committee's members, see Joseph H. Fretz, "The General Problems Committee: Change in the Mennonite General Conference" (student paper, Goshen College, 1976; copy in MHL).

52. [MC] Menn. Gen. Conf. *Report* (1935), 25-26.

53. Ibid. (1943), 51-52.

54. John L. Stauffer, "The Mennonite General Conference at the Crossroads," in f. 6, b. 2, Menn. Gen. Conf. Exec. Comm. files, AMC.

55. Paul Erb, "Introduction," in John C. Wenger, *Historical and Biblical Position of the Mennonite Church on Attire* (Scottdale, Pa.: Herald Press, 1944), 5.

56. Interview with John C. Wenger cited in Fretz, "The General Problems Committee" (n. 51), 14.

57. See Guy F. Hershberger, "Introduction," in *Edward, Pilgrimage* (n. 48), xix.

58. See *Evidences of Modernism at Bluffton College* (Berne, Ind.: First Mennonite Church, 1929).

59. William S. Gottshall to Peter H. Richert, Nov. 27, 1928, f. 46, b. 7, Peter H. Richert papers, MLA.

60. *Official Minutes and Reports of the Twenty-Fifth Session of the General Conference of the Mennonite Church of North America, 1929,* 37 (these reports hereafter cited as [GC] Gen. Conf. *Minutes and Reports,* with years and pages).

61. Ibid. (1933), 138-141.

62. See John E. Hartzler, "Witmarsum Theological Seminary: The Seminary for the Past Fifteen Years, Shall We Move Forward," *Witmarsum Theological Seminary Bulletin* 8 (June, 1929), 1.

63. S. F. Pannabecker, "Scenes from Mennonite Theological Education," *The Mennonite Biblical Seminary and the Mennonite Bible School Bulletin* 11 (Dec. 1947), 9. See also S. F. Pannabecker to J. E. Hartzler, Jan. 24, 1950, copy in f. 173, b. 49, corresp. series, E. G. Kaufman college papers, MLA.

64. See Peter J. Wedel, *The Story of Bethel College,* ed. Edmund G. Kaufman (North Newton, Kan.: Bethel College, 1954); Paul Toews, "Fundamentalist Conflict in Mennonite Colleges: A Response to Cultural Transitions," *MQR* 57 (July, 1983), 241-256.

65. J. W. Kliewer to the Board of Directors, Bethel College Board of Director minutes, Feb. 29, 1930, Bethel College archives, MLA.

66. See corresp. series, f. 343, b. 54, E. G. Kaufman College papers, MLA; boxes 7 and 8, Peter H. Richert papers, MLA.

67. H. P. Krehbiel to H. H. Ewert, Jan. 21, 1932, f. 37, b. 6, H. P. Krehbiel papers, MLA.

68. See a manuscript with the title "Notes by H. P. Krehbiel—Origin and Realization of a School for Preparing Spiritual Workers for Mennonite Churches and Communities" (Aug. 1931), unpaginated, in f. 78, b. 12, H. P. Krehbiel papers, MLA.

69. Ibid.

70. "Overture," and "Provisional Constitution of the Menno Christian Workers School," f. 78, b. 12, H. P. Krehbiel papers, MLA.

71. For more of this story, see Wedel, *Story of Bethel College* (n. 64), 246-253.

72. David A. Haury, *Prairie People: A History of the Western District Conference* (Newton, Kan.: Faith & Life Press, 1981), 238; see also Gregory J. Stucky, "A College Near Death: The Bethel Crisis of 1932" (student paper, Bethel College, 1971; copy in MLA).

73. Jeff A. Steely, "Cornelius German Suckau: Mennonite Fundamentalist?" *ML* 44 (Mar. 1989), 15-21, suggests that all this activity was directly related to the dissatisfaction with Bethel. See also Paul Kuhlmann, *The Story of Grace* (Omaha, Neb.: Grace College of the Bible, 1980), 11-16.

74. Kuhlmann, *The Story of Grace,* 8.

75. C. H. Suckau, *A Miracle of God's Grace: The Marvelous Story of the Beginning of Grace Bible Institute* (Omaha, Neb.: Grace Bible Institute, n.d.), 6.

76. Kuhlmann, *Story of Grace,* 8-9.

77. Ibid; for further information on Suckau's advocacy of noncombatancy, see ch. 6. The general impact of fundamentalism on Mennonite nonresistance is the subject of Rodney Sawatsky, "The Influence of Fundamentalism on Mennonite Nonresistance" (n. 9).

78. Suckau, *Miracle of God's Grace,* 65-67.

79. See Abram J. Klassen, "The Roots and Development of Mennonite Brethren Theology to 1914" (M.A. thesis, Wheaton College, 1966); Albert J. Wardin, Jr., "Baptist Influences on Mennonite Brethren with an Emphasis on the Practice of Immersion," *Direction* 8 (1979), 33-38.

80. Toews, *History of the Mennonite Brethren Church* (n. 24), 375-376.

81. See, e.g., *Year Book of the General Conference of Mennonite Brethren Churches* (1919, 1927) (hereafter cited as [MB] Gen. Conf. *Year Book,* with year); MB

Pacific District Conf. *Year Book* (1920, 1927).

82. See [MB] Gen. Conf. *Year Book* (1943), 47; Minutes of the Committee of Reference and Counsel, Jan. 17-18, 1945, Board of Reference and Counsel file 5, CMBS–F; A. G. Willems, "How to Detect the First Signs of Modernism," *CL* (Feb. 15, 1947), 1-4, and (Mar. 1, 1947), 5-6.

83. For the story of these four see Paul Toews, "Fundamentalist Conflict in the Mennonite Colleges: A Response to Transitions?" *MQR* 57 (July, 1983), 253-254.

84. *Tabor College Bulletin* (Jan. 1950), 1.

85. [MB] Gen. Conf. *Year Book* (1943), 47.

86. Minutes of the Committee of Reference and Counsel, Jan. 17-18, 1945, Board of Reference and Counsel file 5, CMBS-F.

87. See statement by William Neufeld, July 25, 1980, b. 1, Wm. Neufeld papers, CMBS-F.

88. See Paul Toews, "'A Shelter in a Time of Storm': The Establishment of Schools in the Pacific District," in Esther Jost, ed., *75 Years of Fellowship: Pacific District Conference of the Mennonite Brethren Churches, 1912-1987* (Fresno, Calif.: Pacific District Conference of Mennonite Brethren Churches, 1987), 57-70.

89. Kraus, "American Mennonites and the Bible, 1750-1950" (n. 33), 317ff.

90. Marsden, *Fundamentalism and American Culture* (n. 3), 227.

91. Harold S. Bender, "The Anabaptist Vision," *Church History* 13 (Mar. 1944), 3-23 [also in *MQR* 18 (Apr. 1944), 67-88]; Guy F. Hershberger, *War, Peace, and Nonresistance* (Scottdale, Pa.: Herald Press, 1944).

CHAPTER 4

1. American Society of Church History minutes (Dec. 28-29, 1943), *Church History* 13 (Mar., 1944), 56.

2. H. S. Bender to Dr. E. R. Hardy, Dec. 16, 1943, f. 9, b. 17, Bender papers.

3. Bender to Ernst Correll, May 1, 1932, f. 4, b. 6, Bender papers.

4. See "Recent Progress in Anabaptist History," *MQR* 8 (Jan. 1934); a three-part biographical sketch on Grebel in *MQR* 10 (1936); a two-part series on Grebel's theology in *MQR* 12 (1938); and another biographical installment in *MQR* 15 (1941).

5. See Wilhelm Pauck, "The Historiography of the German Reformation During the Past Twenty Years," *Church History* 9 (Dec. 1940), 305-340; and Harold S. Bender, "Recent Progress in Research in Anabaptist History," *MQR* 8 (Jan. 1934), 3–17.

6. Harold S. Bender, "The Anabaptist Vision," *Church History* 13 (Mar. 1944), 3–4.

7. See Carl A. Cornelius, *Geschichte des Muensterischen Aufruhrs*, 2 vols. (Leipzig: T. O. Weigel, 1855-1860); Ludwig Keller, *Die Reformation und die aelteren Reformparteien* (Leipzig: S. Hirzel, 1885); Christian Neff, "Ludwig Keller," *ME*, III, 162-163. Robert Friedmann, "John Horsch and Ludwig Keller," in Harold S. Bender, et al., eds., *John Horsch Memorial Papers* (Scottdale, Pa.: Mennonite Publishing House, 1947), 32-34.

8. Friedmann, "John Horsch and Ludwig Keller," 32-34.

9. Ibid., 34; H. G. Mannhardt, *Jahrbuch der altevangelischen oder taufgesinnten Mennoniten Gemeinden* (Danzig: Selbst-Verlag des Herausgebers, 1888); Peter M. Friesen, *Die alt-evangelische Mennonitische Bruederschaft in Russland (1789-1910) in Nahmen der Mennonitischen* (Halbstadt: Raduga, 1911).

10. Friedmann, "John Horsch and Ludwig Keller," 36-40; for an account of Keller's role in Mennonite historiography, published too late to be used in this chapter, see Abraham Friesen, *History and Renewal in the Anabaptist/Mennonite Tradition*, Cornelius H. Wedel Historical Series no. 7 (N. Newton, Kan.: Bethel College, 1994).

11. See Horsch to Bender, Dec. 17, 1924, f. 7; Lester Hostetler to Bender, Dec. 17, 1924, f. 9; both in b. 2, Bender papers.

12. Harold S. Bender, "Editorial," *MQR* 1 (Jan. 1927), 1.

13. Harold S. Bender, "What Can the Church Do for Her Historical Work? II. The Need for Historical Work," *GH* 20 (Apr. 28, 1927), 90-91.

14. Harold S. Bender, "What Can the Church Do for Her Historical Work? I. Introductory," *GH* 20 (Apr. 21, 1927), 58.

15. Bender, "What Can the Church Do for Her Historical Work? II," 90-91.

16. John Horsch, "The Origins and Faith of the Swiss Brethren," *The College Record: Review Supplement* 27 (Jan. 1926), 1-14.

17. A. H. Newman, "The Significance of the Anabaptist Movement in the History of the Christian Church," *The College Record: Review Supplement* 27 (Jan. 1926), 15-22, 49.

18. John Horsch, "The Origin of the Mennonite Church in the Netherlands," *The College Record: Review Supplement* 27 (May-June, 1926), 20.

19. Ibid., 21. Interpreters might be tempted to see Horsch as an early advocate of what is now called the "polygenesis" view of Anabaptist; for the polygenesis view, see esp. James Stayer, Werner Packull, and Klaus Depperman, "From Monogenesis to Polygenesis: The Historical Discussion of Anabaptist Origins," *MQR* 49 (Apr. 1975), 83-121. But Horsch's intent was very different. Where Stayer and colleagues were searching for a more inclusive reading of the sixteenth-century Anabaptists, Horsch wanted to segregate out and even exclude those Anabaptists whom he considered unsound.

20. Hershberger to Horsch, May 20, 1930, f. H-Z, 1930 corresp., b. 5, John Horsch papers, AMC.

21. Robert Friedmann to Gerald C. Studer, Dec. 15, 1948, quoted in Rodney James Sawatsky, "History and Ideology: American Mennonite Identity Definition Through History" (Ph.D. diss., Princeton University, 1977), 279. Of course Friedmann spent much of his scholarly career seeking to distinguish Anabaptists from Protestants; see his "Anabaptism and Protestantism," *MQR* 24 (Jan. 1950), 12-24.

22. Harold S. Bender, "Editorial," *MQR* 5 (Jan. 1931), 3.

23. Harold S. Bender, "Editorial," *MQR* 5 (Apr. 1931), 85.

24. Wilhelmus Johannes Kühler, *Geschiedenis der nederlandsche Doopsgezinden in de zestiinde eeuw* (Haarlem: H.D., Tjeenk Willink and Zoon, 1932).

25. See Cornelius Krahn, "Kühler, Wilhelmus Johannes," *ME*, III, 253-54; Krahn, "Historiography: IV. Netherlands," *ME*, II, 761-762.

26. *MQR* 7 (Jan., Apr. 1933), 48-60, 97-126.

27. Ibid., 51.

28. Ibid., 60.

29. Ibid., 126.

30. Harold S. Bender, "Editorial," *MQR* 7 (Jan. 1933), 4.

31. GC historians influenced by Keller included C. H. A. van der Smissen, editor of various GC periodicals and author of *Kurzgefaszte Geschichte und Glaubenslehre der Altevangelischer Taufgesinnten oder Mennoniten* (Summerfield, Ill.: privately published, 1895), and Johannes Bartsch, in *Geschichte der Gemeinde Jesu Christi Das Heiszt der Alt-evangelischen und Mennoniten Gemeinden* (Elkhart, Ind.: Mennonite Publishing Co., 1898); see Sawatsky, "History and Ideology" (n. 21), 96-97.

32. Keith L. Sprunger, "Cornelius H. Wedel and Oswald H. Wedel: Two Generations of Mennonite Historians," *ML* 36 (Dec. 1981), 18-19.

33. See Sawatsky, "History and Ideology" (n. 21), 98-99; James C. Juhnke, "*Gemeindechristentum* and Bible Doctrine: Two Mennonite Visions of the Early Twentieth Century," *MQR* 57 (July 1983), 211.

34. Quoted in ibid. (Juhnke), 210.

35. For early years, see C. Henry Smith, *Mennonite Country Boy: The Early Years of C. Henry Smith* (Newton, Kan.: Faith & Life Press, 1962).

36. H. S. Bender to John Horsch, Jan. 15, 1927, f. A-D, corresp. 1927, Horsch papers, AMC.

37. Horsch to H. S. Bender, Mar. 15, 1925, f. 7, b. 2, Bender papers.

38. See Bender to John Horsch, Jan. 16, 1925, f. A-B, corresp. 1925, Horsch papers, AMC; Harold S. Bender, "What the Church Can Do for Her Historical Work: V. The Marbeck Project—An Urgent Present Need," *GH* 20 (May 19, 1927), 154-155.

39. H. S. Bender to C. Henry Smith, June 4, 1926, f. 2, b. 4, Bender papers.

40. See Harold S. Bender, "Reviews and Notes: *Education Among the Mennonites of America*," *The College Record: Review Supplement* 27 (May-June, 1926), 35-41; Lester Hostetler, "The Open Forum Column: *Education Among the Mennonites of America*," *The Christian Exponent* 3 (July 16, 1926), 238-239; Harold S. Bender, "The Open Forum Column: *Education Among the Mennonites of America*," *The Christian Exponent* 3 (Aug. 13, 1926), 269-270.

41. Mosemann to Bender, July 5, 1927, f. 6, b. 3, Bender papers.

42. Both were published by Mennonite Book Concern, Berne, Ind.

43. Edmund G. Kaufman, *The Development of Missionary and Philanthropic Interest Among the Mennonites of North America* (Berne, Ind.: Mennonite Book Concern, 1931), 56.

44. Ibid., ch. 2.

45. Horsch to Bender, July 1, 1929, f. 8, b. 2, Bender papers.

46. Horsch to Bender, n.d., b. 7, Horsch papers, AMC.

47. Horsch to Bender, July 1, 1929, f. 8, b. 2, Bender papers.

48. Bender to Horsch, Aug. 8, 1929, f. A-H, corresp. 1929, Horsch papers, AMC.

49. Bender to Edmund Kaufman, Mar. 16 and Oct. 5, 1929, f. 12, b. 3, Bender papers.

50. C. Henry Smith, *The Story of the Mennonites* (Berne, Ind.: Mennonite Book Concern, 1941), 12.

51. This progressive reading of Mennonite history, apparent throughout Smith's *The Story of the Mennonites*, is most succinctly expressed in his "Mennonites and Culture," *MQR* 12 (Apr. 1938), 71-84.

52. Smith, *Story of the Mennonites*, ch. 16.

53. H. S. Bender and Ernst Correll, "Reviews and Notes: *The Story of the Mennonites*," *MQR* 16 (Oct. 1942), 272.

54. Ibid., 270-75, esp. 272-274.

55. Ibid., 272.

56. "A Communication from C. Henry Smith Concerning the Review of *The Story of the Mennonites*," *MQR* 17 (Oct. 1943), 247.

57. Robert Friedmann, "On Mennonite Historiography and on Individualism and Brotherhood," *MQR* 17 (Apr. 1944), 117.

58. C. Henry Smith, "On Mennonite Historiography," *MQR* 18 (Apr. 1944), 123.

59. On this entire movement, see William L. Bowers, *The Country Life Movement in America, 1900-1920* (Port Washington, N.Y.: Kennikat Press Corp., 1974); Merwin Swanson, "The 'Country Life Movement' and the American Churches," *Church History* 46 (Sep. 1977), 358-373; Jacob H. Dorn, "The Rural Ideal and Agrarian Realities: Arthur E. Holt and the Vision of a Decentralized America in the Inter-War Years," *Church History* 52 (Mar. 1983), 50-65.

60. See J. Winfield Fretz, "Mutual Aid Among the Mennonites," *MQR* 13 (Jan. 1939), 28-58; Fretz, "Mutual Aid Among Mennonites: II. Mutual Aid Activities in a Single Mennonite Community, *MQR* 13 (July 1939), 187-209.

61. Harold S. Bender, "Editorial," *MQR* 13 (Jan. 1939), 4.

62. Fretz, "Mutual Aid Among the Mennonites," 28-29.

63. Cornelius Krahn, J. Winfield Fretz, and Robert Kreider, "Altruism in Mennonite Life," in Pitirim A. Sorokin, *Forms and Techniques of Altruistic and Spiritual Growth* (Boston: The Beacon Press, 1954), 309-328, gives the traditional interpreta-

tion that Mennonite benevolence has grown from Anabaptist-Mennonite belief and principles. Two articles by James C. Juhnke—"Mennonites and the Great Compromise," *TM* 84 (Sept 23, 1969), 562-564, and "Mennonite Benevolence and Civic Identity: The Post-War Compromise," *ML* 25 (Jan 1970), 34-37—offer an interpretation that suggests Mennonites gave out of "civic anxiety," that is, out of wanting to be good citizens, esp. in wartime when Americans looked upon them as slackers.

64. Fretz, "Mutual Aid Among the Mennonites," 31.

65. Ibid., 58.

66. J. Winfield Fretz, "Mennonite Mutual Aid: A Contribution to the Establishment of Christian Community" (Ph.D. diss., University of Chicago, 1941), 231, 236.

67. Ibid., 8.

68. Ibid., 243.

69. J. Winfield Fretz, "Mennonites and Their Economic Problems," *MQR* 14 (Oct. 1940), 201.

70. Karl Baehr, "Secularization Among the Mennonites" (B.D. thesis, University of Chicago, 1942), iii, 150.

71. Melvin Gingerich, "Rural Life Problems and the Mennonites," *MQR* 16 (July 1942), 169.

72. The quotation is from Fretz, "Mennonites and Their Economic Problems," 207; pages 207-213 make the case for land acquisition and community formation. See also Fretz, "Mutual Aid Among Mennonites: II," for a description of how mutual-aid organizations functioned at Mountain Lake, a small Minnesota community with many Mennonites.

73. See Dorn, "The Rural Idea and Agrarian Realities" (n. 59).

74. On Park, see Morton and Lucia White, *The Intellectual Versus the City* (Cambridge: Harvard University Press, 1962), 160-170; Fred H. Matthews, *Quest for an American Sociology: Robert E. Park and the Chicago School* (Montreal: McGill-Queen's University Press, 1977), 121-156.

75. From 1951 onward the name was "Conference on Mennonite Educational and Cultural Problems"; see annual proceedings.

76. Committee on Industrial Problems, "Mennonites and Industrial Organizations," *GH* 30 (Feb 10, 1938), 989-990.

77. Guy F. Hershberger, "Nonresistance and Industrial Conflict," *MQR* 13 (Apr. 1939), 143.

78. Ibid., 147.

79. *Mennonite General Conference: Report of the Twentieth Menonite General Conference Held at Turner, Oregon, August 25-17, 1937*, 22 (these reports hereafter cited as [MC] Menn. Gen. Conf. *Reports*, with dates and pages).

80. See "Report of the Committee on Industrial Relations," [MC] Menn. Gen. Conf. *Report* (1941), 43.

81. Hershberger, "Nonresistance and Industrial Conflict," 149.

82. Ibid., 151.

83. See, e.g., Guy F. Hershberger, "Suggestions for Improving the Small Christian Community," Conference on Mennonite Cultural Problems *Proceedings* (1942), I, 48-59.

84. Hershberger, "Nonresistance and Industrial Conflict" (n. 77), 154.

CHAPTER 5

1. See James C. Juhnke, *Vision, Doctrine, War: Mennonite Identity and Organization in America, 1890-1930*, Mennonite Experience in America vol. 3 (Scottdale, Pa.: Herald Press, 1989), 208-242.

2. The discussion of the peace theology and the activity of these two decades has a rich historiographical tradition. Melvin Gingerich, *Service for Peace: A History of Mennonite Civilian Public Service* (Akron, Pa.: Mennonite Central Committee,

1949), and Guy F. Hershberger, *The Mennonite Church in the Second World War* (Scottdale, Pa.: Mennonite Publishing House, 1951), detail much of the inter-Mennonite and MC activity in the interwar period. James C. Juhnke, *A People of Two Kingdoms: The Political Acculturation of the Kansas Mennonites* (Newton, Kan.: Faith & Life Press, 1975) provides valuable interpretation on Kansas Mennonites. Albert Keim, "Service or Resistance? The Mennonite Response to Conscription in World War II," *MQR* 52 (Apr. 1978), 141-155, traces the discussion and negotiations leading toward the establishment of Civilian Public Service (CPS). Guy F. Hershberger in two unpublished manuscripts—"Questions Raised Concerning the Work of the Committee on Peace and Social Concerns (of the Mennonite Church) and Its Predecessors," and "The Committee on Peace and Social Concerns (of the Mennonite Church) and Its Predecessors," Hershberger papers, AMC—traced the history of the MCs' Peace Problems Committee, as it was called in the 1920s and 1930s. Rodney James Sawatsky's "The Influences of Fundamentalism on Mennonite Nonresistance, 1908-1944" (M.A. thesis, University of Minnesota, 1973) and his "History and Ideology: American Mennonite Identity Definition Through History" (Ph.D. diss., Princeton University, 1977) provide essential categories for understanding the differing positions in the peace dialogue. I am particularly indebted to this last work.

3. C. Henry Smith, *Christian Peace: Four Hundred Years of Mennonite Principles and Practice* (Newton, Kan.: Peace Committee of the General Conference of Mennonites, 1938), 27-28.

4. Guy F. Hershberger, "The Christian's Relation to the State in Time of War: II. Is Alternative Service Desirable and Possible?" *MQR*, 9 (Jan. 1935), 29.

5. Harold S. Bender, "Church and State in Mennonite History," *MQR* 13 (Apr. 1939), 103.

6. See Theron F. Schlabach, "Reveille for *Die Stillen im Lande*: A Stir Among Mennonites in the Late Nineteenth Century," *MQR* 51 (July 1977), 213-226.

7. For a discussion of the war experience and the way in which it, together with the prewar Mennonite identification with American society, now required a new set of responses, see James C. Juhnke's "The Agony of Civic Isolation: Mennonites in World War I," *ML* 25 (Jan. 1970), 27-30, and his "Mennonite Benevolence and Civic Identity: The Post-War Compromise," *ML* 25 (Jan. 1970), 34-37.

8. Lawrence S. Wittner, *Rebels Against War: The American Peace Movement, 1941-1960* (N.Y.: Columbia University Press, 1969), 1-2. For a discussion of interwar pacifism, see Charles Chatfield, *For Peace and Justice: Pacifism in America, 1914-1941* (Knoxville, Tenn.: University of Tennessee Press, 1971).

9. See John E. Wiltz, *In Search of Peace: The Senate Munitions Inquiry, 1934-36* (Baton Rouge: Louisiana State University Press, 1963).

10. Some prominent organizations that emerged in the interwar years include the National Council for the Prevention of War, the Women's International League for Peace and Freedom, the War Resisters League, and the Fellowship of Reconciliation. In 1933 thirty-seven peace organizations united to form the National Peace Conference. Wittner, *Rebels Against War*, 15, estimates that between 45 million and 60 million Americans were sympathetic to pacifism.

11. Paul Erb, *Orie O. Miller: The Story of a Man and an Era* (Scottdale, Pa.: Herald Press, 1969), 206; Hershberger, *Mennonite Church in the Second World War* (n. 2), 5.

12. Erb, *Orie O. Miller*, 206-207.

13. Orie O. Miller, 3 items: "Aggressive Peace Work," *GH* 18 (Jan. 14, 1926), 858-859; "Our Peace Message," *The College Record: Review Supplement* 27 (Sep. 1926), 23-28; "Our Peace Policy," *MQR* 3 (Jan. 1929), 26-32.

14. Miller, "Our Peace Policy," 29.

15. Ibid., 27.

16. Miller, "Our Peace Message," 25.

17. Ibid.

18. Miller, "Our Peace Policy," 30-32.

19. This discussion is carefully reviewed in Sawatsky, "History and Ideology" (n. 2), ch. 7.

20. J. H. Mosemann, "The Modern Peace Movement," *GH* 18 (Jan. 28, 1926), 898.

21. G. R. B., "Pacifism-Nonresistance," *The Sword and Trumpet* (Oct. 1929), 6.

22. J. H. Mosemann to E. L. Frey and O. O. Miller, Mar. 21, 1927, f. 2, b. 9, Peace Problems Committee papers, AMC.

23. J. H. Mosemann to Orie Miller, Aug. 16 and Sep. 10, 1926, f. 1, b. 9, Peace Problems Committee papers, AMC.

24. Ibid.

25. J. H. Mosemann to Orie Miller, Sep. 10, 1926, f. 1, b. 9, Peace Problems Committee papers, AMC.

26. Orie Miller to J. H. Mosemann, Oct. 26, 1926, f. 1, b. 9, Peace Problems Committee papers, AMC.

27. J. H. Mosemann to Orie Miller, Nov. 4, 1926, and Dec. 26, 1926, f. 1, b. 9, Peace Problems Committee papers, AMC.

28. Ibid.

29. Miller to E. L. Frey, Oct. 25, 1927, f. 3, b. 9, Peace Problems Committee papers, AMC. If Miller withdrew his visible connections with these various peace organizations, he remained in correspondence with many, subscribed to their literature, and occasionally offered a small donation. His correspondence for 1930 included the National Committee on the Churches and World Peace, World Alliance for International Friendship Through the Churches, National Council for Prevention of War, Committee on Militarism in Education, League for American Citizenship, World Federation of Education Associations, Pacifist Action Committee, and World Peace Union; see Miller corresp. in f. 1, b. 9, Peace Problems Committee papers, AMC.

30. Mennonite Conference on War and Peace, "A Report of the Conference, Including the Principal Addresses Given" (Goshen College, Goshen, Ind., Feb. 15-17, 1935); mimeographed copies available in various Mennonite historical libraries.

31. John Horsch, "The Difference Between Our Peace Program and the Program of Other Religious Peace Movements," in ibid., 16-20.

32. J. B. Epp, "Refusing to Go to War," *CL* 2 (Feb. 1938), 19.

33. Melvin Gingerich, "The Difference Between Our Peace Program and the Program of Other Peace Movements: I. Non-Religious Peace Movements," in Mennonite Conference . . . , "A Report of the Conference," 15.

34. Ibid., 15-16.

35. Harold S. Bender, "Our Peace Testimony to the World—Goals and Methods," in ibid., 35-36; "all things" hand-underlined in the source.

36. Ibid., 39-40.

37. *Minutes and Reports of the Twenty-Fourth Session of the General Conference of the Mennonite Church of North America* (1926), 17 (these reports cited hereafter as [GC] Gen. Conf. *Minutes and Reports*, with years).

38. J. H. Langenwalter, "What Should Be the Relations of Our General Conference Toward the Conference of Pacifist Churches?" [GC] Gen. Conf. *Minutes and Reports* (1926), 253-265; quot., p. 259.

39. Juhnke, *A People of Two Kingdoms* (n. 2), 72-77 discusses some of Krehbiel's views on faith and politics.

40. Krehbiel to Bowman, Jan. 7, 1933, f. 171, b. 28, H. P. Krehbiel papers, MLA.

41. "An Overture to the Historic Peace Groups of the World," f. 170, b. 28, H. P. Krehbiel papers, MLA.

42. Ibid.

43. H. P. Krehbiel, *What Is a Pacifist?* (Newton, Kan.: Herald Publishing Co., 1931); Krehbiel, *The History of the General Conference of the Mennonite Church of*

North America (Newton, Kan.: privately published, 1938), II, 634-635.

44. Juhnke, *A People of Two Kingdoms* (n. 2), 136-137.

45. H. P. Krehbiel to O. O. Miller, June 26, 1935, f. 172, b. 28, H. P. Krehbiel papers, MLA.

46. "Secretary's Report of the Conference of Historic Peace Churches, October 31-November 2, 1935," f. 173, b. 28, H. P. Krehbiel papers, MLA.

47. Ibid.

48. Ibid.

49. See "A Statement of Our Position on Peace, War and Military Service," in *Mennonite General Conference: Report of the Twentieth Mennonite General Conference Held at Turner, Oregon, August 25-27, 1937*, 123-126; "On Peace, War, Military Service and Patriotism," in [GC] Gen. Conf. *Minutes and Reports* (1941), 163-166; "Resolutions," in [MB] Gen. Conf. *Year Book* (1943), 67-69.

50. "Secretary's Report of the Conference of Historic Peace Churches, October 31-November 2, 1935," f. 173, b. 28, H. P. Krehbiel papers, MLA. For later assessments of the event, see Donald F. Durnbaugh, ed., *On Earth Peace: Discussions on War/Peace Issues Between Friends, Mennonites, Brethren and European Churches, 1935-1975* (Elgin, Ill.: Brethren Press, 1978); Robert Kreider, "The Historic Peace Churches Meeting in 1935," *ML* 31 (June 1976), 21-24.

51. See Mark Unruh, "E. L. Harshbarger: Mennonite Activist" (Bethel College student paper, 1982; copy in MLA).

52. E. L. Harshbarger, "Mennonite Program for Peace," *TM* 51 (Apr. 7, 1936), 2.

53. Ibid., 2.

54. Ibid., 2-5.

55. E. L. Harshbarger circular letter, 1935, f. 2, b. 12, E. L. Harshbarger papers, MLA. The story of the Kansas Institute is well described in Theodore Loewen, "Mennonite Pacifism: The Kansas Institute of International Relations" (Bethel College student paper, 1971; copy in MLA).

56. Ibid. (Loewen).

57. See *Report of General Conference of Mennonites in France in Reconstruction Work, Held at Clermont-en-Argonne, Meuse, France, June 20-22, 1919*, ed. Walter N. Rutt, J. C. Meyer, and C. C. Janzen (n.p., circa, 1919); Guy F. Hershberger, "Historical Background to the Formation of the Mennonite Central Committee," *MQR* 44 (July 1970), 233-235.

58. The Society is obscure in the records, but a Fellowship of Reconciliation (FOR) booklet, *Pacifist Handbook*, lists it (and no other Mennonite organization) as having cooperated with Quakers, Church of the Brethren, Methodists, the Women's International League for Peace and Freedom, and the FOR itself to produce the booklet, and gives the Society's address as Bluffton; A. Warkentin and Melvin Gingerich, comp., *Who's Who Among the Mennonites* (N. Newton, Kan.: Bethel College Press, 1943), 150 lists Landes as the Society's Exec. Sec., 1936-1939.

59. H. S. Bender, "Twenty-Sixth Street Mission," *ME*, IV, 1130.

60. Quotation is from Bert Smucker, "Editorial," *The Plowshare* 1 (1938), 2; for the story of the camp, see Elva May (Schrock) Roth, "Work Camp—Chicago—July 1938" (unpublished paper); both are in the Robert Kreider papers, MLA. "Report of the Executive Director of the Volunteer Citizenship Camp," f. 1, b. 1, Mennonite Peace Society Archives, AMC. See also Lois Barrett, *The Vision and the Reality: The Story of Home Missions in the General Mennonite Church* (Newton, Kan.: Faith & Life Press, 1983), 182-184.

61. O. B. Reimer to P. C. Hiebert, Apr. 19, 1936, f. 344, b. 32, Peter C. Hiebert papers, MLA.

62. Guy F. Hershberger, "Historical Background to the Formation of the Mennonite Central Committee"; see also James C. Juhnke, *Vision, Doctrine, War* (n. 1), 243-257.

63. John D. Unruh, *In the Name of Christ: A History of the Mennonite Central Committee and Its Service, 1920-1951* (Scottdale, Pa.: Herald Press, 1952), 40-41.

64. See Mennonite Central Committee Exec. Comm. minutes, Sep. 30 and Nov. 4, 1939, AMC.

65. Cited in Unruh, *In the Name of Christ*, 43.

66. "MCC Headquarters Letter to the MCC Mailing List," Feb. 4, 1941, copy in f. 38, b. 4, E. L. Harshbarger papers, MLA.

67. H. S. Bender, "Report of a Visit to Mennonite Relief Work in Europe," appended to Minutes of the MCC Executive Committee meeting, Dec. 14, 1940, AMC.

68. M. C. Lehman, "Report to the Executive Committee for the Mennonite Central Committee on Relief Work Done in Poland and Germany," with MCC Exec. Comm. minutes, Feb. 1, 1941, AMC.

69. Guy F. Hershberger, *War, Peace, and Nonresistance* (Scottdale, Pa.: Herald Press, 1944).

70. Ibid., 15.

71. In addition to ibid., ch. 3, see also, Hershberger to Edw. J. Bousma, Dec. 30, 1942, f. 7, b. 3, Hershberger papers, AMC.

72. Hershberger, *War, Peace, and Nonresistance*, 42, 44.

73. J. Irvin Lehman, "Teachers and Teachings," *The Sword and Trumpet* 11 (July 1943), 28.

74. Ibid., 30-31.

75. Hershberger, *War, Peace, and Nonresistance*, 49.

76. Ibid., 73-82.

77. Ibid., 225.

78. Donovan Smucker to Hershberger, Aug. 17, 1943, f. 2, b. 18, Hershberger papers, AMC.

79. Hershberger, *War, Peace, and Nonresistance*, 301.

80. Donovan Smucker, "A Review of *War, Peace, and Nonresistance*," *TM* 59 (Dec. 12, 1944), 11.

81. Hershberger's interest in the relationship between American religious traditions and political-social reform had a long history before 1944; see, e.g., an unpublished 1933 paper "Religion in Politics and Social Reform: A Few Suggestions for Investigations in the Relationship of the American Protestant Churches to Political and Social Reform," f. 18, b. 12, Hershberger papers, AMC.

82. For a discussion of the concept of "alternatives" in Hershberger's thought, see Theron F. Schlabach, "To Focus a Mennonite Vision," in John Richard Burkholder and Calvin Redekops eds., *Kingdom, Cross, and Community: Essays on Mennonite Themes in Honor of Guy F. Hershberger* (Scottdale, Pa: Herald Press, 1976), 15-50.

83. Guy F. Hershberger, *The Way of the Cross in Human Relations* (Scottdale, Pa.: Herald Press, 1958), 43ff., 194-196.

CHAPTER 6

1. Neuenschwander to Fast, Jan. 11, 1941, f. 7, b. 1, Henry A. Fast papers, MLA (hereafter simply Fast papers).

2. Quoted from a report of the Senate Committee on Military Affairs, 78th Congress, 1st session, Feb. 17, 1943, in Mulford Q. Sibley and Philip E. Jacob, *Conscription of Conscience: The American State and the Conscientious Objector, 1940-1947* (Ithaca, N.Y.: Cornell University Press, 1952), 123.

3. Quoted in Godfrey Hodgson, *America in Our Time: From World War II to Nixon, What Happened and Why* (New York: Random House, 1976), 18.

4. See two items by James C. Juhnke: "The Agony of Civic Isolation: Mennonites in World War I," *ML* 25 (Jan. 1970), 27-30; "Mennonite Benevolence and Civic Identi-ty: The Post-War Compromise," *ML* 25 (Jan. 1970), 34-37.

5. Guy F. Hershberger, "The Christian's Relation to the State in Time of War: II. Is Alternative Service Desirable and Possible?" *MQR* 9 (Jan. 1935), 29-30.

6. Ibid., 30.

7. Ibid., 30-31, 33-34.

8. Moravians and Schwenkfelders as well as other peace organizations also took part in some of these meetings.

9. This history is traced in: Melvin Gingerich, *Service for Peace: A History of Mennonite Civilian Public Service* (Akron, Pa.: Mennonite Central Committee, 1949), ch. 3; Albert N. Keim and Grant M. Stoltzfus, *The Politics of Conscience: The Historic Peace Churches and America at War, 1917-1955* (Scottdale, Pa.: Herald Press, 1988), ch. 3. Although at a subsequent meeting with Roosevelt the historic peace churches brought a single statement, at this first meeting the three presented separate ones. The statements appear printed in various places, e.g., *TM* 52 (Mar. 9, 1937), 4-6, which contains the three denominational positions plus the addendum submitted by the Mennonite representatives. MC reservations about ecumenical peace dialogue are reflected in the reporting in the *GH*: in it the report of the visit with the president appeared in the Apr. 15, 1937, issue merely as part of a larger report on peace issues by the Peace Problems Committee, and the discussions among the historic peace churches were described as "informal and unofficial"—although the visit to the president clearly was meant to be more than that.

10. Menn. Central Peace Comm. minutes, Sep. 30, 1939, AMC. "A Plan of Action for Mennonites in Case of War" was printed in various places, most conveniently in Gingerich, *Service for Peace*, 431-433.

11. See "January 10, 1940, letter to President Roosevelt," and "A Plan of Action for Mennonites in Case of War," in Gingerich, *Service for Peace*, 431-435.

12. See Keim and Stoltzfus, *Politics of Conscience* (n. 9), 74-76; quotations on those pages.

13. Letter and memorandum published in various places, e.g., Gingerich, *Service for Peace*, 434-437.

14. Ibid.

15. Report by Orie Miller, Menn. Central Peace Comm. Exec. Comm. minutes, June 9, 1940, AMC.

16. See Keim and Stoltzfus, *Politics of Conscience* (n. 9), 92-93.

17. See ibid., 93-102; Rufus D. Bowman, *The Church of the Brethren and War, 1708-1941* (reprint, New York: Garland Publishing Inc., 1971), 286-294. Both trace the history of the legislative lobbying.

18. The Selective Training and Service Act as finally passed can be found in U.S. Selective Service, *Selective Service in Peacetime: First Report of the Director of Selective Service, 1940-1941* (Washington, D.C.: Government Printing Office, 1942), 189-190; section 5 (g) stipulated the rights of conscientious objectors.

19. Theodore Richard Wachs, "Conscription, Conscientious Objection, and the Context of American Pacifism, 1940-1945" (Ph.D diss., University of Illinois—Champaign-Urbana, 1976), 57.

20. See National Council for Religious Conscientious Objectors minutes, Oct. 11, 1940, AMC (since the council soon became the National Religious Service Board for Religious Objectors, hereafter cited as NSBRO minutes, AMC).

21. See George Q. Flynn, *Lewis B. Hershey, Mr. Selective Service* (Chapel Hill, N.C.: University of North Carolina Press, 1985), 44; pp. 4 and 126 also have reflections on Mennonite connections. See also Paul Comly French diary, Jan. 22, 1941, in Swarthmore College Library, Swarthmore, Pa.; Robert S. Kreider, N. Newton, Kan., furnished me with transcriptions of selected diary portions.

22. Flynn, *Lewis B. Hershey*, 71-76; quot., p. 76.

23. Paul Comly French Memorandum of Conversation with Colonel Hershey, Oct. 15, 1940, in *The Origins of Civilian Public Service* (Washington, D.C.: National Service Board for Religious Objectors, n.d.), 11.

24. Menn. Central Peace Comm. annual meeting minutes, Oct. 4, 1940, AMC. Excerpts from American Friends Service Committee and Brethren Service Committee minutes on this issue are reprinted in *Origins of Civilian Public Service*, 12-15.

25. NSBRO minutes, Oct. 22, 1940, AMC.

26. French to Clarence E. Pickett, Dec. 3, 1940, printed in *Origins of Civilian Public Service*, 21.

27. Clarence A. Dykstra, "Memorandum to the President re: Conscientious Objection," given to Paul Comly French on Dec. 20, 1940, printed in *Origins of Civilian Public Service*, 24-25.

28. Quoted in Keim and Stoltzfus, *Politics of Conscience* (n. 9), 113.

29. John Mosemann, [Jr.,] "The Future of Our Program," *The Olive Branch* 1 (Oct. 11, 1941), 1-2. (A number of libraries collected the various CPS-camp newsletters; especially good collections are in the MHL and the MLA.)

30. Menn. Central Peace Comm. minutes, Oct. 25, 1941, AMC.

31. "The Mennonite Civilian Service Program" (brochure published by MCC in 1940); the item appeared in many Mennonite periodicals, e.g., *GH* 33 (Jan. 9, 1941), 867, 879.

32. Ibid.; J. R. Thierstein, "God Given Opportunities," *TM* 54 (Jan. 21, 1941), 1.

33. "Report of the Peace Problems Committee," *Mennonite General Conference: Twenty-Second Mennonite General Conference* (1941), 17 (these reports hereafter cited as [MC] Menn. Gen. Conf. *Reports*, with dates and pages).

34. Henry Fast, "Mennonites and the Civilian Service Program," *TM* 54 (Jan. 7, 1941), 3.

35. Ibid., 2.

36. Gaeddert, quoted in Gingerich, *Service for Peace* (n. 9), 404.

37. Frank Olmstead to A. J. Muste, Feb. 12, 1941, in f. 8, b. 1, Fast papers.

38. Quoted in Sibley and Jacob, *Conscription of Conscience* (n. 2), 121.

39. Paul Comly French, *Civilian Public Service* (Washington, D.C.: National Service Board for Religious Objectors, 1942), 11-12.

40. Ibid., 12.

41. Orie Miller to MCC Exec. Comm. and Menn. Central Peace Comm., Feb. 28, 1940, f. 8, b. 1, Fast papers.

42. Historians reviewing both church and Selective Service data keep arriving at differing numbers for the various kinds of conscientious objectors in WWII: Gingerich, *Service for Peace* (n. 9), 1, tallies 4,665 Mennonites in CPS; Hershberger, *The Mennonite Church in World War II*, 39, indicates 4,536; Mitchell Lee Robinson, "Civilian Public Service During World War II: The Dilemmas of Conscience and Conscription in a Free Society" (Ph.D. diss., Cornell University, 1990), 110, shows 4,610. Totals for noncombatants vary considerably more: Sibley and Jacob, *Conscription of Conscience* (n. 2), 83, suggests up to 50,000; Cynthia Eller, "Moral and Religious Arguments in Support of Pacifism: Conscientious Objectors and the Second World War (Ph.D. diss., University of Southern California, 1988), 66, indicates 12,000 Seventh-Day Adventists in noncombatancy; for that group's story, see Roger Guinon Davis, "Conscientious Cooperators: The 7th Day Adventists and Military Service, 1860-1945" (Ph.D diss., George Washington University, 1970).

43. Figures on women and children are from Rachel Waltner Goossen, "Conscientious Objection and Gender: Women in Civilian Public Service During the Second World War" (Ph.D. diss., University of Kansas, 1993), 62, 105, 127.

44. See Gingerich, *Service for Peace* (n. 9), ch. 9.

45. Ibid., 177.

46. For a good discussion of the use of CPS men in agricultural service, see Robinson, "Civilian Public Service During World War II" (n. 42), 128-145.

47. See ibid., 139-147; *Smoke Jumpers* (Akron, Pa.: Mennonite Central Committee, 1944).

48. Gingerich, *Service for Peace* (n. 9), 214, 252-275.

49. Harry Van Dyck, *Exercise of Conscience: A WWII Objector Remembers* (Buffalo, N.Y.: Prometheus Books, 1990), 135.

50. Definite numbers are uncertain because some camps were under joint service-agency administration for a period of time, after which they became the responsibilities of single agencies. Generally, the joint administration was early in the camp's history.

51. For Selective Service criteria for judging the CPS program, see U.S. Selective Service, *Selective Service in Peacetime: First Report . . . , 1940-1941* (n. 18), 200-201.

52. Paul Comly French, General Letter no. 53, Oct. 6, 1943, copy in f. 12, b. 2, Albert Gaeddert papers, MLA.

53. Colonel Kosch to M. R. Ziegler, Paul J. Furnas, Henry Fast, Jan. 1942, f. 17, b. 2, Fast papers.

54. See Gingerich, *Service for Peace* (n. 9), 163-165.

55. Bohrer to Fast, Jan. 15, 1942, f. 17, b. 2, Fast papers.

56. See, e.g., Albert Gaeddert to Henry Fast, Mar. 19, 1942, f. 16, b. 2, Fast papers.

57. Paul Comly French diary (n. 21), Nov. 15, 1941.

58. Henry Fast to Paul Comly French, Aug. 23, 1941, f. 4, CPS corresp. 1940-45, MCC Archives IX-6-3, AMC.

59. See Clarence Pickett, *For More Than Bread* (Boston: Little Brown, 1953), 330-331; Sibley and Jacob, *Conscription of Conscience* (n. 2), 311-313.

60. Paul Comly French diary (n. 21), Oct. 17, 1943.

61. Fast to J. H. Langenwalter, Mar. 17, 1941, f. 9, b. 2, Fast papers.

62. E. G. Kaufman to Orie Miller, Apr. 12, 1941, f. 10, b. 2, Fast papers.

63. "Report of the Peace Problems Committee," [MC] Menn. Gen. Conf. *Reports* (1941), 18.

64. Robert Kreider, "Environmental Factors Influencing Decisions of Men of Draft Age," Conference on Mennonite Cultural Problems *Proceedings* (1942), 75-88.

65. Harold S. Bender, "In the Midst of War—Thoughts for Nonresistants: III. Mennonite Men in the Army?" *GH* 35 (Feb. 11, 1943), 986.

66. Russell Lantz to Fast, n.d., f. 6, b. 1, Fast papers.

67. Langenwalter to Fast, Mar. 14, 1941, f. 9, b. 2, Fast papers.

68. Ibid.; Fast to Langenwalter, Mar. 17, 1941, f. 9, b. 2, Fast papers.

69. C. Henry Smith, "Is the General Conference Losing Its Peace Testimony?" *TM* 55 (July 28, 1942), 1-2.

70. Fast to P. K. Derksen, Oct. 1, 1940, f. 6, b. 1, Fast papers.

71. Editorial, "Noncombatant Service," *GH* 37 (June 30, 1944), 243.

72. The sermon is partially reprinted in Emil Waltner, "Difficulties in Applying Nonconformity in the Mennonite Church," Conference on Mennonite Cultural Problems *Proceedings* (1944), 62-63; full copy in f. 3, b. 2, Albert Gaeddert papers, MLA. See also Jeff A. Steely, "Cornelius Herman Suckau: Mennonite Fundamentalist?" *ML* 44 (Mar. 1989), 15-21.

73. Sources cited in n. 72. Berne draft-response figures are in Draft Census Files, MCC Archives IX-7-12, AMC. See also Naomi Lehman, *Pilgrimage of a Congregation: First Mennonite Church, Berne, Indiana* (Berne, Ind.: First Mennonite Church, 1982), 372.

74. See Perry Bush, "Drawing the Line: American Mennonites, The State and Social Change, 1935-1973" (Ph.D. diss., Carnegie-Mellon University, 1990), 171; Guy Hershberger to Emmett L. Harshbarger, Sep. 4, 1940, f. 20, b. 2, Harshbarger papers, MLA.

75. H. A. Fast to Orie Miller, Feb. 11, 1941, f. 8, b. 1, Fast papers.

76. David B. Hoover, *A Testimony of the Truth: No Man Can Serve Two Masters; Ye Cannot Serve God and Mammon* (Ephrata, Pa.: privately published, n.d.), 6-7.

77. Ibid., 9-10; see also Noah Leid, *History of the Bowmansville Mennonites and Related Congregations* (n.p. 1991), 42-43.

78. See Henry Fast to the Members of the Emergency Relief Board (GC), May 5, 1942, and Irwin W. Bauman to Fast, May 9, 1942, f. 17, b. 2, Fast papers.

79. H. A. Fast to Goering, Dec. 30, 1941, f. 15, b. 2, Fast papers.

80. Hiebert to Miller, Jan. 6, 1941, f. 7, b. 2, Fast papers.

81. [MC] Menn. Gen. Conf. *Reports* (1941), 5.

82. See Guy F. Hershberger to Grant Stoltzfus, Oct. 31, 1951; Stoltzfus reply, Nov. 9, 1951; f. 2, b. 14, Hershberger papers, AMC.

83. Lapp to Peace Problems Comm., Feb. 10, 1943, f. 2., b. 17, Peace Problems Comm. papers, AMC.

84. [MC] Menn. Gen. Conf. *Reports* (1943), 46.

CHAPTER 7

1. "Notes from a C.O.'s Journal," *Pike View Peace News* 1 (Sep. 20, 1941), 3. (A number of Mennonite libraries have collected CPS-camp newsletters; excellent collections are in MHL and in MLA.)

2. Irvin Horst, "4th of July Thinking for CPS Men," *The Olive Branch* 1 (July 10, 1942), 8.

3. Harry Van Dyck, *Exercise of Conscience: A WWII Objector Remembers* (Buffalo, N.Y.: Prometheus Books, 1990), 50.

4. See David Wagler, "A Peep at Camp Life," in David Wagler and Roman Raber, eds., *The Story of the Amish in Civilian Public Service* (n.p., n.d. [1945]), 11-20.

5. Van Dyck, *Exercise of Conscience*, chs. 5 and 6.

6. Theodore Grimsrud, "An Ethical Analysis of Conscientious Objection to World War II" (Ph.D. diss., Graduate Theological Union, 1988).

7. "A Star for CPS," *The Olive Branch* 3 (Mar. 1944), 2.

8. Quoted in Perry Bush, "Drawing the Line: American Mennonites, the State, and Social Change, 1935-1973" (Ph.D. diss., Carnegie-Mellon University, 1990), 109.

9. Bill and Helene Ramseyer to Fast, June 22, 1942, f. 17, b. 2, Fast papers.

10. James Steiner to Henry Fast, Oct. 15, 1941, f. 12, b. 2, Fast papers; Jesse Harder to Albert Gaeddert, Feb. 8, 1944, f. 15/55, CPS camp corresp., MCC Archives IX-6-6, AMC.

11. Fast to James Steiner, Oct. 20, 1941, f. 12, b. 2, Fast papers.

12. Fast to John H. Mosemann, Apr. 2, 1941, f. 10, b. 2, Fast papers.

13. See, e.g., Paul Tschetter to Henry Fast, Aug. 17, 1943, and Albert Gaeddert report on Camp Camino, Aug. 18, 1943, f. 11, b. 2, Albert Gaeddert papers, MLA.

14. Arthur A. Ekirch, Jr., "CPS and Slavery," *Pacifica Views* 2 (Aug. 25, 1944), 1, 4.

15. Both quotations are in Bush, "Drawing the Line" (n. 8), 112.

16. Albert Foote, "C.P.S. Camp: A Training School," *The Olive Branch* 1 (Dec. 2, 1941), 6.

17. Edward Yoder and Don Smucker, *The Christian and Conscription: An Inquiry Designed as a Preface to Action* (Akron, Pa.: Mennonite Central Committee, 1945), 53-55.

18. "Powellsville Conscription Confab," *Box 96* 1 (Mar. 1945), 3. (*Box 96* was the Mulberry, Fla., camp paper.)

19. See Rachel Waltner Goossen, "Conscientious Objection and Gender: Women in Civilian Public Service During the Second World War" (Ph.D. diss., University of Kansas, 1993), 62-64.

20. See ibid., 68-74.

21. Ibid., 73.

22. Ibid., 80.

23. Ibid., 77, citing an interview with Maria Lohrenz of Mountain Lake, Minn.

24. Ibid., 74-76, quoting Henry Fast.

25. Harder to Albert Gaeddert, Feb. 8, 1944, f. 15/55, CPS camp corresp., MCC Archives IX-6-3, AMC.

26. See *The Olive Branch* 2 (Nov. 14, 1942); *The Turnpike Echo* 3 (Nov. 1943), 8; "Our Gratitudes," *Whispering Pines* 1 (Nov. 19, 1941); "Donations," *The Olive Branch* 2 (Sep. 1943), 6; "Food Depot," *The Olive Branch* 2 (Dec. 1943), 9.

27. Melvin Gingerich, *Service for Peace: A History of Mennonite Civilian Public Service* (Akron, Pa.: Mennonite Central Committee, 1949), 347.

28. William Chafe, cited in Rachel Waltner Goossen, "The 'Second Sex' and the 'Second Milers': Mennonite Women and Civilian Public Service," *MQR* 66 (Oct. 1992), 528.

29. Cited in Goossen, "The 'Second Sex' and the 'Second Milers,' " 531.

30. Gingerich, *Service for Peace*, 348-349.

31. Ibid., 350-352.

32. See 1944 corresp. between David Suderman and Albert Gaeddert, f. 14/5, CPS camp corresp., MCC Archives IX-6-3, AMC.

33. Dale Nebel to J. N. Weaver, National Service Board, Jan. 10, 1944, f. 16/107, CPS camp corresp., MCC Archives IX-6-3, AMC.

34. Albert M. Gaeddert to David Suderman, July 5, 1944, f. 14/5; Gaeddert to Alfred Zook, Oct. 13, 1944, f. 15/55; CPS camp corresp., MCC Archives IX-6-3, AMC.

35. Goossen, "Conscientious Objection and Gender" (n. 19), 124.

36. Edna Ruth Byler, "Memorandum of My Visit to the New Jersey State Hospital," Jan. 4, 1944, f. 15/63, CPS camp corresp., MCC Archives IX-6-3, AMC.

37. M. C. Lehman to Orie Miller, June 6, 1943, copy in f. 10, b. 2, Albert Gaeddert papers, MLA.

38. See Carl Kreider-H. S. Bender corresp., f. 4a, b. 19, Bender papers.

39. Quoted in Guy F. Hershberger, *The Mennonite Church in the Second World War* (Scottdale, Pa.: Mennonite Publishing House, 1951), 179.

40. Ibid., 179.

41. MCC annual meeting minutes, Dec. 28-29, 1942, AMC.

42. See f. 41, b. 1, CPS collection, MCC Archives IX-13-1, AMC.

43. See "Rules" and other documents about the Relief Workers Training School, in f. 8, b. 1, CPS collection, MCC Archives IX-6-3, AMC.

44. Daniel Kauffman, "Merits of Relief Training," *The Olive Branch* 2 (Aug. 30, 1943), 9.

45. Gingerich, *Service for Peace* (n. 27), 307-308.

46. See *MCC News Letter* 2 (Aug. 1943); *MCC Bulletin* 2 (June 8, 1944); Goossen, "Conscientious Objection and Gender" (n. 19), 163.

47. Charles F. Read, Elgin State Hospital, memorandum to Paul French, with George Reeves to Henry Fast, Sep. 10, 1941, f. 4, CPS corresp. 1940-45, MCC Archives IX-6-3, AMC.

48. See Mulford Sibley and Philip Jacob, *Conscription of Conscience: The American State and the Conscientious Objector, 1940-1947* (Ithaca, N.Y.: Cornell University Press, 1952), 134; William Keeney, "Civilian Public Service and Related World War II Experiences," in Mennonite Mental Health Services, "Papers and Responses Presented at the Twenty-Fifth Anniversary Program . . . [Oct. 1971]" (unpublished, copy in MHL), 1; Gingerich, *Service for Peace* (n. 27), 213-251; Alex Sareyan, *The Turning Point: How Men of Conscience Brought About Major Change in the Care of America's Mentally Ill* (Washington, D.C.: American Psychiatric Press, Inc., 1993; Scottdale, Pa.: Herald Press, 1994), 290; Albert N. Keim, *The CPS Story: An Illustrated History of Civilian Public Service* (Intercourse, Pa.: Good Books, 1990), 107-110.

49. See U.S. Selective Service, *Selective Service in Wartime: Second Report of*

the Director of Selective Service, 1941-1942 (Washington, D.C.: Government Printing Office, 1943), 270; *The Experience of the American Friends Service Committee in Civilian Public Service* (Philadelphia: American Friends Service Committee, 1945), 9; Hershberger, *Mennonite Church in the Second World War* (n. 39), 59; Clarence Pickett, *For More Than Bread* (Boston: Little, Brown, 1953), 326; Sareyan, *The Turning Point.*

50. For a brief historical sketch of these hospitals see Elmer Ediger, "Roots," in Vernon Neufeld, ed., *If We Can Love: The Mennonite Mental Health Story* (Newton, Kan.: Faith & Life Press, 1983), 19-21.

51. In 1937 and 1938 the MBs' Pacific District Conference investigated the possibility of starting a psychiatric hospital; in 1937 similar interest in central Kansas led C. E. Krehbiel to poll the GC congregations to determine support for establishing a psychiatric hospital on a denomination-wide basis.

52. Richert's concern is reflected in Peter H. Unruh to P. C. Hiebert and Orie Miller, Jan. 13, 1941, f. 37, Peter C. Hiebert papers, MLA.

53. Paul Comly French diary, Nov. 10, 1942, in Swarthmore College Library, Swarthmore, Pa.; Robert S. Kreider, N. Newton, Kan., furnished me with transcriptions of selected diary portions.

54. Van Dyck, *Exercise of Conscience* (n. 3), 156.

55. "Mental Hospitals—The Problem," *The Reporter* 2 (Oct. 1, 1943).

56. Gingerich, *Service for Peace* (n. 27), 215; Pickett, *For More Than Bread* (n. 49), 327.

57. Quoted from a Hudson River State Hospital unit report printed in William Keeney, "Experiences in Mental Hospitals in World War II," *MQR* 56 (Jan. 1982), 9.

58. Ibid., 9-10.

59. Ibid., 10-11.

60. Ibid., 11-15; Keeney, "Experiences in Mental Hospitals in World War II," 11-15; Mitchell Lee Robinson, "Civilian Public Service During World War II: The Dilemmas of Conscience in a Free Society" (Ph.D. diss., Cornell University, 1990), 152-153; "M H P Begins Drive," *Mennonite CPS Bulletin* 4 (Aug. 22, 1945).

61. See J. Berkeley Gordon, Medical Director at Marlboro, to Lewis F. Kosch of Selective Service, June 5, 1946, Government Evaluation of CPS file, MCC Archives IX-12, AMC.

62. Keeney, "Experiences in Mental Hospitals in World War II," 7-17.

63. "Psychiatry and Christian Service School," *MCC Bulletin* 3 (Nov. 22, 1944).

64. Goossen, "Conscientious Objection and Gender" (n. 19), 165.

65. Ibid., 168-169.

66. An article in *Sociology and Social Research*, quoted in Doris Crate Cummins, "Civilian Public Service Unit Sixty-Three: Mennonite Conscientious Objectors in World War II" (M.A. thesis, Florida Atlantic University, 1982), 54.

67. Goossen, "Conscientious Objection and Gender," 170, lists the figure of 300 women in service. The data on Mennonite women in summer service is collected in Wilfred J. Unruh, *A Study of Mennonite Service Programs* (Elkhart, Ind.: Institute of Mennonite Studies, 1965), Section A; for a discussion of the women of Marlboro, see also Cummins, "The Civilian Public Service Unit Sixty-Three," 49-57.

68. Albert Gaeddert, "What Have We Learned in Civilian Public Service?" *ML* 1 (July 1946), 16; Gingerich, *Service for Peace* (n. 27), 295, indicates that the educational "opportunity had been foreseen from the beginning by those who planned for alternative service camps."

69. MCC, *Manual for Educational Directors* (1942), 16; copy in AMC.

70. Kreider to Henry Fast, Nov. 11, 1941, f. 14, b. 2, Fast papers.

71. Bender to Henry Fast, Nov. 22, 1941, f. 12, b. 2, Fast papers.

72. No. 1: Harold S. Bender, *Mennonite Origins in Europe* (1942). No. 2: C. Henry Smith, *Mennonites in America* (1942). No. 3: Edward Yoder, *Our Mennonite Heritage*

1943). No. 4: E. G. Kauffman, *Our Missions as a Church of Christ* (1944). No. 5: Guy F. Hershberger, *Christian Relationships to State and Community* (1943). No. 6: P. C. Hiebert, *Life and Service in the Kingdom of God* (1944).

73. Gingerich, *Service for Peace* (n. 27), 295-337; "Educational Memo" #204 (Nov. 4, 1944). The Educational Memos are conveniently bound in MLA.

74. "The Past and Future of the Educational and Recreational Program," *Pike View Peace News* 4 (Oct. 1944), 3.

75. "Our Educational Program," *The Olive Branch* 1 (Apr. 1942).

76. Paul Albrecht, "Civilian Public Service Evaluated by Civilian Public Service Men," *MQR* 22 (Jan. 1948), 12.

77. Hershberger, *Mennonite Church in the Second World War* (n. 39), 39.

78. I.e., the percentage is not based on the total number of Mennonite and Amish men drafted, which would include persons rejected for medical reasons, those deferred as ministers or divinity students, and certain others. A weakness is that the categories reported do not specifically include conscientious objectors who were given occupational deferments, usually to work on farms. On the other hand, the figures may include some such men, either because (1) persons reporting from their congregations may have merged them into the IV-E statistics; or because (2) they may have shifted in and out among the occupationally deferred (II-A) and other categories—with such shifting increased by the fact that occupational deferments ran out unless renewed every six months. For the classification system, see [United States Selective Service System,] *Selective Service Regulations* [1940], Vol. 3: *Classification and Selection.*

79. Several recent articles are among the first attempts by historians to examine the story of Mennonites who chose military options. See Keith L. Sprunger and John D. Thiesen, "Mennonite Military Service in World II: An Oral History Approach," *MQR* 66 (Oct. 1992), 481-491; T. D. Regehr, "Lost Sons: The Canadian Mennonite Soldiers of World War II," *MQR* 66 (Oct. 1992), 461-480; Perry Bush, "Military Service, Religious Faith, and Acculturation: Mennonite G.I.s and Their Church, 1941-1945," *MQR* 67 (July 1993), 261-282.

80. Hershberger, *Mennonite Church in the Second World War* (n. 39), 39.

81. See n. 78.

82. Harold S. Bender, "The Facts About Nonresistance Among the Mennonites of America," appended to Bender to S. H. N. Gorter, Dec. 24, 1947, f. 1, b. 19, Bender papers.

83. Howard Charles, "A Presentation and Evaluation of MCC Draft Status Census," in Conference on Mennonite Cultural Problems *Proceedings* (1945), 88-89.

84. Charles, "A Presentation . . . ," 89-91.

85. Hershberger, *Mennonite Church in the Second World War* (n. 39), 40.

86. Draft Census File, MCC Archives IX-7-12, AMC.

87. Hershberger, *Mennonite Church in the Second World War* (n. 39), 40; Charles, "A Presentation . . . ," 106.

88. Draft Census File, MCC Archives IX-7-12, AMC.

89. Ibid.; see also J. Winfield Fretz, "Draft Status of GC Men in WW II," *TM* 60 (July 24, 1945), 1-2.

90. Walter Dyck, "The Mutual Responsibility of the Church and Returning Service Men," *TM* 60 (Nov. 13, 1945), 5.

91. Bush, "Drawing the Line" (n. 8), 127.

92. B. 1, Arthur Nafziger papers, AMC.

93. Springer to Nafziger, Apr. 19, 1944; Litwiller to Nafziger, n.d.; H. Nafziger to Nafziger, Mar. 3, 1945; all in files 8 or 9, b. 1, Arthur Nafziger papers, AMC.

94. Both quoted in Bush, "Drawing the Line" (n. 8), 128.

95. [MB] Pacific District Conference *Year Book:* (1944), 37; for Hiebert quotation, (1945), 47.

96. Cited in John L. Ruth, *Maintaining the Right Fellowship: A Narrative Account of Life in the Oldest Mennonite Community in North America* (Scottdale, Pa.: Herald Press, 1984), 524.

97. Ibid., 525.

98. Ibid.

99. Ruby Funk, ed., *Peace, Progress, Promise: A 75th Anniversary History of Tabor Mennonite Church* (N. Newton, Kan.: Tabor Mennonite Church, 1983), 100.

100. Hershberger, *Mennonite Church in the Second World War* (n. 39), 116.

101. Ibid., 115-16.

102. Rachel Waltner Goossen, *Prairie Vision: A History of the Pleasant Valley Mennonite Church, 1888-1988* (Hillsboro, Kan.: Pleasant Valley Church, 1988), 72-73.

103. James O. Lehman, *Creative Congregationalism: A History of the Oak Grove Mennonite Church in Wayne County, Ohio* (Smithville, Ohio: Oak Grove Mennonite Church, 1978), 258-259.

104. "Editorial," *GH* 36 (Jan. 20, 1944), 897.

105. Hershberger, *Mennonite Church in the Second World War* (n. 39), 117; Bush, "Drawing the Line" (n. 8), 129-130.

106. See Sprunger and Thiesen, "Mennonite Military Service in World War II" (n. 79), 481-491.

107. See "Report on Present Church Status of Mennonites Who Accepted Military Service," b. 7, Project no.19A, Mennonite Research Foundation collection V-8-20, AMC.

108. Robert S. Kreider, "The Environmental Influences Affecting the Decisions of Mennonite Boys of Draft Age," in Conference on Mennonite Cultural Problems *Proceedings* (1942), 75-88; quot., p. 78; same article reprinted in *MQR* 16 (Oct. 1942), 247-259, 275.

109. Charles, "A Presentation . . ." (n. 83), 101.

110. Gaeddert to Elmer Gingerich, Dec. 19, 1945, f. 15, b. 2, Albert Gaeddert papers, AMC.

111. See Charles, "A Presentation . . . ," 83-106; Gaeddert, "What Have We Learned in Civilian Public Service" (n. 68), 16-20; Albrecht, "Civilian Public Service Evaluated by Civilian Public Service Men" (n. 76), 5-18; Gingerich, *Service for Peace* (n. 27); Hershberger, *Mennonite Church in the Second World War* (n. 39). For assessments at the 25th anniversary of CPS, see various articles in *GH* 59 (May 24, 1966). For assessments anticipating the 50th anniversary, see Keim, *The CPS Story* (n. 48); Paul A. Wilhelm, *Civilian Public Servants: A Report on 210 World War II Conscientious Objectors* (Washington, D.C.: National Interreligious Service Board for Conscientious Objectors, 1990). *MQR* 66 (July 1992) published papers of a conference at Goshen College examining the CPS experience.

112. See John Higham, "Introduction: The Forms of Ethnic Leadership," in Higham, ed., *Ethnic Leadership in America* (Baltimore: The Johns Hopkins University Press, 1978), 1-18.

113. William H. Yoder, "Cooperation or Isolation," *Box 96* 2 (Feb. 1946), 4, 7.

114. Boyd Nelson, "CPS: From Defense to Offense," *GH* 59 (May 24, 1966), 465-466.

115. On the Puidoux Conferences, see Donald F. Durnbaugh, ed., *On Earth Peace: Discussions on War/Peace Issues Between Friends, Mennonites, Brethren and European Churches, 1935-1975* (Elgin, Ill.: The Brethren Press, 1978).

116. Albrecht, "Civilian Public Service Evaluated by Civilian Public Service Men" (n. 76), 12-13 documents the degree to which CPC enhanced inter-Mennonite feelings and relationships.

117. Elmer Ediger, "Do C.P.S. Men Favor a Voluntary Service Program for Peacetime?" *Mennonite CPS Bulletin* 4 (Oct. 22, 1945); see also "C.P.S. Men Enter the Post-

war World," *Mennonite CPS Bulletin* 4 (Sep. 8, 1945).

118. Harry Martens, "Editorially speaking . . . . Graduated from Civilian Public Service," in *Constructive Peace Service: A Supplement to the CPS Bulletin* (Jan. 30, 1947), 1, 3.

119. Hershberger, *Mennonite Church in the Second World War* (n. 39), 286.

120. James Juhnke has made this point repeatedly in articles and books dating back to 1970—e.g., in "Mennonite Benevolence and Revitalization in the Wake of World War I," *MQR* 60 (Jan. 1986), 15-30.

CHAPTER 8

1. Paul Comly French diary, at June 27, 1946, in Swarthmore College Library, Swarthmore, Pa.; Robert S. Kreider, N. Newton, Kan., furnished me with transcriptions of selected diary portions.

2. Ibid., at Sep. 26, 1944.

3. Ibid., at Jan. 3, 1945.

4. John C. Wenger, *The Mennonite Church in America* (Scottdale, Pa.: Herald Press, 1966), 214-215.

5. "The Mennonite Central Committee: A World-Wide Spiritual Influence," *TM* 63 (Jan. 13, 1948), 3.

6. Robert Kreider, "Introduction," in Paul Erb, *Orie O. Miller: The Story of a Man and an Era* (Scottdale, Pa.: Herald Press, 1969), 10.

7. Cornelius Krahn, "Active or Passive Christianity," *ML* 1 (Jan. 1946), 3-4.

8. Robert Kreider, "A Vision for Our Day," *ML* 3 (Jan. 1948), 7.

9. Paul Peachey, *The Church in the City* (Newton,Kan.: Faith & Life Press, 1963), 84.

10. Mininger's comments are in "Report of Meeting of Mennonite Leaders to Consider the Effect of Current Economic and Social Trends on the Life of the Church" (Apr. 10, 1943), in Rural Life Assn. file, b. 15, Guy F. Hershberger papers, AMC.

11. Peachey, *Church in the City*, 84.

12. J. Lawrence Burkholder, *The Problem of Social Responsibility from the Perspective of the Mennonite Church* [printed version of 1958 doctoral diss.] (Elkhart Ind.: Institute of Mennonite Studies, 1989), 23.

13. Peachey, *Church in the City*, 74.

14. Leland Harder, "The Quest for Equilibrium in an Established Sect" (Ph.D. diss., Northwestern University, 1962), 252.

15. Ibid., 234.

16. J. Howard Kauffman and Leland Harder, *Anabaptists Four Centuries Later: A Profile of Five Mennonite and Brethren in Christ Denominations* (Scottdale, Pa.: Herald Press, 1975), 284.

17. Simon G. Gingerich, "Occupations of Mennonite Men, 1940 and 1950," f. 1, b. 12, Mennonite Research Foundation Archives V-7-30, AMC.

18. Ila Eichelberger, "Education and Occcupation of Mennonite Men and Women in Five Conferences" (student paper, Goshen College, 1956; copy in f. 39), 55-56; for more detailed listing, see Melvin Gingerich, "Mennonite Occupations in 1950"; both in b. 10, Mennonite Research Foundation Archives V-7-28, AMC.

19. Harder, "Quest for Equilibrium," 302, summarizing data in J. Lloyd Spaulding, "The Changing Economic Base of the Mennonite Community with Special Reference to Certain Kansas [sic] Counties," in Conference on Mennonite Educational and Cultural Problems *Proceedings* (1957), 94-97.

20. Ibid., 14-15.

21. Melvin Gingerich, "Mennonite Income and Giving in 1951," in f. 1, b. 16, Guy F. Hershberger papers, AMC.

22. Harder, "Quest for Equilibrium," 242.

23. Wilbert G. Lind, "Mennonite Family Census of 1949-50: Marriage Age and the Size of the Family of Mennonite Families" (student paper, Goshen College, 1951; copy in f. 37, b. 10, Mennonite Research Foundation Archives V-7-28, AMC).

24. John R. Smucker, "Mobility Among the Mennonites of Ohio" (student paper, Goshen College, 1956; copy in f. 38, b. 10, Mennonite Research Foundation Archives V-7-28, AMC).

25. Harold S. Bender, "Secondary Education," *ME*, IV, 491-493.

26. *1950 Mennonite Yearbook and Directory* (Scottdale, Pa.: Mennonite Pubishing House, 1950), 32-34.

27. Ibid.

28. Silas Hertzler, "Mennonite Parochial Schools: Why Established and What They Have Achieved," in Conference on Mennonite Cultural Problems *Proceedings* (1949), 78.

29. MCC Peace Section minutes, Aug. 13, 1943, and Feb. 2, 1944, AMC.

30. Ross T. Bender, "An Apology for the Church-Related Secondary School Movement in the Mennonite Church" (unpublished, n.d. [from external sources, 1958]), b. 5, John H. Yoder papers, AMC.

31. Hertzler, "Mennonite Parochial Schools," 69, 77-78.

32. "Information Concerning and Regulation of the Mennonite School Located Near the Lower Deer Creek Congregation" (unpublished, n.d.), f. 13, b. 5, Sanford C. Yoder papers, AMC.

33. Noah Good, "A Mennonite High School—Its Prospects and Problems," in Conference on Mennonite Cultural Problems *Proceedings* (1943), 37.

34. Don E. Smucker, "The Influence of Public Schools on Mennonite Ideals and Its Implication for the Future," Conference on Mennonite Cultural Problems *Proceedings* (1943), 47-48.

35. John R. Smucker, "Mobility Among the Mennonites of Ohio" (n. 24).

36. Harold S. Bender, "The Responsibility of the Mennonite Church School and College for the Preservation and Extension of Mennonitism" (unpublished, n.d. [from external data, 1946]), f. 24, b. 101, Bender papers.

37. "Report of Mennonite Mutual Aid Committee," *Mennonite General Conference Report: Twenty-Sixth Mennonite General Conference* (Aug. 26-29, 1947), 50-53 (MC gen. conf. reports hereafter cited as [MC] Menn. Gen. Conf. *Reports*, with dates and pages).

38. Ibid.

39. "Mennonite Mutual Aid, Inc.," in [MC] Menn. Gen. Conf. *Reports* (1949), 46-51.

40. "General Conference Mutual Aid Board Meeting Held in Chicago," *MWR* (Dec. 27, 1945), 3; J. Winfield Fretz, "Mutual Aid Board," *ME*, III, 801.

41. See, in Conference on Mennonite Cultural Problems *Proceedings*: J. Winfield Fretz, "Helping Mennonite Youth Get a Vocational Start" (1944), 68-86; William Stauffer, "The Rehabilitation of Men in the CPS Camps" (1943), 73.

42. Melvin Gingerich, "Is There a Need for a Mennonite Rural Life Publication?" in Conference on Mennonite Cultural Problems *Proceedings* (1942), 60-66.

43. Paul Erb, "A VISION and Its Realization," *The Mennonite Community* 1 (Jan. 1947), 10.

44. Guy F. Hershberger, "Appreciating THE MENNONITE COMMUNITY," *The Mennonite Community* 1 (Jan. 1947), 6-7.

45. J. Lawrence Burkholder, *Problem of Social Responsibility* (n. 12), 152.

46. See Theron F. Schlabach, "To Focus a Mennonite Vision," in John Richard Burkholder and Calvin Redekop, eds., *Kingdom Cross and Community: Essays on Mennonite Themes in Honor of Guy F. Hershberger* (Scottdale, Pa.: Herald Press, 1976), 33-38.

47. The history of the beginnings of VS is found in many denominational and

MCC sources but is most conveniently collected in Wilfred J. Unruh, *A Study of Mennonite Service Programs* (Elkhart, Ind.: Institute of Mennonite Studies, 1965). Additional sources that compile selected materials are Myron Ebersole, "History of Mennonite Central Committee Voluntary Services," History of Voluntary Service File, MCC Archives IX-12, AMC; Cornelius J. Dyck, ed., *Witness and Service in North America: Documents*, The Mennonite Central Committee Story vol. 3 (Scottdale, Pa.: Herald Press, 1980); John D. Unruh, *In the Name of Christ: A History of the Mennonite Central Committee and Its Service, 1920-1951* (Scottdale, Pa.: Herald Press, 1952), 294-309.

48. For the beginnings of the MC denominational program see Anne Birky, "The Development and a Case Study of the Voluntary Service Program of the (old) Mennonite Church" (student paper, Goshen, College, 1976; copy in MHL); the GC story is told in Lois Barrett, *The Vision and the Reality: The Story of Home Missions in the General Conference Mennonite Church* (Newton, Kan.: Faith & Life Press, 1983), and in "General Conference Voluntary and Summer Units for 1948," *TM* 63 (Feb. 10, 1948), 13. The MB story remains untold; manuscript sources dealing with its beginning are in the Board of General Welfare and Public Relations collection, CMBS-F.

49. "Mennonite Brethren VS Begins," *MWR* (May 19, 1949), 3; Arthur Jost, "Be It Resolved That We Serve," *CL* (Dec. 15, 1948), 8.

50. "Annual Report of the Voluntary Service Section," MCC Annual Meetings Report, Mar. 17-18, 1950, AMC.

51. Unruh, *A Study of Mennonite Service Programs*, A-109, A-110.

52. Quoted in ibid., A-20, A-21.

53. Quoted in ibid., A-25.

54. Ibid., A-21.

55. Quoted in Willard H. Smith, *Mennonites in Illinois* (Scottdale, Pa.: Herald Press, 1983), 365.

56. Wilton E. Hartzler, "Should the Church Administer a Program of Voluntary Service," *CPS Bulletin* 4 (Jan. 4, 1946).

57. Ibid.; *Minutes and Reports of the Fifty-Ninth Session of the Western District Conference* (Oct. 1950), 53.

58. Robert Kreider and Rachel Waltner Goossen, *Hungry, Thirsty, a Stranger: The MCC Experience* (Scottdale, Pa.: Herald Press, 1988), 385-386; Unruh, *In the Name of Christ* (n. 47); Irvin B. Horst, *A Ministry of Goodwill* (Akron, Pa.: MCC, 1950).

59. Peter and Elfrieda Dyck, *Up from the Rubble* (Scottdale, Pa.: Herald Press, 1991), 63. For the CRALOG story and MCC participation in this larger ecumenical agency, see Eileen Egan and Elizabeth Clark Reiss, *Transfigured Night: The CRALOG Experience* (Philadelphia: Livingston Publishing Company, 1964).

60. Frank H. Epp, *Mennonite Exodus, The Rescue and Resettlement of the Russian Mennonites Since the Communist Revolution* (Altona, Man.: Canadian Mennonite Relief and Immigration Council, 1962); P. and E. Dyck, *Up from the Rubble*; Herbert and Maureen Klassen, *Ambassador to His People: C. F. Klassen and the Russian Mennonite Refugees* (Winnipeg, Man.: Kindred Press, 1990); T. D. Regehr, "Anatomy of a Mennonite Miracle: The Berlin Rescue of 30-31 January 1947," *Journal of Mennonite Studies* 9 (1991), 11-33; T. D. Regehr, "Polish and Prussian Mennonite Displaced Persons, 1944-50," *MQR* 66 (Apr. 1992), 247-266.

61. P. and E. Dyck, *Up from the Rubble*, 132-139.

62. Ibid., 147-150.

63. See ibid., 132-161; Regehr, "Anatomy of a Miracle," 15-16, 19-21.

64. Frank Epp, *Mennonite Exodus*, 363-364; Regehr, "Polish and Prussian Mennonite Displaced Persons," 247-266; William I. Schreiber, *The Fate of the Prussian Mennonites* (Goettingen: Goettingen Research Committee, 1955), 37-41.

65. MCC press release "Europe Confronted by Stark Famine," *MWR* (May 31, 1945), 8. Many similar articles appeared. The *MWR* listing for 1945 alone is substantial, e.g.: S. J. Goering, "MCC Representative Visits Mennonites in France" (June 7,

1945), 3; S. H. N. Gorter, "Severe Suffering Among Mennonites in Holland" (July 12, 1945), 1; Cornelius Krahn, "Holland Writes" (Aug. 9, 1945), 2; "Shoes and Winter Clothing Scarce in Holland" (Sep. 6, 1945), 1; "Four Thousand Displaced Mennonites Arrive in Denmark" (Sep. 6, 1945), 1; "Conditions Extremely Serious in Europe" (Sep. 13, 1945), 1; "Food Conditions Extremely Critical: Desperate Circumstances of French People Necessitate Unlimited Assistance from America" (Oct. 4, 1945), 1, 8; M. C. Lehman, "Diseases Incident to War-Suffering" (Oct. 18, 1945), 4; L. D. S. Knipscheer, "Critical Winter Ahead for People of Holland" (Dec. 27, 1945), 4.

66. P. and E. Dyck, *Up from the Rubble* (n. 59), 253.

67. Ibid., 246-253.

68. " 'Flour for Relief Program' Gets Under Way in Moundridge," *MWR* (Sep. 20, 1945), 3.

69. "Flour and Wheat Donated by Mennonites on Way to Europe," *MWR* (Dec. 6, 1945), 1.

70. "Liberal Relief Contributions at Whitewater," *MWR* (Feb. 7, 1945), 1.

71. "Relief Canning Project at Wayland, Iowa," *MWR* (Feb. 21, 1946), 1.

72. "Large Food Shipment Collected by Mountain Lake Churches," *MWR* (Nov. 22, 1945), 1.

73. "Ohio Cattle En Route to Europe," *MWR* (Dec. 27, 1945), 3.

74. From *MWR:* "Relief Sale at Goshen" (Mar. 7, 1946), 1; "Community-Wide Relief Sale" (Mar. 21, 1946), 1; "Correspondence—Pratum, Oregon" (Mar. 21, 1946), 7.

75. "Generous Clothing Contributions," *MWR* (Apr. 19, 1945), 1; "Pack over 200 Bales Relief Clothing," *MWR* (Dec. 13, 1945), 1.

76. "Raisins Packed in Steel Buckets Here," *Reedley Exponent* (Jan. 6, 1949), 1.

77. Unruh, *In the Name of Christ* (n. 47), Appendix IV.

78. Ibid.

79. "Annual Report of the Mennonite Aid Section," MCC Annual Meeting, Mar. 17-18, 1950, AMC.

80. See James C. Juhnke, *A People of Mission: A History of General Conference Mennonites Overseas* (Newton, Kan.: Faith & Life Press, 1979); Melvin Gingerich, "North American Mennonite Overseas Outreach in Perspective, 1890-1965," *MQR* 39 (Oct. 1965), 262-279; Samuel F. Pannabecker, "Missions, Foreign Mennonite," *ME,* III, 712-717; Henry F. Garber, "Eastern Mennonite Board of Missions and Charities," *ME,* II, 133; Paul Classen, "Statistics on Mennonite Central Committee Personnel," *MQR* 44 (July 1970), 324-329; Paul N. Kraybill, ed., *Called to Be Sent: Essays in Honor of the Fiftieth Anniversary of the Founding of the Eastern Mennonite Board of Missions and Charities, 1914-1964* (Scottdale, Pa.: Herald Press, 1964).

81. Paul N. Kraybill and William T. Snyder, "Identification of Areas Where the Interests of the Mission and Service Agencies Converge," *Proceedings of Consultation on Relief, Services, and Missions Relationships Overseas, May 7-8, 1964* (Akron, Pa.: MCC, 1964). For a specific example of how MCC work aided the development of Mennonite missions, see Justus G. Holsinger, *Serving Rural Puerto Rico* (Scottdale, Pa.: Mennonite Publishing House, 1952).

82. J. D. Graber, "Mennonite Board of Missions and Charities," *Mennonite Yearbook 1949* (Scottdale, Pa.: Mennonite Publishing House, 1949), 6.

83. See Robert Kreider, "The Impact of MCC Service on American Mennonites," *MQR* 44 (July 1970), 245-261; Larry Kehler, "A Profile of Mennonite Personnel Involved in International Experience," in Conference on Mennonite Educational and Cultural Problems *Proceedings* (1967), 9-39.

84. J. Winfield Fretz, *The MEDA Experiment: Twenty-Five Years of Economic Development* (Waterloo, Ont.: Conrad Press, 1978), 1-37.

85. See Elmer Ediger, "Excerpts, Considerations and Recommendations on Possibility of Utilizing Leitsburg, Maryland Farm as Mental Rest Home," in Dyck, ed., *Witness and Service in North America* (n. 47), 84; see also pages 80-94 for other documents on the early history of Mennonite Mental Health. For narrative of the entire

program's beginnings, see Elmer Ediger, "Roots" and Vernon Neufeld, "Mennonite Mental Health Services," in Vernon Neufeld, ed., *If We Can Love: The Mennonite Mental Health Story* (Newton, Kan.: Faith & Life Press, 1983), 3-54. See also: Alex Sareyan, *The Turning Point: How Men of Conscience Brought About Major Change in the Care of America's Mentally Ill* (Washington, D.C.: American Psychiatric Press, Inc., 1994); a special issue of the *MQR* 56 (Jan. 1982), which deals with the history, theory, and practice of Mennonite mental health centers; Otto D. Klassen, "The Church Creates a Mental Health Center: Oaklawn Psychiatric Center," *McCormick Quarterly* 21 (1967), 40-54; William Klassen, "The Role of the Church in Community Psychiatry," *McCormick Quarterly* 21 (1967), 23-39.

86. Sources listed in n. 85.

87. Delmar Stahly, C. J. Rempel, John R. Schmidt, C. Krahn, "Mennonites and Mental Health: I. Programs for Mental Illness," *ML* 9 (July 1954), 118-126; Dyck, ed., *Witness and Service in North America* (n. 47), 80-95; Neufeld, *If We Can Love*, 3-225; see also Titus Bender, "The Development of the Mennonite Mental Health Movement, 1942-1971" (D.S.W. diss., Tulane University, 1976).

88. Katie Funk Wiebe, *Day of Disaster* (Scottdale, Pa.: Herald Press, 1976), 107; ch. 7 offers the early history of MDS. An earlier, brief history of the MDS beginnings is Vernon Wiebe, "Mennonites: A Brief History of Mennonite Disaster Service" (1960), conveniently printed in Dyck, ed., *Witness and Service in North America* (n. 47), 114-15.

89. Sources listed in n. 88.

90. See "Statement of Guiding Principles About Civil Defense," approved at a joint meeting of MDS and MCC, Mar. 1-2, 1956, printed in Dyck, ed., *Witness and Service in North America* (n. 47), 120-121.

91. See Donald B. Kraybill, "Modernity and Identity: The Transformation of Mennonite Ethnicity," in Calvin Wall Redekop, ed., *Mennonite Identity: Historical and Contemporary Perspectives* (Lanham, Md.: University Press of America, 1988), 164-172.

92. Robert Kreider, "Introduction" in Erb, *Orie O. Miller* (n. 6), 10.

CHAPTER 9

1. Harold S. Bender, "Editorial," *MQR* 24 (Jan. 1950), 4.

2. Sanford C. Yoder, *The Days of My Years* (Scottdale, Pa.: Herald Press, 1959), 227-228.

3. John R. Mumaw, "To the General Council of the Mennonite General Conference," f. 2, b. 1, Mennonite Church [MC] Gen. Conf. Exec. Comm. papers, AMC. "Board of Reference and Counsel Report," *Year Book of the 45th General Conference of the Mennonite Brethren Church of North America, 1951*, 125-127 (hereafter cited as [MB] Gen. Conf. *Year Book*, with year).

4. "Board of Reference and Counsel Report" (n. 3).

5. Sanford Shetler, "Progress or Drift," *The Sword and Trumpet* 25 (First Quarter, 1957), 11-15; quot., p. 14.

6. Robert Friedmann, *The Theology of Anabaptism* (Scottdale, Pa.: Herald Press, 1973), 25.

7. See Walter Klaassen, *Anabaptism: Neither Catholic nor Protestant* (Waterloo, Ont.: Conrad Press, 1973); Werner O. Packull, *Mysticism and the Early South German-Austrian Anabaptist Movement, 1525-1531* (Scottdale, Pa.: Herald Press, 1977); Marlin Miller, "Theology," *ME*, V, 881-884; Rodney J. Sawatsky, "Defining 'Mennonite' Diversity and Unity," *MQR* 57 (July 1983), 284-285.

8. Harold Bender, "Outside Influences on Mennonite Thought," in Conference on Educational and Cultural Problems *Proceedings* (1953), 33-41; Robert Friedmann, *Mennonite Piety Through the Centuries: Its Genius and Its Literature* (Goshen, Ind.: The Mennonite Historical Society, 1949).

9. "1952 a Year of Evangelism," *TM* 66 (Dec. 11, 1951), 774.

10. *Minutes and Reports of . . . Convention*[s] *of Mennonite Brethren Churches of the United States*: (1963), 41-48; (1974), 28.

11. See Theron F. Schlabach, *Peace, Faith, Nation: Mennonites and Amish in Nineteenth-Century America*, Mennonite Experience in America vol. 2 (Scottdale, Pa.: Herald Press, 1988), 110-116, 236-240, and ch. 11.

12. Harold S. Bender, "Evangelism," *ME*, II, 273.

13. Paul Lederach, "Revival in Franconia," *GH* 44 (Sep. 18, 1951), 902-903.

14. Barbara Bowie Wiesel, "From Separatism to Evangelism: A Case Study of Social and Cultural Change among the Franconia Conference Mennonites, 1945-1970" (Ph.D. diss., University of Pennsylvania, 1973), 95, 97.

15. Dale F. Dickey, "The Tent Evangelism Movement of the Mennonite Church" (Ph.D. diss., Bowling Green State University, 1980), 41.

16. C. F. Yake, "The Brunk Meetings: An Evaluation of the Movement," *GH* 45 (June 10, 1952), 566.

17. See, e.g., in *GH* 44: J. D. Graber, "Men Work" (Sep. 11, 1951), 890; A. C. Brunk, "Evangelization the Chief Work of the Church" (Oct. 23, 1951), 1017-1018; Lester W. Yoder, "Lay Evangelism" (Oct. 30, 1951), 1044-1045; Robert Detweiler, "Personal Evangelism—A Christian Laymen's Duty" (Dec. 11, 1951), 1189-1190.

18. Edward Gerber, "Christian Laymen's Tent Evangelism," *GH* 45 (June 10, 1952), 567; Nelson E. Kauffman, "Report of the First Annual Meeting of Christian Laymen's Evangelism, Inc.," *GH* 46 (Feb. 3, 1953), 102-103.

19. John A. Toews, *A History of the Mennonite Brethren Church: Pilgrims and Pioneers*, ed. A. J. Klassen (Fresno, Calif.: Board of Christian Literature of the General Conference of Mennonite Brethren Churches, 1975), 316-318.

20. Paul Erb, "The Evangelism Conference," *GH* 46 (May 12, 1953), 435.

21. Dale F. Dickey, "Tent Evangelism Movement" (n. 15), 86.

22. Paul Erb, "Evangelism for Full Discipleship," *GH* 46 (June 9, 1953), 555; see also Beulah Stauffer Hostetler, *American Mennonites and Protestant Movements: A Community Paradigm* (Scottdale, Pa.: Herald Press, 1987), 284.

23. From *CL* 16: Rueben Baerg, "Will Revival Come to Our Church in This Day?" (Mar. 15, 1952), 7-8; George W. Peters, "Revival Echoes" (May 15, 1952), 3-5; J. W. Vogt, "A Revival Is Just a Beginning" (Aug. 15, 1952), 3.

24. Baerg, "Will Revival Come . . . ?" 7.

25. Katie Florence Shank, *Revival Fires* (Broadway, Va.: privately published, 1952). See also: Frank H. Epp, ed., *Revival Fires in Manitoba* (Denbigh, Va.: Brunk Revivals, Inc., 1957); A. J. Klassen, ed., *Revival Fires in British Columbia* (Denbigh, Va: Brunk Revivals, Inc., 1958).

26. William G. McLoughlin, *Revivals, Awakenings, and Reforms: An Essay on Religion and Social Change in America, 1607-1977* (Chicago: University of Chicago Press, 1978), 2.

27. Beyond McLoughlin's, other works with perceptive interpretations of the social role of revivalism in American culture include: Richard Bushman, *From Puritan to Yankee: Character and the Social Order in Connecticut, 1690-1765* (Cambridge: Harvard University Press, 1967); Perry Miller, *Errand into the Wilderness* (Cambridge: Harvard University Press, 1964); Perry Miller, *Nature's Nation* (Cambridge: Harvard University Press, 1967).

28. See George Marsden, "From Fundamentalism to Evangelicalism: A Historical Analysis," in David F. Wells and John D. Woodbridge, eds., *The Evangelicals: What They Believe, Who They Are, Where They Are Changing* (Nashville: Abingdon Press, 1974), 128ff.

29. Regarding the GCs, see *General Conference Mennonite Church Report 1965, 37th session, July 10-17, Estes Park, Colorado*, 5.

30. On Hershberger's NAE linkages, see Theron F. Schlabach, "To Focus a Vision," in John Richard Burkholder and Calvin Redekop, eds., *Kingdom Cross and Community: Essays on Mennonite Themes in Honor of Guy F. Hershberger* (Scott-

dale, Pa.: Herald Press, 1976), 45.

31. Kevin Enns-Rempel, "The Fellowship of Evangelical Bible Churches and the Quest for Religious Identity," *MQR* 63 (July 1989), 256.

32. [MB] Gen. Conf. *Year Book* (1945), 74; see also Toews, *A History of the Mennonite Brethren Church* (n. 19), 387.

33. Minutes of [MB] Board of Reference and Counsel, Aug. 2-6, 1950, Board of Reference and Counsel files, CMBS-F.

34. Minutes of Board of Reference and Counsel, Sep. 14-15, 1966, Board of Reference and Counsel files, CMBS-F. On Brethren in Christ influencing NAE, see David Zercher, "Opting for the Mainstream: The Brethren Join the National Association of Evangelicals," *Brethren in Christ History and Life* 10 (Apr. 1987), 48-70.

35. Myron Augsburger, "The 20th Annual Convention, The National Association of Evangelicals," *GH* 60 (May 15, 1962), 445.

36. Paul S. Rees, "Evangelical Hawks and Doves," *Christianity Today* 12 (Dec. 22, 1967), 39. See also "Seminar a Unique Experience," *GH* 60 (Dec. 19, 1967), 1136.

37. Stan Nussbaum, *You Must Be Born Again: A History of the Evangelical Mennonite Church* (Fort Wayne, Ind.: Evangelical Mennonite Church, 1991), 38, 45-46.

38. Ibid., 57.

39. Ibid., 53-57.

40. Everek Richard Storms, *History of the United Missionary Church* (Elkhart, Ind.: Bethel Publishing Company, 1958), 69; discussion of the name change is on pp. 68-75.

41. Frank Wald, "The History and Evolution of the Missionary Church: Faith versus Culture" (student paper, Conrad Grebel College [Waterloo, Ont.], 1982), 20-22, hints at such an interpretation.

42. Clarence Hiebert, *The Holdeman People: The Church of God in Christ, Mennonite, 1859-1969* (Pasadena, Calif.: William Carey Library, 1973), 299-310.

43. Ibid., 311-315.

44. Richard Burkholder, "What's Wrong with Nonconformity?" *GH* 43 (Sep. 5, 1950), 879.

45. Daniel Hertzler, "What Basis Nonconformity?" *GH* 43 (Oct. 10, 1950), 996.

46. Ibid., 997.

47. Burkholder, "What's Wrong with Nonconformity?" 879.

48. John Christian Wenger, *Separated unto God: A Plea for Christian Simplicity of Life and for a Scriptural Nonconformity to the World* (Scottdale, Pa.: Mennonite Publishing House, 1951); "Declaration of Commitment in Respect to Christian Separation and Nonconformity to the World," *Twenty-Ninth Mennonite General Conference Proceedings, August 23-26, 1955*, 26-32 (these reports hereafter cited as [MC] Menn. Gen. Conf. *Reports*, with dates and pages).

49. John R. Mumaw, "A New Vitality," *GH* 55 (May 15, 1962), 442.

50. Hostetler, *American Mennonites and Protestant Movements* (n. 22), 289, notes that by 1960 in the Franconia Conference (historically one of the more conservative district conferences) "persons in leadership positions were sometimes bypassing dress codes."

51. Conrad G. Brunk, "Rediscovering Biblical Nonconformity," *GH* 66 (Sep. 25, 1973), 729.

52. See Carlton O. Wittlinger, *Quest for Piety and Obedience: The Story of the Brethren in Christ* (Nappanee, Ind.: Evangel Press, 1978), 475-492; E. Morris Sider, *Messenger of Grace: A Biography of C. N. Hostetter, Jr.* (Nappanee, Ind.: Evangel Press, 1982), 145-150.

53. See Oscar Burkholder, "Introduction," and Paul Erb, "Summary," in *Prophecy Conference: Report of Conference Held at Elkhart, Indiana, April 3-5, 1952* (Scottdale, Pa.: Mennonite Publishing House, 1953).

54. Erb to Barney Ovensen, Nov. 9, 1953, cited in Kevin Enns-Rempel, "Paul Erb: Mennonite Diplomat" (M.A. thesis, University of California—Riverside, 1984), 116-117.

55. Paul Erb, *The Alpha and the Omega: A Restatement of the Christian Hope in Christ's Coming* (Scottdale, Pa.: Herald Press, 1955), vii.

56. Quoted in ibid., 40-41.

57. See "Church Planting," in *ME*, V, 157-159.

58. David A. Haury, *Prairie People: A History of the Western District Conference* (Newton, Kan.: Faith & Life Press, 1981), ch. 12.

59. Samuel Floyd Pannabecker, *Open Doors: The History of the General Conference Mennonite Church* (Newton, Kan.: Faith & Life Press, 1975), 230.

60. Orlando Harms, *A Conference in Pilgrimage: The Story of the Southern District Mennonite Brethren Conference and Its Churches* (Hillsboro, Kan.: The Center for Mennonite Brethren Studies, 1992), 100.

61. Ibid., ch. 7; the chapter's title is "Establishing New Churches Takes Priority (1956-1972)."

62. This paragraph and the next one are drawn from ch. 3 of an unpublished history of the Eastern Mennonite Board of Missions and Charities, written by A. Grace Wenger and furnished to me by courtesy of the Lancaster Mennonite Historical Society, Lancaster, Pa.

63. Ibid.; the last several sentences rest on Wenger's p. 109.

64. Lois Barrett, *The Vision and the Reality: The Story of Home Missions in the General Conference Mennonite Church* (Newton, Kan.: Faith & Life Press, 1983), 235.

65. Cornelius Krahn, "Prolegomena to an Anabaptist Theology," *MQR* 24 (July 1950), 7.

66. Robert Friedmann, "Anabaptism and Protestantism," *MQR* 24 (Jan. 1950), 21-24.

67. Harold S. Bender, "The Anabaptist Theology of Discipleship," *MQR* 24 (Jan. 1950), 30-32.

68. Erland Waltner, "The Anabaptist Conception of the Church," *MQR* 25 (Jan. 1951), 16.

69. See "A Tentative Plan for a General Council of the Mennonite General Conference" and letters to Paul Mininger, Sec. of the [MC] Mennonite Church Gen. Conf., in f. 2, b. 3, [MC] Mennonite Gen. Conf. Archives, AMC.

70. Ivan J. Miller, *History of the Conservative Mennonite Conference, 1910-1985* (Grantsville, Md.: Ivan J. and Della Miller, 1985), 66-67.

71. See Leland Harder, "The Quest for Equilibrium in an Established Sect: A Study of Social Change in the General Conference Mennonite Church" (Ph.D. dissertation, Northwestern University, 1962).

72. John L. Horst, "Mennonite District Conference Trends in Change of Pattern," in *Church Organization and Administration: Proceedings of the Study Conference on Church Organization and Administration* (Scottdale, Pa.: Mennonite Publishing House, lithograph, 1955; copy in MHL), 39-40.

73. Howard Charles, "The New Testament Pattern of Church Organization," in *Church Organization and Administration*, 9.

74. Paul Peachey, "The Growth of the Mennonite Pattern of Church Organization," in *Church Organization and Administration*, 19.

75. Ibid., 23.

76. Ibid., 25.

77. Ibid., 32.

78. [MB] Gen. Conf. *Year Book* (1951), 125-133.

79. Ibid. It was a strategy that Beulah Hostetler, borrowing from Bernard Siegal to analyze the creation of stronger authority systems in the MC Franconia Confer-

ence, has termed "defensive structuring." See Bernard Siegal, "Defensive Structuring and Environmental Stress," *The American Journal of Sociology* 76 (July 1970), 11-12; Beulah Hostetler, "Defensive Structuring and Codification of Practice: Franconia Mennonite Conference," *MQR* 60 (July 1986), 429-444; Hostetler, *American Mennonites and Protestant Movements* (n. 22), 246-247.

80. Elmer Ediger, "Statement of Our Task in This Study Conference," in *Proceedings of the Study Conference on the Believers' Church* (Newton, Kan.: General Conference Mennonite Church, 1955), 45-47.

81. Cornelius J. Dyck, "Discipline in the General Conference," in proceedings just cited, 125-134.

82. E. G. Kaufman, "The General Conference Mennonites and the Biblical Church," in proceedings just cited, 106.

83. See John Howard Yoder, "Anabaptist Vision and Mennonite Reality," in A. J. Klassen, ed., *Consultation on Anabaptist-Mennonite Theology* (Fresno, Calif.: Council of Mennonite Seminaries, 1970).

84. Paul Peachey, "Toward an Understanding of the Decline of the West," *Concern* 1 (June 1954), 8-44.

85. John Howard Yoder, "The Anabaptist Dissent: The Logic of the Place of the Disciple in Society," *Concern* 1 (June 1954), 58.

86. Ibid., 46.

87. Ibid., 58.

88. Orley Swartzentruber, "An Estimate of Current American Mennonitism," in f. 2, b. 16, Guy F. Hershberger papers, AMC; Swartzentruber's point was somewhat like that of Robert Kreider in "The Anabaptist Conception of the Church in the Russian Environment, 1789-1870," *MQR* 25 (Jan. 1951), 17-34; while not using the "*corpus Mennonitarium*" language, at the second of the Goshen-Mennonite Biblical seminary consultations on Anabaptist theology, Kreider made similar observations about the Russian story.

89. John Howard Yoder to John C. Wenger, July 10, 1954; Yoder to H. S. Bender, July 2, 1954; b. 11, John H. Yoder papers, AMC. For further interpretation of the generational issues at stake in the conflict, as well as a fuller interpretation of the Concern movement, see Paul Toews, "The Concern Movement: Its Origins and Early History," *The Conrad Grebel Review* 8 (Spring 1990), 109-126. See also reflections by six of the original seven members of the Concern movement in the same issue of the *Review*.

90. Yoder to Bender, July 2, 1954, b. 11, John H. Yoder papers, AMC.

91. See Cal Redekop, Paul Peachey, and Irvin Horst letters to MCC, Aug. 6, 1952, all in f. 3, b. 1, Calvin Redekop papers, AMC.

92. Yoder to "Amsterdam Club," Feb. 2, 1954, b. 11, John H. Yoder papers, AMC.

93. Yoder to Gerald Studer, Feb. 2, 1954, b. 11, John H. Yoder papers, AMC.

94. Peachey to Calvin Redekop, Irvin Horst, and John Howard Yoder, Jan. 18, 1952, made available by Redekop who now lives at Harrisonburg, Va.

95. Paul Peachey, "Social Background and Social Philosophy of the Swiss Anabaptists, 1525-1540," *MQR* 28 (Apr. 1954), 102-127.

96. Gordon D. Kaufman, "Nonresistance and Responsibility," *Concern* 6 (Nov. 1958), 6.

97. Ibid., 28. This Kaufman paper not only appeared in *Concern* but also received wide attention in a predominantly GC "Theological Study Group." Formed in 1956 and 1957, that group gathered a membership of some thirty leading GC academic and church leaders. While not modeled after the Concern group, it functioned analogously. The leaders were generally young. Being GC they were not reacting to the MC-style bishop authority or to the towering presences of a Harold S. Bender and an Orie O. Miller. However, like Concern people, they wanted to connect the newly reconceptualized Anabaptist tradition with modern theological discussions. Kaufman's piece, the first to circulate, suggested how central the church-world issue was to their

quest. Various "Theological Study Group" papers circulated among the group; see materials dated Oct. 1956, Jan. 1957, Aug. 5, 1957, and Oct. 3, 1957 in the Esko Loewen papers, MLA, and in b. 7, John H. Yoder papers, AMC.

98. J. Lawrence Burkholder, *The Problem of Social Responsibility from the Perspective of the Mennonite Church* (Elkhart, Ind.: Institute of Mennonite Studies, 1989), 152-153. Burkholder wrote the work as a Princeton Th.D. diss. already in 1958; the publication delay is a commentary on the interest which Mennonite thinkers eventually took in this position in the years following its appearance.

99. Ibid., 223.

CHAPTER 10

1. Quoted in Patricia Shelly, "Winona Lake Memories," *Peace Office Newsletter* 21 (Nov.-Dec. 1991), 1. This newsletter is in various Mennonite libraries, e.g., MHL and MLA.

2. "A Declaration of Christian Faith and Commitment," in *Report of the MCC Peace Section Study Conference Held at Winona Lake, Indiana, on November 9 to 12, 1950* (MCC mimeographed book, 1950), 20-21; item is more accessible in MCC's *Peace Office Newsletter* 21 (Nov.-Dec. 1991), 3-4.

3. Orie Miller, "Our Witness to Government," *GH* 41 (Mar. 30, 1948), 294-295.

4. Paul Goering, "How to Secure Information from Washington, *TM* 63 (Apr. 28, 1948), 8.

5. From *TM* 63 (1948): Gordon Kaufman, "Should Mennonites Register for the Draft?" (June 8), 4-5; Paul Goering, "Should We Make Registration the Issue" (June 22), 3; Albert Gaeddert, "Should I Register Under the Draft Act" (July 27), 3; Roland Brown, "The Implications of Registering for War" (Oct. 12), 13-14; Austin Regier, "Christianity and Conscription" (Nov. 30), 14. From *TM* 64 (1949): Austin Regier, "The Faith of a Convict" (Feb. 15), 8-10; Robert Hartzler, "The Christian and the Draft Law" (Sep. 6), 15.

6. "Is It Time to Read Prophecy? An Editorial," *TM* 63 (Apr. 20, 1948), 1.

7. See *Year Book of the 44th General Conference of the Mennonite Brethren Church of North America* (Mountain Lake, Minnesota, Aug. 28 to Sep. 2, 1948), 104 (hereafter cited as [MB] Gen. Conf. *Year Book*, with year). On B. B. Janz's search for a form of medical noncombatancy in both Canada and the United States, see John B. Toews, *With Courage to Spare the Life of B. B. Janz (1877-1964)* (Winnipeg, Man.: The Board of Christian Literature of the General Conference of the Mennonite Brethren Churches, 1978), ch. 10.

8. [MB] Gen. Conf. *Year Book* (1954), 120.

9. Ibid.

10. Zelle Andrews Larson, "An Unbroken Witness: Conscientious Objection to War, 1948-1953" (Ph.D. diss., University of Hawaii, 1975), 59. Lawrence S. Wittner, *Rebels Against War: The American Peace Movement, 1941-1960* (New York: Columbia University Press, 1969), 186, describes the doubleness of the new legislation: "The 1948 draft act represented, in pacifist eyes, an advance over the 1940 legislation because it granted C.O.'s complete exemption, and a regression for requiring a stricter religious test for C.O. status."

11. Minutes of Peace Section Meeting, Chicago, Apr. 23, 1948, and Exhibit IV, "Statement Expressing Attitude Toward Deferment of CO's," cited in Perry Bush, "Drawing the Line: American Mennonites, the State, and Social Change, 1935-1973" (Ph.D. diss., Carnegie-Mellon University, 1990), 183.

12. "Guiding Principles on Alternatives to Military Service," MCC memorandum from J. Harold Sherk to Peace Section members, Apr. 16, 1951, cited in Dirk W. Eitzen and Timothy R. Falb, "An Overview of the Mennonite I-W Program," *MQR* 56 (Oct. 1982), 367.

13. Eitzen and Falb, "Overview," 367-368, 365.

14. For an introduction to the Pax program, see Urie Bender, *Soldiers of Compassion* (Scottdale, Pa.: Herald Press, 1969).

15. Editorial, "The Present Opportunity," *GH* 45 (Mar. 25, 1952), 291.

16. J. S. Schultz, *Report of the 1-W Program Evaluation Study of Mennonite and Brethren in Christ 1-W Men* (n.p., 1955), 12.

17. "I-W Service—Kingdom of God Work?" *The I-W Mirror* 1 (June 3, 1953), 2-4. *The I-W Mirror* is available in various Mennonite libraries, e.g., MHL and MLA.

18. Both GC and MC figures are cited in Perry Bush, "Drawing the Line" (n. 11), 188-189.

19. "Location and Church Affiliation of 1-W Men," f. 14, b. 8, Mennonite Research Foundation Archives, AMC.

20. Data is from an address by Victor Olsen, Administrator of 1-W services, National Office of Selective Service, attached to a memo from J. Harold Sherk to Peace Section members, Oct. 3, 1956, I-W Misc. File #5, MCC Archives IX-12, AMC.

21. *The I-W Mirror* 1 (Oct. 21, 1953), 1.

22. "Location and Church Affiliation of I-W Men," f. 14, b. 8, Mennonite Research Foundation Archives, AMC.

23. See, e.g., "Discussions Centering on the Work of the Board of Christian Service" [1956], f. 128, b. 15, Albert Gaeddert papers, MLA.

24. Gaeddert to Wilfred Unruh, Apr. 25, 1959, f. 563, b. 22, [GC] Board of Christian Service collection, MLA.

25. "What Mennonite and Brethren in Christ I-W's Do. . . ," *The I-W Mirror* 2 (July 28, 1954), 2.

26. Data is from an address by Victor Olsen, Administrator of 1-W Services, National Office of Selective Service, attached to a memo from J. Harold Sherk to Peace Section Members, Oct. 3, 1956, I-W Misc. File #5, MCC Archives IX-12, AMC.

27. Minutes of "MCC I-W Representatives, Unit Leaders and Area Pastors," Chicago, Sep. 30, 1953, I-W Misc. File #2, MCC Archives IX-12, AMC. See also from MCC Archives IX-12: "Report on Visit of John Lapp and Paul Gross to Denver and Their Meeting with the Advisory Board of the 1-W Service at Denver, Colorado, October 15, 1960," I-W Coordinating Board Minutes, 1958-1960, Peace Section; Eldon King, "A Review of Current 1-W Operations and Procedures," attachment 1 of "1-W Evaluation Conference, Elkhart, Indiana, October 6-7, 1959 Proceedings Report," Data File #1, b. 20. See also Minutes of the Committee on Peace and I-W of the Board of Christian Service, June 11-12, 1957, f. 129, b. 15, Albert Gaeddert papers, MLA. For Amish sources, see N. J. B. Miller, "Our C-O Boys in Hospital Service," *The Budget* 64 (Mar. 4, 1954), 2; Harvey Bender, "I-W Service," *Witnessing* 4 (Jan. 1956), 4.

28. "A Statistical Analysis of the Denver Unit," *The Denver Post-Mortem* 4 (Apr. 15, 1956).

29. Edgar Stoesz to Dwight Wiebe, Oct. 27, 1959, f. 36, b. 3, Denver Unit corresp., Peace Section, MCC Archives IX-7-12, AMC.

30. *The I-W Mirror* 1 (Aug. 26, 1953), 2. "Current Denver 1-W Program, May 1964"; "1-W Men in Denver, June 1, 1966"; "Denver 1-W Report" (July 26, 1966); all in 1962-70 file, I-W Coordinating Board, Peace Section, MCC Archives IX-7-12, AMC. *The I-W Mirror* 3 (June 15, 1956), 4. John Lapp and Esko Loewen, "Visit to the Denver 1-W Unit, June 15-17, 1959" (p. 1), I-W Program Review Committee files; "Denver 1-W Directory," I-W Misc. File; both in MCC Archives IX-12, AMC.

31. Dwight Wiebe and Arlo Kasper, "I-W Visitation Report," Aug. 13, 1958-Sep. 7, 1958 (p. 14), 1958-1960 file, I-W Coordinating Board Minutes, Peace Section, MCC Archives IX-7-12, AMC.

32. Edgar Stoesz to William Snyder, Oct. 30, 1959, f. 65, Data File #3, MCC Archives IX-7-12, AMC.

33. Albert Gaeddert, H. B. Schmidt, and Fred Unruh, "Reporting Visit to Denver on January 8, 9 and 10, 1959" (p. 4), I-W Program Review Committee files, Data Files, MCC Archives IX-12, AMC.

34. Ibid.

35. Lapp and Loewen, "Visit to the Denver I-W Unit, June 15-17, 1959," 2.

36. "Report on visit of John Lapp and Paul Gross to Denver . . . October 15, 1960" (n. 27), 2.

37. E. M. Yost, "Current Denver I-W Program" (May 1964; p. 4), 1962-1970 file, I-W Coordinating Board, Peace Section, MCC Archives IX-7-12, AMC.

38. From *The Denver Post-Mortem*: Delbert Schrag, "Do Your Own Thinking," 3 (Dec. 3, 1955); "Genuine or Counterfeit," 1 (June 11, 1953).

39. Ralph Lehman, "Essay on the State of the I-W Unit," *The Denver Post-Mortem* 2 (Feb. 27, 1954).

40. Chester Flickinger, "Thinking with Chet," *The Denver Post-Mortem* 2 (Apr. 15, 1954).

41. Paul Moyer to Ray Horst and Wilfred Unruh, Apr. 19, 1962, f. 1418, b. 72, [GC] Christian Service Board collection, MLA.

42. The story of gaining this cooperation from Colorado Selective Service is told in Eitzen and Falb, "Overview" (n. 12), 374-375; quot. from Perry Bush, "Drawing the Line" (n. 11), 207.

43. John Lapp and Esko Loewen, "Visit to the Denver I-W Unit, June 15-17, 1959" (p. 2), I-W Program Review Committee files, Data Files, MCC Archives IX-12, AMC.

44. Pekrul's assessments are included in E. M. Yost, "Current Denver I-W Program" (May 1964; p. 2), 1962-1970 file, I-W Coordinating Board, Peace Section, MCC Archives IX-7-12, AMC.

45. See, e.g.: Elbert Koontz, "A Report to the Western District Committee of a visit to the Denver 1-W Unit to Discuss the spiritual ministry to the G.C. boys" (Oct. 4, 1955), and Cornelius J. Dyck, "Report on my visit to the Denver 1-W Unit, May 21, 1955," both in f. 22, b. 1, [GC] Board of Christian Service Archives, MLA; Dwight Wiebe reports to the 1-W Coordinating Committee, Mar. 13, 17, 1959, on visits to employing institutions in Kansas, Colorado, Ohio, and Indiana, in f. 15, b. 3, MCC Archives IX-7-12-1, #1, AMC.

46. Late 1953 or early 1954 untitled document reflecting on a Dec. 10, 1953, summary of the location of men in I-W service under MCC supervision; see also Minutes I-W Services Study Committee Meeting, Feb. 26, 1954, and Exhibit I of Atlee Beechy, "Some Difference in the Organizational Pattern Program and Conditions as Between I-W and CPS"; both in b. 20, I-W Misc. Files, Data Files, MCC Archives IX-12-1, AMC.

47. "Findings of the I-W Evaluation and Planning Conference, Elkhart, Ind., April 9-10, 1957," I-W Program Evaluation Files, MCC Archives IX-12, AMC.

48. John W. Miller, "Can CO's Survive Tolerance?" *The I-W Mirror* 2 (Mar. 10, 1954), 1-2.

49. Quoted in "Nuggets Cleaned at Goshen," *Witnessing* 3 (Oct. 1955), 10. See also, from *GH*: John Miller, "Are COs Dangerous?" 47 (Feb. 16, 1954), 153; "Findings of the 1-W Evaluation-Planning Conference" 50 (May 21, 1957), 489; Edgar Metzler, "Another Alternative for Draft-Age Youth" 52 (Nov. 17, 1959), 997; Paul Landis, "From a I-W Council Member" 54 (Aug. 8, 1961), 153.

50. William Keeney, "Report of Visit to Michigan I-W Men, March 27, 28, 1954," I-W Misc. Files #4, MCC Archives IX-12, AMC.

51. See several documents: Minutes of MCC I-W Representatives Meeting; Exhibit 1 of "Mennonite Relief and Service Committee," Dec. 9, 1954; Albert Gaeddert, "I-W Program Administration Through Local Congregations and/or Conference Organization or Institutions"; Elmer Ediger "Report on Chicago 1-W meeting and miscellaneous matters, Dec. 9, 10, 1954"; all in b. 20, I-W Misc. File, MCC Archives IX-12-1, AMC. See also "Minutes of the Co-Ordination Committee for 1-W Services" Dec. 31, 1954, f. 20, b. 3, Peace Section, MCC Archives IX-7-12, #1, AMC.

52. Paul Peachey, "Report to Peace Problems Committee," Sep. 8, 1956; "Find-

ings of the I-W Evaluation and Planning Conference, Elkhart, Ind., April 9-10, 1957";
both in b. 20, I-W Program Evaluation Files, Data Files, MCC Archives IX-12-1, AMC.

53. Gordon Dyck, "Discussion Presentation for VS and 1-W at Estes Park General Conference," with July 21, 1965, mailing by Wilfred Unruh to GC Board of Christian Service members, f. 345, b. 13, [GC] Board of Christian Service Archives, MLA.

54. Wilfred J. Unruh, "Perspectives on the 1-W Earning Work Program Presented to the 1-W Coordinating Board, June 15, 1967," f. 1419, b. 72, Board of Christian Service Archives, MLA.

55. "I-W Coordinating Board Expires," 1962-1970 file, I-W Coordinating Board, Peace Section, MCC Archives IX-7-12, AMC.

56. Eitzen and Falb, "Overview" (n. 12), 380.

57. Edgar Metzler, "Report of Stabbing Incident at Spring Grove State Hospital," Feb. 8, 1955, I-W Misc. File #4, Peace Section, MCC Archives IX-12, AMC; "Report of a Conference of John E. Lapp and Paul Gross with the Church of God in Christ Mennonites, October 17, 1960, Moundridge, Kansas," f. 13, b. 3, I-W Coordinating Committee files, Peace Section, MCC Archives, IX-7-12, AMC. See also *History and Report of the 1-W Program of the Church of God in Christ* (Galva, Kan.: The Christian Public Service, Inc. [1960]).

58. For example see Paul Gross, "Report on 1-W Visitation Trip, November 12-25, 1960," b. 3, I-W Coordination Committee files, Peace Section, MCC Archives IX-7-12, AMC.

59. *Minutes of the Old Order Amish Steering Committee: October 20, 1966 to October 25, 1972*, vol. 1 (Gordonville, Pa.: Gordonville Print Shop, n.d.), 5.

60. See, e.g., from *The Budget*: Jonas E. Beachy, "Plain City, Ohio," 64 (Dec. 31, 1953), 5; Raymond Wagler, "Partridge, Kansas," 64 (Jan. 7, 1954), 1; Joe Bontrager, "Subjection to Magistrates," 64 (Jan. 21, 1954), 6; and "To Whom It May Concern" 64 (Feb. 25, 1954), 6. The last item includes letters by Joe Bontrager, Thomas, Okla.; William T. Snyder, MCC Akron office; and an unidentified person from Shipshewana, Ind.

61. Ervin Hershberger, "Who Is Responsible for the Draft?" *Witnessing* 3 (Dec. 1955), 1-2.

62. *Minutes of the Old Order Amish Steering Committee*, 13.

63. Figures are in Abbie Gertrude Enders Huntington, "Dove at the Window: A Study of an Old Order Amish Community in Ohio," (Ph.D. diss., Yale University, 1957), 567.

64. *Minutes of the Old Order Amish Steering Committee*, 1.

65. *Ambassador of Peace* was published monthly, Jan. 1966-Dec. 1970, after which the title was *Young Companion*.

66. *Minutes of the Old Order Amish Steering Committee*, 10; Albert N. Keim, "Military Service and Conscription," in Donald B. Kraybill, ed., *The Amish and the State* (Baltimore: The Johns Hopkins University Press, 1993), 62.

67. Andrew Kinsinger, "The Steering Committee," in Susan Kinsinger, comp., *Family and History of Lydia Beachy's Descendants, 1889-1989* (Gordonville, Pa.: Gordonville Print Shop, 1988), 131.

68. *Minutes of the Old Order Amish Steering Committee*, 18-20.

69. Andrew Kinsinger in "The Steering Committee," 131-132; Marc Olshan, "The National Steering Committee," in Kraybill, ed., *The Amish and the State*, 67-84.

70. Quot. from Edgar Stoesz to William T. Snyder, Oct. 3, 1959, cited in Eitzen and Falb, "Mennonite I-W Program," 375.

71. Paul H. Holdeman, "Report from Colorado, Kansas, Nebraska and South Dakota Area, March 1, 1955," I-W Misc. file #4, b. 20, Data Files, MCC Archives IX-12-1, AMC.

72. Joseph Stoll, "Have We Neglected Our I-W Men?" *Ambassador of Peace* 1 (Apr. 1966), 14-15.

73. Minutes of the Committee on Peace and I-W of the Board of Christian Ser-

vice, May 2-3, 1958, I-W Misc. file #5, b. 20, Data Files, MCC Archives IX-12-1, AMC.

74. Quoted in Larson, "An Unbroken Witness" (n. 10), 27.

75. Larson, "An Unbroken Witness" (n. 10), 1-27, quot. p. 24.

76. Boyd Nelson to William Snyder, Oct. 22, 1959, Data File #3, MCC Archives IX-7-12, AMC.

77. Unidentified mother quoted in *Sponsors' Bulletin* (Nov. 3, 1964). The *Bulletin* was sent out, usually monthly, from the MCs' I-W Services Office to its CPS-unit sponsors.

78. See Eitzen and Falb, "Mennonite I-W Program" (n. 12), 381; J. S. Schultz, *Report of the 1-W Program Evaluation Study* (n. 16).

79. For the history of these contacts see Marlin Adrian, "Mennonites, Missionaries and Native Americans: Religious Paradigms and Cultural Encounters" (Ph.D. diss., University of Virginia, 1989); James C. Juhnke, "General Conference Missions to the American Indians in the Late Nineteenth Century," *MQR* 54 (Apr. 1980), 117-134.

80. Rafael Falcón, *The Hispanic Mennonite Church in North America, 1932-1982* (Scottdale, Pa.: Herald Press, 1986), 182, 195.

81. Grant M. Stoltzfus, "The History of Mennonites in the South with Particular Attention to Race Relations," *Papers Presented at the Conference on Race Relations, Atlanta Georgia, February 25-26, 1964* (Akron, Pa.: MCC Peace Section mimeograph; available in various Mennonite libraries), 5-8.

82. LeRoy Bechler, *The Black Mennonite Church in North America, 1886-1986* (Scottdale, Pa.: Herald Press, 1986), ch. 3.

83. The MC figures are from Bechler, *The Black Mennonite Church*, 172; the KMB figures are from *ME*, III, 915.

84. Martin Luther King, *Stride Toward Freedom: The Montgomery Story* (New York: Harper & Row, 1958), 84-85. This passage is quoted in Leo Driedger and Donald B. Kraybill, *Mennonite Peacemaking: From Quietism to Activism* (Scottdale, Pa.: Herald Press, 1994), 110.

85. Guy F. Hershberger, "Mennonites and the Current Race Issue: Observations, Reflections and Recommendations Following a Visitation to Southern Mennonite Churches, July-August 1963, with a Review of Historical Background" (mimeographed; copy in MHL).

86. Paul Peachey, "Nonviolence in the South," *GH* 50 (Feb. 19, 1957), 177.

87. Guy F. Hershberger, "Nonresistance, the Mennonite Church and the Race Question," *GH* 53 (June 28, 1960), 578.

88. *Mennonite General Conference Proceedings: Twenty-Ninth Mennonite General Conference* (Aug. 23-26, 1955, Hesston, Kan.), 22.

89. Ervin Ray Stutzman, "From Nonresistance to Peace and Justice: Mennonite Peace Rhetoric, 1951-1991" (Ph.D. diss., Temple University, 1993), 94.

90. For this entire section on Gulfport I am drawing from David A. Haury, *The Quiet Demonstration: The Mennonite Mission in Gulfport, Mississippi* (Newton, Kan.: Faith & Life Press, 1979); quot. p. 33.

91. Ibid., 35.

92. Ibid., 62.

93. Ibid., 78-79.

94. See Frieda Claassen, ed., *The Woodlawn Story* (Chicago, Ill.: Mennonite Biblical Seminary Alumni Association, 1958); some further names are from C. J. Dyck, tel. convers. with Theron Schlabach, Jan. 23, 1995.

95. Minutes of the Committee on Peace and I-W of the Board of Christian Service, June 11-12, 1957, f. 129, b. 15, Albert Gaeddert papers, MLA.

96. Minutes of the Committee on Peace and I-W of the Board of Christian Service, May 2-3, 1958, I-W Misc. File #5, b. 20, Data Files, MCC Archives IX-12-1, AMC.

97. Claassen, ed., *The Woodlawn Story*; for a statement by Harding expressing deep appreciation for his work with Mennonites of that Woodlawn community,

plus more prophetic challenge, consult an address, "Mennonites and the Anabaptist Vision: Reflections and Observations," Oct. 14, 1994, at a conference, "Anabaptist Vision(s) in the 20th Century: Ideas and Outcomes," at Goshen College, tapes in AMC; quot. cited in Bush, "Drawing the Line" (n. 11), 231. See also Driedger and Kraybill, *Mennonite Peacemaking* (n. 84), 111.

98. Vincent Harding, "The Task of the Mennonite Church in Establishing Racial Unity," in "Report of a Seminar on Christ, The Mennonite Churches and Race, April 17-19, Woodlawn Mennonite Church, Chicago, Illinois" (MCC Peace Section mimeograph [these mimeographs are in various Mennonite libraries or archives]), 32-34.

99. Ibid., 29.

100. Ibid., 31.

101. Paul Peachey, "What Can Be Done to Improve Race Relations in the Mennonite Church?" *Christian Race Relations: Proceedings of the Conference on Christian Community Relations* (Apr. 22-24, 1955; Goshen, Ind.: Committee on Economic and Social Relations of the Mennonite Church, 1955), 68; copies are in various Mennonite libraries, e.g., MHL and MLA.

102. Vincent Harding, "The Peace Witness and Modern Revolutionary Movements," in Cornelius J. Dyck, ed., *The Witness of the Holy Spirit: Proceedings of the Eighth Mennonite World Conference, Amsterdam, The Netherlands, July 22-30, 1967* (Elkhart Ind.: Mennonite World Conference, 1967), 337-344.

103. Ervin Ray Stutzman, in "From Nonresistance to Peace and Justice: Mennonite Peace Rhetoric, 1951-1991" (Ph.D. diss., Temple University, 1993) presents Burkholder's experience as paradigmatic for Mennonites; see esp. pp. 81-82. For further context see esp.: Driedger and Kraybill, *Mennonite Peacemaking* (n. 84); John Richard Burkholder, *Continuity and Change: A Search for a Mennonite Social Ethic* (Akron, Pa.: MCC Peace Section, 1977); Bush, "Drawing the Line" (n. 18); Beulah Stauffer Hostetler, "Nonresistance and Social Responsibility: Mennonites and Mainline Peace Emphasis, ca. 1950 to 1985," *MQR* 64 (Jan. 1990), 49-73.

104. For key writings of J. Lawrence Burkholder, see *The Problem of Social Responsibility from the Perspective of the Mennonite Church* [unaltered publication of 1958 doctoral diss.] (Elkhart, Ind.: Institute of Mennonite Studies, 1989), and "The Limits of Perfection: Autobiographical Reflections," in Rodney J. Sawatsky and Scott Holland, eds., *The Limits of Perfection: Conversations with J. Lawrence Burkholder* (Waterloo, Ont.: Institute of Anabaptist-Mennonite Studies, Conrad Grebel College, 1993), 1-54.

105. Burkholder, *Problem of Social Responsibility*, iv.

106. Burkholder, *Problem of Social Responsibility*; Stutzman, "From Nonresistance," 81-82.

107. Guy F. Hershberger, *The Way of the Cross in Human Relations* (Scottdale, Pa.: Herald Press, 1958), 102-110. For analysis of Hershberger book see Theron F. Schlabach, "To Focus a Mennonite Vision," in John Richard Burkholder and Calvin Redekop, eds., *Kingdom Cross and Community: Essays on Mennonite Themes in Honor of Guy F. Hershberger* (Scottdale, Pa.: Herald Press, 1976), 43-44; Driedger and Kraybill, *Mennonite Peacemaking* (n. 84), 100-101; J. R. Burkholder, *Continuity and Change*, 11-12.

108. See Donald Durnbaugh, ed., *On Earth Peace: Discussions on War/Peace Issues Between Friends, Mennonites, Brethren, and European Churches, 1935-1975* (Elgin, Ill.: The Brethren Press, 1978), 19-20, 46-90; Hostetler, "Nonresistance and Social Responsibility" (n. 103), 51-52.

109. John Howard Yoder, "Reinhold Niebuhr and Christian Pacifism," *MQR* 27 (Apr. 1953), 101-117; quot., p. 104.

110. John Howard Yoder, "The Theological Basis of the Christian Witness to the State," in Durnbaugh, ed., *On Earth Peace*, 135-143; for discussion of this address, see Hostetler, "Nonresistance and Social Responsibility" (n. 103), 53-54. See also John

Howard Yoder, *The Christian Witness to the State* (Newton, Kan.: Faith & Life Press, 1964).

111. Elmer Neufeld, "Christian Responsibility in the Political Situation," *MQR* 32 (Apr. 1958), 143.

112. Ibid., 150-162.

113. Driedger and Kraybill, *Mennonite Peacemaking* (n. 84), 122.

114. Harold S. Bender, "Editorial," *MQR* 32 (Apr. 1958), 110.

115. Edgar Metzler, "Another Alternative for Draft-Age Youth," *GH* 52 (Nov. 17, 1959), 977-978, 997.

116. Harold S. Bender, "When May Christians Disobey the Government?" *GH* 53 (Jan. 12, 1960), 25-26, 44; quot. p. 25.

CHAPTER 11

1. H. S. Bender to S. C. Yoder, Nov. 2, 1938, f. 13, b. 13, Bender papers.

2. "Editorial," *TM* 45 (Sep. 4, 1930), 1-2.

3. For a brief history of the All-Mennonite Conferences, see Harold S. Bender, "Inter-Mennonite Relations," *ME*, III, 44-48. For origins of MCC, see Guy F. Hershberger, "Historical Background to the Formation of the Mennonite Central Committee," *MQR* 44 (July 1970), 213-244; James C. Juhnke, "Mennonite Benevolence and Revitalization in the Wake of World War I," *MQR* 60 (Jan. 1986), 15-30. On the Amish-Mennonite mergers, see James C. Juhnke, *Vision, Doctrine, War: Mennonite Identity and Organization in America, 1890-1930*, Mennonite Experience in America vol. 3 (Scottdale, Pa.: Herald Press, 1989), 121-122.

4. Harold S. Bender, "Inter-Mennonite Relations," *ME*, III, 46. For elaboration of Bender's claim see Ken Neufeld, "Factors Associated with the Growth in Number of Inter-Mennonite Organizations" (unpublished student paper, University of Southern California, n.d.; copy at CMBS-F); Paul N. Kraybill, "North American Inter-Mennonite Relationships" (unpublished paper, 1974; copy in MHL). On the role of World War II for advancing inter-Mennonitism, see Melvin Gingerich, "*The Mennonite Church in World War II*: A Review and Evaluation," *MQR* 25 (July 1951), 193-194.

5. Kraybill, "North American Inter-Mennonite Relationships."

6. See Neufeld, "Factors Associated . . . ," 16-18, 23.

7. Ibid.

8. William B. Weaver, "Central Conference Mennonite Church," *ME*, I, 540-541. For an interesting analysis of the Central Conference and its movement toward merger, see also R. L. Hartzler, "Significant Eras in Our Conference: History and Our Present Status," *The Christian Evangel* 41 (Sep.-Oct. 1953), 163-165.

9. "Editorial: Christian Unity," *The Christian Evangel* 20 (Feb. 1930), 27. For a detailed history of this merger see Samuel Floyd Pannabecker, *Faith in Ferment: A History of the Central District Conference* (Newton, Kan.: Faith & Life Press, 1968), ch. 12.

10. See selected reports in *The Christian Evangel*, on the various meetings: "Report of a Meeting of the Comity Committees" 20 (Apr. 1930), 82-83; "Definite Steps Towards Unity" 20 (May 1930), 99; "Minutes of a Meeting of the Joint Committees on Publication Interests" 20 (June 1930), 123-124; "United Publication Work" 23 (Sep. 1933), 195; "United Publication Work" 23 (Oct. 1933), 219-220.

11. Editorial, "*The Mennonite* Again a Weekly," *TM* 51 (Jan. 7, 1936), 1.

12. "The Editor's Greetings," *The Christian Evangel* 24 (Jan. 1936), 3.

13. Pannabecker, *Faith in Ferment*, 332.

14. "Editorial," *The Christian Evangel* 33 (Apr. 1945), 75-76; quot., p. 76.

15. For the history of the Evangelical Mennonite Conference, see Stan Nussbaum, *You Must Be Born Again: A History of the Evangelical Mennonite Church* (Fort Wayne, Ind.: Evangelical Mennonite Church, 1991). For that of the Evangelical Mennonite Brethren, see Evelyn Regier, "An Historical Study of the Develop-

ment of the Evangelical Mennonite Brethren" (M.R.E. thesis, Biblical Seminary in New York, 1948); Calvin Redekop, "The Embarrassment of a Religious Tradition," *ML* 36 (Sep. 1981), 17-21; Kevin Enns-Rempel, "The Evangelical Mennonite Brethren: In Search of Religious Identity" (unpublished senior thesis, Fresno Pacific College, 1982; copy in CMBS-F); Enns-Rempel, "The Fellowship of Evangelical Bible Churches and the Quest for Religious Identity," *MQR* 63 (July 1989), 247-264; Enns-Rempel, "A Merger That Never Was: The Conference of Evangelical Mennonites, 1953-1962," *ML* 48 (Mar. 1993), 16-21.

16. Enns-Rempel, "A Merger That Never Was," 17.

17. John R. Dick, "Too Old to Marry?" *The Evangelical Mennonite* (Nov. 15, 1957), 3.

18. Nussbaum, *You Must Be Born Again*, 52.

19. See the standard history of each group: John A. Toews, *A History of the Mennonite Brethren Church: Pilgrims and Pioneers*, ed. A. J. Klassen (Fresno, Calif.: The Board of Christian Literature of the General Conference of the Menonite Brethren, 1975); Cornelius F. Plett, *The Story of the Krimmer Mennonite Brethren Church* (Winnipeg, Man.: Kindred Press, 1985).

20. Plett, *Story of the Krimmer Mennonite Brethren*, 313.

21. On these various discussions, see Paul Toews, "The Long Road to Union," *CL* 48 (Nov. 12, 1985), 5-6, for brief summary; for lengthier, Plett, *The Story of the Krimmer Mennonite Brethren Church*, 311-317.

22. *Year Book of the Krimmer Mennonite Brethren Conference* (1938), 9.

23. Exec. Comm. of the MB general conference, letter to the chairman of the KMB conference, Oct. 10, 1949, Board of Reference and Counsel Minutes/Reports (hereafter BORAC Minutes/Reports) 1949-1950, CMBS-F.

24. See, e.g.: "Joint Session of the Executive Committee of the Krimmer Mennonite Brethren Conference with the Committee of Reference and Counsel of the General Conference of the Mennonite Brethren Church of North America at Hillsboro, Kansas, September 9, 1952...," BORAC Minutes/Reports, CMBS-F; files of the Merger Committee and the Conference Exec. Comm., KMB Conference files, CMBS-F; *Krimmer Mennonite Brethren Conference Year Book, 1957*, 16; Plett, *Story of the Krimmer Mennonite Brethren*, 324.

25. On the Gnadenau withdrawal and merger see the Conference Exec. Comm., KMB Conference files, CMBS-F. The merger documents and ceremonies are reported in the *Year Book, Centennial Conference and 48th Session of the General Conference of the Mennonite Brethren Church in North America* (1960), 26-29 (hereafter cited as [MB] Gen. Conf. *Year Book*, with year).

26. Harold S. Bender, "Lessons to be Learned from Past Divisions," *GH* 53 (May 17, 1960), 441-442.

27. Ed G. Kaufman, "The Problem of Unity in the General Conference," in *Christian Unity in Faith and Witness: Proceedings of the Centennial Study Conference* (General Conference Mennonite Church, Donnellson, Iowa, June 20-23, 1960), E-8.

28. *General Conference Mennonite Church Minutes 1959*, 15 (hereafter cited as [GC] Gen. Conf. *Minutes and Reports*, with years).

29. William Klassen, "The Future of Inter-Mennonite Co-operation," in *Christian Unity in Faith and Witness: Proceedings of the Centennial Study Conference* (General Conference Mennonite Church, Donnellson, Iowa, June 20-23, 1960), E-12.

30. [MB] Gen. Conf. *Year Book* (1960), 36-38, 135-136.

31. See "Statement on Church Unity," [GC] Gen. Conf. *Minutes and Reports* (1965), 22-23.

32. Orlando A. Waltner, Exec. Sec. of the GC church, to MB Conference Moderator Frank C. Peters; A. J. Metzler, Exec. Sec. of the MC, to Peters; and MB response; all in [MB] Gen. Conf. *Year Book* (1966), 30-33.

33. John A. Toews, "Mennonite Brethren in Inter-Mennonite Endeavors," *Direction* 7 (July 1978), 4.

34. "Eastern District Talks Union," *TM* 80 (June 9, 1965), 383.

35. "Statement on Church Unity," [GC] Gen. Conf. *Minutes and Reports* (1965), 23.

36. John Drescher, "A Call to Unity," *GH* 58 (Aug. 24, 1965), 737.

37. James A. Goering, "Response to 'A Call to Unity,' " *GH* 58 (Oct. 26, 1965), 945-946; reprinted as "Mennonite Differences," *TM* 80 (Nov. 16, 1965), 719-720.

38. See "The Challenge of the Divided State of American Protestantism," and "Christian Unity in a Divided Mennonitism," *Reports Submitted to* [MC] *Mennonite General Conference* (1967), 55-62; "Text on the Organizational Expression of Christian Unity," [MC] *Mennonite General Conference Proceedings* (1969), 54-63 (these proceedings, variously named, hereafter cited as [MC] Menn. Gen. Conf. *Reports*, with dates); "Principles and Guidelines for Interchurch Relations" (pamphlet of the Interchurch Relations Committee of the Mennonite General Conference, Aug. 1971).

39. See "The Challenge," 55-57. The number of National Council of Churches and National Association for Evangelicals linkages was reported in "Interchurch Relations Committee," *Reports Submitted to Mennonite* [MC] *General Conference* (1969), 38.

40. John Howard Yoder memo to Interchurch Relations Committee, with letter by A. J. Metzler to members of the committee, Sep. 9, 1966, Interchurch Relations Comm. file 3, b. 3, Paul N. Kraybill papers, AMC.

41. "Christian Unity in a Divided Mennonitism," 58-62.

42. "Interchurch Relations," *Report to General Conference Mennonite Church* (1971), 4.

43. For summary of some of these bilateral discussions, see Interchurch Relations Committee minutes, May 18, 1967; on the hesitancy of the MC church, see same, Mar. 19, 1969; both in f. 1, b. 1, A. J. Metzler papers, AMC. Included in the discussions was the recognition that certain sections of the "Mennonite Church constituency . . . feel threatened by interchurch openness." Moving too aggressively on interchurch questions could jeopardize "*intra*church relations."

44. Heinz Janzen to Gary Shrag, Rainbow Boulevard Mennonite Church, May 21, 1970, f. 1, b. 2, [MC] Interchurch Relations Comm. collection, AMC.

45. [MC] Interchurch Relations Comm. minutes, Mar. 18, 1969, f. 1, b. 1, A. J. Metzler papers, AMC.

46. See Samuel Floyd Pannabecker, *Ventures of Faith: The Story of Mennonite Biblical Seminary* (Elkhart, Ind.: Mennonite Biblical Seminary, 1975), 7-24.

47. Ibid., 26.

48. Harold S. Bender, "Inaugural Address," *Goshen College Bulletin* 38 (Dec. 1944), 6-7.

49. Don E. Smucker, "Warning from Witmarsum," *The Bulletin: The Mennonite Biblical Seminary-Mennonite Bible School* 12 (Apr. 1949), 4-5.

50. Smucker to Ed G. Kaufman, Oct. 23, 1943, f. 386, b. 55, corresp. series, E. G. Kaufman College papers, MLA.

51. See Rodney J. Sawatsky, *Authority and Identity: The Dynamics of the General Conference Mennonite Church* (N. Newton, Kan.: Bethel College, 1987), 48-49.

52. John B. Toews, "Focusing the Vision: The M.B. Biblical Seminary," in A. J. Klassen, ed., *The Seminary Story: Twenty Years of Education in Ministry, 1955-1975* (Fresno, Calif.: Mennonite Brethren Biblical Seminary, 1975), 17-24.

53. See Toews, *A History of the Mennonite Brethren Church* (n. 19).

54. These paragraphs are adapted from Paul Toews, "Differing Historical Imaginations and the Changing Identity of the Mennonite Brethren," in Walter Klaassen, ed., *Anabaptism Revisited: Essays on Anabaptist/Mennonite Studies in Honor of C. J. Dyck* (Scottdale, Pa.: Herald Press, 1992), 166-169.

55. See Robert Wuthnow, *The Restructuring of American Religion: Society and Faith Since World War II* (Princeton: Princeton University Press, 1988), 100-132;

Samuel McCrea Cavert, *The American Churches in the Ecumenical Movement, 1900-1968* (New York: Association Press, 1968), 189-208.

56. Quoted in Willard H. Smith, *Mennonites in Illinois* (Scottdale, Pa.: Herald Press, 1983), 108.

CHAPTER 12

1. Victor Stoltzfus, "Amish Agriculture: Adaptive Strategies for Economic Survival of Community Life," *Rural Sociology* 38 (Summer, 1973), 203.

2. Donald B. Kraybill, *The Riddle of Amish Culture* (Baltimore: The Johns Hopkins University Press, 1989), 228.

3. Thomas W. Foster, "Occcupational Differentiation and Change in an Ohio Amish Settlement," *Ohio Journal of Science* 84 (June 1984), 75, notes these modern elements in the construction of some Amish buggies.

4. The notion of "negotiating" or "bargaining" as the way to understand the Amish relationship to the larger culture is central to Kraybill's *The Riddle*, and to his "Negotiating with Caesar" in Donald B. Kraybill, ed., *The Amish and the State* (Baltimore: The Johns Hopkins University Press, 1993), 3-22.

5. See Beulah Hostetler, "The Formation of the Old Orders," *MQR* 66 (Jan. 1992), 5-25; Theron F. Schlabach, *Peace, Faith, Nation: Mennonites and Amish in Nineteenth-Century America*, The Mennonite Experience in America vol. 2 (Scottdale, Pa.: Herald Press, 1988), ch. 8.

6. James C. Juhnke, *Vision, Doctrine, War: Mennonite Identity and Organization in America, 1890-1930*, The Mennonite Experience in America vol. 3 (Scottdale, Pa.: Herald Press, 1989), 45-46; Amos Hoover, "The Old Order Mennonites," in Paul N. Kraybill, ed., *Mennonite World Handbook* (Lombard, Ill.: Mennonite World Conference, 1984), 374-381.

7. Donald B. Kraybill to Paul Toews, Aug. 29, 1994.

8. See John A. Hostetler, *Amish Society* (2nd ed.; Baltimore: The Johns Hopkins University Press, 1968), 38-42; James E. Landing, "The Spatial Developments and Organization of an Old Order Amish-Beachy Amish Settlement: Nappanee, Indiana" (Ph.D. diss., Pennsylvania State University, 1967), 27; Steven Nolt, "The Mennonite Eclipse," *Festival Quarterly* 19 (Summer, 1992), 8-12.

9. David Luthy, "Amish Migration Patterns, 1972-1992," in Donald B. Kraybill and Marc A. Olshan, eds., *The Amish Struggle with Modernity* (Hanover, N.H.: University Press of New England, 1994), 243-260.

10. William K. Crowley, "Old Order Amish Settlement: Diffusion and Growth," *Annals of the Association of American Geographers* 65 (June 1978), 261; Crowley offered a different accounting of the establishment of Amish settlements from that of Luthy.

11. Noah Leid, *History of the Bowmansville Mennonites and Related Congregations* (privately published, 1991), 47.

12. David and Edna Miller, *Families of the Indiana and Michigan Wisler Mennonite Church* (privately published, 1981), 4; Hoover, "The Old Order Mennonites" (n. 6), 374-375.

13. Allen B. Clark, *This Is Good Country: A History of the Amish of Delaware, 1915-1988* (Gordonville, Pa.: Gordonville Print Shop, 1988), 158.

14. Thomas J. Meyers, "Population Growth and Its Consequences in the Elkhart-Lagrange Old Order Amish Settlement," *MQR* 65 (July 1991), 313-314.

15. Judith A. Nagata, *Continuity and Change Among the Old Order Amish of Illinois*, Immigrant Communities & Ethnic Minorities in the United States & Canada no. 18 (New York: AMS Press, 1989), 301-304.

16. Ibid., 314-318.

17. See Leo Driedger, "The Anabaptist Identification Ladder: Plain-Urbane Continuity in Diversity," *MQR* 51 (Oct. 1977), 278-291.

18. Nagata, *Continuity and Change*, 327.

19. John A. Hostetler, *Amish Society* (3rd ed.; Baltimore: The Johns Hopkins University Press, 1980), 93-94.

20. Steven Nolt, *A History of the Amish* (Intercourse, Pa.: Good Books, 1992), 280; Hostetler, *Amish Society* (3rd ed.), 95-97; some points added by Theron Schlabach from personal knowledge and observation.

21. Eugene P. Ericksen, Julia A. Ericksen, and John A. Hostetler, "The Cultivation of the Soil as a Moral Directive: Population Growth, Family Ties and the Maintenance of Community Among the Old Order Amish," *Rural Sociology* 45 (Spring 1980), 52.

22. Figures are summarized in Nolt, *A History of the Amish*, 280-281; Nolt took them from David Luthy, "Old Order Amish Settlements in 1974," *Family Life* 8 (Dec. 1974), 13-16, and *Mennonite Yearbook 1972* (Scottdale, Pa.: Mennonite Publishing House). On the origin of the Beachy Amish and the factors that distinguish them from the Old Order Amish, see ch. 1 of this book.

23. Hostetler, *Amish Society* (3rd ed.), 96-97.

24. See Marc A. Olshan, "The National Amish Steering Committee," in Kraybill, ed., *The Amish and the State* (n. 4), 67-86.

25. "Rules-Regulations-Duties and Guidelines Regarding Old Order Amish Steering Committee and Its State Directors," attached to "5th Annual Old Order Amish Steering Committee Meeting Minutes, Oct. 27, 1971," in *Minutes of Old Order Amish Steering Committee from Oct. 20, 1966 to Oct. 25, 1972*, vol. 1 (Gordonville, Pa.: Gordonville Print Shop, n.d.), 63.

26. Hoover, "Old Order Mennonites" (n. 6), 376.

27. Hostetler, *Amish Society* (3rd ed.) (n. 19), 75-77.

28. For a history of the ban among the Old Orders, see Elmer S. Yoder, *The Beachy Amish Mennonite Fellowship Churches* (Hartville, Ohio: Diakonia Ministries, 1987), ch. 5.

29. See Sandra Lee Cronk, "Gelassenheit: The Rites of the Redemptive Process in Old Order Amish and Old Order Mennonite Communities" (Ph.D. diss., University of Chicago, 1977); Kraybill, *The Riddle* (n. 2), ch. 2.

30. See Walter Kollmorgen, *Culture of a Contemporary Rural Community: The Old Order Amish of Lancaster County, Pennsylvania*, Rural Life Studies no. 4 (Washington, D.C.: U.S. Department of Agriculture, 1942), 76.

31. Kraybill, *The Riddle* (n. 2), ch. 2.

32. Hostetler, *Amish Society* (3rd ed.) (n. 19), 277-280.

33. John A. Hostetler, *Amish Society* (4th ed.; Baltimore: The Johns Hopkins University Press, 1993), 281.

34. For a discussion of Beachy Amish origins, see ch. 1.

35. Elmer S. Yoder, *Beachy Amish Mennonite Fellowship Churches* (n. 28), 128-136.

36. Ibid., 136-137.

37. Hostetler, *Amish Society* (4th ed.) (n. 33), 284.

38. Nolt, *History of the Amish* (n. 20), 264.

39. Harvey Graber, "Spiritual Awakening in the Old Order Amish Church" (student paper, Goshen College, 1956; copy in MHL), 5.

40. Graber, "Spiritual Awakening," 6.

41. Nolt, *History of the Amish* (n. 20), 265.

42. Abbie Gertrude Enders Huntington, "Dove at the Window: A Study of an Old Order Amish Community in Ohio" (Ph.D. diss., Yale University, 1957), 692-695.

43. Nolt, *History of the Amish* (n. 20), 266-267; Abner F. Beiler, "A Brief History of the New Order Amish Church, 1966-1976" (typescript, copy in MHL).

44. Amos Hoover, "Historical Sketches of the Weaverland Conference Mennonite Congregations," in Mary Edna Hoover, comp., *Directory of the Members and*

Their Families Who Attend the Weaverland Conference Mennonite Churches (n.p.: Weaverland Conference Mennonite Congregations, 1985), 5-6.

45. Leid, *History of the Bowmansville* . . . (n. 11), 27, 29.

46. Hoover, "The Old Order Mennonites" (n. 6), 376-377.

47. Edward Weaver, "Editor's Comments," *Home Messenger* 2 (May 1974), 2.

48. See Nagata, *Continuity and Change* (n. 15), 68-143; Calvin Bachman, *The Old Order Amish of Lancaster County*, Publications of the Pennsylvania German Society vol. 60 (Lancaster, Pa.: Pennsylvania German Society, 1961), 79-88.

49. Ericksen, Ericksen, and Hostetler, "Cultivation of the Soil as . . . " (n. 21), 57-61.

50. Stoltzfus, "Amish Agriculture: Adaptive Strategies" (n. 1), 199-200.

51. Kollmorgen, *Culture of a Contemporary Rural Community* (n. 30), 12, 30.

52. Stoltzfus, "Amish Agriculture: Adaptive Strategies" (n. 1), 201.

53. Nagata, *Continuity and Change* (n. 15), 135-136.

54. Foster, "Occupational Differentiation and Change" (n. 3), 78, 81.

55. Clark, *This Is Good Country* (n. 13), 143-148.

56. Isaac R. Horst, *Separate and Peculiar* (privately printed, 1979), 67.

57. Nagata, *Continuity and Change* (n. 15), 125-135.

58. Foster, "Occupational Change and Differentiation" (n. 3), 80.

59. "Farm vs. Factory," *Family Life* (May 1971), 22—article brought to my attention through Thomas J. Meyers, "Stress and the Amish Community in Transition" (Ph.D. diss., Boston University, 1983), 72.

60. That debate goes back to the nineteenth century; for a discussion of the social science debate over the degree to which distinctive groups can carry their communal, *Gemeinschaft* relations into a less separated and more integrated, *Gesellschaft* world, see Meyers, "Stress and . . . ," ch. 3.

61. See Albert N. Keim, "Military Service and Conscription," in Kraybill, ed., *The Amish and the State* (n. 4), 43-66.

62. Joseph Stoll, "Who Shall Educate Our Children?" in Albert Keim, ed., *Compulsory Education and the Amish: The Right Not to Be Modern* (Boston: Beacon Press, 1975), 31; see also John A. Hostetler and Gertrude Enders Huntington, *Children in Amish Society: Socialization and Community Education* (New York: Holt, Rinehart and Winston, 1971), 105-116.

63. Quot. is from Kraybill, *The Riddle* (n. 2), 131; for insightful yet brief discussions of the purposes of Amish schools, see same source and also Thomas J. Meyers, "Education and Schooling," in Kraybill, ed., *The Amish and the State* (n. 4), 102-106; for Old Order Mennonite schools, see Mark W. Dewalt and Bonnie Troxell, "Old Order Mennonite One-Room School: A Case Study," *Anthropology and Education Quarterly* 20 (Dec. 1989), 308-325.

64. Herbert V. Ferster, "The Development of the Amish School System," *Pennsylvania Mennonite Heritage* 6 (Apr. 1983), 7-9; Albert N. Keim, "From Erlanbach to New Glarus," in Keim, ed., *Compulsory Education and the Amish*, 1-15.

65. The decade listing is taken from Nolt, *History of the Amish* (n. 20), 260. See also: "Schools Directory, 1982-1983," *Blackboard Bulletin* (Nov. 1982), 9-22; Meyers, "Education and Schooling," 87-108.

66. Listing of attendees is included in *Background of the Old Order Mennonite Parochial Schools of Pennsylvania* (Gordonville, Pa.: Gordonville Print Shop, 1969), 5-7.

67. For the story of these educational conflicts in Pennsylvania, see John A. Hostetler, *Amish Society* (4th ed.) (n. 33), 261-263; Ferster, "The Development of the Amish School System," 9; Levi Esh, "Research Notes: The Amish Parochial School Movement," *MQR* 51 (Jan. 1977), 69-75; Kraybill, *The Riddle* (n. 2), 120-129; *Background of the Old Order Mennonite Parochial Schools of Pennsylvania*; *Report of Committee of Plain People Making Pleas for Leniency from Depressive School Laws*

(n.p., 1939); Eli M. Shirk, *History of Our School Controversy* (privately printed, 1959). Hostetler and Huntington, *Children in Amish Society*, 73, reprints two of these required vocational diaries.

68. Andrew Kinsinger, "The Heating System," in Susan Kinsinger, comp., *Family and History of Lydia Beachy's Descendants, 1889 to 1989* (Gordonville, Pa.: Gordonville Print Shop, 1988), 120, 124.

69. A short summary and analysis of this conflict is in Hostetler, *Amish Society* (4th ed.) (n. 33), 264-268. The Iowa conflict prompted Donald A. Erickson of the University of Chicago to convene a two-day conference on "Freeedom and Control in Education: National Invitational Conference on State Regulation of Nonpublic Schools" (Center for Continuing Education, University of Chicago, Mar. 28-29, 1967). Erickson's paper "Showdown at an Amish Schoolhouse," delivered and distributed at the conference, is a blow-by-blow account of the conflict; it is printed in Donald Erickson, *Public Controls for Non-Public Schools* (Chicago: University of Chicago Press, 1969), ch. 5, and as ch. 3 of Keim, ed., *Compulsory Education and the Amish* (n. 62).

70. Nolt, *History of the Amish* (n. 20), 261.

71. See ibid., 261; Hostetler, *Amish Society* (4th ed.) (n. 33), 267-268.

72. William B. Ball, "Building a Landmark Case: *Wisconsin* v. *Yoder*," in Keim, ed., *Compulsory Education and the Amish* (n. 62), 120.

73. Text of the U.S. Supreme Court decision, "*State of Wisconsin, Petitioner,* v. *Jonas Yoder et al.*," in Keim, ed., *Compulsory Education and the Amish* (n. 62), 159.

74. Leo Pfeffer, "The Many Meanings of the Yoder Case," in Keim, ed., *Compulsory Education and the Amish* (n. 62), 136, 144.

75. Andrew Kinsinger, "The Social Security Subject," in *Family and History of Lydia Beachy's Descendants* (n. 68), 128-129.

76. Glenn D. Everett, "Amish Seek Social Security Exemption," *The Budget* 64 (Jan. 21, 1954), 1.

77. "Our Religious Convictions Against Social Security" (leaflet published by the Amish, n.p., Apr. 1960; copy in MHL); Peter J. Ferrara, "Social Security and Taxes," in Kraybill, ed., *The Amish and the State* (n. 4), 127-133; Paul Charles Cline, "Relations Between the 'Plain People' and Government in the United States" (Ph.D. diss., The American University, 1968), 122-131.

78. Nolt, *History of the Amish* (n. 20), 270-71; Ferrara, "Social Security and Taxes," 132.

79. Ferrara, "Social Security and Taxes," 132-133.

80. Kraybill, *The Riddle* (n. 2), 220.

81. "Rules-Regulations-Duties and Guidelines" (n. 25), 56-57.

CHAPTER 13

1. Sydney Alhstrom, *A Religious History of the American People* (New Haven: Yale University, 1972).

2. Ibid., 1093.

3. "Repent for Vietnam Action" (MCC news release) *TM* 81 (Feb. 8, 1966), 95-96.

4. Luke Martin, "An Evaluation of a Generation of Mennonite Mission, Service and Peacemaking in Vietnam, 1954-1976" (commissioned by MCC, MCC Peace Section, and Eastern Mennonite Board of Missions and Charities; mimeographed, 1976, copies in various Mennonite libraries and archives); this citation is from pp. 6-15 of a summary version of the same. Also consult the first "Voluntary Agency Agreement with the Government of Viet-Nam," signed in Saigon, Aug. 20, 1954, and in Akron, Aug. 26, 1954; copy in 1960 files, Vietnam corresp., MCC Archives IX-6-3, AMC (hereafter MCC VN corresp., AMC); subsequent agreements, renegotiated at various intervals, are also in the MCC Archives.

5. Donald E. Voth to MCC, Nov. 9, 1960, MCC VN corresp., AMC.

6. See Carl D. Hurst to MCC, Sep. 7, 21, 1957; Robert Miller to Willard Kraybill, n.d. (in 1957 files); Donald Voth to MCC, Aug. 11, 1960; all in MCC VN corresp., AMC.

7. Willard Kraybill, "Reply to Questionnaire to Directors of MCC Foreign Units on Material Aid Need and Material Aid Program," Apr. 6, 1957; Donald Voth, "Vietnamese Land Development Material Aid Request," n.d. (in 1960 files); MCC VN corresp., AMC.

8. Donald Voth to MCC, Sep. 23, 1961, MCC VN corresp., AMC.

9. Longacre to MCC, Dec. 30, 1964, MCC VN corresp., AMC.

10. Hostetter, "Vietnam Journal," Nov. 17, 1966, Doug Hostetter papers, AMC.

11. Longacre, "Relief Strategy," *Occasional Bulletin* (Jan. 11, 1965), 1965 files, MCC VN corresp., AMC.

12. Paul Longacre, "Hospital Future: Church Relatedness," *Occasional Bulletin* (Jan. 12, 1965), 1965 files, MCC VN corresp., AMC.

13. Earl Martin, "Activity Report," Dec. 26, 1966, but in 1967 files, VN Reports, MCC Archives IX-6-3, AMC.

14. William Keeney, "Report to the Peace Section on Trip to Vietnam," May 1-16, 1967, VN-MCC Data File #5, 1966-68, MCC Archives IX-12, AMC.

15. Robert W. Miller, "The Role and Contribution of the Foreign Voluntary Agencies in South Vietnam" (M.A. thesis, University of Pittsburgh, 1972), 32.

16. Ibid., 55.

17. "Vietnam Christian Service Objectives and Philosophy," Vietnam Christian Service (herafter VNCS) files, 1968, MCC Archives IX-6-3, AMC; Atlee Beechy, "Report of Vietnam Christian Service" (VNCS), Aug. 20, 1966, VN-MCC Data File #6, 1966-68, MCC Archives IX-12, AMC.

18. Longacre to MCC, Oct. 6, 1965, MCC VN corresp., AMC.

19. Ibid.; Martin to MCC, Oct. (n. day), 1967, MCC VN corresp., AMC.

20. David Stowe to Tracey Jones, Jr., Chairman, National Council of Churches Advisory Committee on the Peace Priority Program, Oct. 30, 1967, VNCS files, MCC Archives IX-6-3, AMC.

21. MCC News Service release, VN-MCC Data File #5, MCC Archives IX-12, AMC.

22. Doug Hostetter, "untitled statement," dated Feb. 1968 but in 1967 files, MCC VN corresp., AMC.

23. Judy Danielson, "On Being a Western Presence," in Midge Meinertz, ed., *Vietnam Christian Service: Witness in Anguish* (New York: Church World Services, 1976), 92-102.

24. Miller, "The Role and Contribution . . ." (n. 15), 59.

25. Quoted in Earl Martin, "Reflections on the Mennonite Role in Viet Nam" (unpubl., Jan. 1976), MCC-Vietnam Study Project files, Doug Hostetter papers, AMC.

26. Atlee Beechy, "The Fruits of War: Reflections on Viet Nam" (convocation address, Bethel College [N. Newton, Kan.], Dec. 5, 1975), MCC-Vietnam Study Project files, Doug Hostetter papers, AMC.

27. Luke Martin, "An Evaluation . . ." (n. 4), 108-110.

28. Atlee Beechy, "A Report on Conferences with Representatives of the Democratic Republic of Viet Nam and the Provisional Revolutionary Government" (Apr. 14, 1971), MCC files, Doug Hostetter papers, AMC.

29. Beechy, "Fruits of War."

30. Earl S. Martin, *Reaching the Other Side: The Journal of an American Who Stayed to Witness Vietnam's Postwar Transition* (New York: Crown Publishers, 1978), 39.

31. Ibid., 13.

32. Longacre to MCC, May 7, 1966, MCC VN corresp., AMC.

33. William Snyder, "Vietnam Christian Service and the 'Tet Offensive,' " VNCS 1968 files, MCC Archives IX-6-3, AMC.

34. Minutes and Attachments of MCC Peace Section Meeting, Sep. 1, 1966, f. 2, b. 4, MCC Archives IX-7-8, AMC.

35. James Metzler to President Johnson, Oct. 21, 1967, MCC VN corresp., AMC.

36. C. N. Hostetter to President Johnson, Nov. 2, 1967, VNCS files, Doug Hostetter papers, AMC. While in Hostetter's name, the letter was drafted by Paul Longacre; see Oct. 18, 1967, draft in, VN-MCC Data File #6, 1966-68 MCC Archives IX-12, AMC.

37. "Letter to American Christians," written by the Eastern Mennonite Board of Missions and Charities personnel in Vietnam, Nov. 1967, MCC VN corresp., AMC.

38. Sam R. Hope, "The Challenge to Christian Missions in Southeast Asia Today" (an address to the World Missions Conference, Montreat, N.C., July 30, 1968), VNCS 1968 files, MCC Archives IX-6-3, AMC.

39. Earl S. Martin, "Reflections on the Mennonite Role in Viet Nam" (Jan. 1976), MCC-Vietnam Study Project files, Doug Hostetter papers, AMC.

40. Paul Longacre, "Vietnam: The Church's Dilemma," MCC news release, Sep. 22, 1967, b. 8, MCC Archives, AMC.

41. "Editorial," *TM* 80 (June 1, 1965), 372.

42. Maynard Shelly, "Journal," *TM* 83 (June 11, 1968), 24.

43. Vincent Harding, "Our Crisis of Obedience," *TM* 81 (Feb. 15, 1966), 110.

44. Vincent Harding, "Vietnam: What Shall We Do?" *TM* 80 (Sep. 21, 1965), 582-584.

45. Dan Dalke, "Revolting Alliance," *TM* 80 (Sep. 7, 1965), 560.

46. Vernon Stucky, "Hot or Cold," *TM* 80 (Sep. 7, 1965), 560.

47. See, in *TM*: Marie Regier, "Focus on Demonstrations" 80 (Oct. 5, 1965), 624; Mike Schmidt, "How Awful Is War" 81 (Jan. 4, 1966), 13; Mrs. D. P. Ewert, "Voice for the Voiceless Ones" 81 (Jan. 18, 1966), 43-44; Ronald Woelk, "Credibility in Vietnam" 80 (Oct. 12, 1965), 640.

48. "A Manual for Action and Witness," *TM* 81 (Jan. 25, 1966), 51.

49. See, e.g., Willard Kraybill, "Soul Sick and War Weary," *TM* 81 (Jan. 25, 1966), 50-52; Paul Peachey, "America's Hour of Truth in Vietnam," *TM* 81 (Jan. 1966), 64-66.

50. John Howard Yoder, "Our Witness to Government," *TM* 81 (Jan. 25, 1966), 58-59.

51. "Congregations Begin to Look at Vietnam: Concerns Expressed Through Prayer and Acts," *TM* 81 (Feb. 22, 1966), 128.

52. Perry Bush, "Drawing the Line: American Mennonites, the State and Social Change, 1935-1973" (Ph.D. diss., Carnegie-Mellon University, 1990), 264-267.

53. Quoted in ibid., 266.

54. Quoted in ibid., 265.

55. Minutes and Attachments of MCC Peace Section Meeting, June 8, 1966, f. 2, b. 1, MCC Archives IX-7-8, AMC.

56. Ibid., June 10, 1967.

57. Guy Hershberger, "A Mennonite Office in Washington?" *GH* 51 (Feb. 27, 1968), 186.

58. William Keeney, memo to Peace Section Exec. Comm., Jan. 13, 1968, MCC Peace Section Exec. Comm. 1963-69 files, MCC Archives IX-12-4, AMC.

59. "An Urgent Message to Our Churches from the 1967 Council of Boards," *TM* 82 (Dec. 12, 1967), 753-754.

60. "On Vietnam," *The Sword and Trumpet* 34 (First Quarter 1966), 1-3.

61. Quoted in Bush, "Drawing the Line" (n. 52), 254.

62. "Disarming America—A Real Cause for Alarm," *Guidelines for Today* (May-June, 1969), 2.

63. Quoted in Bush, "Drawing the Line," 256.

64. John E. Lapp, "Study of Church-State Relations," *GH* 61 (Mar. 12, 1968), 236.

65. On World War I resisters, see C. Henry Smith, *Smith's Story of the Mennonites,* revised and enlarged by Cornelius Krahn (Newton, Kan.: Faith & Life Press, 1981), 794-795; James C. Juhnke, *Vision, Doctrine, War: Mennonite Identity and Organization in America, 1890-1930,* The Mennonite Experience in America vol. 3 (Scottdale, Pa.: Herald Press, 1989), 208-242; Lloyd Kniss, *I Couldn't Fight: The Story of a C.O. in World War I* (Scottdale, Pa.: Herald Press, 1971); Gerlof D. Homan, *American Mennonites and the Great War, 1914-1918* (Scottdale, Pa.: Herald Press, 1994). The best estimate on Mennonites in prison is in Ted Grimsrud, "An Ethical Analysis of Conscientious Objection to World War II" (Ph.D. diss., Graduate Theological Union, 1988), 111-112, 177. The most accessible accounting of those imprisoned following the 1948 draft law is in Melissa Miller and Phil M. Shenk, *The Path of Most Resistance: Stories of Mennonite Conscientious Objectors Who Did Not Cooperate with the Vietnam Draft* (Scottdale, Pa.: Herald Press, 1982), 226-229.

66. Miller and Shenk, *Path of Most Resistance,* 13.

67. Ibid., 44-45.

68. "General Conference, 1969," *The Sword and Trumpet* 37 (Oct. 1969), 8.

69. Miller and Shenk, *Path of Most Resistance,* 45-52.

70. *Mennonite General Conference Proceedings, August 15-19, 1969,* 119-121 (hereafter cited as [MC] Menn. Gen. Conf. *Reports,* with dates); the resolution is more accessible in Miller and Shenk, *Path of Most Resistance,* 232-235.

71. "General Conference, 1969," *The Sword and Trumpet* 37 (Oct. 1969), 9.

72. Ibid.; see also J. Otis Yoder, "Observations Regarding General Conference, 1969," *The Sword and Trumpet* 37 (Nov. 1969), 9-11.

73. See, e.g., the stories of Ivan Schantz and Jim Hochstedler in Miller and Shenk, *Path of Most Resistance* (n. 65), 113-148.

74. "Mennonite Ghetto Faces Eviction," *TM* 84 (Oct. 28, 1969), 645; see also "Draft Resistance Makes the Scene," *TM* 84 (Dec. 16, 1969), 758-759.

75. Baker's sentiments are recorded in Miller and Shenk, *Path of Most Resistance* (n. 65), 56-57.

76. David Toews, "How to Be a Radical in One Easy Weekend" (n.d.), MCC Peace Section 1961-72 files, MCC Archives IX-7-12, AMC. See also a report on the conference—"The Meaning of Shalom in a Militarized Society"—as Exhibit 14 of in the MCC Peace Section Report Dec. 10-11, 1970, AMC.

77. John A. Lapp, "The Purpose of Our Meeting Together," Peace Section 1961-72 files, MCC Archives IX-7-12, AMC.

78. Both are quoted in J. R. Burkholder, "Christ, Conscience, Church and Conscription: Toward an Ethical Analysis of Mennonite Draft Resistance," in *Conscience and Conscription: Papers from an MCC Peace Section Assembly, November 20-22, 1969* (Akron, Pa.: MCC, 1970), 11.

79. Ibid., 14-15.

80. James C. Juhnke, "Conflicts and Compromises of Mennonites and the Draft," in *Conscience and Conscription,* 23. The two subsequent essays were: Juhnke, "The Agony of Civic Isolation: Mennonites in World War I," *ML* 25 (Jan. 1970), 27-33; Juhnke, "Mennonite Benevolence and Civic Identity: The Post-War Compromise," *ML* 25 (Jan. 1970), 34-37.

81. Juhnke, "Conflicts and Compromises . . . ," 25.

82. Ibid., 32-33.

83. Ibid.

84. Ibid.

85. Findings Committee Report, "A Message from the Consultation Conscience and Conscription," in *Conscience and Conscription* (n. 78), 46.

86. *The Draft Should Be Abolished* (MCC pamphlet, May 1970; copies in various Mennonite libraries).

87. "Non-Cooperation with the Draft," May 29, 1973, Draft Dodgers 1966-70 files, MCC Archives, AMC.

88. Miller and Shenk, *Path of Most Resistance* (n. 65), 220.

89. See "Visit to Mennonite Men in the Military Service in Vietnam," Exhibit 7 of MCC Exec. Comm. minutes, Apr. 14, 1970; and a similar report, also Exhibit 7 of MCC Exec. Comm. minutes, May 21-22, 1970; AMC.

90. [MCC] Peace Section Newsletter 2 (Oct. 15, 1971), 5. This serial publication is in various Mennonite libraries.

91. "Summary Report of Discussions with the Executive Committee of the Evangelical Mennonite Brethren Conference" (Apr. 7, 1970), Exhibit 1 of MCC Exec. Comm. minutes, May 21-22, 1970, AMC.

92. Kevin Rempel, "The Evangelical Mennonite Brethren: In Search of a Religious Identity" (senior thesis, Fresno Pacific College, 1982; copy in CMBS-F), 93, 97.

93. "Regarding Political Involvement," *Yearbook of the 50th Session, General Conference of Mennonite Brethren Churches, November 25-29, 1966,* 24-25 (hereafter cited as [MB] Gen. Conf. *Yearbook,* with year).

94. "General Conference: 'Christian Responsibility' . . . Words or Deeds?" *CL* 32 (Sep. 9, 1969), 5.

95. [MB] Gen. Conf. *Yearbook* (1969), 113-114.

96. [MB] Board of Reference and Council (hereafter BORAC) minutes, Dec. 3-4, 1970, General Conference BORAC files, CMBS-F.

97. John A. Toews, "Our Ministry of Reconciliation in a Broken World" (pamphlet of Board of Reference and Council, General Conference of Mennonite Brethren Churches, n.d.).

98. [MB] Gen. Conf. *Yearbook* (1972), 8-9.

99. BORAC minutes, Dec. 3-4, 1970, Gen. Conf. BORAC files, CMBS-F.

100. Victor Adrian, "The Whole Gospel to the Whole Man" (paper presented to a BORAC Study Conference, Aug. 16-17, 1971; copy in Gen. Conf. BORAC files, CMBS-F), p. 10; underlining is Adrian's.

101. William Keeney, "Conditions for a Revolutionary Century," *ML* 25 (Jan. 1970), 6.

102. Alvin Beachy, "The Biblical Basis for Civil Disobedience," *ML* 25 (Jan. 1970), 6-11; quot., p. 11.

103. Alvin Beachy, "A Case Study in Civil Disobedience: Pilgrim Marbeck," *ML* 25 (Jan. 1970), 12.

104. This issue of *Mennonite Life*—Jan. 1970—also contained the two articles by James Juhnke on the great Mennonite compromise with the state—"The Agony of Civic Isolation: Mennonites in World War I" and "Mennonite Benevolence and Civic Identity: The Post-War Compromise."

105. J. R. Burkholder, "Forms of Christian Witness to the State" (address at Goshen College, Mar. 12, 1976; copy in MHL).

106. Ibid., 6.

107. See J. Howard Kauffman and Leland Harder, *Anabaptists Four Centuries Later: A Profile of Five Mennonite and Brethren in Christ Denominations* (Scottdale, Pa.: Herald Press, 1975), ch. 9.

108. John Howard Yoder, *The Politics of Jesus* (Grand Rapids, Mich.: Eerdmans, 1972).

109. Ibid., 62-63.

110. Ibid., 64-77.

111. Ibid., 108.

112. Ibid., 116. For an elaboration of this point, see Helmut Harder, "The Pacifism of the Messianic Community," in John Richard Burkholder and Barbara Nelson Gingerich, eds., *Mennonite Peace Theology: A Panorama of Types* (Akron, Pa.: MCC, 1991), 35-41.

113. Yoder, *Politics of Jesus,* 106-114.

114. Mark Nation (of Fuller Theological Seminary, Pasadena, Calif.) to author,

Aug. 15, 1994; *Christian Century*, 99 (Jan. 20, 1982), 44. Nation, who is currently preparing a dissertation on Yoder, noted that by the early 1990s more than 75,000 copies of Yoder's *Politics of Jesus* had been sold.

EPILOGUE NOTES

1. Paul Peachey, "Identity Crisis Among American Mennonites," *MQR* 42 (Oct. 1968), 244.

2. Ibid., 244.

3. Ibid., 245.

4. John A. Toews, "In Search of Identity," *Mennonite Brethren Herald* 11 (Mar. 10, 1972), 2.

5. Ibid., 3.

6. J. Howard Kauffman and Leland Harder, *Anabaptists Four Centuries Later: A Profile of Five Mennonite and Brethren in Christ Denominations* (Scottdale, Pa.: Herald Press, 1975), 338-342.

7. Peachey, "Identity Crisis," 246.

8. By the mid-1970s the power of the Bender vision was on the wane. That story is beyond the boundaries of this volume, but the publication of James M. Stayer, Werner O. Packull, and Klaus Deppermann, "From Monogenesis to Polygenesis: The Historical Discussion of Anabaptist Origins," *MQR* 49 (Apr. 1975), 83-121, was more or less the opening of a scholarly discussion that, by questioning Bender's category of "Evangelical Anabaptism," also questioned the normative role of Bender's formulation in shaping Mennonite identity. For further discussion of this revising of Bender, see James Stayer, "The Easy Demise of a Normative Vision," in Calvin Wall Redekop, ed., *Mennonite Identity: Historical and Contemporary Perspectives* (Lanham, Md.: University Press of America, Inc., 1988), 109-116; Rodney Sawatsky, "The One and the Many: The Recovery of Mennonite Pluralism," in Walter Klaassen, ed., *Anabaptism Revisited: Essays on Anabaptist/Mennonite Studies in Honor of C. J. Dyck* (Scottdale, Pa.: Herald Press, 1992), 141-154.

9. Thomas Bender, *Community and Social Change in America* (Baltimore: Johns Hopkins University Press, 1978), 4.

BIBLIOGRAPHY

Archival Sources

The archival resources for twentieth-century North American Mennonite history are rich. The development of Mennonite archives during the twentieth century, most of them attached to academic institutions, is itself a rich story. This book's research included consulting but not exhausting nearly fifty archival collections.

The largest set of such collections is in the Archives of the Mennonite Church (AMC), located on the campus of Goshen College, Goshen, Indiana. The AMC houses the records of the Mennonite Church (MC) and of many inter-Mennonite agencies including Mennonite Central Committee (MCC), plus numerous personal papers. Especially helpful for this study were the MCC and MCC Peace Section Archives, the MC Peace Problems Committee collection, and the papers respectively of Harold S. Bender, John H. Yoder, Doug Hostetter, Guy F. Hershberger, and Calvin Redekop.

Other valuable collections consulted at AMC include those of the MC Interchurch Relations Committee, the MC Conference Executive Committee, Moses Beachy, John Horsch, Daniel Kauffman, Abram (A. J.) Metzler, Sanford (S. C.) Yoder, Arthur Nafziger, the Mennonite Peace Society, and the Mennonite Research Foundation, along with the Minutes of the National Council for Religious Conscientious Objectors.

The Mennonite Library and Archives at Bethel College, North Newton, Kansas, holds records of the General Conference Mennonite Church (GC) and many significant personal collections. Central to this study were the GC Board of Christian Service collection, the Henry A. Fast papers, and the Albert Gaeddert papers. Other relevant holdings include the minutes of the Bethel College Board of Directors and the College papers of Bethel's president Edmund (E. G.) Kaufman, plus the papers of, respectively, Peter S. Goertz, Emmet (E. L.) Harshbarger, Peter (P. C.) Hiebert, Robert

Kreider, Esko Loewen, Henry (H. P.) Krehbiel, and Peter (P. H.) Richert.

The Centers for Mennonite Brethren Studies in Hillsboro, Kansas (attached to Tabor College), and in Fresno, California (attached to the Mennonite Brethren Biblical Seminary and Fresno Pacific College), hold Mennonite Brethren (MB) conference papers, Krimmer Mennonite Brethren (KMB) conference papers, the archives of various MB institutions, and personal papers.

Collections consulted at the Center at Fresno (CMBS-F) were those of the MB Board of Reference and Counsel, of the MB Board of General Welfare and Public Relations, of the KMB conference, and of Reedley (California) Mennonite Brethren congregations, plus personal papers of Henry W. Lohrenz and of William Neufeld. At the Center at Hillsboro (CMBS-H) the study used the Tabor College faculty minutes and the Peter (P. C.) Hiebert papers.

The Menno Simons Library and Archives at Eastern Mennonite University, Harrisonburg, Virginia, holds the records of the Virginia Conference (MC) and those of various institutions and individuals of that conference. Particularly helpful were the personal papers respectively of George R. Brunk (I), John (J. L.) Stauffer, and Chester (C. K.) Lehman, and the collections of two executive committees—those of the Virginia Conference and of its Board of Missions.

Two regional archives in Pennsylvania—the Lancaster Mennonite Historical Society (LMHS) in Lancaster, Pennsylvania, and the Eastern Pennsylvania Mennonite Historical Library (EPMHL) at the Meetinghouse in Souderton—hold collections important for Pennsylvania Mennonite history. The Jacob B. Clemens papers and John E. Lapp papers at EPMHL and the Lancaster Conference's Bishop Board minutes at LMHS were especially useful.

SELECTED PUBLISHED BOOKS AND ARTICLES

Albrecht, Paul. "Civilian Public Service Evaluated by Civilian Public Service Men." *MQR* 22 (Jan. 1948).

Alhstrom, Sydney. *A Religious History of the American People.* New Haven: Yale University Press, 1972.

American Friends Service Committee. [*The Experience of the American Friends Service Committee in Civilian Public Service.*] Philadelphia, Pa.: American Friends Service Committee, 1945.

"The Automobile Issue Among the Old Order Mennonites: 1920." *MHB* 27 (Oct. 1976).

Barrett, Lois. *The Vision and the Reality: The Story of Home Missions in the General Conference Mennonite Church.* Newton, Kan.: Faith & Life Press, 1983.

Beachy, Alvin. "The Rise and Development of the Beachy Amish Mennonite Churches." *MQR* 29 (Apr. 1955).

Beachy, Alvin. "The Amish Settlement in Somerset County, Pennsylvania." *MQR*, 28 (Oct. 1954).

Bechler, Le Roy. *The Black Mennonite Church in North America, 1889-1986.* Scottdale, Pa.: Herald Press, 1986.

Bender, Harold S. "Anabaptism and Protestantism." *MQR* 24 (Jan. 1950).

_____. "Anabaptist Theology of Discipleship." *MQR* 24 (Jan. 1950).

_____. "Anabaptist Vision," *Church History* 13 (Mar. 1944).

_____. *Mennonite Origins in Europe. Mennonites and Their Heritage,* no. 1. 3rd ed. Akron, Pa.: MCC, 1945.

_____. "Outside Influences on Mennonite Thought." *ML* 10 (Jan. 1955).

_____. "Recent Progress in Research in Anabaptist History." *MQR* 8 (Jan. 1934).

_____. Review of C. Henry Smith, *The Story of the Mennonites. MQR* 16 (Oct. 1942).

_____. Review of J[ohn]. E. Hartzler, "Education Among the Mennonites of America." *The* [Goshen] *College Record: Review Supplement* 27 (May-June 1926).

_____. "When May Christians Disobey the Government?" *GH* 53 (Jan. 12, 1960).

Bender, Thomas. *Community and Social Change in America.* Baltimore: Johns Hopkins University Press, 1978.

Bender, Urie. *Soldiers of Compassion.* Scottdale, Pa.: Herald Press, 1969.

Bendroth, Margaret. "Fundamentalism and Femininity: The Reorientation of Women's Role in the 1920s." *Evangelical Studies Bulletin* 5 (Mar. 1988).

Bowman, Rufus D. *The Church of the Brethren and War, 1708-1941.* New York: Garland Publishing Inc., 1971.

Bratt, James D. *Dutch Calvinism in Modern America: A History of a Conservative Subculture.* Grand Rapids, Mich.: Eerdmans, 1984.

Brunk, Harry Anthony. *History of Mennonites in Virginia, 1900-1960,* vol. 2. Harrisonburg, Va.: privately published, 1972.

Brunk, G[eorge]. R. "Peace Witness." *The Sword and Trumpet* 3 (Apr. 1931).

_____. "Pacifism-Nonresistance." *The Sword and Trumpet* 3 (Apr. 1931).

Burkholder, J. Lawrence. "The Limits of Perfection: Autobiographical Reflections," in *The Limits of Perfection: Conversations with J. Lawrence Burkholder*. Eds. Rodney J. Sawatsky and Scott Holland. Waterloo, Ont.: Institute of Anabaptist-Mennonite Studies, Conrad Grebel College, 1993.

_____. *The Problem of Social Responsibility from the Perspective of the Mennonite Church* [unaltered publication of 1958 doctoral dissertation]. Elkhart, Ind.: Institute of Mennonite Studies, 1989.

Burkholder, John Richard. *Continuity and Change: A Search for a Mennonite Social Ethic.* Akron, Pa.: MCC Peace Section, 1977.

Bush, Perry. "Military Service, Religious Faith, and Acculturation: Mennonite G.I.s and Their Church, 1941-1945." *MQR* 67 (July 1993).

Called to be Sent: Essays in Honor of the Fiftieth Anniversary of the Founding of the Eastern Mennonite Board of Missions and Charities, 1914-1964. Ed. Paul N. Kraybill. Scottdale, Pa.: Herald Press, 1964.

Carpenter, Joel A. "Fundamentalist Institutions and the Rise of Evangelical Protestantism, 1929-1942." *Church History* 49 (Mar. 1980).

Cauthen, Kenneth. *The Impact of American Religious Liberalism.* N.Y.: Harper & Row, 1962.

Clark, Allen B. *This Is Good Country: A History of the Amish of Delaware, 1915-1988.* Gordonville, Pa.: Gordonville Print Shop, 1988.

Compulsory Education and the Amish: The Right Not to Be Modern. Ed. Albert N. Keim. Boston: Beacon Press, 1975.

Driedger, Leo. "The Anabaptist Identification Ladder: Plain-Urbane Continuity in Diversity." *MQR* 51 (Oct. 1977).

_____. "Mennonite Community Change: From Ethnic Enclaves to Social Networks." *MQR* 60 (July 1986).

_____. "*MQR* 60: Weaving Scholarly Mennonite Networks." *MQR* 61 (Oct. 1987).

Driedger, Leo, and Donald B. Kraybill. *Mennonite Peacemaking: From Quietism to Activism.* Scottdale, Pa.: Herald Press, 1994.

Dyck, C. J. *An Introduction to Mennonite History.* 2nd ed. Scottdale, Pa.: Herald Press, 1983. 3rd., revised ed., 1993.

Dyck, Harry Van. *Exercise of Conscience: A WWII Objector Remembers.* Buffalo, N.Y.: Prometheus Books, 1990.

Dyck, Peter J. and Elfrieda. *Up from the Rubble*. Scottdale, Pa.: Herald Press, 1991.

Ediger, Elmer. "Roots," in *If We Can Love: The Mennonite Mental Health Story*. Ed. Vernon Neufeld. Newton, Kan.: Faith & Life Press, 1983.

Egan, Eileen, and Elizabeth Clark Reissl. *Transfigured Night: The CRALOG Experience*. Philadelphia: Livingston Publishing Company, 1964.

Eitzen, Dirk W., and Timothy R. Falb. "An Overview of the Mennonite I-W Program." *MQR* 56 (Oct. 1982).

Enns-Rempel, Kevin. "The Fellowship of Evangelical Bible Churches and the Quest for Religious Identity." *MQR* 63 (July 1989).

_____. "They Came from Many Places: Sources of Mennonite Migration to California, 1887-1939." *California Mennonite Historical Society Bulletin* 28 (May 1993).

Epp, Frank. *Mennonites in Canada, 1920-1940: A People's Struggle for Survival*. Mennonites in Canada vol. 2. Scottdale, Pa.: Herald Press, 1982.

_____. *Mennonite Exodus: The Rescue and Resettlement of the Russian Mennonites Since the Communist Revolution*. Altona, Man.: Canadian Mennonite Relief and Immigration Council, 1962.

Erb, Paul. *The Alpha and the Omega: A Restatement of the Christian Hope in Christ's Coming*. Scottdale, Pa.: Herald Press, 1965.

_____. *Orie O. Miller: The Story of a Man and an Era*. Scottdale, Pa.; Herald Press, 1969.

_____. *South Central Frontiers: A History of the South Central Mennnonite Conference*. Scottdale, Pa.: Herald Press, 1974.

Evidences of Modernism at Bluffton College. Berne, Ind.: First Mennonite Church, 1929.

Falcón, Rafael. *The Hispanic Mennonite Church in North America, 1932-1982*. Scottdale, Pa.: Herald Press, 1986.

Fast, Henry. "Mennonites and the Civilian Service Program." *TM* 54 (Jan. 7, 1941).

Flynn, George Q. *Lewis B. Hershey, Mr. Selective Service*. Chapel Hill, N.C.: University of North Carolina Press, 1985.

French, Paul Comly. *Civilian Public Service*. Washington, D.C.: National Service Board for Religious Objectors, 1942.

_____. *The Origins of Civilian Public Service*. Washington, D.C.: National Service Board for Religious Objectors, n.d.

Fretz, J. Winfield. *The MEDA Experiment: Twenty-Five Years of Economic Development.* Waterloo, Ont.: Conrad Press, 1978.

_____. "Mennonites and Their Economic Problems." *MQR* 14 (Oct. 1940).

Friedmann, Robert. "Anabaptism and Protestantism." *MQR* 24 (Jan. 1950).

_____. "John Horsch and Ludwig Keller." *John Horsch Memorial Papers.* Ed. Harold Bender et al. Scottdale, Pa.: Mennonite Publishing House, 1947.

_____. *Mennonite Piety Through the Centuries: Its Genius and Its Literature.* Goshen, Ind.: Mennonite Historical Society, 1949.

_____. "On Mennonite Historiography and on Individualism and Brotherhood." *MQR* 17 (Apr. 1944).

_____. *The Theology of Anabaptism: An Interpretation.* Scottdale, Pa.: Herald Press, 1973.

Full Circle: Stories of Mennonite Women. Ed. Mary Lou Cummings. Newton, Kan.: Faith & Life Press, 1978.

Gaeddert, Albert. "What Have We Learned in Civilian Public Service?" *ML* 1 (July, 1946).

Gingerich, Melvin. *Mennonite Attire Through Four Centuries.* Breinigsville, Pa.: The Pennsylvania German Society, 1970.

_____. "The Mennonite Church in World War II: A Review and Evaluation." *MQR* 25 (July 1951).

_____. "Rural Life Problems and the Mennonites." *MQR* (16 July 1942).

_____. *Service for Peace: A History of Mennonite Civilian Public Service.* Akron, Pa.: Mennonite Central Committee, 1949.

Goering, Gladys. *Women in Search of Mission: A History of the General Conference Mennonite Women's Organization.* Newton, Kan.: Faith & Life Press, 1980.

Goossen, Rachel Waltner. "The 'Second Sex' and the 'Second Milers': Mennonite Women and Civilian Public Service." *MQR* 66 (Oct. 1992).

_____. *Prairie Vision: A History of the Pleasant Valley Mennonite Church, 1888-1988.* Hillsboro, Kan.: Pleasant Valley Church, 1988.

Gross, Leonard. "Mennonite Leadership: Holding the Church Together." *MHB* 47 (Apr. 1986).

Harms, Orlando. *The Journey of a Church.* Hillsboro, Kan.: Center for Mennonite Brethren Studies, Hillsboro, 1987.

Hartzler, John E. *Education Among the Mennonites of America.* Danvers, Ill.: Central Mennonite Publishing Board, 1925.

_____. "Witmarsum Theological Seminary: The Seminary for the Past Fifteen Years, Shall We More Forward." *Witmarsum Theological Seminary Bulletin* 8 (June 1920).

Haury, David. "Hard the Road to Oklahoma," in *Growing Faith: General Conference Mennonites in Oklahoma.* Ed. Wilma McKee. Newton, Kan.: Faith & Life Press, 1988.

_____. *Prairie People: A History of the Western District Conference.* Newton, Kan.: Faith & Life Press, 1981.

_____. *The Quiet Demonstration: The Mennonite Mission in Gulfport, Mississippi.* Newton, Kan.: Faith & Life Press, 1979.

Henderson Mennonites: From Holland to Henderson. Ed. Stanley E. Voth. N.p.: Henderson Centennial Committee, 1975.

Hershberger, Guy F. "Appreciating THE MENNONITE COMMUNITY." *The Mennonite Community* 1 (Jan. 1947).

_____. *Christian Relationships to State and Community.* Mennonites and Their Heritage, no. 5. Akron, Pa.: MCC, 1943.

_____. "The Christian's Relation to the State in Time of War: II. Is Alternative Service Desirable and Possible?" *MQR* (9 Jan. 1935).

_____. *The Mennonite Church in the Second World War.* Scottdale, Pa.: Mennonite Publishing House, 1951.

_____. "Nonresistance and Industrial Conflict." *MQR* 13 (April 1939).

_____. "Nonresistance, the Mennonite Church and the Race Question." *GH* 53 (June 28, 1956).

_____. "The Times of Sanford Calvin Yoder: The Mennonite Church and the First Fifty Years of Goshen College," in *An Evening to Honor Sanford Calvin Yoder.* Goshen, Ind.: Goshen College, 1974.

_____. *The Way of the Cross in Human Relations.* Scottdale, Pa.: Herald Press, 1958.

_____. *War, Peace, and Nonresistance.* Scottdale, Pa.: Herald Press, 1944.

Hertzler, R. L. "Significant Eras in Our Conference History and Our Present Status." *The Christian Evangel* 41 (Sep.-Oct. 1953).

Hiebert, Clarence. *The Holdeman People: The Church of God in Christ, Mennonite, 1859-1969.* Pasadena, Calif.: William Carey Library, 1979.

Higham, John. "Introduction: The Forms of Ethnic Leadership," in *Ethnic Leadership in America.* Ed. John Higham. Johns Hopkins Symposia in Comparative History no. 9. Baltimore: Johns Hopkins University Press, 1978.

_____. "Hanging Together: Divergent Unities in American History." *The Journal of American History* 61 (1974).

History and Report of the 1-W Program of the Church of God in Christ. Galva, Kan.: The Christian Public Service, Inc. [1960].

Holsinger, Justus G. *Upon This Rock: Remembering Together the 75-Year Story of the Hesston Mennonite Church*. Hillsboro, Kan.: Hesston Mennonite Church, 1984.

_____. *Serving Rural Puerto Rico*. Scottdale, Pa.: Mennonite Publishing House, 1952.

Hoover, Amos. *The Jonas Martin Era*. Denver, Pa.: the author, 1982.

_____. "The Old Order Mennonites," in *Mennonite World Handbook*. Ed. Paul N. Kraybill. Lombard, Ill.: Mennonite World Conference, 1984.

Hoover, David B. *A Testimony of the Truth: No Man Can Serve Two Masters; Ye Cannot Serve God and Mammon*. Ephrata, Pa.: privately published, n.d.

Horsch, John. *The Mennonite Church and Modernism*. Scottdale, Pa.: Mennonite Publishing House, 1924.

Hostetler, Beulah Stauffer. *American Mennonites and Protestant Movements: A Community Paradigm*. Scottdale, Pa.: Herald Press, 1987.

_____. "Defensive Structuring and Codification of Practice: Franconia Mennonite Conference." *MQR* 60 (July 1986).

_____. "Nonresistance and Social Responsibility: Mennonites and Mainline Peace Emphasis, ca. 1950 to 1985." *MQR* 64 (Jan. 1990).

Hostetler, John A. *Amish Society*, 3rd and 4th eds. Baltimore: Johns Hopkins University Press, 1980, 1993.

_____. *The Sociology of Mennonite Evangelism*. Scottdale, Pa.: Herald Press, 1954.

Hurst, Emma. "Moses G. Horning and the Old Order Divisions in Pennsylvania." *MHB* 21 (Apr. 1960).

If We Can Love: The Mennonite Mental Health Story. Ed. Vernon Neufeld, Newton, Kan.: Faith & Life Press, 1983.

Juhnke, James. "Mennonites and the Great Compromise." *TM* 84 (Sept. 23, 1969).

_____. "The Agony of Civic Isolation: Mennonites in World War I." *ML* 25 (Jan. 1970).

_____. "Mennonite Benevolence and Civic Identity: The Post-

War Compromise." *ML* 25 (Jan. 1970).

_____. "Mennonite Benevolence and Revitalization in the Wake of World War I." *MQR* 60 (Jan. 1986).

_____. "Mennonite Church Theological and Social Boundaries, 1920-1930—Loyalists, Liberals and Laxitarians." *ML* 38 (June 1983).

_____. "Mennonite History and Self-Understanding: North American Mennonitism as a Bi-Polar Mosaic," in *Mennonite Identity: Historical and Contemporary Perspectives.* Ed. Calvin Wall Redekop. Lanham, Md.: University Press of America, 1988.

_____. *A People of Mission: A History of General Conference Mennonites Overseas.* Newton, Kan.: Faith & Life Press, 1979.

_____. *A People of Two Kingdoms: The Political Acculturation of the Kansas Mennonites.* Newton, Kan.: Faith & Life Press, 1975.

_____. *Vision, Doctrine, War: Mennonite Identity and Organization in America, 1890-1930.* The Mennonite Experience in America vol. 3. Scottdale, Pa.: Herald Press, 1989.

Kauffman, J. Howard, and Leland Harder. *Anabaptists Four Centuries Later: A Profile of Five Mennonite and Brethren in Christ Denominations.* Scottdale, Pa.: Herald Press, 1975.

Kaufman, Edmund G. *Our Mission as a Church of Christ.* Mennonites and Their Heritage, no. 4. Akron, Pa.: MCC, 1944.

_____. *The Development of Missionary and Philanthropic Interest Among the Mennonites of North America.* Berne, Ind.: Mennonite Book Concern, 1931.

Kaufman, Gordon D. "Nonresistance and Responsibility." *Concern* 6 (Nov. 1958).

Keeney, William. "Experiences in Mental Hospitals in World War II." *MQR* 56 (Jan. 1982).

Keim, Albert N. "Military Service and Conscription," in *The Amish and the State.* Ed. Donald B. Kraybill. Baltimore: Johns Hopkins University Press, 1993.

_____. *The CPS Story: An Illustrated History of Civilian Public Service.* Intercourse, Pa.: Good Books, 1990.

Keim, Albert N., and Grant M. Stoltzfus. *The Politics of Conscience: The Historic Peace Churches and America at War, 1917-1955.* Scottdale, Pa.: Herald Press, 1988.

Keim, Albert N. "Service or Resistance? The Mennonite Response to Conscription in World War II." *MQR* 52 (Apr. 1978).

Kissinger, Andrew. "The Steering Committee," in *Family and History of Lydia Beachy's Descendants, 1889-1989.* Ed. Susan

Kinsinger. Gordonville, Pa.: Gordonville Print Shop, 1988.

Klaassen, Walter ed. *Anabaptism Revisited: Essays on Anabaptist/Mennonite Studies in Honor of C. J. Dyck.* Scottdale, Pa.: Herald Press, 1992.

Klassen, Herbert and Maureen. *Ambassador to His People: C. F. Klassen and the Russian Mennonite Refugees.* Winnipeg, Man.: Kindred Press, 1990.

Klassen, Peter J. *A Homeland for Strangers: An Introduction to Mennonites in Poland and Prussia.* Fresno, Calif.: Center for Mennonite Brethren Studies—Fresno, 1989.

Klingelsmith, Sharon. "Women in the Mennonite Church, 1900-1930." *MQR* 54 (July 1980).

Krahn, Cornelius. "Active or Passive Christianity." *ML* 1 (Jan. 1946).

_____. "Prolegomena to an Anabaptist Theology." *MQR* 24 (July 1950).

Kraus, C. Norman. "American Mennonites and the Bible." *MQR* 41 (Oct. 1967).

Kraybill, Donald B. ed. *The Amish and the State.* Baltimore: Johns Hopkins University Press, 1993.

_____. *The Riddle of Amish Culture.* Baltimore: Johns Hopkins University Press, 1989.

Krehbiel, H[enry]. P. *What Is a Pacifist?* Newton, Kan.: Herald Publishing Co., 1931.

_____. *The History of the General Conference of the Mennonite Church of North America,* vol. 2. Newton, Kan.: the author, 1938.

Kreider, Robert. "The Anabaptist Conception of the Church in the Russian Environment, 1789-1870." *MQR* 25 (Jan. 1951).

_____. "The Historic Peace Churches Meeting in 1935." *ML* 31 (June 1976).

_____. "The Impact of MCC Service on American Mennonites." *MQR* 44 (July 1970).

_____. "A Vision for Our Day." *ML* 3 (Jan. 1948).

Kreider, Robert S., and Rachel Waltner Goossen. *Hungry, Thirsty, a Stranger: The MCC Experience.* The Mennonite Central Committee Story no. 5. Scottdale, Pa.: Herald Press, 1988.

Kuhlmann, Paul. *The Story of Grace.* Omaha, Neb.: Grace College of the Bible, 1980.

Lageer, Elieen. *Merging Streams: Story of the Missionary Church.* Elkhart, Ind.: Bethel Publishing Co., 1979.

Lederach, Paul. "Revival in Franconia." *GH* 44 (Sep. 18, 1951).

Lehman, J. Irvin. "Teachers and Teachings." *The Sword and Trumpet* 11 (July 1943).

Lehman, James O. *Salem's First Century: Worship and Witness.* Kidron, Ohio: Salem Mennonite Church, 1986.

_____. *Creative Congregationalism: A History of the Oak Grove Mennonite Church in Wayne County, Ohio.* Smithville, Ohio: Oak Grove Mennonite Church, 1978.

_____. *Seedbed for Leadership: A Centennial History of the Pike Mennonite Church.* Elida, Ohio: Pike Mennonite Church, 1974.

_____. *Sonnennberg, a Haven and a Heritage: A Sesquicentennial History of the Swiss Mennonite Community of Southeastern Wayne County, Ohio.* Kidron, Ohio: Kidron Community Council, Inc., 1969.

Lehman, Naomi. *Pilgrimage of a Congregation: First Mennonite Church, Berne, Indiana.* Berne, Ind.: First Mennonite Church, 1982.

Leid, Noah. *History of the Bowmansville Mennonites and Related Congregations.* N.p., 1991.

Lind, Hope Kauffman. *Apart and Together: Mennonites in Oregon and Neighboring States, 1876-1976.* Scottdale, Pa.: Herald Press, 1990.

Loewen, Howard John. *One Lord, One Church, One Hope and One God: Mennonite Confessions of Faith in North America.* Elkhart, Ind.: Institute of Mennonite Studies, 1985.

_____. "Augustus H. Strong: Baptist Theologian for the Mennonite Brethren," in *Mennonites and Baptists: A Continuing Conversation.* Ed. Paul Toews. Winnipeg, Man.: Kindred Press, 1993.

Longfield, Bradley. *The Presbyterian Controversy: Fundamentalists, Modernists, and Moderates.* New York: Oxford University Press, 1991.

Luthy, David. *The Amish in America: Settlements That Failed, 1840-1960.* Aylmer. Ont.: Pathway Publishers, 1986.

Mack, Noah. "The Situation in American Mennonitism." *The Sword and Trumpet* 2 (Oct. 1930).

McLoughlin, William G. *Revivals, Awakenings, and Reforms: An Essay on Religion and Social Change in America, 1607-1977.* Chicago: University of Chicago Press, 1978.

Marsden, George R. *Fundamentalism and American Culture: The Shaping of Twentieth-Century Evangelicalism, 1870-1925.* New York: Oxford University Press, 1980.

Martin, Earl S. *Reaching the Other Side: The Journal of an American Who Stayed to Witness Vietnam's Postwar Transition.* New York: Crown Publishers, 1978.

Martin, Luke. "An Evaluation of a Generation of Mennonite Mission, Service and Peacemaking in Vietnam, 1954-1976." Mimeographed and distributed by Mennonite Central Committee and Eastern Mennonite Board of Missions and Charities, 1976.

Mennonite Encylopedia, vols. 1-4, ed. Harold S. Bender et al., and vol. 5, ed. Cornelius J. Dyck and Dennis Martin. Scottdale, Pa.: Herald Press, 1955-1959, 1990.

Mennonite Identity: Historical and Contemporary Perspectives. Ed. Calvin Wall Redekop. Lanham, Md.: University Press of America, 1988.

Mennonite Peace Theology: A Panorama of Types. Ed. John Richard Burkholder and Barbara Nelson Gingerich. Akron, Pa.: MCC, 1991.

Miller, Ivan J. *History of the Conservative Mennonite Conference, 1910-1985.* Grantsville, Md.: the author, 1985.

Miller, John. "Can CO's Survive Tolerance?" *The 1-W Mirror* 2 (Mar. 10, 1954).

Miller, Joseph P. *Beyond the Mystic Borders: 100 Year History of the Whitestone Mennonite Church.* Hesston, Kan.: Whitestone Mennonite Church, 1985.

Miller, Mary. *A Pillar of Cloud: The Story of Hesston College, 1909-1959.* N. Newton, Kan.: Mennonite Press, 1959.

Miller, Melissa and Phil M. Shank. *The Path of Most Resistance: Stories of Mennonite Conscientious Objectors Who Did Not Cooperate with the Vietnam Draft.* Scottdale, Pa.: Herald Press, 1982.

Miller, Orie O. "Aggressive Peace Work." *GH* 18 (Jan. 14, 1926).

_____. "Our Peace Message." *The College Record: Review Supplement* 27 (Sep. 1926).

_____. "Our Witness to Government." *GH* 41 (Mar. 30, 1948).

"Minutes of the Fifty-Fifth Consecutive Meeting of the American Society of Church History, December 28 and 29, 1943." *Church History* (Mar. 1944).

Minutes of Old Order Amish Steering Committee, vol. 1. Gordonville, Pa.: Gordonville Print Shop, n.d.

Nagata, Judith A. *Continuity and Change Among the Old Order Amish of Illinois. Immigrant Communities and Ethnic Minorities in the United States and Canada*, no. 18. New York: AMS Press, 1989.

Neufeld, Elmer. "Christian Responsibility in the Political Situation." *MQR* 32 (April 1958).

Newman, A[lbert]. H. "The Significance of the Anabaptist Movement in the History of the Christian Church." *The College Record: Review Supplement* 27 (Jan. 1926).

Nolt, Steven M. *A History of the Amish.* Intercourse, Pa.: Good Books, 1992.

Nussbaum, Stan. *You Must Be Born Again: A History of the Evangelical Mennonite Church.* Fort Wayne, Ind.: Evangelical Mennonite Church, 1981.

Olshan, Marc. "The National Steering Committee," in *The Amish and the State.* Ed. Donald B. Kraybill (Baltimore: Johns Hopkins University Press, 1993).

On Earth Peace: Discussions on War/Peace Issues Between Friends, Mennonites, Brethren and European Churches, 1935-1975. Ed. Donald F. Durnbaugh. Elgin, Ill.: The Brethren Press, 1978.

Pannabecker, Samuel Floyd. *Faith in Ferment: A History of the Central District Conference.* Newton, Kan.: Faith & Life Press, 1968.

_____. *Open Doors: A History of the General Conference Mennonite Church.* Newton, Kan.: Faith & Life Press, 1975.

_____. "Scenes from Mennonite Theological Education." *The Mennonite Biblical Seminary and the Mennonite Bible School Bulletin* 11 (Dec. 1947).

_____. *Ventures of Faith: The Story of Mennonite Biblical Seminary.* Elkhart, Ind.: Mennonite Biblical Seminary, 1975.

Peace, Progress, Promise: A 75th Anniversary History of Tabor Mennonite Church. Ed. Ruby Funk. N. Newton, Kan.: Tabor Mennonite Church, 1983.

Peacemakers in a Broken World. Ed. John A. Lapp. Scottdale, Pa.: Herald Press, 1969.

Peachey, Paul. "Identity Crisis Among American Mennonites." *MQR* 42 (Oct. 1968).

_____. "Toward an Understanding of the Decline of the West." *Concern* 1 (June 1954).

Pickett, Clarence. *For More Than Bread.* Boston: Little Brown, 1953.

Plett, Cornelius F. *The Story of the Krimmer Mennonite Brethren Church.* Winnipeg, Man.: Kindred Press, 1985.

The Recovery of the Anabaptist Vision: A Sixtieth Anniversary Tribute to Harold S. Bender. Ed. Guy F. Hershberger, Scottdale, Pa.: Herald Press, 1957.

Redekop, Calvin. "The Embarrassment of a Religious Tradition." *ML* 36 (Sep. 1981).

_____. *Mennonite Society.* Baltimore: Johns Hopkins University Press, 1989.

Regehr, T. D. "Lost Sons: The Canadian Mennonite Soldiers of World War II." *MQR* 66 (Oct. 1992).

_____. "Polish and Prussian Mennonite Displaced Persons, 1944-50." *MQR* 66 (Apr. 1992).

_____. "Anatomy of a Mennonite Miracle: The Berlin Rescue of 30-31 January 1947." *Journal of Mennonite Studies* 9 (1991).

Rich, Elaine Sommers. *Mennonite Women: A Story of God's Faithfulness, 1683-1983.* Scottdale, Pa.: Herald Press, 1983.

Ruth, John L. *Maintaining the Right Fellowship: A Narrative Account of Life in the Oldest Mennonite Community in America.* Scottdale, Pa.: Herald Press, 1984.

Sareyan, Alex. *The Turning Point: How Men of Conscience Brought About Major Change in the Care of America's Mentally Ill.* Washington, D.C.: American Psychiatric Press, Inc., 1993; Herald Press, Scottdale, Pa. 1994.

Sawatsky, Rodney J. *Authority and Identity: The Dynamics of the General Conference Mennonite Church.* N. Newton, Kan.: Bethel College, 1987.

_____. "Defining Mennonite Diversity and Unity." *MQR* 57 (July 1983).

_____. "The One and the Many: The Recovery of Mennonite Pluralism," in *Anabaptism Revisited: Essays on Anabaptist/Mennonite Studies in Honor of C. J. Dyck.* Ed. Walter Klaassen. Scottdale, Pa.: Herald Press, 1992.

Schlabach, Theron F. *Gospel Versus Gospel: Mission and the Mennonite Church, 1863-1944.* Scottdale, Pa.: Herald Press, 1980.

_____. *Peace, Faith, Nation: Mennonites and Amish in Nineteenth-Century America.* The Mennonite Experience in America vol. 2. Scottdale, Pa.: Herald Press, 1988.

_____. "Reveille for *die Stillen im Lande*: A Stir Among Mennonites in the Late Nineteenth Century." *MQR* 51 (July 1977).

_____. "To Focus a Mennonite Vision," in *Kingdom, Cross, and Community: Essays on Mennonite Themes in Honor of Guy F. Hershberger.* Ed. John Richard Burkholder and Calvin Redekop. Scottdale, Pa.: Herald Press, 1976.

Schultz, J. S. *Report of the 1-W Program Evaluation Study of Mennonite and Brethren in Christ 1-W Men.* N.p., 1955.

*The Seminary Story: Twenty Years of Education in Ministry,
1955-1975.* Ed. A[bram]. J. Klassen. Fresno, Calif.: Mennonite
Brethren Biblical Seminary, 1975.

Shetler, Sanford G. *Two Centuries of Struggle and Growth, 1763-
1963: A History of the Allegheny Mennonite Conference.*
Scottdale, Pa.: Herald Press, 1963.

Sibley, Mulford, and Philip Jacob. *Conscription of Conscience:
The American State and the Conscientious Objector, 1940-
1947.* Ithaca, N.Y.: Cornell University Press, 1952.

Sider, E. Morris. *Messenger of Grace: A Biography of C. N. Hostetter Jr.* Nappanee, Ind.: Evangel Press, 1982.

Smith, C. Henry. "A Communication from C. Henry Smith Regarding the Story of the Mennonites." *MQR* 17 (Oct. 1943).

_____. *Christian Peace: Four Hundred Years of Mennonite
Principles and Practice.* Newton, Kan.: Peace Committee of
the General Conference of Mennonites, 1938.

_____. "On Mennonite Historiography." *MQR* 18 (Apr. 1944).

_____. "The Mennonites and Culture." *MQR* 12 (Apr. 1938).

_____. *The Story of the Mennonites.* Berne, Ind.: Mennonite
Book Concern, 1941.

Smith, Willard H. *Mennonites in Illinois.* Scottdale, Pa.: Herald
Press, 1983.

*Something Meaningful for God. The Mennonite Central Commit-
tee Story,* vol. 4. Ed. Cornelius J. Dyck. Scottdale, Pa.: Herald
Press, 1981.

Sprunger, Keith L., and John D. Thiesen. "Mennonite Military Service in World War II: An Oral History Approach." *MQR* 66 (Oct.
1992).

Sprunger, Keith. "Cornelius H. Wedel and Oswald H. Wedel: Two
Generations of Mennonite Historians." *ML* (Dec. 1981).

Stayer, James, Werner Packull, and Klaus Depperman. "From Monogenesis to Polygenesis: The Historical Discussion of Anabaptist Origins." *MQR* 49 (Apr. 1975).

Steely, Jeff A. "Cornelius Herman Suckau: Mennonite Fundamentalist?" *ML* 44 (Mar. 1989).

Stoltzfus, Grant M. *Mennonites of the Ohio and Eastern Conference: The Colonial Period in Pennsylvania to 1968.* Scottdale, Pa.: Herald Press, 1969.

Storms, Everek Richard. *History of the United Missionary
Church.* Elkhart, Ind.: Bethel Publishing Co., 1958.

Suckau, C[ornelius]. H. *A Miracle of God's Grace: The Marvelous
Story of the Beginning of Grace Bible Institute.* Omaha, Neb.:
Grace Bible Institute, n.d.

Thiesen, John D. *Prussian Roots, Kansas Branches: A History of the First Mennonite Church.* Newton, Kan.: First Mennonite Church, 1986.

Toews, John A. *A History of the Mennonite Brethren Church: Pilgrims and Pioneers.* Ed. A[bram]. J. Klassen. Fresno, Calif.: Board of Christian Literature, General Conference of Mennonite Brethren Churches, 1975.

Toews, John A. "In Search of Identity." *Mennonite Brethren Herald* 11 (Mar. 10, 1972).

Toews, J. B. "The Influence of Fundamentalism on Mennonite Brethren Theology." *Direction* 10 (July 1981).

Toews, John B. *With Courage to Spare: The Life of B. B. Janz (1877-1964).* Winnipeg, Man.: Board of Christian Literature, General Conference of the Mennonite Brethren Churches, 1978.

Toews, Paul. "Dissolving the Boundaries and Strengthening the Nuclei." *CL* 45 (July 27, 1982).

_____. "Fundamentalist Conflict in Mennonite Colleges: A Response to Cultural Transitions." *MQR* 57 (July 1983).

_____. "Henry W. Lohrenz and Tabor College." *ML* 38 (Sep. 1983).

_____. "The Concern Movement: Its Origins and Early History." *Conrad Grebel Review* 8 (Spring 1990).

Umble, John Sylvanus. *Goshen College, 1894-1954: A Mennonite Venture in Christian Higher Education.* Goshen, Ind.: Goshen College, 1954.

Unruh, John D. *In the Name of Christ: A History of the Mennonite Central Committee and Its Service, 1920-1951.* Scottdale, Pa.: Herald Press, 1952.

Unruh, Wilfred J. *A Study of Mennonite Service Programs.* Elkhart, Ind.: Institute of Mennonite Studies, 1965.

U.S. Bureau of the Census, Census of Religious Bodies, 1936: Mennonite Bodies; Statistics Denominational History, Doctrines and Organization. Washington, D.C.: Government Printing Office, 1940.

U.S. Selective Service. *Selective Service in Peacetime: First Report of the Director of Selective Service, 1940-41.* Washington, D.C.: Government Printing Office, 1942.

U.S. Selective Service. *Selective Service in Wartime: Second Report of the Director of Selective Service, 1941-42.* Washington, D.C.: Government Printing Office, 1943.

U.S. Selection Service System. *Conscientious Objection. Special Monograph,* no. 11. Washington, D.C.: Government Printing Office, 1950.

Unrau, Ruth. *Encircled: Stories of Mennonite Women.* Newton, Kan.: Faith & Life Press, 1986.

Waltner, Erland, "The Anabaptist Conception of the Church." *MQR* 25 (Jan. 1951).

Wardin, Albert J. Jr. "Baptist Influences on Mennonite Brethren with an Emphasis on the Practice of Immersion." *Direction* 8 (Oct. 1979).

Warkentin, Abraham, and Gingerich, Melvin. *Who's Who Among the Mennonites.* N. Newton, Kan.: Bethel College Press, 1944.

Wedel, Peter J. *The Story of Bethel College.* Ed. Edmund G. Kaufman. N. Newton, Kan.: Bethel College, 1954.

Wenger, J[ohn]. C. *The Mennonite Church in America.* Scottdale, Pa.: Herald Press, 1966.

Wenger, John Christian. *The Mennonites in Indiana and Michigan.* Scottdale, Pa.: Herald Press, 1961.

Wenger, John C. *Historical and Biblical Position of the Mennonite Church on Attire.* Intro. Paul Erb. Scottdale, Pa.: Herald Press, 1944.

Wenger, John C., et al. *Harold S. Bender: Educator, Historian, Churchman.* Scottdale, Pa.; Herald Press, 1964.

Whitmer, Paul. "The Future of the Mennonite Church: In the United States and Canada." *TM* 44 (Aug. 29, 1929).

_____. "The Future of the Mennonite Church, Part II." *TM* 44 (Sep. 5, 1929).

Wiebe, Katie Funk. *Day of Disaster.* Scottdale, Pa.: Herald Press, 1976.

Wilhelm, Paul A. *Civilian Public Servants: A Report on 210 World War II Conscientious Objectors.* Washington D.C.: National Interreligious Service Board for Conscientious Objectors, 1990.

Witness and Service in North America. The Mennonite Central Committee Story, vol. 3, Documents. Ed. Cornelius J. Dyck. Scottdale, Pa.: Herald Press, 1980.

Wittlinger, Carlton O. *Quest for Piety and Obedience: The Story of the Brethren in Christ.* Nappanee, Ind.: Evangel Press, 1978.

Wittner, Lawrence S. *Rebels Against War: The American Peace Movement, 1941-1960.* New York: Columbia University Press, 1969.

Women Among the Brethren: Stories of Fifteen Mennonite Brethren and Krimmer Mennonite Brethren Women. Ed. Katie Funk Wiebe. Hillsboro, Kan.: Board of Christian Literature of the General Conference of Mennonite Brethren Churches, 1979.

The Woodlawn Story. Ed. Frieda Claassen. Chicago, Ill.: Mennonite Biblical Seminary Alumni Association, 1958.

Wuthnow, Robert. *The Restructuring of American Religion: Society and Faith Since World War II.* Princeton: Princeton University Press, 1988.

Yake, C[layton]. F. "The Brunk Meetings: An Evaluation of the Movement." *GH* 45 (June 10, 1952).

Yoder, Edward, and Don Smucker. *The Christian and Conscription: An Inquiry Designed as a Preface to Action.* Akron, Pa.: Mennonite Central Committee, 1945.

Yoder, Elmer S. *The Beachy Amish Mennonite Fellowship Churches.* Hartville, Ohio: Diakonia Ministries, 1987.

Yoder, Edward. *Edward, Pilgrimage of a Mind: The Journal of Edward Yoder, 1931-1945.* Ed. Ida Yoder. Privately published, 1985.

Yoder, John Howard. "The Anabaptist Dissent: The Logic of the Place of the Disciple in Society." *Concern* 1 (June 1954)

_____. "Anabaptist Vision and Mennonite Reality," in *Consultation on Anabaptist-Mennonite Theology.* Ed. A. J. Klassen (Fresno, Calif.: Council of Mennonite Seminaries, 1970).

_____. "Reinhold Niebuhr and Christian Pacifism." *MQR* 27 (Apr. 1953).

_____. *The Christian Witness to the State.* Newton, Kan.: Faith & Life Press, 1964.

_____. *The Politics of Jesus.* Grand Rapids, Mich.: Eerdmans, 1972.

Yoder, Paton. *Tradition and Transition: Amish Mennonites and Old Order Amish, 1800-1900.* Scottdale, Pa.: Herald Press, 1991.

Yoder, Sanford C. *The Days of My Years.* Scottdale, Pa.: Herald Press, 1959.

Yousey, Arlene. *Strangers and Pilgrims: History of Lewis County Mennonites.* Croghan, N.Y.: privately published, 1987.

Zercher, David. "Opting for the Mainstream: The Brethren Join the National Association of Evangelicals." *Brethren in Christ History and Life* 10 (Apr. 1987).

SELECTED PROCEEDINGS

Christian Race Relations. Proceedings of the Conference on Christian Community Relations. Goshen, Ind.: Committee on Economic and Social Relations of the Mennonite Church, 1955.

Christian Unity in Faith and Witness. Proceedings of the Centennial Study Conference. Newton, Kan.: General Conference Mennonite Church, 1960.

Church Organization and Administration. Proceedings of the Study Conference on Church Organization and Administration. Scottdale, Pa.: Mennonite Publishing House, 1955.

Conscience and Conscription. Papers from an MCC Peace Section Assembly, November 20-22, 1969. Akron, Pa.: MCC Peace Section, 1970. [MCC=Mennonite Central Committee.]

Mennonite General Conference Report (1927-1953); *Mennonite General Conference Proceedings* (1955); *Reports Submitted to Mennonite General Conference;* and *Mennonite General Conference Proceedings* (1957-1969); *Proceedings, Mennonite Church* (1971). [Pertain to the "old" or "MC" Mennonite Church.]

Mennonite Conference of War and Peace. (Goshen College, Goshen, Ind., Feb. 15-17, 1935).

Minutes of the Virginia Mennonite Conference: vol. 1 (1835-1950); vol. 2 (1951-1966). Harrisonburg, Va.: Virginia Mennonite Conference, 1950, 1967.

Minutes, Reports and Papers of Session of the General Conference of the Mennonites of North America (1929); *Official Minutes and Reports of Session of the General Conference of the Mennonite Church of North America* (1933-1947); *Reports and Official Minutes of the General Conference of the Mennonite Church of North America* (1950); *Reports and Official Minutes of the General Conference Mennonite Church* (1953-1956); *The General Conference Mennonite Church Reports and the General Conference Mennonite Minutes* (1959); *Report, General Conference Mennonite Church and Minutes, General Conference Mennonite Church* (1962-1974).

Papers Presented at the Conference on Race Relations, Atlanta, Georgia, February 25-26, 1964. Akron, Pa.: MCC Peace Section, 1964.

Proceedings, Conference on Mennonite Cultural Problems (1942-1949); *Proceedings,* Conference on Mennonite Educational and Cultural Problems (1951-1967).

Proceedings of Consultation on Relief, Services, and Missions Relationships Overseas, May 7-8, 1964. Akron, Pa.: MCC, 1964.

Proceedings of the Study Conference on the Believers' Church. Newton, Kan.: General Conference Mennonite Church, 1955.

Prophecy Conference. Report of Conference Held at Elkhart, Indiana, April 3-5, 1952. Scottdale, Pa.: Mennonite Publishing House, 1953.

Protocol, Western District Conference (1938-1941); *Minutes*, Western District Conference (1942-1945); *Minutes and Reports*, Western District Conference (1948-1953); *Reports and Minutes*, Western District Conference (1954-1965); *Minutes and Reports*, Western District Conference (1966-1974).

Report of the Conservative Mennonite Conference, August 9-12, 1955.

Report of General Conference of Mennonites in France in Reconstruction Work. Held at Clermont-en-Argonne, Meuse, France, June 20-22, 1919. Ed. Walter N. Rutt, J. C. Meyer, and C. C. Janzen. N.p., [ca. 1919].

Report of the MCC Peace Section Study Conference. Held at Winona Lake, Indiana, on November 8 to 12, 1955. Akron, Pa.: MCC, 1950.

The Mennonite Churches and Race. Report of a Seminar on Christ, April 17-19, Woodlawn Mennonite Church, Chicago, Illinois. Akron, Pa.: MCC Peace Section, [1959].

The Witness of the Holy Spirit. Proceedings of the Eighth Mennonite World Conference, Amsterdam, The Netherlands, July 22-30, 1967. Ed. Cornelius J. Dyck. Elkhart, Ind.: Mennonite World Conference, 1967.

Year Book of the General Conference of the Mennonite Brethren Church of North America (1919-1960); *Year Book of the General Conference of the Mennonite Brethren Churches* (1963-1975).

Year Book, Pacific District Conference of the Mennonite Brethren Church of North America (1920-1962); *Year Book, Pacific District Conference of the Conference of the Mennonite Brethren Churches* (1963-1971).

UNPUBLISHED DISSERTATIONS, THESES, AND PAPERS

Doctoral Dissertations

(Ph.D. dissertations unless indicated otherwise. U.=University.)

Adrian, Marlin. "Mennonites, Missionaries and Native Americans:

Religious Paradigms and Cultural Encounters." U. of Virginia, 1989.

Bender, Titus. "The Development of the Mennonite Mental Health Movement, 1942-1971." D.S.W., Tulane U., 1976.

Bush, Perry. "Drawing the Line: American Mennonites, the State and Social Change, 1935-1973." Carnegie-Mellon U., 1990.

Cline, Paul Charles. "Relations Between the 'Plain People' and Government in the United States." The American U., 1968.

Cronk, Sandra Lee. "Gelassenheit: The Rites of the Redemptive Process in Old Order Amish and Old Order Mennonite Communities." U. of Chicago, 1977.

Davis, Roger Guinon. "Conscientious Cooperators: The Seventh-Day Adventists and Military Service, 1860-1945." George Washington U., 1970.

Dickey, Dale F. "The Tent Evangelism Movement of the Mennonite Church: A Dramatistic Analysis." Bowling Green State U., 1980.

Eller, Cynthia. "Moral and Religious Arguments in Support of Pacifism: Conscientious Objectors and the Second World War." U. of Southern California, 1988.

Fretz, Joseph Winfield. "Mennonite Mutual Aid: A Contribution to the Establishment of Christian Community." U. of Chicago, 1941.

Gallagher, Thomas Edward, Jr. "Clinging to the Past or Preparing for the Future? The Structure of Selective Modernization Among Old Order Amish of Lancaster County." Temple·U., 1981.

Goossen, Rachel Waltner. "Conscientious Objection and Gender: Women in Civilian Public Service During the Second World War." U. of Kansas, 1993.

Graber, Robert Bates. "The Sociocultural Differentiation of a Religious Sect: Schisms Among the Pennsylvania German Mennonites." U. of Wisconsin—Milwaukee, 1979.

Grimsrud, Theodore. "An Ethical Analyses of Conscientious Objection to World War II." Graduate Theological Union, 1988.

Harder, Leland. "The Quest for Equilibrium in an Established Sect: A Study of Social Change in the General Conference Mennonite Church." Northwestern U., 1962.

Huntington, Abbie Gertrude Enders. "Dove at the Window: A Study of an Old Order Amish Community in Ohio." Yale U., 1957.

Landing, James E. "The Spatial Developments and Organization of an Old Order Amish-Beachy Amish Settlement: Nappanee, Indiana." Pennsylvania State U., 1967.

Larson, Zelle Andrews. "An Unbroken Witness: Conscientious Objection to War, 1948-1953." U. of Hawaii, 1975.

Meyers, Thomas J. "Stress and the Amish Community in Transition." Boston U., 1983.

Robinson, Mitchell Lee. "Civilian Public Service During World War II: The Dilemmas of Conscience and Conscription in a Free Society." Cornell U., 1990.

Sawatsky, Rodney J. "History and Ideology: American Mennonite Identity Definition Through History." Princeton U., 1977.

Stutzman, Ervin. "From Nonresistance to Peace and Justice: Mennonite Peace Rhetoric, 1951-1991." Temple U., 1993.

Wachs, Theodore Richard. "Conscription, Conscientious Objection, and the Context of American Pacifism, 1940-45." U. of Illinois—Champaign-Urbana, 1976.

Wiesel, Barbara Bowie, "From Separatism to Evangelism: A Case Study of Social and Cultural Change Among the Franconia Conference Mennonites, 1945-1970." U. of Pennsylvania, 1973.

Master's and B.D. Theses

(M.A. thesis unless indicated otherwise. U.=University.)

Baehr, Karl. "Secularization Among the Mennonites." B.D., U. of Chicago, 1942.

Cummins, Doris Crate. "Civilian Public Service Unit Sixty-Three: Mennonite Conscientious Objectors in World War II." Florida Atlantic U., 1982.

Enns-Rempel, Kevin. "Paul Erb: Mennonite Diplomat." U. of California, Riverside, 1984.

Klassen, Abram J. "The Roots and Development of Mennonite Brethren Theology to 1914." Wheaton College, 1966.

Miller, Robert W. "The Role and Contribution of the Foreign Voluntary Agencies in South Vietnam." U. of Pittsburgh, 1972.

Peterson, David Chris. "Children of Freedom or Children of Menno? The Oregon Mennonite Church in the Two World Wars." U. of Oregon, 1981.

Rempel, Valerie G. " 'She Hath Done What She Could:' The Development of the Women's Missionary Services in the Mennonite Brethren Churches of the United States." Mennonite Brethren Biblical Seminary, 1992.

Student and Other Unpublished Papers

(Note: For Goshen College papers, check with the MHL; for Bethel

College papers, with the MLA; for Fresno Pacific College papers, with CMBS-F.)

Beiler, Abner F. "A Brief History of the New Order Amish Church, 1966-1976." Available at the MHL.

Birky, Anne. "The Development and a Case Study of the Voluntary Service Program of the (old) Mennonite Church." Student paper, Goshen College, 1976.

Fretz, Joseph. "The General Problems Committee: Change in the Mennonite General Confrence." Student paper, Goshen College, 1976.

Graber, Harvey. "Spiritual Awakening in the Old Order Amish Church." Student paper, Goshen College, 1956.

Kraybill, Paul N. "North American Inter-Mennonite Relationships." 1974. Available at the MHL.

Lind, Wilbert G. "Mennonite Family Census of 1949-50: Marriage Age and the Size of the Family of Mennonite Families." Student paper, Goshen College, 1951.

Loewen, Theodore. "Mennonite Pacifism: The Kansas Institute of International Relations." Student paper, Bethel College, 1971.

Neufeld, Ken. "Factors Associated with the Growth in Number of Inter-Mennonite Organizations." Student paper, U. of Southern California, n.d. Available at CMBS-F.

Redekop, Benjamin Wall. "Mennonite Peace Identity Through Three Wars, 1914-1975." Student paper, Fresno Pacific College, 1985.

Rempel, Kevin. "The Evangelical Mennonite Brethren: In Search of Religious Identity." Student paper, Fresno Pacific College, 1982.

Smucker, John R. "Mobility Among the Mennonites of Ohio." Student paper, Goshen College, 1956.

Stucky, Gregory J. "A College Near Death: The Bethel Crisis of 1932." Student paper, Bethel College, 1971.

Unruh, Mark. "E. L. Harshbarger: Mennonite Activist." Student paper, Bethel College, 1982.

INDEX

Conference on Mennonite Cultural
    Problems, 102, 280
Conference on Nonresistance and
    Political Responsibility,
    264
Conscience and Conscription Con-
    ference, 326
Conscientious Objector Girls
    (COGs), 168
Conscientious objectors, 123, 129,
    135, 142, 146, 158
    absolutists, 133
    resisters, 155
    separatists, 155
    servants, 155
    transformers, 155. *See also*
        Civilian Public Service;
        World War I; World War II;
        Korean War; Vietnam
        War; Pacifism; Nonresis-
        tance; Conference of Paci-
        fist Churches; Burke-
        Wadsworth; I-W; Menno-
        nite conscription choices.
Conscription institutes, 158
Conservative Mennonite Church,
    28, 54, 173, 207, 219, 229,
    289
Consumer cooperatives, 53
Cornelius, Carl A., 87
Correll, Ernst, 36, 88, 97-98
Corry, Pennsylvania, 209
Costa Rica, 207
Council of Mennonite Colleges,
    163, 269
Council of Mennonite Seminaries,
    269
Council of Moderators and
    Secretaries, 269
Council of Relief Agencies Licensed
    for Operation in Germany,
    201-202
Croghan congregation, New York
    (MC), 60
Crowley, William, 288
Culp, Arkansas, 191
Cultural accommodation, 180
Cultural assimilation, 26, 32, 95
Cultural integration, 26, 32, 83,
    105, 108, 186
    Mennonites, 26

Cultural resistance, 83, 95, 185,
    339
Cultural separation, 109, 185-186,
    191
Czech Brethren, 333

D
Dadville, New York congregation
    (MC), 60
Dallas Theological Seminary, 223
Darby, John, 70
"Declaration of Christian Faith and
    Commitment," 238
Deep Run congregation, Pennsylva-
    nia (GC), 177
DeFehr, Cornelius A., 209
Defender, The, 52
Defenseless Mennonite Brethren in
    Christ of North America,
    272
Defenseless Mennonite Church, 29,
    272, 279. *See also* Evan-
    gelical Mennonites.
Defenseless Mennonites, 28, 70,
    174. *See also* Evangelical
    Mennonites.
Denmark, 201, 203
Dennison CPS camp (Iowa), 155,
    160
Denominationalism, 29
Denver I-W Council, 247
Denver Post-Mortem, The, 247
Denver, Colorado, 243, 247, 249
    I-Ws in Denver, 245
Department of Agriculture, 143
*Development of the Missionary
    and Philanthropic Inter-
    est Among the Menno-
    nites of North America,
    The,* 95
Dick, John R., 272
Dickey, Dale, 219
Dien Bien Phu, Vietnam, 312
Diener, Harry A., 75
Dinuba, California, 50
Dispensationalism, 68
District of Columbia, 243
Doctrines of the Bible, 69. *See also*
    Daniel Kauffman.
Dominican Republic, 207
Donnellson, Iowa, 275

Index

Dover, Delaware, 192, 288, 303
Draft Should Be Abolished, The,
329
Draft. *See also* Military service;
Conscientious Objectors.
Drescher, John, 277
Driedger, Leo, 259, 265
Dutch Anabaptists and Menno-
nites, 26-28, 90-92
Dutch Calvinism, 33
Dutch-north German
Mennonites, 27
Dyck, Cornelius (C. J.), 232, 259
Dyck, Elfrieda, 202
Dyck, Harry Van, 154
Dyck, Peter, 201-202
1947 speaking tour, 204-205
Dyck, Walter, 176
Dykstra, Clarence, 138

E
East Prussia, 23
East Swamp congregation, Penn-
sylvania (GC), 177
Eastern District Conference (GC),
41-43, 149, 175, 177
Eastern Mennonite Board of Mis-
sions and Charities, 207,
312, 318
Eastern Mennonite College, 217,
223-225, 232, 325
Eastern Mennonite School, 69, 71.
See also Eastern Menno-
nite College-University.
Ediger, Elmer, 120, 181, 210, 232
*Education Among the Mennonites
of America*, 94
Egly, Henry, 272
Egypt, 199
Eicher Mennonite Church, Iowa
(GC), 205
Ekirch, Arthur A., 157
Elbing, Kansas, 191
Elgin, Illinois, 165
Elida, Ohio, 47
Eliot, T. S., 127
Elk Park, North Carolina, 256
Elkhart County, Indiana, 101, 288
Elkhart, Indiana, 186, 226, 244,
281
Elkhart Institute, 93

England, 122, 199
Episcopalians, 134
Epp, Jacob (J. B.), 113
Erb, Paul, 76, 118, 196, 219, 226
Erikson, Erik, 337
Ethiopia, 199, 207-208
Europe, 24, 121-123, 134, 185, 201,
240
Eastern, 24, 130
European Trainee Program, 268
Evangelical Mennonite Brethren,
40, 80, 174, 191, 222, 271-
273, 330
Evangelical Mennonite Brethren
Conference, 271-272. *See
also* Fellowship of Evan-
gelical Bible Churches.
Evangelical Mennonite Church,
188, 207, 223, 330, 338
affiliation with Evangelical
Mennonite conference,
271
Evangelical Mennonite Conference,
271. *See also* Fellowship
of Evangelical Bible
Churches.
Evangelical Mennonite, The, 272
Evangelical Mennonites, 28
Evangelicalism, 30, 221-222
American, 221-222, 338
European, 30, 283
history, 221
*Evidences of Modernism at Bluff-
ton College*, 77
Ewert, Bruno, 203

F
Fairview, Oklahoma, 50
Family Life, 302
Fast, Aganetha, 160
Fast, Henry A., 120, 129, 136, 140,
147-151, 156, 159, 170
Federal Security Administration,
143
Fellowship of Evangelical Bible
Churches, 273. *See also*
Evangelical Mennonite
Brethren.
Fellowship of Reconciliation, 120,
126, 134, 170
First Mennonite congregation,

257, 260, 262, 281, 322,
327, 334-335
Hershberger, Neil, 308
Hershey, Lewis B., 130, 136, 147,
253
Hertzler, Daniel, 225
Hertzler, Silas, 192-193
Hesston College, 45, 49-51
accreditation, 51
Hesston, Kansas, 49-50, 211
Hiebert, Nicholas, 82
Hiebert, Peter C., 21-23, 118, 132,
151, 171, 177, 210
Hiebert, Peter N., 82
Hill City CPS camp (South Dakota),
146, 159
Hillsboro, Kansas, 44, 50, 222, 244
Hindu Sikhs, 199
Hiroshima, Japan, 232
Hispanic Mennonite, 255
Lawndale Mennonite congre-
gation, Chicago (MC), 255
Mission, Texas, 255
Historic Peace Church Conference,
116, 118-119
World War II cooperation, 131,
133
Historical rediscovery, 84-101. *See
also* Goshen historical
renaissance.
1960s revisionism, 333
GC/MC historiographical de-
bates, 95-99
General Conference historical
renaissance, 95-99
Mennonite Brethren histori-
cal renaissance, 283
Ho Chi Minh, 312
Hofer, Jonas D., 82
Holdeman, Paul, 254
Holdemans, 28, 251. *See also*
Church of God in Christ
Mennonites.
Holmes County, Ohio, 191, 295
Home Messenger, 298
Home Missions Committee, 227
Honduras, 207
Hong Kong, 208
Hoover, David B., 150
Hopedale, Illinois, 176
Horning, Moses, 35

Horsch, John, 36-37, 66, 72, 77, 86-
87, 90, 92, 94, 96-97, 113,
115
Horst, Irvin, 154, 198, 232, 235, 263
Horst, John L., 230
Hostetler, John A., 287-288, 295,
299
Hostetler, Lester, 72
Hostetter, Christian (C. N.) Jr., 318
Hostetter, Doug, 314-316
Howard, Rhode Island, 169
Huebert, George B., 82
Hughes, Harold E., 307
Hungary, 199
Huntington, Gertrude, 296
Hutchinson, Kansas, 44, 61, 191
Hutterian Brethren, 90, 100, 278

I
I-W, 242
I-W Mirror, The, 249
I-W service, 243, 260, 268
Amish farm deferments, 253
assessing the I-W experience,
253-255
assessment, 265
Board of Christian Service,
251
census, 242-244
church concern about, 245-
251
compared to CPS service, 243,
249
conservative groups, 251-253
Denver I-Ws, 245-249
European Trainee Program,
268
I-W Coordination Committee,
250
I-W earning service, 242-244
impact on Mennonite peace
witness, 249
institutional settings of I-W
workers, 244
Mennonite Relief and Service
Commission, 250
pastoral visits, 250
Pax service, 241-244
structure, 240-242
Voluntary Service, 241-244,
268

The Author

Paul Toews is professor of history at Fresno (Calif.) Pacific College, a Mennonite Brethren school. He teaches both American and Mennonite history.

Born into the family of a 1920s Russian Mennonite immigrant, Toews grew up in Russian Mennonite villages across the United States and Canada. Toews spent a decade outside Mennonite communities while pursuing graduate degrees (including a 1972 Ph.D. in history from the University of Southern California), and teaching at the University of Wisconsin-Parkside. His move to Fresno Pacific College involved a conscious re-embrace of the Mennonite tradition.

Since the early 1980s, Toews has brought to the writing of American Mennonite history the insights and interpretations of his years of working in the broader field of American religious history. He had edited four volumes and published over thirty articles on North American Mennonite history.

In addition to teaching history at Fresno Pacific, he is director of the Center for Mennonite Brethren Studies, a Mennonite historical library and archive attached to the college and the adjacent Mennonite Brethren Biblical Seminary. He is also executive secretary of the Historical Commission of the Mennonite Brethren Church.

He has traveled extensively to visit Mennonite communities, past and present, in Western Europe, Eastern Europe, the Commonwealth of Independent States (former USSR), and South America.

Toews is married to Barbara (Reimer) Toews. They are the parents of two grown children—Renee and Matthew—and one grandchild. They are members of the Mennonite Brethren College Community congregation in Clovis, California.